W9-BLO-472

Dumb-Bell of Brookfield, Pocono Shot, and Other Great Dog Stories

Dumb-Bell of Brookfield, Pocono Shot,

& Other Great Dog Stories

John Taintor Foote

Edited & with an Introduction by Timothy Foote

Lyons & Burford, Publishers

Printed in the United States of America

Design by Kathy Kikkert

10 9 8 7 6 5 4 3 2 1

Library of Congress Cataloging-in-Publication Data

Foote, John Taintor, 1881–1950.
Dumb-Bell of Brookfield, Pocono Shot & other great dog stories/
John Taintor Foote; edited & with an introduction by Timothy Foote.
p. cm.
Contents: Dumb-Bell of Brookfield—Allegheny—Trub's diary—
Jing—Dog upon the waters—The white grouse—Pocono Shot.
ISBN 1–55821–262–0
1. Hunting dogs—Fiction. 2. Hunting stories, American.
I. Foote, Timothy. II. Title.
PS3511.0345D86 1993
813'.52—dc20 93–28707
CIP

CONTENTS

THE HANDSOME LINE DRAWINGS ARE BY

Gordon Allen

INTRODUCTION

For years now, and more and more often lately, since Lyons & Burford reissued John Taintor Foote's fishing stories, I've heard from people who wonder where they can find copies of his famous dog stories. The remote and dedicated dealers who specialize in book searches, they say, can no longer be counted on. So it seems time to offer *Dumb-Bell, Trub*, and all the others, gathered in one volume.

In the Foreword to *Dumb-Bell of Brookfield*, when it was first published as a separate title more than sixty years ago, novelist and adventure writer Rex Beach admitted that he had laughed—and cried—over the story, and guessed that anyone who knows dogs at all would do the same. That is certainly true for me, and I hope it proves true for anyone who picks up these stories, even though fashions in writing about dogs, and nearly everything else, have changed considerably in the intervening years.

Dumb-Bell, for instance, involves rich folk, a great country estate, Irish gardeners, Scandinavian maids, etc., whose comic doings do not seem as funny as they may once have done. It is fair to say that Dumb-Bell's owners now and then sound like Melvin Douglas, say, and Claudette Colbert in a sentimental movie from the 1930s. But their dogs are dogs we know, and the people's affection and knowledge are real, too, and entirely compelling.

My father hunted with, and extravagantly admired, a number of setters and pointers. Some of them, I remember, would hunt until they were so tired that you had to carry them back to the car at the end of the day. Some, like Dumb-Bell and Pocono Shot and Jing, whose tales are told here, had uncanny noses that allowed them to find birds where other dogs had failed. Dumb-Bell's sire, my father wrote, had a nose that allowed him "to go down wind, running like fire, stiffen in the middle of one of his effortless bounds, twist himself in the air, and light rigid at a bevy a hundred feet away."

So, though these stories are works of fiction, you can learn a lot from them about what hunting dogs can do. Dumb-Bell is a setter who will hold his point till hell freezes over. But anyone who doubts his prowess might consider Eugenia Hawk, a setter belonging to famous Texas trainer Jack Harper, who was once photographed still on point, after having held point for three hours.

Other skills of the dogs in this book, though they may seem preternatural to a casual reader, tend to be based on dogs my father knew, or knew of. "Dog Upon the Waters" is a slightly fictionalized version of an incident that happened to him. Dumb-Bell's size and field-trial wizardry are almost certainly based on the exploits of a tiny (hardly more than twenty pounds) setter with the odd name of Wun Lung, who won nearly every trial going in the 1890s when my father was a boy. In the story, Dumb-Bell's bloodline runs back to Roderigo, a famous sire celebrated in the *Field Trial Stud Book* who fathered twenty-seven field trial winners as well. Gladstone's Nellie, the beautiful but lackadaisical setter who appears in the curious fantasy entitled "The White Grouse," is descended from one of the greatest dogs of all time.

My father's other favorite dog, an earlier yet enduring love, was the bull terrier. Whence came *Trub* and *Allegheny*. As a boy in Ohio he had a bull terrier named Mr. Dooley after the cagey commentator invented by pundit Finley Peter Dunne. I can remember him telling me that the first time he ever hit a man was when a stranger kicked Mr. Dooley hard in the ribs for sitting too close to the door of the local post office. The intensity of feeling that launched that defense of his dog turns up in far bloodier and more somber form at the end of "Pocono Shot," a story that by current standards is quite savage in a number of ways.

Essentially, though, bull terriers, like terriers generally, are comedians. And "*Trub's Diary*," many readers think, is the funniest story John Taintor Foote ever wrote, as well as the only one to depend heavily on that trickiest of techniques, a narrative told by the dog himself.

People who know dogs at all, especially working dogs who hunt, retrieve, track, or herd sheep like border collies, have never doubted that dogs think. Fortunately, most of the old fuss with behavioral scientists about anthropomorphism has withered away. Of course, nobody believes that dogs speak English when conducting the interior monologues that we attribute to them. But human speech is the only language we have to describe what they appear to have on their minds. And often that is clearly more complex and more admirable than just the contrary pulls of blindly opposed instincts that die-hard behaviorists would have us believe.

Trub is short for Trouble. The people I used to train with in the world of literature would describe his adventures as picaresque, and happily I leave them to the reader to enjoy. There are people as well as dogs in his world, including a love-sick college kid and a pretty girl who is up to no good. Among the dogs are a touchy chow, a bone-proud greyhound, and a Pekinese who manages great hauteur though he is often referred to as "the penwiper."

Trub has some great lines. My favorite: "All this fuss about fleas makes me sick. If you are busy, you don't notice them. If you aren't, they give you something to do." When a supercilious retriever asks him what he does best, he truthfully replies: "Eat and chase cats." A moment comes when he invades the premises of two ladies who keep scores of cats. At first he can hardly believe his luck. "Cats began going in every direction. They went up the backs of chairs. They went up curtains. They went round and round the room. "I thought, 'This is the life!' But it wasn't. You can't chase ten or twelve cats at once. I had an idea. It came to me in a quick way. The idea was—Pick a cat!'"

It is a useful concept.

—TIMOTHY FOOTE
Washington, D.C.
Spring 1993

Dumb-bell of Brookfield

·I·

The Runt

The king sat on his throne and blinked at the sunlight streaming through the French window. His eyes were pools of liquid amber filled with a brooding dignity, and kind beyond expression. His throne was a big leather chair, worn and slouchy, that stood in the bay window of the Brookfield living-room. He had slept there all night, and it was time for a maid to come, open the French window, and let him out into the dew-washed rose garden.

The king was old. He had seized the throne years before. He had been put on the train one day, with nothing but his pedigree and a prayer. He had come home, six months later, champion of champions, greatest field trial setter of his time, lion-hearted defender of the honor of Brookfield.

He never saw the inside of the kennels again. He had been given humbly the freedom of the house. After due sniffings at one place and another he had taken the leather chair for his own. From then on visitors were asked to sit elsewhere, if they didn't mind, because *he* might want his chair, and *he* was Champion Brookfield Roderigo.

So now the king sat on his throne, or rather lay curled up in it, with his long, deep muzzle resting on his paws. At the end of that muzzle was a nose. A nose uncanny in its swift certainty. A nose which had allowed him to go down wind, running like fire, stiffen in the middle of one of his effortless bounds, twist himself in the air, and light rigid at a bevy a hundred feet away. He had done this again and again when only a "derby." He had done it in the National Championship until hard-riding men, galloping behind him, had yelled like boys, and Judge Beldon, mad beyond all ethics, had called across to another judge, "The dog never lived that could beat him, Tom!"

This was a flagrant breach of form. It was unpardonable for a field trial judge to indicate his choice before the official vote. That night Judge Beldon apologized to the owner of the pointer, Rip Rap Messenger, who was running with, or rather far behind, the king at the time.

But the owner of the pointer said: "Forget it, Judge! Why, I was as crazy as any of you. Man, oh, man, ain't he some dog!"

All this was long ago. It was no longer part of the king's life, and he was not thinking of those triumphant days of his youth. He wondered how soon the maid would come and let him out. Once in the garden he might find a toad under a rosebush at which to paw tentatively. Perhaps he would dig up the piece of dog cake he had buried in the black earth near the sundial. And there was that mole the terrier had killed, it was certainly worth a sniff or two. No doubt a gardener had removed it by this time, though ... meddlesome things, gardeners — an unguarded bone was scarcely safe a moment when one of them was about!

Where was that maid? Why didn't she come? Perhaps he had better take a little nap. He closed his eyes.... He never opened them again. The heart that had pumped so staunch a beat for Brookfield decided to pump no more. A shudder passed over the king's body ... then it was still.

The maid came presently and called his name. When he didn't stir she went to the leather chair and looked, her eyes growing wide. She hurried from the room and up the stairs.

"Mister Gregory, sir," she panted at a door, "won't you come down, please? Roderigo — he don't move. He don't move at all, sir!"

She was beside the chair again when the master of Brookfield arrived in his dressing gown.

"He don't move — " she repeated.

The master of Brookfield put his hand on the king's head. He slid his other hand under the king's body between the fore legs and held it there for a moment. Then he stooped, gathered a dangling paw, and rubbed the raspy pad of it against his cheek.

"No. He won't move—any more," he said. "Ask Mrs. Gregory to come down."

When the mistress of Brookfield came, she kneeled before the king in a patch of the streaming sunlight at which he had blinked early that morning. She kneeled a long time, twisting one of the king's soft ears between her fingers.

"He liked to have me do that," she said, looking up.

The master of Brookfield nodded.

The mistress of Brookfield bent until her lips were close to the ear she had been stroking.

"Old lover ... old lover!" she whispered. Then she got up suddenly and went out into the rose garden.

And so there was a chair which no one ever sat in standing in the bay window of the living-room. And it was understood that the chair would remain empty until a dog was born at Brookfield who could lie in it without shame.

Highland Lassie was in disgrace. Her field trial record was forgotten. She had brought three puppies into the world and had smothered two of them before they were six hours old.

"An' to think," wailed Peter, head kennel man at Brookfield, "the 'ussy's went an' rolled on the only Roderigo puppies this world'll ever see again! Look what she's got left—one pup, an' 'im the runt!"

He poked the pinky-white atom with a stumpy forefinger, and Highland Lassie cuddled the puppy hastily to her side.

Leona, the big blond waitress, removed a straw from Peter's coat and allowed her hand to linger on his sleeve.

"Are you not to your breakfast coming?" she asked.

But Peter had forgotten for the time that her eyes were blue, that her bosom was deep, and that she looked like gold and milk and roses.

"Breakfast?" he snorted. "An' what do I care about breakfust?

'Aven't I just told you she's gone an' killed two Roderigo pups, an' 'im layin' out there in the orchard?"

Leona gave a gentle tug at his sleeve.

"Always more puppies there will be," she said, and her words were like the notes of a flute.

Peter straightened up and glared at her.

"Always more puppies there will be!" he repeated with dreadful scorn. "You go back to the 'ouse!"

Leona departed with a quivering lip, to have her statement swiftly verified. That very day Black-Eyed Susan became the mother of seven, of whom Dan Gath, winner of the Manitoba All Age, was the indifferent father.

"A fine litter by a good young sire!" said Peter. "Brookfield ain't done yet. 'Ow's that for a grand pup—the second one there? 'E'll be a movin' picture, you 'ear me!"

"Maybe he'll be champion," suggested a kennel boy, hopefully.

"Champion!" said Peter. "So'll your grandmother. 'Ere, put some fresh straw in that corner an' don't you bother the bitch whilst you're doin' it, neither."

But when the boy had gone Peter filled his pipe and stared thoughtfully at Black-Eyed Susan, her eyes still fever bright from birth pangs.

"'E might at that, old gel," said Peter softly. "'E might at that."

Four months later the second puppy in the row of seven had grown into a thing of beauty that make you gasp when you saw him. From his proudly chiseled head to the glistening plume of his tail he was a triumph.

"The grandest pup we've ever bred at Brookfield!" said Peter. "For looks, that is," he added, glancing out toward the orchard. "Only for looks."

Highland Lassie's puppy grew also. He lived in a land of plenty unshared by crowding brothers and sisters. He did not dine in frantic haste, but deliberately and at his ease, his soft-eyed mother watching.

He was seldom disturbed by callers. Even the abundance he received failed to give him size. He could add nothing, therefore, to the honor of Brookfield. He could only dim, a little, the glory of his sire—and so they let him alone.

Then weaning time came, and his mother neglected him more and more. At last she gave him up altogether, and he was left to his own devices.

He tried hard to make the time pass. A sparrow lighting in his runway was a great event. He would creep toward it, and at the proper distance would halt and stand rigid until the sparrow flew away. Sometimes the sparrow would fly to a wire above the kennel and make a shadow on the ground. When this happened he pointed the shadow very carefully until it, too, was gone. Always he wished to pounce upon the sparrow, or its shadow; but he was a son of Roderigo—the great Roderigo who never flushed a bird—and so he held his point, with no one there to see.

Sparrows were few, however. They seldom came to his yard. In the long hours between their visits he was lonesome. He grew to have a wistful expression, and a grin that went to the heart. He seemed to be grinning at himself. The last son of Roderigo was a runt! it was a joke, a grim joke, and he grinned at it.

When winter withdrew at last and spring marched over the hills to Brookfield, a great washing descended upon the kennels and no one escaped.

Highland Lassie's puppy was smitten with the rest. He was taken by a kennel boy to the washroom and there he suffered in silence. The bath brought out his markings clearly, and after a casual glance at him Peter bent over and examined his left side.

"Now ain't that a curious mark?" he said. "It might 'ave been painted on 'im, it's that perfect. It's like one of them things the strong man 'olds up in the cirrcus—I forget what you call 'em. 'E's the runt, by the old dog out of the Lassie bitch, ain't 'e?"

"Yep," said the kennel boy. "He's all alone in No. 9 runway."

"You 'aven't growed much, 'ave you?" said Peter.

The wee son of Roderigo, his eyes still smarting from carbolic soap, looked up at Peter and grinned.

Peter drew in his breath sharply.

"Bli' me!" he said. "The beggar knows.... Not much doin' down there in No.9, is there? 'Ow'd you like to see the world for a while?" Once more the puppy grinned up at him.

"All right," said Peter. "I'll come an' get you when I'm through."

An hour later Peter opened the gate of runway No. 9.

"Come on out, Runt!" he said cheerfully. And the runt, for that, it seemed, was to be his name, came out. He stood for a moment, dazed by sudden freedom, then sped like an arrow far across the lawn. Peter's eyes lighted.

"'E can move!" he said. Then his face fell. "But what'll that get him?" he muttered. "'E couldn't step over a lead pencil!"

Each morning from then on the runt was let out to follow Peter about the place. Peter was in a cheerful mood these days. The master and mistress of Brookfield would soon return from Florida, and he was anticipating a triumph.

"Won't the missus squeal when she sees 'im!" he thought, as he brushed the shining coat of the Dan Gath puppy. "Eh, Runt?" he said aloud. And the runt, who had been gravely watching, grinned.

"I wish you'd quit that!" Peter told him. "It gives me the creeps!"

When at last the great day came, Peter scorned delay. The mistress of Brookfield was still in her hat and gloves when she heard that he was waiting in the rose garden.

"What does he want?" she asked. "I've hardly caught my breath!"

She was told that he had something to show her.

"Oh!" she said, and went to the terrace that looked lown into the garden.

Then Peter hid his triumph. He was standing at the foot of the terrace in the sunshine, and by his side was a living marvel, new washed and glistening.

The mistress of Brookfield stared, breathless for a moment.

"Oh, Peter!" she gasped. "He's a wonder dog! Bring him inside!"

"Yes, mem," said Peter, beaming.

"Bring him to the living-room, Peter. Mr. Gregory's in there!"

She turned to the door, failing to see that other who had followed Peter uncertainly into the rose garden. She was excited to begin with, and *he* was very small. Also, he felt that he did not belong in the sunshine beside the wonder dog; so he had hidden himself behind a rosebush and watched her through the leaves.

When they went into the house and left him, he crept up the

steps, crossed the terrace, and halted at the open door.... Peter had gone in here with the pretty lady, and it was his habit to follow Peter. He put a timid forepaw across the threshold — nothing happened. He tried the other paw — still nothing happened. He caught the scent of Peter now, so slowly and with caution he took up the trail.

Presently he came to a big room, and saw Peter and the pretty lady and a tall man looking at the wonder dog. He wished to keep out of sight until Peter was ready to go. The recess of the bay window seemed an excellent retreat and he slipped into it. A doggy smell came to him as he did so. He advanced and found a huge chair with bulging arms and a well-hollowed seat.

He loved the chair at sight. It seemed so friendly and safe. It seemed to hold out its arms to him in welcome. Why, it actually seemed glad to see him! Perhaps it didn't know that he was a runt.... He curled down into its soft hollow with a deep sigh of contentment.

The master of Brookfield was still staring at the wonder dog.

"How did you do it, Peter?" he said at last. "He's too good to be true!"

"'E'll be true," said Peter, "if breedin'll do it. 'E's by Dan Gath, out of Black-Eyed Susan. You get one like 'im out of a thousand matin's — maybe."

"He's handsome enough," said the master of Brookfield. "But — what will he do in the field?"

"Listen," said Peter; "I've 'ad 'im on larks a time or two, an' I'm tellin' you now, we never bred a faster, wider, 'igher-'eaded goin' pup ... but one." He glanced toward the leather chair, and a look of bewilderment came into his face, which changed to one of horror. "'Eavens above!" he said. "Look there!"

They followed his gaze, conscious for the first time of a strange sound which rose and fell steadily in the bay window.

Curled deep in Roderigo's chair was the runt, and, as Peter told the kennel men afterward, "'E was snorin' that 'eavy you could 'ear 'im all through the room."

"And what the devil is that?" said the master of Brookfield, after a stunned silence.

"The runt of the last litter by the old dog," said Peter. "'E just come along."

"Yes—I see he did," said the master of Brookfield. "Come here, you!" he called.

The runt opened one eye, twitched his tail sleepily, and closed the eye again. That was all.

A whip sung in the bay window. The terrier who lived at the house could have told the runt what that whip was for. In a moment the tall man stood above him.

"Get down out of that!" he said, and flicked the whip over the chair.

The runt was frightened. The big chair was his only friend, it seemed. He shrank deeper into it as the whip was raised above him.

"Don't! Please, Jim!" said the mistress of Brookfield. "He's so little. He'll learn soon enough." She came and took the runt by his scruff. "Get down, little mannie," she said, "this place isn't for you."

"I 'ope not!" said Peter.

"Never mind, Peter," she said. "It isn't his fault that he's little, and that was his daddy's chair.... Oh, Jim! See that dumb-bell on his side! Look! It's perfect!"

"That's too bad!" said the master of Brookfield, examining the mark.

"Why too bad?" asked Mrs. Gregory.

The master of Brookfield winked at Peter.

"We'll never be able to lose him," he explained. "Will we?" he said to the runt, and the runt looked up and grinned.

Mrs. Gregory gave a quick little gasp.

"I hate such jokes!" she said. "Is he registered, Peter?"

"No, mem," said Peter.

"Well, register him as Brookfield Dumb-Bell—and give him every chance." Suddenly she stepped close to the runt. "You two may have the *beauty* there," she flashed; "and his missy will look after *him*!"

"Why, Chief!" said the master of Brookfield.

"I don't care!" she said. "He's little—and I think he knows it—and it isn't his fault!" Then she went out of the room.

The master of Brookfield rubbed his chin thoughtfully.

"Now what did *we* do, Peter?" he asked.

It was a hot summer that year. Day after day the sun glared down at Brookfield, and the runt panted as he followed Peter. Often when visitors arrived and Peter was told to bring the wonder dog to the house the runt came along.

He was always embarrassed during these visits. He felt smaller than ever in the stately rooms of the big house. But he remembered his friend the chair, and while the visitors were exclaiming over the wonder dog he would slip away quietly and crawl into it.

He was whipped for this several times, but he never seemed to learn; so at last he was put back in runway No. 9, where there were no chairs at all, only loneliness and an occasional sparrow.

One day the master of Brookfield visited the kennels.

"Peter," he said, "ship the Dan Gath puppy to Ramsey, in Tennessee. Ship him tomorrow night. Wire Ramsey.... Hot, isn't it?"

"What about *'im*?" said Peter, jerking his thumb toward a runway.

"What do you mean?" asked the master of Brookfield. Then he saw the occupant of No. 9 staring wistfully out at Peter.

"Oh!" he said, "*you* break him this fall for a shooting dog. He ought to have a nose on him."

As Peter was going over a dog crate next day, he looked up to find the mistress of Brookfield watching him.

"Good morning, Peter," she said. "What's that crate forer"

"I'm shippin' the Dan Gath pup away tonight, mem," said Peter. "'E's to 'ave a chance at the trials."

"Why have you brought out only one crate?" asked the mistress of Brookfield.

"I'm only shippin' one dog," said Peter, tapping away with his hammer.

"Ah!" said she. "And when does the runt go?"

"'E don't go," said Peter. "I'm to break 'im myself—for a shootin' dog."

"Peter!" said the mistress of Brookfield.

"Yes, mem," said Peter uneasily.

"Get out another crate, please." And when two crates stood side by side, the mistress of Brookfield touched one of them with her fingertips.

"The little chap," she said, "goes in this crate tonight. Do you understand me, Peter?"

"Yes, mem," said Peter.

"And, Peter—tell Ramsey to send the training bills to *me*."

"Yes, mem," said Peter.

Two weeks later the mails brought a letter to Brookfield. It was addressed to Peter, and this is how it ran:

Emeryville, Tennessee, R. R. No.4
Sept. 6, 19—

FRIEND PETER:

I take shame in telling you the small pup is lost. He found a bevy the first day I took him out, chased when they flushed, and I ain't seen him since. I've hunted the country over and offered big rewards. Tell Mrs. Gregory, and say a good word for me. The big pup is doing fine. I like every move he makes. I'll keep on looking for the little pup, and that's all at present.

Yours in friendship,
W. RAMSEY.

Peter sat on a sawhorse and slowly read his letter. He moved to an overturned grindstone, seeking a better light, and read it again. He looked up toward the house, a black pile against the setting sun, and whistled softly.

"'Ell will be to pay shortly," he muttered, and moved reluctantly to his doom.

The master of Brookfield had been to the cattle barns to watch the milking. When he returned he found that Peter was something of a prophet. He found his lady bathed in tears, Peter standing miserably before her, and maids running in all directions.

"I'm going to Tennessee tonight!" she gasped. "Read that!"

"But, Chief!" said the master of Brookfield when he had read the letter. "You couldn't possibly do any good down there. If Ramsey, who knows every foot of the country, can't find him, how can you expect to?"

"I'll send down a motor and ride all day," she told him. "You can come too—and Peter—and Felix to drive..."

"Is that all?" he said. "We'll be quite a party. It's out of the question, my dear.... I'll tell Ramsey to double the reward and do everything possible.... You'll make yourself sick if you don't stop crying!"

"We *have* lost him, you see! In spite of your horrid joke about it. *Now* I hope you and Peter are satisfied! I'll write to Ramsey!" she added ominously. "Oh, I'll write to *him*!"

When W. Ramsey, Esq., received a letter a few days later he whistled over it much as Peter had whistled over his.

"I guess I'd better quit trainin'," he muttered, "an' go to pup huntin' for a perfession!"

And until he went West with his "string," the redoubtable Bill Ramsey, high-priced specialist in the training and handling of field trial setters, turned his fieldwork and yard-breaking over to an assistant, and scoured the country day after day. But no one had seen a "real small setter with a funny mark on his side," and he never found a trace of what he sought.

Brookfield Beau Brummell No.43721 F. D. S. B., for such was now the wonder dog's official title, was taken to a country where he could go far, and fast, and wide.

In the cramped valleys and thicket-rimmed fields of the East, bobwhite lives close to cover, and field trial dogs are educated in the land of the prairie chicken, where their handlers can keep them in sight for mile after level mile.

The Beau was put down one morning with the veteran Rappahannock as guide, counselor, and friend. The sun was beginning to climb the eastern side of the huge blue void that domed an ocean of grass.

"Hi, yah! Get away!" yelled Ramsey. Rappahannock, free of the leash, shot over a gentle rise and was gone. He had eaten up a good half-mile of country when the frostbitten grass began to whisper just behind him. He flattened out in a desperate effort to shake off the whisper, but the whisper grew to the soft pad, pad of flying feet, as the Beau, moving like oil, flowed past.

Ramsey lowered his field glasses and smiled.

"Look out for that one, Mike!" he called to his assistant. "They've bred another bird dog at Brookfield!"

As time went on and the Beau developed into a prodigy of speed, range, and nose, Peter went about his work with a far-away look in his eyes. His body was at Brookfield, his spirit in Manitoba. The Beau would make his first start in the great Canadian stake, and—"They can't beat him!" was the word that came from Ramsey.

On the day the stake was run Peter sat on the grindstone and whittled. He spoke no word to anyone. Late in the evening the telephone bell rang in the kennels, but Peter never stirred. A kennel boy approached him timidly.

"They want you up to the house," said the boy; and Peter closed his knife and rose.

He found the mistress of Brookfield in the living-room. Her cheeks were flushed, her eyes like stars. She was dancing about the master of Brookfield with a fluttering telegram in her hand.

"*Peter*!" she said, "*Oh, Peter! See what our boy's done*!"

Peter read the telegram, then looked at the master of Brookfield through half shut lids.

"If they don't watch 'im 'e'll likely take the National," he said.

"It's possible," said the master of Brookfield. "Yes, it's possible."

"Why, of course," said Mrs. Gregory. "Didn't you know that? He's to be champion.... Outclassed his field!" she sang. "Did you read that, Peter? Read it again."

This was only the beginning. The Beau swept through field trial after field trial, piling victory upon victory. He won again in Canada. He came nearer home, into Illinois, to take the Independent All Age from the best dogs in the land. He went down into Georgia, and left his field gasping behind him in the select Continental. He won "off by himself," as Ramsey said, in the Eastern Subscription against twenty-five starters, and "every dog worth a million dollars!"

He was certain to take the National. No other dog could stand his pace in the three-hour running of the Championship. Rival handlers conceded this, and Black-Eyed Susan came into her own.

"Susan is trying not to look down on the rest of us, Peter," explained the mistress of Brookfield.

Peter watched Black-Eyed Susan partake of crackers and cream languidly, and from a silver spoon.

"I can't say as 'ow you're 'elpin' 'er much," he said.

Then suddenly Ramsey was smitten with inflammatory rheumatism, and the Beau was turned over to Scott Benson, who would handle him in his other engagements.

"Don't worry," Peter told the master of Brookfield. "Scott's a good 'andler. It's all over, anyway, but the United States *and* the Championship.... Are you goin' down?"

"To the National? Why, yes," said the master of Brookfield. He caught a wistful look in Peter's eyes. "Would *you* care to go?" he asked.

Peter bent over and picked up a willow twig for whittling purposes.

"Why, I expect the boys could look after things here for a day or two," he said.

The United States All Age was the last big stake before the Championship. On the morning after it was run, Peter was whistling as he sprinkled the whelping shed with disinfectant. Footsteps crunched on the gravel outside and he stepped to the door. The master of Brookfield stood there with a newspaper in his hand.

"He was beaten, Peter," he said.

"*No*!" said Peter. And after a silence—"What beat 'im?"

"Little Sam," said the master of Brookfield.

"An' who is Little Sam?" asked Peter.

"I don't know," said the master of Brookfield. "I never heard of him before. Our dog was second. Here! Read it yourself."

The dispatch was short:

Grand Junction, Tenn., Jan. 8.

In the All Age stake of the United States Field Trial Club, Little Sam, lemon and white setter, handled by C.E. Todd, was first. Brookfield Beau Brummell, black, white, and ticked setter, handled by Scott Benson, was second. Thirty-two starters.

"C.E. Todd!" said Peter. "Why, that's Old Man Todd—'e's eighty years old if 'e's a day! What's 'e doin' back in the game?"

"Don't ask me!" said the master of Brookfield. "He's back, it would seem, and he's brought a dog."

"Do you think 'e'll start 'im in the National?" Peter inquired.

"I presume so," said the master of Brookfield. "You're to bring the Beau home, Peter—if he wins."

"An' if 'e don't—win?" asked Peter.

"Why, then," said the master of Brookfield, "he can stay in training and try again next year."

Three days later the mistress of Brookfield stood with Black-Eyed Susan in the high stone arch of the front entrance. "You're to bring home the champion, Peter!" she called. "Don't fail us, will you?—Susy and me? There's some light underwear in the black bag, Jim; it may be warm in Tennessee. Good-by ... Good-by, Peter.... Your shaving things are in the small bag, Jim! Peter—Peter! Don't forget Susy and me—we'll be waiting!"

"No, mem," said Peter stoutly. But as he watched the landscape slide steadily northward the ties clicked a fearsome refrain: "*Little Sam*!" they said, "*Little Sam*!"

Grand Junction was reached at last. Scott Benson was the first to greet them at the packed and roaring hotel.

"Well," said the master of Brookfield, "how does it look?"

The trainer shook his head.

"Bad, Mr. Gregory," he said. "We've got an awful dog to beat."

"You mean the dog that old Todd's got?" said Peter.

"Yes," said Scott, "That's what I mean—but he ain't a dog."

"What is 'e, then?" asked Peter.

"He's a flying machine, with a telescope nose. You got a grand dog, Mr. Gregory, a grand dog. A gamer dog never lived—he'll try all the way; but this here dog that old fool's got a hold of somehow ain't human. In three hours he'll find all the quail in the state!"

"What's 'e look like, an' 'ow's 'e bred?" Peter inquired.

"Get ready to laugh," said Scott. "I forgot to tell you. His breedin's unknown, an' he ain't as big as a stud beagle."

That evening was a trial. Beau Brummell seemed forgotten. The hotel lobby echoed with the name of Little Sam.

"He must be a great dog," smiled the master of Brookfield. "I'll enjoy seeing him run. I think I'll turn in now, Major, if you'll excuse me. I'm a little tired from the trip."

Peter sat up longer, half listening to the babble about him. At last he became conscious of a hissing for silence as the secretary climbed to a tabletop and began to read the drawings for the National.

"Belwin with Dan's Lady!" read the secretary. "Opal Jane with Rappahannock! Bingo with Prince Rodney!" and so the starters in the Championship were paired. At last, at the very end, the secretary paused an instant and smiled grimly. "Brookfield Beau Brummell Little Sam!" he read, and there was a roar that shook the hotel.

Chuck Sellers leaped upon Peter and took him to his bosom.

"Stick around, Pete!" he yelled. "Stick around fur the big show!"

Peter shoved him aside.

"I'm goin' to bed," he growled. "I 'ope I get a decent 'oss tomorrow."

But fate had a blow in store for Peter. In the scramble for mounts next morning, a big gray mule with a will of his own was "wished on him" as Chuck Sellers put it, and he devoted the next few hours to equestrianship. By the time the second brace was cast off he had conquered, and he saw good old Rappahannock win on his courage from dashing Opal Jane, who failed to last the three hot hours and was running slower and slower, with a dull nose, when they took her up.

The Championship was run off smoothly. Brace after brace was put down, until at last came Thursday morning and the pair for which they waited.

Peter had been having an arguement with his mount, who hated to start in for the day. When it was settled he looked up to see an old man standing ahead of the judges, with a lemon and white setter who tugged and tugged to be gone. He was small beyond belief, this setter, so small that Peter rubbed his eyes. Then he rode down the line of horsemen until he found Chuck Sellers.

"Don't tell me that's 'im, Chuck?" he said.

"That's him," said Chuck.

"Why, a bunch of grass'll stop 'im!" said Peter. "'E ain't big enough to jump it."

"*He* don't jump nothin'," Chuck informed him. "He's got wings."

"'E may lose 'em before three hours," said Peter. "'Im an' 'is breedin' unknown."

"May be," said Chuck. "Here's the dog to clip 'em, or it can't be done," and he pointed to Beau Brummell going out to his position.

He was still the wonder dog, a glory every inch of him, and a murmur of admiration rippled down the line of horsemen.... Peter felt a sudden glow of pride and hope.

But it didn't last. The next moment he was watching a white speck fade away across the stubble. As it grew dimmer and dimmer so did Peter's hopes. The white speck was Little Sam breeding unknown. When he whirled and came to point, at the far edge of the woods, Brookfield Beau Brummell was a hundred feet behind.

Peter was among the stragglers in the stampede across the field that followed. When he reached the mass of waiting horsemen, Old Man Todd was being helped out of his saddle to shoot over his dog.

With a feeling of numb despair Peter looked for the master of Brookfield. He saw him at last, sitting his horse a little apart from the crowd, his face the color of ashes.

Peter rode to him quickly.

"What's the matter, sir?" he asked. "Are you unwell?"

The master of Brookfield kept his eyes on the pointing dog.

"*Look*!" he said, "*look*!" And Peter looked at Little Sam. Then his heart skipped a beat, fluttered, and sent the blood surging against his eardrums.

Little Sam had his bevy nailed. He stood as though of stone. He looked like white marble against the dark of the woods. And on his side, his left and nearest side, was a perfect lemon dumb-bell....

"My Gawd," said Peter. "My Gawd."

He swung his eyes along the woods and found another statue. It was Beau Brummell, still as death itself, in honor of his brace mate.

"My Gawd!" said Peter again. "What'll we do?"

"Nothing—*now*," said the master of Brookfield, "Let the best dog win."

A man should only whisper while the championship is run, but Peter rose in his stirrups, not fifty feet from a brace on point, and disgraced himself forever.

"My money's on the old dog's blood," he howled; "*an' let the best dog win*!"

"*Peter! Peter*!" said the master of Brookfield, and took him by the arm.

"I forgot," said Peter sheepishly.

There have been field trials in the past, there will be field trials in the future. But those who saw the whirlwind struggle between the great Beau Brummell and the white ghost with the magic nose will not listen while you tell of them. Eighteen bevies they found that day, and they went at top speed to do it. Not a bird was flushed as they flashed into point after dazzling point, backing each other like gentlemen.

It was perfect bird work, done with marvelous speed, and the Beau had the sympathy of those who watched, for they knew that he was beaten. He had everything that makes a champion, including looks and heart. But the little white dog who skimmed from one covey to the next was more than a champion—he was a miracle. The blazing soul of Roderigo had leaped to life in this, his son, and would not be denied.

An hour or more had passed when Chuck Sellers thought of Peter and sought him out to offer what consolation he could.

"The little dog may quit, Pete," he said, "any time now. It's the last half that tells on the short-bred ones."

Then Peter gave the puzzled Chuck a wide calm smile.

"Nothing is certain in this 'ere world," he said. "But I'll tell you one thing that is. That little dog won't quit till the pads wear off his feet."

And Peter was right. The announcement of the new champion finished with "breeding unknown."

The crowd swarmed toward the winner, who grinned as they closed about him. They had never seen a National Champion without a pedigree, and they pushed and pulled and laughed and hooted.

A *Field* reporter was yelling at Old Man Todd above the noise.

"The country wants to know this dog's breeding, old man," he said. "And it's got to be traced, if possible."

"He ain' got no breedin', I tell you!" screamed Old Man Todd.

"He's a niggah-ralsed dawg—jes' a niggah-raised dawg!"

The runt was frightened. It must be terrible to be a nigger-raised dog, or all these men wouldn't glare at him and yell! He remembered leaving the place where the big house was, long ago, and riding on a train. He remembered running for miles and miles until he had found that nice shed where he could rest. A black man had come to the shed and given him some mi1k. He drank it all and went to sleep.

Next he remembered hunting birds with the black man every day. One day an old man had watched him find some birds and had talked with the black man. Then he was taken away by the old man, and had hunted birds with him ever since.

They had had a good hunt today. But now he was tired, and they all yelled at him so— Then someone pushed and fought his way through the crowd, and the runt was glad to see him, for it was Peter, whom he had followed long ago.

The runt went to him quickly, and Peter fell on one knee and put an arm about him.

"Runt!" said Peter. "Runt!—You're yer daddy's own son!"

The runt grinned, and Peter put him down and took hold of the leash.

"Let go of this, Old Man," he said.

It is not a good thing to win the championship with a "niggah-raised" dog when that dog has been advertised over an entire state as lost. Old Man Todd looked into Peter's eyes.

"Why—why—" he began, and stopped. Then his fingers unclosed from the leash and he backed slowly into the crowd. Peter whirled about and faced the reporter, with the runt close at his side.

"Now, Mr. Reporter," he said, "you can put in your paper that Brookfield Dumb-Bell by Champion Brookfield Roderigo 'as won the National. You can say the new champion is out of Brookfield 'Ighland Lassie. You can tell 'em 'e was bred and whelped at Brookfield—and now 'e's goin' 'ome."

The reporter was dancing up and down. His face was red and he had lost his hat.

"How can I verify this?" he yelled. "How can I verify this?"

Suddenly the runt saw the tall man who lived in the big house he dimly remembered. He had always been afraid of the tall man—he was so quiet. He was quiet now. He didn't yell at all, but when he held up his hand everybody kept still.

"I can verify it for you," he said.

"Mr. Gregory!" said the reporter. "Good, very good—excellent! Will you let me have the facts as quickly as possible, please? I've got to catch the evening papers!"

Peter didn't stay to hear what the tall man said, and the runt was glad for he was tired. But Peter put him on a train and he couldn't sleep it jiggled so, and the baggage man gave him part of his supper. When other men came into the car, the baggage man pointed to him and said something about "National Champion," and "worth ten thousand dollars," and the men came and stared at the runt.

At last they got out of the train, and he and Peter and the tall man rode in an automobile till they went through some gates, and the runt saw the lights of the big house shining through the trees.

"Where shall I take him," asked Peter, "to the kennels?"

The tall man dropped his hand on the runt's head.

"I think not, Peter," he said; and they all got out at the front door.

As they came into the hall someone called from upstairs, and the runt recognized the voice of the pretty lady.

"Oh, Jim!" said the voice. "Why didn't you wire? Did Beau Brummell win?"

"No," said the tall man. "He was runner up."

"Oh!" said the voice, and then nothing more for a while, and the runt could hear the big clock ticking in the hall.

"Is Peter there?" said the voice at last.

"Yes, mem," said Peter.

"You went back on Susy and me, didn't you, Peter?" said the voice.

"Come down here, Chief!" said the tall man. "Unleash him!" he directed in a low voice, and Peter did so.

The runt threw up his head and sniffed. He was so tired by now that his legs were beginning to shake, and he wanted a place to lie down... then suddenly he remembered. He walked to the living-room and peered in... Yes, there was his friend the chair, holding out its arms to him.... The runt gave a deep sigh as he curled himself into it.

The tall man who had followed laughed softly.

"And *that's* all right!" he said.

Just then the pretty lady came in.

"Why—what dog is that?" she asked.

"Don't you know?" said the tall man.

The pretty lady stared at the runt very hard. He became uneasy, and grinned. The pretty lady shrieked and ran to him.

"Little mannie!" she said, hugging him until he could feel her heart beating against his side. "Where did they find you, little mannie?"

"At Grand Junction," said the tall man.

"What was he doing there?" asked the pretty lady.

"A good deal." said the tall man.

The pretty lady gave the runt a last big squeeze, then she straightened up.

"Oh, Runt!" she said. "Darling Runt—you're just as bad as ever!"

She put her hand on his collar. "Come!" she said. "This place isn't for you."

But the tall man stepped forward, and took her hand from the collar. His eyes were shining queerly and his voice was husky.

"Let him alone, my dear!" he said. "Let him alone!"

It was nice of the tall man to do this, thought the runt. He must have known how tired, how very tired, he was. He curled himself deep in the chair and began to snore.... In his dreams he heard the tall man talking, and then the pretty lady bent above him, and a wet drop fell on his nose.

· II ·

A Reluctant Traveler

Leona was a Catholic. Also, she, adored church weddings. Also, she was aided and abetted in her madness, and Peter was sunk in gloom.

From the bottom of his soul he favored an unostentatious, not to say stealthy, visit to the justice of the peace. Why prolong this hour of pain? Why be butchered to make a Brookfield holiday?

Beyond all doubt his new shoes would hurt him. His boiled shirt would creak when he breathed. He would have to wear suspenders, which he loathed, and lately there had been a growing murmur in favor of kid gloves.

His collar would choke him; but this would be a transitory affliction. Nature, kind nature, would aid him here: before, during, and immediately following the ceremony he would, as he told himself, "sweat to beat 'ell."

"He was justified in this prophecy. At the mere recollection of the wedding of Felix and Minnie he broke into a gentle perspiration. He remembered how that laundress, the fat one, who was by nature a tearful person, had turned the ceremony into a catacylsm of grief. He remembered how at the dance that followed the wedding he himself had been forced to take a turn with the bride, and how, after one round of the carriage house, she had informed him that it was lucky she was going to Niagara Falls because it was now doubtful if she could ever find enough cold water to relieve her feet.

Well, at any rate, there would be no trip to Niagara Falls for him; there were certain limits beyond which he would not be driven. Leona had suggested it, of course. But the new brick cottage near the kennels was finished and furnished and waiting. He would make no "'oly show" of himself at the station, "dodgin' shoes an' such!" That was final.

Then one morning he was passing the stables and halted by a harrowing spectacle. The doors of the carriage house stood open. Clustered about the victoria was a chattering feminine group who bent to their dreadful task with giggles and much white ribbon.

Between a rage and a panic Peter sought the master of Brookfield.

"Beggin' your pardon," he began. "But this 'ere 'as gone far enough."

The master of Brookfield was spending a dreamy hour in the gun room among a welter of firearms, fishing tackle, the game heads of four continents, and the smell of oil and leather. He looked up vaguely from a battered tin box choked with salmon flies, and blinked at Peter.

"If that's the case, let's stop it," he said. "But what are you talking about?"

Peter raised a quivering finger. "I am a plain man!" he roared.

"Granted," said the master of Brookfield.

"I'm no frog-eatin' French shofer!"

"True," said the master of Brookfield.

"An'," declared Peter, "I'll not drive 'ome in nothing with ribbons on it!"

The master of Brookfield picked up a patent reel and turned quickly to the window. He became absorbed in the reel's mechanism for some moments.

At last, with his back to Peter, he spoke. "I suppose you've told Leona?"

"I 'ave not," said Peter, "an' 'ere's why: She 'as every female on the place behind 'er. I 'ave gave up on this 'ere church notion, with 'alf the town there an' Father Vincent in 'is shirt tail sayin' 'okus pokus at me. I 'ave gave up on kid gloves. I 'ave gave up on 'avin' a stinkin' posy pinned to me. But drivin' 'ome in a bloomin' birdcage is more than I will do."

"Well, that settles it, doesn't it? Why do you come to me?"

Peter glanced cautiously about him, and directed a meaning look at the master of Brookfield. "Be'ind all this," he confided hoarsely, "is the missus!"

"Ah!" said the master of Brookfield.

"Could you now," said Peter, "be of 'elp to me in that quarter?"

The master of Brookfield shook with a sudden spasm of coughing. When he was sufficiently recovered he extended his hand to Peter.

"We'll make a try of it," he said. "But I'm afraid we don't amount to much at a time like this, Peter."

A moment later they were advancing manfully on the breakfast-room.

"Chief," began the master of Brookfield, "we have a complaint to make."

Mrs. Gregory broke a French roll crisply in half.

"The cream, please, Leona," she said. "Well, what is it?" she inquired over her coffee cup.

"Peter shrinks from the spectacular," explained the master of Brookfield. "He is a believer in—er—quiet simplicity. He objects, particularly, to ribbons on his carriage. Couldn't you get along without this feature?"

As the last words fell from the lips of the master of Brookfield, Leona forgot a lifetime's training. She shot one venomous glance at Peter, and burst into tears.

"Like that he is!" she sobbed. "Always like that he is. Nothing does he think of but p-p-puppies." She made a hasty clutch at her apron and the cream jug tilted a yellow pool straight into Mrs. Gregory's lap. "Ah!" came a wail of horror from Leona. "Pardon, madam."

Confusion and the flourishing of napkins followed. Despite them, when the mistress of Brookfield could rise from the table the front of her morning gown was a woeful sight. She patted the grief-stricken Leona reassuringly, and turned to Peter.

"Now, I hope you're satisfied!" She said, and swept from the room.

"You see?" said the master of Brookfield when they were safely in the gun-room once more.

Peter nodded gloomily. "Oh, I've gave up on that," he said; "but you 'ear me now—I'll not go to Nihagara Falls!"

Leona had accused Peter of thinking only of puppies. This, however, was not true. For instance, as his wedding day drew near he was particularly concerned over Peg o' My Heart, who was on the verge of motherhood and who turned listlessly from the most tempting morsels he could offer.

"What is it, old lady?" asked Peter. " 'Ere's a nice piece of liver now. Be a good gel and take it! No? Well 'ow about this good warm milk? The little 'uns'll need it. Come on now, Peggy dear!"

At his urging Peggy sniffed at the milk bowl, then lapped a swallow or two. She drew back, thanked Peter with a wave of her tail, and sank down into the straw.

Peter lifted her muzzle and stared into her eyes. He found them dark and glittering, and his own narrowed with anxiety.

"What is it?" he asked once more, and Peggy voiced her trouble with a gentle whine. "Yes, I know," Peter told her softly; but this was not the truth. He could only, like the most pompous of whiskered medicos, guess and guess again.

However, he got his thermometer from the medicine chest, and shook his head over the tiny line of quicksilver a moment later.... This much he knew: Brookfield Peg o' My Heart, bench and field trial winner, with the blood of twenty champions in her veins, faced her *accouchement* with a temperature of one hundred and three.

Peter looked up from the thermometer to find Leona standing in the doorway. She had a slim white box in her hand and a warm, shy look in her eyes.

"For you," she said. "From me. Tomorrow you wear it when—when—" She became speechless, flushing hotly.

Peter took the box automatically, opened it, and beheld a lavender tie of knitted silk. He gazed at the tie vaguely for a moment, replaced the cover, and put the box in his pocket.

"This 'ere bitch," he said, "ain't well by no means." He stooped over Peg o' My Heart. "If you're going to the 'ouse," he threw over his shoulder, "telephone Slosson to come out 'ere."

The warm, shy look fled swiftly from Leona's eyes. The flush left her cheeks as they paled with indignation. She had knitted the tie with her own fair hands and had gone back through rows and rows to recover a stitch not even dropped but loosely woven.

A silence that bristled followed Peter's words. At last he glanced her way.

"Did you 'ear me?" he inquired, and was shocked by the countenance of his bride-to-be. Wrath blazed in her eyes. Scorn curled her lips. Her chin quivered ominously. Even as he opened his lips to ascertain the cause of her displeasure she turned stiffly from him and was gone.

Peter regarded the empty doorway for a moment with a puzzled frown.

"Now what?" he said aloud. Then he shut his jaws. "If it's Nihagara Falls," he muttered, "she can take on till the cows come 'ome—'er an' the missus, too."

He spent the next few hours with Peg o' My Heart, and Powder and Shot howled a protest to him as he passed their runway. They were the pick of the first litter by Brookfield Dumb-Bell, were through with yard breaking, and should have gone afield that day.

"I'll thank you for less noise," Peter told them. "You'll get your run tomorrow." He made the promise in good faith, and then it dawned on him what day tomorrow was. He grinned sheepishly. "On the 'ole," he decided, staring at the wildly eager Powder and Shot, "I'll 'ave my 'ands full tomorrow, I expect."

Then he remembered that Peg o' My Heart had never had distemper. She showed no signs of the disease, but he did not know what ailed her as yet, and until her malady developed these youngsters would be better farther from the whelping shed. He put them on leash and took them to a runway at the extreme end of the line.

"In you go," he said, and closed the gate in their despairing faces.

Through such small incidents as this come large affairs. The runways at Brookfield have two feet of grouting below the fences. In this particular runway the frost had been at work that winter. It had lifted the grouting and forced up the east fence several inches. Peter had noticed this some months before and had removed the inmate of the runway—also the loose grouting, intending to repair the damage later.

And now, with the pressure of events distracting him, he had forgotten; and Powder and Shot, after a careful inspection of their new quarters, set joyfully to work. Inside that fence was a dreary world in which the hours dragged by on leaden feet. Outside was a heaven containing Peter and the rolling fields. To reach it one must dig industriously; but what was a little digging?

They dug until the moon came up to watch their labors. They rested toward morning, and when the sun rose a kennel boy brought them food and went his way, and then for hours they were undisturbed.

It was queer how quiet it was at the kennels. They missed Peter's morning inspection. They missed his footsteps and his voice and his whistle. Well, he was somewhere outside, that was certain.... The situation seemed to require more digging.

By nine o'clock, Powder, who was a shade the smaller, squeezed, with a whimper of excitement, to freedom.

Shot wailed in agony and flung himself at the hole. By a desperate effort he won through, leaving a tuft of hair behind him.

He gave a triumphant yelp, then shot down the line of runways. He met Powder, a white flash, returning, and together they explored the kennel house. The scent of Peter was all about, but Peter himself was strangely absent. Well, he had worked them over the marshy ground by the creek the last time he had taken them out. There were snipe in the marsh. Perhaps Peter was looking for snipe!... They went over the hill toward the maarsh like twin streaks.

Peter was not at the marsh, but they found a fat jacksnipe, and they chased it madly across the oozy meadows while the snipe said: "Scai-ip! Scai-ip!" and they acquired a coating of black muck and green slime.

The snipe became disgusted at last and disappeared in the sky, and their thoughts returned uneasily to Peter. They had chased, which was wrong. Guilt was heavy on their souls. They must find Peter, take a whipping if necessary, and be forgiven.

They turned homeward and scoured the place from end to end. At last Shot found a trace of Peter in the drive. He followed the scent until it disappeared unaccountably. It was replaced by the smell of rubber tires. Ah, that was it! Peter had gone away on the thing that made the rubber smell. To find Peter it was necessary to follow the rubber smell. He explained this to Powder, and a moment later they arrived at the main gates and the wide road leading out into the world.

They hesitated here. They had never been off the place before. It was a tremendous venture; but the trail of the rubber smell led straight away from the gates. They sniffed at it, whined anxiously, then slowly it drew them on.

There had been friction between the groom and the best man. It had developed over the groom's toilet. In particular, a fawn-colored waistcoat that the best man had extracted from his own wardrobe had proved an irritant. It had taken all of ten minutes to persuade the groom that its splendors would not transform its wearer into a "'oly show."

At last this was accomplished, a coat was slipped on over the waistcoat, and a whisk broom applied to the *tout ensemble*.

"An' now," said Peter ungratefully, "I 'ope to Gawd you're through."

Griggs, the butler, stepped back and surveyed his work with growing pride. He had felt his task to be hopeless until now; but he had builded better than he knew. The result surprised him.

"Not bad," he said, revolving slowly and with half-shut eyes about Peter's person. "Very genteel, I should say, if you ask me. Try to stand more as if you was made of something besides cement."

He smoothed a lapel, tweaked the lavender silk tie, and withdrew a *boutonnière* from Peter's shaving mug.

"Mrs. Gregory's orders," he said firmly, as he pinned the flowers to a shrinking bosom. "If you'd take things as they come," he suggested, "you'd 'elp appearances by sweating less profuse."

A gleam of satisfaction flickered for an instant in Peter's dripping countenance.

"I'll 'andle that matter to suit myself," he stated.

Griggs consulted his watch.

"Well, take 'old of yourself," he advised. "I must 'ave you at the church in ten minutes. 'Ere's the motor now.... Kindly put that chewing tobacco back where you got it!"

Ten minutes later Peter was staring fixedly at nothing. His eyes were glazed, his knees shook, his hands had become extraordinarily prominent. There stretched before him a white-ribboned aisle that cut a blurred mass of rustling, whispering, staring humanity squarely in half. All Brookfield was there, of course, and most of the village besides; but Peter knew them not as individuals. They were nothing but eyes, devouring eyes, that feasted on the very soul of him as it palpitated somewhere beneath the fawn-colored waistcoat.

Then a face swam out of the blurred mass before him, and it was the face of the master of Brookfield, and it grinned mockingly at him and then faded away.

There was a sort of moaning sound, and Peter knew that it came from the organ, and then the church door filled and there bore down on him a floating cloudy whiteness, and somewhere in it was a new pair of eyes, big and blue and mysterious.

"The mistress of Brookfield cooed once with delight.

Isn't she adorable, Jim?" she gasped. "And Peter, I'm proud of Peter, too .... It's going splendidly!"

The master of Brookfield gave the bride a brief glance. Then his fascinated eye swung back and settled on a lavender tie, white *boutonnière*, and fawn-colored waistcoat.

"Superb!" he murmured, and bowed his head in the darkest corner of the pew. He looked up at last just as Father Vincent rolled forth the first sonorous Latin of the service.

Then the master of Brookfield became conscious of a vague and rustling murmur from the back of the church. He heard the booming voice of Father Vincent falter. He turned toward the growing murmur, and a look of such unhallowed joy came into his face that the mistress of Brookfield marveled, and quickly followed his glance with her own. Her face froze with horror as she did so.

Down the ribboned aisle, the rubber smell discarded for the more certain scent of Peter's footsteps, came two animated mops of dust and swamp ooze. They came swiftly, surely, and they threw themselves with abandon at Peter, whom they had come so far to find.

The next few moments were full to overflowing. It is a pleasure to record that the best man was equal to the emergency. He plunged to the rescue of the groom—or was it the fawn-colored waistcoat?— at the expense of his own apparel. He succeeded in fastening a pudgy hand on Powder's collar, but the fingers of his other hand closed wildly on one of Shot's long, silky, sensitive ears, and Shot raised his voice in a despairing wail.

Father Vincent had thus far proved his mettle. He had no more than hesitated for an instant at the first whirlwind entrance of the puppies. Then, without a visible tremor, he continued the service.

But now the groom was moved to speech. He glared once at the worthy Griggs, and addressed Father Vincent briefly.

"'Old your 'orses," he said. He whirled and advanced on the best man, and fire was in his eye. "'Aven't you no sense?" he inquired. "Do you think you can 'old a setter by the ear? 'E ain't a 'og nor yet a calf! Leggo of 'im!"

Griggs obeyed, and Shot flew to his rescuer with a whine of gratitude.

"'Ow," said Peter, advancing another step, "would you like for a big fat-'anded bum to take 'old of your ear?"

Griggs backed hurriedly against the chancel railing, still holding Powder mechanically by the collar. Peter pointed to the puppy.

"Leggo of 'im, too," he ordered, and Grigg's nerveless fingers unclosed from the collar.

"A setter's ear," explained Peter to the awestricken front pews, "is that delicate it ought never to be touched, 'ardly, let alone 'anging to it."

At these words a distressing thing occurred. For some moments the master of Brookfield, unnoticed for the time being, had been rocking back and forth as though in terrible agony. But now attention swung his way, for there burst from him a sound difficult to describe. It was as though a hen, afflicted with bronchitis, were attempting to cackle. That he was suffering there could be no doubt, for he writhed in his seat. Quite suddenly he disappeared altogether, and those nearest him realized that he had collapsed entirely, and now half sat, half lay, in the corner of the pew.

The mistress of Brookfield bent over him. Her attitude was one of tender solicitude. It was deceiving, however.

"Jim Gregory," she hissed, "sit up this instant!"

Strange words, harsh words, to a man overtaken by a dire seizure, and the master of Brookfield sent back a husky appeal for mercy.

"'I am dying, Egypt, dying,'" he informed her.

His life partner proved herself a cruel, a heartless woman. She straightened up and sat stiffly erect, coldly, proudly pale.

"I'll not forgive you!" she told him, looking straight before her, and added, regardless of her grammar, "*Never*!"

All this is minor detail. The central figure was Peter, who proved at this moment his right to the attention of the audience. He turned from the abashed and shrinking Griggs and uttered one word.

"'Eel!" he said.

Powder and Shot now did their mentor proud. They obeyed the command instantly, and halted just behind Peter, one to the right, one to the left of him. Peter took his place at Leona's side, the puppies following.

"Charge!" he ordered.

Powder and Shot sank dutifully down behind him. Peter gave Father Vincent a look of supreme triumph.

"'Ow's that," he inquired in a confidential whisper, "for only eight months?"

Father Vincent did not reply. His face, which had been cherry red, became a vivid purple. Above all else he wished to meet the eye of the master of Brookfield. He knew, however, that to do so would be fatal. He made a supreme effort.

"Join hands," he directed; and then, despite the countenance of the bride, which seemed to hold in check the lightning's blast, he went on with the service, while Powder and Shot, their heads tilting now and then to hear the better, gave his Latin a close, a respectful attention.

They were good. They were good as gold, and Peter swelled with pride. His face shone with it as he turned at last from the altar, a bachelor no longer. There remained, however, the long journey down a lane of whispering humans. Would Powder and Shot stand this acid test?

"'Eel!" commanded Peter with some anxiety. He was rewarded by such prompt obedience that he was reassured. He began the march down the aisle in visible triumph. Then, as he passed the pew wherein was the mistress of Brookfield, he received a dagger glance that made him falter. He looked uneasily behind him to see if the puppies were at heel. They were; but Leona, unfortunately, was three paces in the rear of them.

Then Peter remembered. He had been told to bear his bride from the altar on his right arm. He slackened his pace until she came abreast of him, then poked his elbow at her invitingly.

"'Ere," he muttered, "take 'old of this!"

And then Leona repudiated her marriage vows with startling swiftness. The echo of her promise to obey had scarcely ceased to whisper from the vaulted ceiling, yet at this first connubial command she became insurgent. She shrank from Peter's offered arm as though it were an adder. Without acknowledging his presence by so much as the quiver of an eyelash, she swept on—at Peter's side, to be sure, but as far from physical contact with him as the width of the aisle would permit.

They reached the door at last, to find the victoria and a pair of hunters, pressed into unaccustomed service, waiting at the curb. Peter surveyed the victoria dubiously. Once, long ago, it had been Brookfield's pride. He glanced from its cloth upholstering to the bedraggled Powder and Shot. The comparison was odious; but this was an emergency, and what must be must be.

"I'll keep 'em on the floor like," he explained to old Marcus, who was on the box. "They'd be 'ell-'ooping over 'alf the country if I let 'em go.' Op in!" he told Leona, "an' 'old on to one of 'em when I 'and 'im to you."

Then, for the first time in her married life, Leona addressed her husband.

"Assassin!" she gasped, and fled.

Peter's mouth opened with amazement as he watched her. She went as though pursued, her veil trailing behind her, her hands clasped at her bosom. As she reached the Brookfield limousine she swerved, climbed wildly in, and sank, a sobbling heap, into the deep cushions of the back seat.

Peter's mouth was still open as the mistress of Brookfield appeared hurriedly in the church door. Her eyes swept past the victoria and caught the huddled figure in the limousine. She favored Peter with one crushing look as she flew to Leona's side.

The master of Brookfield followed her leisurely. As he reached the car its door closed in his face.

"Home, Felix," said the mistress of Brookfield succinctly, and the big car rolled like a battleship from the curb.

Peter and the master of Brookfield watched it until it turned the corner and disappeared. Then their eyes met.

Peter put Powder and Shot into the victoria, climbed in himself, and looked uncertainly at the master of Brookfield.

"'Ow about a lift?" he suggested with an apologetic glance at the bows of white ribbon that gleamed like snow against the dark running gear of the victoria.

The master of Brookfield accepted the invitation with alacrity.

"You're on," he said with a gleam.

At the end of two strenuously tearful hours the mistress of Brookfield had succeeded in convincing the bride that her life was not wrecked beyond repair.

"And now," said the mistress of Brookfield, "drink your tea and no more crying. I'll see that you have your wedding trip."

"Yes, madam," said Leona.

"I'm going to send for Peter now. You can leave on the six o'clock train tonight."

"To Niagara Falls we will go, madam?" questioned Leona.

"If you prefer," promised the mistress of Brookfield, and was rewarded by a quivering smile.

When Peter entered, hat in hand, a few moments later, he too, was smiling. He beamed joyfully at Leona and the mistress of Brookfield.

"The Peg bitch," he said, "'as 'ad six grand pups. 'Er fever's gone down, an' Slosson says she'll be 'erself in no tune. 'E thinks mebby as 'ow—"

"Peter," cried the mistress of Brookfield, "stop this instant! There, there," she said soothingly to Leona, "he doesn't mean it. Don't you dare," she threw at Peter, "mention dogs again!"

Peter swallowed hastily, reached for his chewing tobacco, recollected himself in time, and touched his forehead.

"No, mem," he said dazedly.

There was a moment's pause.

"Peter," said the mistress of Brookfield at last, "are you fond of Leona?"

Peter blushed to the roots of his hair and dropped his eyes. He raised them then until they met a pair of moist blue ones, into which he gazed.

"Why," he burst out suddenly, "she's just the finest gel that ever stood on two legs!"

"Yes," said the mistress of Brookfield. "Now give her a kiss." She became busy at her desk for a moment, then turned to Peter and put a folded piece of paper in his hand. "You're going on a little trip together," she explained. "You leave at six o'clock. Drive to town now and have that cashed."

Peter's face fell as he unfolded the paper mechanically. He brightened somewhat when his eye took in the check's figures.

"Why, now," he said, "I've been thinking as 'ow I'd like to go down to Chuck Sellers's place in Tennessee. 'E's got a strain of these 'ere Pointin' Griffons 'e wants me to look over."

A quavering moan came from Leona. The mistress of Brookfield shot Peter an icy glance.

"You will go," she said frigidly, "to Niagara Falls. Felix will take you to the train."

"Yes, mem," said Peter, and withdrew.

At five forty-five that evening he struggled with a bulging suitcase into the limousine and took his seat beside his beaming bride.

The master of Brookfield strolled out of the dusk, cigarette in hand, and halted by the car.

"Where to now?" he inquired.

"Nihagara Falls," said Peter.

"But I thought—" began the master of Brookfield.

Peter kicked the suitcase viciously, and slumped down in his seat.

"Oh, I've gave up on *that*," he said.

· III ·

Dumb-Bell's Check

During the summer months early dinner was the custom at Brookfield. It was served out of doors, weather permitting, either on the terrace or beneath the canopy of vines that crept with artful abandon from end to end of the pergola.

In the latter case it meant that the master and mistress of Brookfield were alone and it would be a "cozy" dinner, as they called it, hidden from the many staring windows of the big house by the dumb and eyeless vine.

At such times those who served them did so swiftly, and withdrew. Then they helped themselves and stole choice morsels from each other's plates, and giggled, and "scrapped," as in days gone by, and sometimes upset things, which was dreadful. But no one would come except at the voice of the silver bell with the carved ivory handle, and they were careful not to touch it lest its fatal clamor occur.

"Chief," said the master of Brookfield, one August evening, "pass the jam!" He indicated with a lordly gesture a mound of currant jelly glowing in a crystal dish.

Since jam had to do with childhood his words were a challenge. which Mrs. Gregory at once accepted.

"Why, certainly," she said politely, and placed a buttered ear of corn in his extended palm.

The master of Brookfield scooped a lump of ice from his drinking goblet, encircled his lady with his arm, and drew her slowly to him.

It's not fair to use strength," she wailed. "You know it's not. You're breaking a rule."

At that exact moment Leona stood round-eyed in the entrance to the pergola.

The mistress of Brookfield became particularly dignified. She returned to her chair unhurriedly, patted her hair, and then addressed Leona.

"What is it?" she said. "I didn't ring."

"Peter to you weesh to speak," explained Leona with a gulp.

Mrs. Gregory looked at Leona in amazement.

"Peter?" she said. "Why, what's got into the man?" Then apprehension seized her. "Is anything wrong at the kennels?" she asked quickly. "Where is Peter?"

"'Ere, mem, beggin' your pardon," said Peter, and appeared miraculously beside Leona. "I thought as 'ow you'd like to see this 'ere," he explained, as he pulled a copy of *The American Field* from his pocket. "It's just come."

"What's the matter with you, Peter?" asked the master of Brookfield. "Have you lost your mind?"

"No, sir, beggin' your pardon," said Peter. "They've challenged with the big pointer to run a three-hour match against Dumb-Bell for a thousand dollars. It's all in 'ere," he added, flourishing the paper. "You can see for yourself."

The master of Brookfield scowled at Peter.

"What of it?" he said. "Why do you come here with it *now*?"

"Well, you see," said Peter, a shade uncertainly, "the quicker you knew about it, the quicker you could take 'em up. You can wire yet tonight, sir."

Mrs. Gregory watched the master of Brookfield with dancing eyes. But the master of Brookfield did not smile. "Why should I 'take em up'?" he asked.

Peter's jaw dropped.

"Why, now—er" he began, and became speechless as his world fell about him At last he looked up, dull-eyed. "I never thought," he said, "as 'ow you'd let 'em say we was afraid to race the big 'ound.... I ax your pardon for disturbin' of you." He folded the paper, stuffed it into his pocket, and turned slowly away. "Good night, mem," he threw over his shoulder, and was gone.

"Oh, Jim!" said Mrs. Gregory. "He's heartbroken—he thinks you mean it! Peter!" she called, "Peter!" But Peter was out of earshot, and she rang the silver bell.

While someone went to summon Peter, the master of Brookfield wrote a telegram. As he finished, Peter again appeared.

"They said as 'ow you wanted me," he muttered, looking straight before him.

"Why, yes," said the master of Brookfield "You left in such a hurry you forgot to take this with you.... I want it sent tonight."

Peter took the telegram and read it carefully. He looked up with blazing eyes.

"That's tellin' 'em!" he said. "I'll start workin' the little dog tomorrow. We'll need all of two months to get 'im ready—'e'll 'ave to go to Ramsey for a month on chicken."

There are two championships in which field trial dogs compete. The winning of either means everlasting glory. One, the National, is run in Tennessee on quail. The other, the All America, is run in the Far West on prairie chicken.

The winner of the National or the All America has Champion written before his name from that day on, and never again may he compete in open trials. He is a crowned king, whose sons and daughters are of the blood royal. He may not stoop to struggle with more common clay.

But a champion may run a match race against any dog with the temerity to meet him. And now Champion Brookfield Dumb-Bell, winner of the National, had been defied in public print by the owner of Champion Windem Bang, winner of the All America, and Peter was in a fever.

The telegram he sent that night read:

Meet you any time after October first, at any place, for any sum.

And it meant that "the little white ghost" must leave his leather chair in the living-room and take to the open for the honor of Brookfield.

So, early next morning, Peter, a kennel boy, and the small champion went over the hill to the broad meadows across which the brook lay like a silver serpent.

Peter rode a good horse. Dumb-Bell had not been hunted for pleasure as yet, and no man on foot could keep within sight of the ghost at his work.

"Turn 'im loose!" said Peter to the kennel boy. "An' meet me by them willows in thirty minutes."

"O-o-o-o!" said the kennel boy a moment later, his eyes on something white fading, fading in the distance.

"'E's 'ell, ain't he!" said Peter, gathering up his reins. "Come on, 'oss! You wouldn't let a little thing like that get away from you, would you?"

Morning after morning from then on they went forth, and little by little the thirty minutes were increased until at last Dumb-Bell could do the full three hours at top speed, wolf down his meat that night, and ask for more.

According to science, fatigue produces a toxin. When an animal is overworked he cannot throw this off. The poison dulls the nerves of his stomach and plays havoc with his appetite. Peter knew nothing of science, but he scanned a tin plate anxiously every evening. When, after the full three hours, it was licked to mirror brightness—

"'E's ready," said Peter, "to beat anybody's dog!"

Meanwhile the field trial world divided over this meeting of champions. Pointer men prayed, in private, for big slashing, smashing Windem Bang. In public they admitted that perhaps the Brookfield setter had a shade in nose and bird sense, but for courage and headlong brilliancy there was "nothing to it" but the pointer. Furthermore, since Gregory had allowed his adversary to name the place for the meeting, the owner of the pointer had of course chosen North Dakota, the home of the prairie chicken. The country and the birds were an old story to the pointer, whereas the Brookfield dog was more familiar with the haunts of quail.

Setter men thought of the white ghost with his uncanny nose, and smiled. *Their* champion was to have a month's work on the prairies before the battle.

"And," said Scott Benson, "if they just let him go, in a month he'll be an old friend to every chicken from the Gulf to Canada."

On one subject, however, everyone was in accord. Dog men all over the land had learned to hate the owner of the pointer. For years he had bred dogs — good dogs, they regretfully admitted — and at last fate had breathed the spirit of a champion into one of them. Furthermore, he was a great champion. This they admitted, also, but with more than regrets. That Emmett Fry should own such a dog was beyond mere regretting — it was a calamity.

Chuck Sellers relieved himself on the subject with a few well-chosen words.

"There's more class in the tip of that pointer's tail," he said, "than Emmett's got in his whole blame carcass."

Since the tail of Champion Windem Bang was needle pointed, this was repeated broadcast and found much favor.

All this was man's talk, and not for women's ears, so the mistress of Brookfield heard no word of it; but she felt cold steel in the air when Emmett Fry was mentioned, and it puzzled her.

"You don't like this man Fry, do you?" she said to Gregory one morning, and felt his arm stiffen within her own.

"I don't know him," said the master of Brookfield shortly. "Are you sure you want to go out to this match, Chief? It's a hard trip."

"I'm going," she stated. "I've never seen Dumb-Bell run, you know, and this may be my last chance.... Why don't you like him?" she asked, returning to the charge.

"I don't know him," he repeated. "How can I like him or dislike him?"

She knew this to be an evasion, but let it pass, and questioned Peter the next day.

"What sort of a man is Mr. Fry?" she asked him.

Peter was dusting a puppy with flea powder. He straightened up and spoke with difficulty, for flea powder is as certain in its action as snuff.

"A-choo-o! " he said. "Just plain skunk... a-choo-o! ... beggin' your pardon!"

"What has he done, what does he do, that makes you say that, Peter? " she questioned.

"Well," said Peter, "I'll tell you one thing he done. Six years ago, come November, Emmett Fry starts a pointer derby, by Damascus out of Old Rose, in the Continental. 'E was a nice-going pup but a leetle gun-shy—just flinchy-like. 'E run a good 'eat an' it was between 'im an' a young bitch by Gladstone in the finals. The judges were 'ard put to it for a decision, but they noticed that Emmett don't stand close to 'is pup when 'e fires.

"'At his next point, Mr. Fry, shoot directly over your dog,' they tells Emmett, an' he done so. At the crack of the gun the pup breaks for the woods, 'is tail between 'is legs—an' that lets 'im out.

Well, Emmett goes into the woods after 'is pup, an' next we 'ear 'is gun—both barrels. When 'e comes out of the woods.. .'e's alone. 'An',' says Emmett, 'e'll not run away from a gun no more."

Peter caught up the can of flea powder, and bent abruptly to his work.

"Oh!" said Mrs. Gregory. "The beast ... the beast!"

And presently the master of Brookfield looked up from his desk into a white and quivering face.

"Good Lord, Chief?" he said, "what's happened?"

"You knew about it all along!" she accused. "And let Dumb-Bell meet his dog ... a man like that! How could you do such a thing! ... How could you!"

"I've never met this man," the master of Brookfield said slowly. "When he did ... what he did, I used what influence I had to have his entries refused by all field trial clubs in America. Since then I have made it a point never to enter a dog where he was a competitor. But now—it is a question of setter against pointer; and because I believe in the setter as the greatest of all bird dogs, and many men agree with me and look to my dog to prove it, we owe it to them to beat this pointer—if we can .... Don't you think so?"

There was a moment's silence.

"What about the thousand dollars you may win from him?"

The master of Brookfield regarded her gravely. Then the corners of his mouth twitched ever so little.

"Why," he said, with a bow, "*you* may have that, Chief."

She had him by the coat lapels in an instant, and did her futile best to shake him.

"I'll tear it up!" she said, between her teeth.

"Indeed?" said Gregory. "And what about that family on Rock Ridge who haven't a shoe to their back, and the lame man who needs a wooden leg or an aëroplane or something, and the woman who has delirium trem—Excuse me, it's her husband—isn't it? And that girl who should have her voice cultivated, and—er—all the rest of 'em?"

The mistress of Brookfield knitted her brows in thought.

"They won't get a cent of it!" she announced at last. "If Dumb-Bell wins it, *he* will send it to the S.P.C.A.!"

The hotel at Belmont, North Dakota, was packed to bursting. Its occupants lifted up their voices and discussed bird dogs, past, present, and to come. The noise was bewildering. From a little distance it sounded like the roar of falling waters, and seemed as endless.

Back in the kennels it was comparatively quiet. Derbys might bay a neighbor, old veterans might rustle the straw as they dreamed of whirring birds; but though the match between Brookfield Dumb-Bell and Windem Bang was to be run as a final to the Great Western Trials, and a hundred dogs were all about them, Peter spoke almost in a whisper to Bill Ramsey as they examined the white ghost by lantern light.

"I don't like it!" said Peter. "'E never ate a bite.... 'Is eyes don't look good to me, neither."

"Pshaw, Pete!" said Ramsey. "There's nothin' wrong with him. He knows why he's here as well as you an' me. He's excited, that's all. Why, look how you passed up them ham an' eggs yourself tonight! Let him alone — let him get his rest!"

"Feel 'is nose!" said Peter. "An' why don't 'e lie down like 'e'd ought?"

Ramsey took Peter by the arm.

"Come on out of here!" he urged. "If a big mutt was to keep a-rubbin' at your nose you wouldn't go to sleep, neither. He'll run his race if you let him alone. If you mess with him all night Emmett'll beat me tomorrow. *I've* got charge of this dog... now, come on out of here!"

So Peter, with a last troubled look at the suspiciously bright eyes of the Brookfield champion, followed the handler from the kennels; and Dumb-Bell dropped his head on his paws to pass the night in a twitching and uneasy slumber.

A pale blue sky appeared next morning and hung above an endless rolling stubble. Two months before this stubble had been wheat, a golden guaranty that North Dakota could put bread into the mouths of half a continent. But the gold had been garnered and now in its place was a lesser metal, for the stubble was heavy with frost and the rising sun had turned it to a plain of glistening silver.

Calm to majesty was this plain of silver, unruffled by the fact that it would soon become a battlefield. The last day of the Great Western Trials had arrived; two champions would meet that morning, and over the stubble would prove the mettle of their sires.

When the sun was an hour high, black dots appeared at the far edge of the plain. Presently they became horsemen — hundreds of horsemen — with a sprinkling, of buggies, buckboards, and even an automobile or so, strung about a wagon from which came, now and then, a beseeching whine.

This whine was the voice of Champion Windem Bang, who gazed out through the slats that penned him in and longed to be away.

His small rival was quieter. The white ghost knew what all these horsemen meant; he knew what was expected of him that day; but he knew that his body ached, that his throat was dry, and that the rolling stubble called but faintly to him. The day before he had eaten a piece of tainted meat no bigger than a lump of sugar, and now it was better to lie quietly in the soft straw than to pit one's speed and nose against another over those long, long miles.

So the gulf which never can be crossed, between the human animal and his most passionately devoted friend, was between the little setter and fair play. One word would have told these humans, one word—and yet it was denied him. He would be judged by what he did that day, without it.... And so he lay in the wagon and grinned a hopeless grin when the big pointer yelped reproaches at those about him, or scratched and bit at the slats.

An iron-gray man on a big roan horse drew rein at last.

"I think we might put them down here, Frank," he said. "What time is it?"

A man riding beside him nodded and took out his watch.

"All right, Mr. Fry! All right, Mr. Ramsey!" he called. "We'll let them go at eight sharp—that gives you five minutes."

It was only after a struggle that his handler snapped the leash on Windem Bang. When this was done, the pointer soared out of the wagon with a yelp, and bounded like a rubber ball to the end of his tether. Emmett Fry threw his weight against the leash and smiled.

Chuck Sellers saw the smile, and leaned down confidentially from the saddle.

"Better save some of that, Emmett!" he advised. "You'll need it."

The handler looked up with a sneer.

"A hundred even on him!" he said.

"Got you," said Chuck cheerfully. "Come again!"

"Make it two!" said Fry.

"Got you!" Chuck repeated. "Are you through?" But the pointer had dragged his handler out of earshot, and Chuck turned to Ramsey. "You heard that, Bill?" he asked.

Ramsey nodded as he snapped the leash on the white ghost.

"We'll give you a run for your money," he promised, and led his dog to the starting point.

With the feel of the stubble underfoot, with the big pointer straining at his leash beside him, Dumb-Bell's spirits revived a little. He was better; there was no doubt of that. The water that Ramsey had given him a moment before had cooled his throat. His legs felt stronger, too. He even wanted to run. He *would* run, that was sure! Fast enough, perhaps, to beat an ordinary dog. But Windem Bang, big, splendid Windem Bang, was not an ordinary dog. And in addition to the running the white ghost must read the crisp wind that sang across a thousand miles of prairie, and miss no word of its message.

The little setter lifted his head. His nostrils quivered as they explored the wind. Then he knew that his nose would betray him. It was no longer the nose of a champion, but a dull, uncertain thing—the kind with which ordinary shooting dogs go slowly and make mistakes. As he heard the "Get away!" of his handler, which is the field trial call to battle, he grinned his hopeless grin.

When his leash is slipped, a field trial dog races straight away. He is driven to this first exultant rush by an overwhelming energy. A pair of high-class dogs make this preliminary flight a trial of pure speed. It was the custom of the white ghost to give his rival fifty feet or so and then sweep by him.

That Windem Bang could go like a comet made no difference to him. Had Dumb-Bell been himself, he would have matched the pointer stride for stride, with joy in his heart. But now his heels had failed him and he called on the big brain of Roderigo that was in his little head. He let Windem Bang go on alone into the far distance, while he shot away to the left.

He saw a patch of green alfalfa as he ran, and he headed for it. It was a likely place for chickens; there was a good half mile of it and he went down the lower edge, his head well up, as fast as he could go.

But Windem Bang did not run blindly long. He, too, had brains; a champion always has. When he found himself alone, he looked about him. Then he caught the green of the alfalfa, and he swung in a magnificent curve to strike the lower edge, down wind. He was moving like a race horse, directly behind the ghost. At each terrific bound he made he cut down the distance between them.

Dumb-Bell heard him coming. He must get wind of the covey somewhere in the green alfalfa before the pointer passed him! He put every ounce of strength he had into his running. He no longer heard the pointer. Good! He could still run, it seemed. Then he heard, far away, another sound. It was the spectators shouting. He turned his head, and there was Windem Bang, on the very spot where he himself had passed ten seconds before, tense as steel, as moveless as a stone.

There could be no mistaking what that panther crouch of the big pointer meant. From his eager lifted muzzle, to his stiff and lancelike tall, every line of him said: "Birds!"

Dumb-Bell's heart was bitter within him as he whirled and acknowledged his rival's find with an honor point.

"Missed'em!" burst out a pointer man. "Missed 'em clean! *There's* your setter champion for you! Oh, mamma! Did you see that Bang dog nail 'em?"

"He—he didn't d-do very well that time, did he, Jim?" said the mistress of Brookfield, as their buckboard swayed and bounded toward the pointing dogs.

"No," said Gregory. "I don't understand it. It may be a false point."

But it wasn't a false point. Emmett Fry flushed a mighty bevy of prairie chickens thirty feet ahead of Windem Bang. They rose like one bird, and sailed off in stately flight to scatter in the stubble nearly a mile away.

The man on the roan horse kept his eyes on the two champions. Neither moved.

"Send them on, gentlemen!" he called to the handlers. "We'll follow this covey up. We'll let them work on singles for a while."

Then followed a terrible half-hour for Dumb-Bell. In the race to the scattered covey he was beaten, and he saw the pointer make a smashing find two hundred feet ahead of him. Once more he came to an honor point. Once more a yell of delight went up from those who favored Windem Bang. Once more the setter men looked at each other and were silent.

And now it was a race among a scattered covey at top speed, for champions must catch the faint scent of a lone bird while going like a rocket; and this takes nose, and nose, and nose, fine as a hair and certain as a compass ... Dumb-Bell's was hot with fever.

So he drove his aching body along, while Emmett Fry called, "Point, judge!" again and again, as his dog cut down the singles with swift precision.

For Dumb-Bell the wind was a blank. Had he slowed down he might have read it, but he was a champion, and he must make his points high-headed and like a flash of lightning, or not at all. He worked in a frenzy, his sides heaving, his eyes shot with blood, only to honor Windem Bang, who was going faster than he, and with a razor nose.

"Why, Pete!" said Chuck Sellers at last in wide amazement. "They're goin' to beat us!"

Peter turned to him with a set and stony face.

"Beat us!" he said. "An' why wouldn't they beat us? 'E 'asn't no more nose than I 'ave! I knowed it last night, an' I let Bill talk me out of it! 'E's a sick dog! An' we're tryin' to beat the best pointer that ever lived, with 'im. I ain't a trainer, I'm a bum! An' *Bill*! ... They'd ought to shoot 'im! 'E's sick, I tell you ... 'e's sick this minute!" He turned his horse and galloped back to the master of Brookfield.

"'Ave him took up, sir!" he said. "'E's off—away off—'e ain't got nothin'. 'Ave him took up!"

The master of Brookfield hesitated.

"It won't do, Peter," he said finally. "We should have known that before they started."

"*I* knowed it!" said Peter. "I knowed it last night! I'm a big slob—beggin' your pardon—I ain't fit to 'andle 'untin' dogs, let alone '*im*! You can fire me tomorrow, sir; but take the little dog up! 'E's sick—we may be 'armin' of 'im!"

They had come to a halt while a chicken was flushed to the credit of Windem Bang. Peter's voice had risen to a wail, and many heard what he had said.

"That's right, Gregory!" called a pointer man. "Take him up! He's got no business with *that* kind of a dog. *He's* sick, all right, and gettin' sicker! ... Take him up!"

The master of Brookfield felt a slender hand creep into his own. He squeezed it slightly, and smiled a grim smile.

"He'll have to take a beating, Peter," he said quietly. "Go on, driver!"

So Dumb-Bell took his beating for half of the three hours that he must run, and a fearful beating it was. For an hour and thirty minutes he ran, gasping for air, slobbering at the mouth, while his nose told him nothing.

Then as he passed a patch of ragweed he caught a faint trace on the wind. He turned like a flash and froze into a statue. He had taken a desperate chance of making a false point. He had acted with the certainty of a good nose when he was far from certain. He grinned with anxiety as he waited for his handler, while faint, very faint, came that trace on the wind.

"Steady, boy!" said Ramsey. An instant later twenty feathered bombs shot up from the stubble and sailed away.

"Some find!" said Chuck Sellers, brightening. "How does that suit you, Pete?"

But Peter did not reply. He was watching a white streak flash along the stubble, neck and neck with Windem Bang.

This was the turning of the tide. The violent effort he had made on courage alone was the little setter's salvation. His pounding heart had at last cleared his blood of the ptomaine that had drugged him.

As he raced for the scattered covey he felt a new vitality surge within him.... Ten minutes more and Dumb-Bell was himself again—a white ghost with a magic nose.

But Windem Bang was a great dog, backed by a tremendous lead. Only a miracle could save the day for Brookfield. The white ghost knew this as well as those who watched, and from that moment he became a miracle in nose and range and speed. Windem Bang was still going like the wind—few dogs could have held him even. But now ahead of him, always ahead of him, was a white and fleeting thing that skimmed the stubble with no apparent effort, and found birds in all directions.

The big pointer was puzzled. For the first time in his life he was being outpaced, and he couldn't understand it. He had run rings around this little setter until now! He would do it again, he told himself—then every sinew in his body drank deep of his vitality while he ran as he had never run before.

An hour went by, and Windem Bang began to wonder. A shadow came and dimmed the eager light in his eyes. The shadow was fatigue, and it frightened him.

He fled from it in a tremendous burst of speed, found a bevy, and went on. But the shadow grew deeper. It was blotting out all the fire, all the brilliancy of his efforts. In nose and heels and heart he felt it now, and he looked anxiously ahead. Despair seized him as he looked; for Brookfield Dumb-Bell was going like a driven spirit, immune from the weakness of flesh.

"Call in your dogs, gentleman!"said the man on the roan horse. "They have been down three hours."

In another moment he was the center of a crowding mass of horsemen that grew larger every instant.

"Who wins?" they howled. "Who wins?" And many answered the question themselves.

The man on the roan horse held up his hand for silence, and obtained it.

"Gentlemen," he began, "the judges have decided that this match, so far, is a draw. We— " He got no further.

"Draw! Hell! The setter couldn't smell nothin' for two hours!" ... "Two hours! Forget it! Look what he done all the last end! The setter wins!"... "You're a liar!" ... "Get down off that horse an' say it again!"

At last quiet was restored.

"As I have said before, gentleman, this match, as it now stands, is a *draw*. It becomes a matter of stamina. The judges ask that the dogs go on until we can render a decision!"

"Why, certainly," said the master of Brookfield when Peter brought him the word.

But Emmett Fry faced the judges with the panting Windem Bang on leash beside him.

"Do you think these are huntin' dogs?" he inquired. "Do you want 'em to go all day? This was a three-hour match. I've run it *and* won it, and I want a decision *now*! I won't turn this dog loose again for nobody!"

The man on the roan horse looked at Emmett coldly.

"Very well, Mr. Fry," he said. "If you refuse to go on, we shall decide now—in favor of the setter."

The handler's face became gray with rage. He took a step forward, opened his lips, closed them again, and turned abruptly to Bill Ramsey.

"I'm ready whenever you are," he said hoarsely.

Ramsey stooped and cast off his dog.

"Get away!" he said, with a wave of bis hand—and the white ghost was gone.

An instant later Windem Bang flung himself across the stubble at the top of his clip, and the battle was on again.

The short rest had helped the big pointer. He went away with a rush. For twenty minutes more he went, a splendid thing to see. Then suddenly a red darkness fell about him. it was hot and suffocating; it filled his nostrils so that his breath came in struggling gasps.

It was hard to go in in this darkness. But champions must go on and on until they hear a whistle. He went on until a weight, an immense weight, seemed to fall across his loins. It was not fair to make him carry such a weight, he thought, and faltered in his stride .... The voice of his handler came like the lash of a whip:

"You Bang!—Go on!" it said.

Yes, he must go on. He had forgotten for a moment. He saw a swale ahead and to the right. Its edge was dark with ragweed, and he plunged toward it. The swale was half a mile away, and he called on the last of his strength to reach it. He was nearly there when a white flash shot from the left, cut in ahead of him, and stiffened into marble. Windem Bang lurched to a point in acknowledgment, swaying where he stood.

This was the end. As the birds were flushed, the pointer staggered on—he didn't know where. The voice of his handler had lost its meaning. He must go on, he knew that. So he went—in an aimless circle.

The man on the roan horse rode forward to the pointer's handler. His eyes were full of pity.

"You have a great dog, Mr. Fry," he said, "but—call him in, please."

"Damn his heart ... damn his yellow heart!" said Emmett Fry, and blew his whistle.

Windem Bang swung toward the sound of it, and came in. He was too far gone to dodge the loaded butt of the heavy dog whip, and he went down without a sound when it descended across his back. Nor did he make much of an outcry as it descended again and again. Only a moan came from him. He was too exhausted to do more....

The mistress of Brookfield gave a choking cry, flung herself from the buckboard, and rushed forward like a fury. Emmett Fry heard her coming, and looked up blindly.

"The dirty hound quit!" he said. "He had it won ... the dirty hound... but he quit!"

"You vile beast!" flamed the mistress of Brookfield. "Don't you dare touch him again!" She dropped in the stubble beside Windem Bang, throwing her coat over him as she did so.

The master of Broofield lifted her up.

"This won't do, Chief," he said, and all but carried her to the buckboard.

"Oh, Jim!" she pleaded. "He tried so hard!"

Then a thumping sound, followed by a moaning whimper, came to her. She covered her ears and sank in a heap to the floor of the buckboard.

"If Dumb-Bell had only lost!" she sobbed. "If Dumb-Bell had only lost...."

"Never mind, little Chief!" said the master of Broofield. *"I'll* take care of that."

He strode back until he faced the owner of Windem Bang.

"I have taken—a fancy—to your dog..." he managed to say, but could get no further. Suddenly he tore a checkbook from his pocket and wrote with a shaking hand. He held out a signed check for the other to see. "Fill it in—quick—for God's sake!" he said.

No one will ever know what Champion Windem Bang cost the master of Brookfield. He said no word to any man as he led the first pointer he had ever owned to the buckboard. But as he drove away a pair of dog eyes, trusting, faithful, looked up into his face, and a slim arm went about his neck. So, perhaps, everything considered, he did not pay too much.

A few days later the secretary of a certain benevolent society received the following letter:

Being heartily in sympathy with the work you do, it gives me great pleasure to inclose my check for one thousand dollars.

Faithfully Yours,

Champion BROOKFIELD DUMB-BELL.

· IV ·

A Permanent Intruder

The last thirty miles had been slid over somehow, and the car, sheathed in the mud of five counties, shot between brick gateposts to decent footing at last. I went into high gear—for the first time in hours, it seemed to me—with a sigh of relief. The mile spin up the graveled drive was a humming flash, and soon I was getting out of my coat in the dusky paneled hall which bisects the house, clean as a knife cut, from front to back.

The man disappeared with my bags after telling me that Mr. and Mrs. Gregory were out on the place somewhere "huntin' mush-rooms." I went to the dining-room, poured myself a drink of raw Scotch, and then drifted, as one does at Brookfield, to the living-room with its big open fire. I was halfway across the room when there came a hoarse rumble from the fireplace that nailed my feet to the floor.

"That-a-boy!" I said cheerfully, and took a step toward the fire-place.

There was another cavernous rumble.

"Now see here," I said with authority. "You stop this nonsense."

A gargoyle head was lifted from the bricks before the fireplace, a pair of bloodshot eyes were rolled in my direction and the rumble ceased. The eyes inspected me lazily and—I was glad to note this—without malice. Presently thump, thump went a clublike tail on the bricks. At the invitation I advanced.

He was an astonishing thing to find in his present surroundings. He was huge, he was a tawny yellow, he had lost an ear. He had been arrived at through the haphazard matings of bull terriers, English bulls, mastiffs, and heaven knows what else. Yet here he was, stretched comfortably before the living-room fire at Brookfield, where chickens, pigeons, cats, cattle, horses, and, above all, dogs, show an impeccable line of ancestors who made no steps aside.

He was a mystery, a friendly mystery, after that first deep-throated challenge, and my curiosity grew as I examined the unlovely bulk of him. I wondered in what disreputable proceedings he had lost his ear. I wondered why four of his lower front teeth were gone. Most of all I wondered at his serene contentment; at his air of being perfectly at home.

At last I pushed his bullet head aside, pulled his one good ear, gave him a solid thump on the ribs, and took my way to the kennels, and Peter, for an explanation.

"Peter," I said, while shaking hands, "why is that"—I hesitated—"bulldog allowed in the living-room?"

Peter took his stumpy fingers from mine and grinned.

"You 'ad 'ard work gettin' it out, didn't you?" he said. "Oh 'e belongs 'ere all right. 'Aven't you seen the people?"

"No," I replied. "They don't know I've come. He looks like bad medicine. I should think you'd be afraid he'd take hold of one of the setters."

"I was," said Peter thoughtfully—"at first. I put up a 'ell of a row about 'im. 'E come 'ere all along of horchids."

"Orchids!" I repeated. "What have orchids got to do with it?"

Peter indicated a sawhorse.

"'Ave a seat," he invited, and wadded a startling handful of fine cut into his mouth.

"You know," he began, after a necessary pause, "the missus was all for raisin' these 'ere horchids awhile back?"

I nodded.

"Well," said Peter, "we 'ad our troubles till it was over. Whilst we was goin' through this horchid business everything else was forgot. Why, she wouldn't come 'ere once a month, an' my best litters by Dumb-Bell bein' whelped at the time. I'd go up to the 'ouse after breakfast and I'd say: 'Beggin' your pardon, mem, but Sue Whitestone 'as nine grand ones by the little dog."

"'Yes,' she'd say; 'that's fine, Peter. I'll come down in a little while —just as soon as I see Jerry.'

"Then she'd start for the green'ouses, an' 'er an' ole Jerry 'ud 'ave their 'eads together the rest of the day.

"For all Jerry's sweatin' an' stewin', though, an' 'er an' 'im readin' books an' such, it seemed like the horchids was too shifty for 'em. Jerry 'as been a good gardener in 'is time, but 'e 'adn't never messed with horchids an' 'e couldn't seem to get the 'ang of 'em somehow.

"Right in the midst of it comes woodcock season, an' I got the missus' Lampton 20 oiled up nice for 'er. The day before the season opened the mister tells me we'll go over to the big 'ollow after cock next mornin'.

"'We'll take Bang and Beau,' 'e says. 'We'll start at five o'clock.'

"'I've been workin' a pair of young Dumb-Bells on cock,' I says; 'an' while they're not finished yet they 'ave sweet noses on 'em—that Bang sets a 'ot pace for the missus.'

"She's not going,' 'e says. 'She's too busy to get away.'

"'Well, I 'ardly expected it,' I says. 'She 'asn't looked in this direction for a month.'

"'Try flowers, Peter,' 'e says, grinnin' at me. 'Why don't you plant some nice geraniums along the runways?'

"'Me an' the mister 'unted cock alone all that week an' the next. One noon we're 'aving a bite at the 'ickory grove spring.

"''Ow long now,' I says, 'do you think it'll last?"

"'Last?' 'e says. 'Why, ten days more, of course.'

"'I don't mean the season,' I says. 'I mean horchids.'

"'E was just reachin' for a sandwich, but 'e didn't take it. Instead 'e rolls in the leaves.

"'Don't ask me,"'e says, settin' up with dead leaves in 'is 'air. 'She's sent to Scotland for an expert. 'E'll be 'ere soon, I fancy. Then we'll see some regular horchids. Cheer up, Peter; perhaps she'll let us wear one now and then.'

"Well, it was so. One day 'ere comes a specimin up the drive—it 's a long-necked Scotchman with reddish 'air like. 'E 'as a shiny black 'amper in one 'and an' a bundle tied with rope in the other. At 'is 'eels was a yellow—'ided butcher's bull as big as 'e was ugly.

"'Where,' I says to 'im, 'did you find little Buttercup?'

"'Mon,' 'e says, 'will ye tell Missus MacGregor I'm koom?'

"'I will that,' I says. 'I'll mention both of you to 'er. Stay 'ere till I'm back.'

"I found the missus in a green'ouse. 'Er sleeves was rolled up an' she 'ad loam on 'er 'ands an' face.

"'Mem,' I says, 'your horchid man 'as come with something that'll 'ave to be got off the place in a 'urry.'

"'Bring him 'ere to me, Peter,' she says; an' I done so. But first I 'ad 'im shut 'is dog in a runway.'

"When we got to the greenouse I points inside, an' Scotty an' 'is 'amper an' 'is bundle all goes in. 'E took a look at the missus.

"'Lassic,' 'e says, 'whur's your lady?'

"The missus gave me a look out of the corner of her eye.

"Won't I do?' she says.

"I must say this—Scotty, for all 'is long neck, surprised me. But then 'e 'ad red 'air. 'E put down 'is 'amper an' 'is bundle.

"'Aye, lass,' 'e says, 'ye'll do, though soap an' watter would na harm ye.' With that 'e steps to the missus an' takes a kiss at 'er. An' as I'm a livin' man she never moved an inch.

"'Thank you,' she says. 'Now what else can I do for you? I'm Mrs. Gregory.'

"Scotty looked at 'er close. 'Er rings was layin' on the window edge where she'd been diggin', an' the flash of 'em in the sunlight caught 'is eye. It 'it 'im all at once. Man, I'm tellin' you it was 'ard to tell where 'is face stopped and 'is 'air begun. Next 'e grabbed up 'is bundle an' out an' away 'e went.

"''E climbed the stone wall at the edge of the south lawn an' 'is coat tails goin' over it was the last we ever saw of 'im. The missus come to the green'ouse door an' watched 'im streak it across the lawn.

"''E seems to be going, Peter,' she says, an' 'er eyes was dancin' in 'er 'ead.

"''E 'as that appearance, mem,' I says.

"She looked anxious all of a sudden.

"''E'll surely come back, won't 'e?" she says. 'I paid his passage from Aberdeen."

"'Beggin' your pardon, mem,' I says, 'but just at the wall there 'e didn't strike me, take it all in all, like a person who 'ad 'opes of returning.' Then I remembered something.

"'Oh, Lord!' I says. "E's went an' left Buttercup.'

"'Buttercup?' says the missus. 'What's Buttercup?'

"'If the horchids,' I says, 'could get on by themselves, mem, whilst you're walkin' down to the kennels,' I says, 'you can see for yourself.'

"She 'adn't nothing to say to that an' we started for the kennels.

"'Peter,' she says all of a sudden, 'I 'aven't treated you very well lately. I'm sorry.'

"'Who am I to complain, mem?'" I says.

"'I'm going for woodcock tomorrow,' she says. 'But, Peter,' she says, 'this mustn't get out, you know—I'd never 'ear the last of it.'

"We'd got to the runways by now. Buttercup was in No. 4 an' I 'eaded for it.

" ''Ave no fear of me, mem,' I says. 'But,' I says, stoppin' at the runway gate, 'what's to be done with 'im? 'E'll need a lot of explainin'.'

"Buttercup was settin' on 'is 'unkers, lookin' mournful an' lettin' a kind of low thunder come off 'is chest.

"''Eavens, what a brute!' says the missus. 'Where did 'e come from?'

"''E belonged,' I says, 'to our late friend from Scotland. 'E don't seem to like the climate 'ere, does 'e?'

"'This is dreadful, Peter,' she says. 'What'll we do with 'im?'

"'Give him away to somebody,' I says, 'for a pet.'

"'Peter!' she says. 'Open that gate!'

"'Yes, mem,' I says, an' put my 'and to the gate latch. With that Buttercup goes plumb crazy. 'E let out a roar 'an 'it the gate like a tornado.

"'Oh, that's the way you feel about it, is it?' I says. 'Then I went to the carpenter shop and got me a piece of lead pipe about two foot long.

"'What are you goin' to do, Peter?' says the missus when I'm back.

"'I'm goin' in,' I says, 'an' explain about 'is disposition to 'im.'

"'No, no,' she says. 'Just let 'im alone for awhile. Get water to 'im somehow, then drive to town as fast as you can and find 'is master. If you find him, telephone me.'

"I done what she said, but I couldn't find 'ide nor 'air of Scotty until I thought of the junction a mile this side of town. I drove out there, an' the man at the tower told me Scotty 'ad climbed the noon train goin' east when she stopped for water.

"Well, that left Buttercup on our 'ands. I was for puttin' a charge of shot in 'is ugly 'ead, but the missus wouldn't hear of it. She says that Scotty may send for 'im.

"'An' suppose he does,' I says. 'Who'll get 'im out of there an' ship 'im?'

"'I thought you were a dog trainer,' says the missus.

"'I am,' I says; 'I'm just that. But I'm no lion tamer. An' then suppose 'e don't send for 'im — will 'e live an' die in a runway?'

"'No,' she says; 'I'm going to 'andle 'im myself. 'E'll be fond of me in a month, Peter.'

"I done all I could to change 'er mind, but she wouldn't listen, an' she tells me not to feed Buttercup nothin' that day.

"The next mornin' she's 'ere bright an' early with a package of meat. The dog is back in 'is kennel an' all you can see of 'im is 'is green eyes shinin', but you can 'ear 'im easy enough, if you go up to the gate.

"The missus stands by the runway an' begins a conversation with 'im.

"'What's the matter?' says the missus. 'Lonesome?'

"'Gr-r-r-rh!' says Buttercup.

"'Come out an' get acquainted,' says the missus.

"'Gr-r-rh!' says Buttercup; an' that's the way it goes.

"'You want 'im out of there, mem?' I says after a while.

"'Yes,' she says. 'I'd like to have 'im come 'ere to the fence.'

"'That can be arranged,' I says. I stepped up to the gate an' rattled the catch, an' 'e come out all right. 'E kep' comin' too, till 'e 'it the gate, an' 'e tried to tear it down when 'e got there.

"The missus flinched back a step or two. I didn't blame 'er neither.

"'Better let me put a charge of shot in 'im an' get it over with, mem,' I says.

"But she looks at me as pleased as Punch.

"'Why, Peter,' she says, 'I wouldn't miss it for anything. Isn't he splendid! It's just what you said it was—lion taming.'

"She throws the meat over the fence, tells me not to feed the dog, an' goes up to the 'ouse. Anybody could see she was 'aving the time of 'er life.

"She comes every day for a week with meat, or dog cakes, or something, an' puts in an hour with Buttercup; but it never fazed 'im. 'E 'ad the worst disposition on 'im I ever saw. She'd set by the gate an' call 'im a lamb an' such, an' 'im ragin' inside with 'is back like a 'airbrush.

"Despite what she'd told me, she tells the whole business to the mister, an' never warned me neither. So when 'e asks me about Buttercup I horiginates 'ow the horchid man, not likin' the place, 'ad left without 'is dog.

"'Why didn't 'e like it 'ere?' 'e says when I'm done.

"''E didn't say,' I says. ' 'E just left 'urriedly.'

"'Is eyes crinkled up the way they do when 'e's tickled.

"''Urriedly, eh?' 'e says, 'I think that describes it. Talk some more, Peter; I like to 'ear you."

"'She's told you,' I says. 'An' never let me know.'

"'Well, anyway,' 'e says, 'I think we're through with horchids. But be careful, Peter; lion taming is all right if it isn't overdone, you understand?"

"I shows 'im the butt of a thirty-eight stickin' out of my 'ip pocket.

"'If the fence should 'appen to bust,' I says, 'we'll lose a lion round 'ere sudden.'

"'Exactly,' 'e says, an' goes over to the cattle barns.

"Well, the lion tamin' goes on as usual for a week or so more, an' then 'er work begun to tell. Buttercup got so 'e begun to look for 'er when ten o'clock came, which was the time she always showed up.

"'E'd give 'er a growl or two just to show 'e 'adn't lost 'is voice, but 'e left the gate alone an' 'e begun to listen to what she 'ad to say.

"One day she 'olds a piece of meat in 'er 'and an' pokes it through the fence. 'E looks at it an' then looks away like 'e 'asn't no interest in meat.

"'Come on!' she says. 'You know you want it.'

"'Gr-r-r-rh!' 'e says, an' took another look at the meat.

"They argued about it for a while, but 'e wouldn't touch it. Next day she done the same thing, an' at last 'e come up careful, grabbed the meat, takes it back in the runway an' drops it.

"'Very good!' she says. 'But never snatch; it's not polite. Aren't you going to eat it?'

"'E smelled it an' then ate it an' come back for more. I don't think 'e ever growled at 'er after that.

"'When 'e wags 'is tail, Peter, I'm going in,' she says, an' that's what she done. She 'ad fed 'im by 'and for quite a while. Then one morning she was late an' 'e stood at the fence lookin' up the drive toward the 'ouse. After a while 'e give a whine or two, an' all of a sudden 'is tail begun to go. I looked up the drive an 'ere she come.

"'E stood up on 'is 'ind legs pawin' at the gate when she got there, 'is tail as busy as a bee.

"'Good morning, Big Boy!' she says. An' before ever I knowed what she was at she opened the gate an' stepped in. I 'ollered an' run for it, but she shut it in my face.

"'You stay outside with your fine large revolver,' she says. I didn't know she 'ad noticed the gun till then.

"She goes to feedin' 'im by 'and, a piece at a time. 'E grabbed at the first one, an' I'm tellin' you now she give 'im a slap on the nose.

"'Table manners!' she says, an' 'e took the rest more careful. When 'e'd ate it all she 'ad me get 'er a chair. Then she sets an' talks to 'im, an' after a while 'e puts 'is ugly mug in 'er lap.

"Well, that ended the lion tamin'. But 'e 'ad to be shut up for fear 'e'd kill a real dog for us, an' the missus took 'im out on a leash every day. She'd go way over in the fields with 'im an' let 'im run there, an' I will say 'e minded 'er good.

"I 'ated the sight of 'im at the kennels, more especial when dog men came to see my stuff. Chuck Sellers, 'e visited me once, an' I was goin' down the runways with 'im.

"'This,' I says, pointin' to a dog we'd just brought over, 'is the Duke of Kent. We himported 'im for an outcross on the Roderigo blood. 'Andsome, ain't 'e?'

"'Yes, says Chuck, an' looks over in the next runway where the big mongrel was kep'. 'What you goin' to do with Count Cesspool?' 'e says. 'Raise little 'ippopotamuses?'

"I got so I 'ated the big slob like a skunk, but the missus wouldn't get rid of 'im. She says that Scotty may send for 'im; but that wasn't it. You see 'e would 'ave bit a leg off any but 'er that monkeyed with 'im, an' she knowed it an' it tickled 'er.

"'E 'ad been on the place three months or so when one day 'ere comes a man from the cattle barns on the run.

"'Get a gun quick an' come on!' he 'ollers. 'The Regent is loose.'

"'E meant Cordova Regent. You've 'eard of 'im, I expect—the worst Jersey bull that ever stood on four feet.

"'That's a fine business,' I says. 'Who let 'im loose?'

"'We tried to put another ring in 'is nose an' 'e broke the ropes,' 'e says. ''Urry up!'

"I grabbed an automatic from the kennel gun rack with a 'andful of shells, an' started for the barns. As I went down the runways I banged into an open gate. It was Buttercup's runway, so 'e was out with the missus somewhere, an' I cussed 'im an' run on.

"I run through the dairy 'ouse, thinkin' to go out the back way an' save time. Well, the back door was locked, 'eaven knows why, so I come out again an' went round.

"At the barnyard was the men, some up on sheds, some on the straw stack, an' one or two on the barn. They 'ad clubs an' pitchforks an' such, but I didn't see nobody on the ground.

"There was a panel of the barnyard fence tore down, an' the Regent was trottin' across the fields toward a bunch of cows, shakin' 'is big black 'ead an' bellerin'.

"Then something came up out of the 'ollow just ahead of the Regent. It was the missus an' she 'ad her back to 'm, an' then I lost my mind.

"'Run, mem!' I says. 'For God's sake, run!' I whispered it, that's what I done, an' 'er a 'alf mile away.

"The Regent put down 'is 'ead when 'e saw 'er, gave a roar, an' started. She 'ad stooped down for something—she told afterward she 'ad seen a four-leaf clover—but she 'eard 'im an' straightened up. Then she tried to run.

"Do you 'appen to know 'ow fast a bull can move? I didn't until then. She might as well 'ave stood still in 'er tracks.

"Just about as the bull 'it 'er, Buttercup come up over the bank at the brook. 'E 'ad been diggin' at a ground 'og 'ole or something, an' 'is 'ead an' chest was covered with mud.

"The Regent seemed to strike the missus fair—that's the way it looked, any'ow. Man, it was 'orrible! The fact is, 'is left 'orn went through 'er skirt, whirled her in the air like, an' tore it clean off of 'er. 'E never touched 'er else.

"The Regent stopped an' turned to come back, but 'e didn't get far. 'E 'ad no more than turned, I'll say to you, when the dog 'ad im by the nose.

"I don't know 'ow long it took for me to get to where they were—long enough. The Regent would swing 'is 'ead in the air, then bring it down an' batter Buttercup against the ground. I was 'opin' the dog would 'ave enough life left in 'im to 'old 'is grip until I come, an' 'e done it, although the Regent got 'im under 'is feet at the last.

"As I come up the missus got on 'er knees—she'd been lyin' still till then.

"'Shoot—quick!' she says. ''E's killin' 'im!' An' I done so.

"Well, sir, when the missus tells me she ain't 'urt, I tried to make that dog let go the dead bull's nose; but 'e wouldn't think of it. 'E ad 'is jaws an' eyes shut tight an' 'e didn't open neither of 'em.

"At last the missus tries what she can do. She puts 'er 'and on 'is 'ead.

"'Let go, Big Boy!' she says. 'It's all over.' She keeps talkin' to 'im, an' after a while 'e lets go an' rolls on 'is side.

"''E lay there very limp, one ear gone an'bleedin' from the mouth. One of the men gets 'is 'at full of water from the brook an' the missus pours it over Buttercup's 'ead, an' then bathes 'is muzzle.

"I got 'er skirt where the Regent 'ad tossed it an' brought it to 'er.

"'Don't you want this, mem?' I says. 'You can wrap it round you like.'

"'What difference does it make?' she says. ''E's going to die, Peter.'

"''Ow do you know, mem?' I says. 'We'll carry 'im up to the kennels an' 'ave a vet take a look at 'im.'

"'What a fool I am!' she says. 'Of course. 'Ave Felix go for Doctor Slosson as fast as 'e can. Tell 'im to take the roadster.'

"'Yes, mem,' I says, an' the men carried the dog to the stables whilst I went to 'ustle Felix off.

"By the time Felix drove in with the vet Buttercup was settin' up an' takin' notice.

"The vet went over 'im careful. 'Two ribs,' 'e says, 'one car an' four front teeth. Outside of that 'e'll do. 'E's not worth much, is 'e?'

"'Not much, Doc,' I says. 'Just 'is weight in gold, that's all.'

"The missus looks at me quick an' I see 'er eyes flood up.

"'Thank you, Peter, dear old Peter,' she says. 'There's quite a lot of 'im, you know.'

"With that she drops 'er 'ead in 'er 'ands an' cries like 'er 'eart would break. Ain't that funny, now—she 'adn't shed a tear till then.

"Well, that's about all, an' 'ere she comes down the drive. She's after you, I expect."

I got to my feet and waved to the slender figure approaching.

"But, Peter," I said, "how can a dog as cross as that be kept at the house?"

"Cross!" said Peter. "Huh! 'E's old 'ome folks now."

· V ·

Dumb-Bell's Guest

How long can you stay?" asked Mrs. Cregory.

"Three days, three whole blissful days," I answered. I put my arm about her and I led her to the north end of the terrace, from which point Brookfield rolls away in emerald or flame or duns and browns, depending on the season.

The rose garden lapping the terrace was bare. Stiff, thorny spikes were all that November had left of a riot of bending, lifting, swaying roses and green-enamel leaves. The white marble shaft of the sundial was bold against a flat background of chocolate brown earth. The garden wall was edged with hydrangeas. Their creamy petals had become ghosts in Japanese grays and tans that the afterglow was changing to heliotrope. Beyond the garden was the north, some of the east, and nearly all of the west lawn. These flowed away to far vine-clad flint walls guessed at in the half-light where they passed a vista in the trees.

Drives, maple bordered, swept in curves to stables, garage, greenhouses, and gates. Oaks, hickories, elms, and the dark mystery of scattered pines broke the red of the western sky. Behind us was the black pile of the house itself, in which friendly lights were springing up. And behind that the meadows of Brookfield ran and ran to distant hills.

"It is lovely, isn't it?" said Mrs. Gregory after a time. Her hand tightened on my arm. "My dear, we nearly lost it!"

I turned and met her eyes. "Lost it!" I said. "What do you mean?"

"Money!" she explained.

"But that's impossible. Jim wrote me the works were running night and day on war orders."

"That was it—war orders. Jim will tell you. You'll find him changed, a little. Things like that change people. We go along for years never knowing. Life seems so simple, so easy, then—something happens, some small thing, a little human thing, and you're ground to pieces, nearly. We were saved by—a miracle, I think."

I heard well-known footsteps on the terrace behind us. They had the swinging stride that comes from mile on mile of stubble or briars, or crackling leaves.

"Spooning, eh?" said the master of Brookfield.

"Of course," said Mrs. Gregory.

"What's all this the Chief's been telling me?" I demanded.

"Spare me," said Gregory, releasing my hand. "What does a lady tell a gentleman when he stands with his arm about her in the gloaming?" Then he grew serious. "After dinner," he said.

"He's not changed much, that I can see," I told Mrs. Gregory.

But at dinner I did see a change. His grin, his irrepressible boyish grin, had become a smile. And in those comfortable silences that are the hallmark of abiding friendship I had time to wonder.

So they had nearly lost it! I glanced about the big shadow-filled room. It seemed incredible. It was all so secure, so permanent. Why, the sideboard alone was immovable! It stood there, ponderous, majestic, defying mortal hands to budge it. And the serving tables—stolid, silent. I felt that they would set their broad backs and massive legs and remain stubbornly against those walls while we who dined, and our children's children, became dust.

And yet, what kept them there? What made Brookfield, every stick and stone of it, a thing of joy, a place that filled all those who entered its gates with indescribable contentment? I knew, I had seen it. It was six miles down the valley. It was referred to, casually, as "the works." It was a place of din and dirt and sweat. Tall stacks belched sootily into the face of heaven while white-hot mouths of hell opened and closed below. In infancy it had been a tiny forge at which a great-great-grandfather had labored placidly. It had grown into a huge black demon disgorging thousands of tons of greasy gray ingots in a manner that was beyond my understanding. Gregory, shouting above the terrifying noise, had attempted to explain; but my head was aching and I very much desired to leave that place to its own infernal devices.

I had never seen it since. Submerged in the tranquillity of Brookfield, I had forgotten it entirely. Even Gregory gave it scant attention. He motored down the valley once or twice a month, was gone perhaps three hours, and returned to his dogs and his guns.

But something had gone amiss, apparently. Perhaps the trouble had been in the demon's entrails. Perhaps it had refused to digest the ore and lime and coke that pygmies poured down its gullet.

A gray shadow padded through the doorway. It stopped just at the entrance and surveyed us silently.

"Good evening," said Gregory. "Won't you join us?"

The shadow waved a plumed tail. It advanced unhurriedly until the candlelight showed a small white setter with a lemon dumb-bell on his side.

He was quite small, as setters go, but he had the dignity of kings. He was the double champion Brookfield Dumb-Bell who had won the National and All America and twenty lesser stakes besides. He outclassed the setters and pointers of the world, and I think he knew it.

With all this he was not above the duties of hospitality. Straight to my chair he came, sniffed once to assure himself of my identity, then raised his eyes to mine.

"How do you do?" I said and slid my hand along his head until one of his ears slipped through my fingers.

He waved his tail and stretched his lips in the suggestion of a grin, an uncanny habit he had—and I remembered how many birds I had missed the year before after some of his matchless finds.

"It's not polite to laugh at a duffer," I told him.

He poked a cold nose into the hollow of my hand, then sauntered around the table. He waved his tail as he passed both his master and mistress, stood a moment in thought, and withdrew as unhurriedly as he had come. We heard his nails click as he passed from rug to rug on the hardwood floor of the main hall and we listened until the sound grew fainter and was gone.

"Back to the throne," I said, and this proved to be true. When we went to the living-room a few moments later he was curled up in his chair with his eyes closed. "Asleep, eh?" I said; but he denied it feebly with a slight thump of his tail against the leather chair seat. Presently he was snoring.

"How much could you get for him?" I asked.

"Oh, I don't know," said Gregory. "His size is against him for a stud dog."

"How much would you take?"

Gregory joined me by the chair. He looked down at the sleeping Dumb-Bell. "Well, I hadn't thought of selling him. Had you, Chief?"

"Oh, yes, often. He tracks the house up so, with his blessed muddy paws. Come here, you silly things, and drink your coffee."

Gregory took a gold and white egg-shell of a cup to the fireplace. He stood with his back to the fire stirring his coffee thoughtfully.

"I can tell you how much he is worth," he said suddenly: "one million, two hundred and fifteen thousand dollars."

"He should find a pleasant home for that," I said. "Would you throw off the fifteen thousand for cash?" Then I saw that he was serious. "What do you mean?" I asked. "Why the exact sum?"

"Do you happen to know an old Mr. Parmalee, of Chicago, R. H. Parmalee?"

I considered a moment. "Yes, I think I do. That is, I knew of him when I was scratching for the *Tribune*. He's the *bête noir* of the higher-ups in Wall Street. He lives in Chicago, won't leave it, and is chairman of the board or a big stockholder in heaven knows how many Eastern concerns. He won't go East to board meetings, so board meetings go to him, and the elect groan and moan at the trip. He hates ostentation like the devil, and looks like a tramp. Is he the man you mean?"

"Yes, that's the man. Especially the tramp part."

"He's a queer old codger," I said. "He supports a flock of no-account relatives who are ashamed to meet him on the street."

A coffee spoon clattered. "He's not a queer old codger!" said Mrs. Gregory. "He's a dear! I adore him. Imagine being ashamed to meet him! What do his clothes matter? Why—"

"Hold on there," Gregory put in. "What did you say when Griggs took him upstairs?—Griggs was carrying his bag as though it might explode at any moment—What was it you said?"

Mrs. Gregory recovered her spoon. "I'm sure I've forgotten."

"You asked me where I'd picked him up, didn't you?"

"Well, perhaps I did, but I simply meant—"

Gregory turned to me. "If you should hear your hostess ask where you had been picked up, how would it strike you?"

"Why, has he been here?" I asked. "Where did you meet him? What's all this about, anyway?"

"It's about—what the Chief was telling you on the terrace. Are you ready to smoke? Cigarettes in that silver doodab. Cigars just behind you. Want a liqueur? Well, take that other chair; it's more comfortable. Don't interrupt at mere exaggeration, Chief. Man, it would make a play! Perhaps you can do something with it. And I thought I was doing a kind act." He grinned at his wife. "Succoring the poor and needy, eh, Chief? She was Lady Bountiful—Oh, golly! And then Dumb-Bell saved the day. And the Chief—I think he was fond of the Chief, too, she'd been so sweet to the poor old man. He—"

"Are you going to tell what happened, or are you going to stand there and—"

"Well, you tell him!"

"Indeed I'll not. Sit down here and be serious. You were serious enough—then."

Gregory's smile was gone the instant she had spoken. "Yes, Chief," he said gravely. "We were both a bit serious, I thought." He left the fireplace and let himself slowly down into a chair close to where his wife was sitting. "I hope we'll never be quite so serious again." He crossed his long legs, lit a cigar, and stared into the bluish flames of the applewood fire. "The war did it," he said at last. "And playing a new game. Do you know anything about high explosive shells?"

"Not a thing," I said. "Except that they go off with a bang, and everybody's getting rich making them."

"Just so. That's what I knew, last year. Of course I thought, still think, the Allies are doing our work. We didn't have the sweepers to get into the housecleaning properly and — they needed brooms. Well, things'll be more tidy when they get through, but it's been a dirty job. A year ago it looked bad. I rather wanted to help in a small way.

"Of course you know I'm not very active at the works. Braithwaite runs things to suit himself, and that lets me knock about pretty much as I please. He loves work and I love play, and there you are — everybody satisfied.

"Well, along comes a chap from the Midland Iron Company with his pockets full of subcontracts and his head full of everything from barbed wire to aëroplanes. He spent two days with Braithwaite and Gaston, and they came up here, all mad as hatters, and routed me out. The idea was to build a plant in nine or ten minutes and take on the machining of three million three-inch high explosives for Russia on a subcontract from Midland Iron, who'd furnish the rough casings.

"All play and no work makes Jack a bright boy, and I inquired gently about Midland Iron.

"They smiled at me pityingly. 'You tell him,' said Braithwaite. So the subcontract chap mentioned the names of the directors in a hushed voice, and I blinked. 'But,' I said, 'I've never heard of it before, and outside of hunting season I do read the papers now and then.' They explained that it was a lot of junk consolidated solely for war business with 'all the money in the world' behind it. This was so, all right. Both Dun and Bradstreet sent a report a few days later that made me blink again.

"Well, there seemed to be a quarter of a million in it sure, but I went in more for the reason I've told you than for the profit on the job. Business had been bad for two years and I was down pretty fine; but all you had to do was to mention Midland Iron at any bank and you could walk in and help yourself. We built a plant — equipment, three hundred lathes, three hundred electric motors, and a lot of odds and ends. I went on the paper, of course.

"There was some delay at first. We wanted master gauges, and Midland couldn't let us have 'em. When we hollered they passed the buck to Russia. The Grand Dukes were too busy or too tired or something to send on the drawings, so we paid three hundred machinists for an eight-hour day and they sat among the lathes and played pinochle. We didn't dare let 'em go. Skilled labor is skilled labor these days. That was all right, because we put it up to Midland and they never whimpered. Just O.K.'d our payroll and charged it to—the Czar, I guess.

"This went on for two months. Then we got our gauges and a Russian inspector who talked French, all in one day; and the rough cases began to roll in from Midland in trainload lots, and pinochle ceased to be a vocation around there.

"All during this the field trial season was on, and it was breaking my heart. We had a nice birdy pup by Dumb-Bell out of Miss Nance in the derbys, and Peter went to a trial or two. He came home quite gloomy, though, because the pointers were winning all down the line. "'Ell-'ooping all over the country like a lot o' gray-'ounds,' is what he told me. 'Don't they find birds?' I asked, and I rathered from what he said that when a pointer stumbled over a bevy he stopped in astonishment.

"War or no war, I was going to see the National at least, and things got to running, so nicely I decided to make it three weeks and take in the United States and another stake. Braithwaite said to go—he was glad to get rid of me, I think. I left for the South with everybody happy and the Russian inspector walking around twisting his little stick-up mustache and saying *'C'est très bien,'* at everything, including the three-star Hennessey, which he liked and we furnished. He drank a quart a day without a quiver. Think of it!

"Peter was right about the pointers. It was a pointer year. They were a poor lot, too; but the setters were worse, and our crowd was in the dumps. There was a lot of grumbling about the judging. Some of us think that first of all a bird dog must find birds. We believe he can go just as fast as his nose will let him and no faster. And that brings me to old Mr. Parmalee.

"He got in the second night of the United States. He had the same old frowsy leather bag he has brought to every field trial as long as anybody can remember. He was looking seedy, even for him, and that's saying a good deal. He came in the door of the hotel, and the boys yelled at him and grabbed him and hammered him on the back, and he blushed—he's a diffident little old cuss.

"Nobody knew anything about him, except that he came down to the trials year after year, that he loved a setter as well as any man in the world, and that he was a stickler for nose rather than speed. He'd forget all embarrassment and speak right up when it came to arguing about that.

"He had a bully round with Fosdick of the Argot strain that first night. Fosdick was a little overbearing, I thought—he has a twenty-thousand-acre preserve on the James River and twenty feet of water at his own dock when he runs down in his yacht—and finally he said: 'Well, if you don't like the kind of dogs we're sending to the trials, why don't you breed some to suit you?'

"Everybody felt uncomfortable. You don't hear things like that often at the trials.

"But the old gentleman looked Fosdick in the eye and came back as pat as you please. 'I don't have to breed one,' he said; 'it's already been done. If you want to find out just what you've got, pick out the best one you ever bred and put him down for three hours with Brookfield Dumb-Bell.'

"Well, the setter men yelled at that—everybody did, in fact—and Fosdick shut up like a clam. The old gentleman came over to where I was sitting, and we talked for the rest of the evening.

"He said that he was from Chicago, and that he took his vacation each year when the National was run. He said he hoped to 'slip out of the harness some day' and spend the rest of his life with a twenty gauge and a pair of Llewellyns. I thought perhaps he was keeping books; I don't know why, except that he was stoop-shouldered and spoke of having to work too hard at his age. I had a vision of him perched on a high stool doing double entry.

"I didn't see much of him after that until the finals of the Championship. He rode with me that afternoon, and we followed the dogs as best we could, hoping for bird work, which we didn't get. He was fairly chipper when we started, but as the dogs ran he got more and more quiet. I don't think he spoke once during the last hour.

"Well, they gave it to a rangy, wild-eyed, bitch-headed pointer who had covered most of a county and found two bevies and one single in three hours' running; and I rode home with old Mr. Parmalee. He got off his horse and sighed, and went into the hotel without a word.

"I went upstairs and packed. When I came down he was standing looking out the window, and I walked over to him.

"The new champion was on leash in front of the hotel with a crowd around him. His handler was telling everybody what a great dog they were looking at. Once he said: 'He's a bird dog, men!' and old Mr. Parmalee snorted. He turned to me and, by George, he looked all broken up. 'This is my last trip,' he said; 'I'm getting too old to come down here and see—what we saw today.'

"I said something about it being an off year, but he didn't answer. He looked out the window and clicked with his tongue. 'So that's a National Champion!' he said. Then he turned to me again. 'Five years ago today,' he said, 'I saw a real champion win this stake. I can remember every move he made. He found sixteen bevies and twenty-three singles, and he went a mile at every cast. I have wanted to see something like that again ... but I don't think I shall... I don't think I shall.'

"I'm something of a soft ass at times, and he looked rather old and forlorn; so I took hold of his arm and said, 'You come back to Brookfield with me, and we'll shoot some quail over him and watch him work for a week or so. What do you say?'

"He said a lot about being an old nuisance and that sort of thing, but his eyes were shining like a child's, and I hustled him upstairs and helped him pack his duds—you should have seen 'em—and we caught the five o'clock train. The Chief met us at the front door next day and Dumb-Bell was standing beside her.

"I didn't see much of him after that—I had other things on my mind—but the Chief took him under her wing and he took to it all like a wet setter to a wood fire. Didn't he, Chief?"

"He was just sweet; one of the very nicest guests we ever had. He understood everything so. Of course at first I was—well, not startled exactly, but Jim chums with terrible creatures if they shoot well or can walk as far as he can. You know he adores that Slade man who's been in jail I don't know how many times, and sells whisky on the sly, and fights bulldogs and game chickens. Jim takes him to the gun room and they sit and roar at each other. Sometimes I wonder who tells the worst stories, the Slade man or Jim.

"Jim hadn't told me he was bringing anyone home with him, and when they got out of the motor and I saw Mr. Parmalee for the first time, well!—really his clothes are shocking. And his collars and cuffs and ties! And his hat! Where do you suppose he got that hat, Jim? Then he was not at all at his ease when Jim presented him; I didn't know how diffident he was, then, so when he went upstairs I asked Jim—what he told you just now."

Gregory chuckled. "About picking him up, she means. He's worth a hundred million."

"What of it? If he hadn't been the charming old thing he is what difference would that make?"

"Of course, of course; but, even so, 'picking up' a multimillionaire isn't the way I'd put it—exactly."

"It wasn't any time until I knew. He had beautiful old-school manners when his shyness wore off. Mr. Braithwaite had been telephoning for Jim, so he went off to the works, and I showed Mr. Parmalee the place, and he loved it all. We spent most of the afternoon at the kennels. He knew Peter, he'd seen him somewhere at the trials, and they looked at all the dogs and talked and talked. Then I showed him Roderigo's grave in the orchard, and he stood looking down at it, and I knew I was going to like him.

"We came to the house because he wanted to see Dumb-Bell again, but the mannie was out in the garden digging for moles with his face all dirty. He was having a splendid time and I didn't want to call him in, and Mr. Parmalee said, 'Of course not.'

"We had tea in here and Mr. Parmalee sat down in Dumb-Bell's chair—not knowing—and I asked him if he would mind changing his seat. He tooked surprised and embarrassed, and said, 'Why, certainly.' So when he had taken another chair I told him.

"I said that Roderigo had had it first and it was his very own chair. And then it was empty for a long time, and then Dumb-Bell did—what he did, and now it was his, and nobody else sat in it.

"Mr. Parmalee said, 'I see, I see,' and went over and looked at the chair, and then he said, rather to himself, 'It's not for mere humans, is it?' and then he blew his nose.

"'Sometimes,' I said, 'people sit in it and hold him in their laps. That's all right, of course.' And he said, 'I should like to do that very much'; and then we had our tea. We got along splendidly after that."

"I should say they did," said Gregory. "She took to the Lady Bountiful business like a duck. She fancied she was showing the poor old man the time of his life."

"I was," said Mrs. Gregory calmly.

"He's coming back, at any rate. And the Lord knows I didn't do so much to make his visit pleasant. After I saw Braithwaite I didn't have time to work dogs for old Mr. Parmalce or anybody else. I told him I was busy, and Peter took him out every morning and he knocked about with the Chief in the afternoon. It was out of season, but I told Peter to let the old man kill a few quail over Dumb-Bell just to say he'd done it. I thought Peter would shoot me.

"He came up to the house that night, though, and looked at me as though I were a convict. It seems the old man had refused point blank to take a gun along out of season. ''E's a sportsman,' said Peter, 'and, 'eaven knows, they're rare enough!' I admitted it, and Peter left with his head in the air.

"This was at first. I saw the old chap each night of course and he'd describe every point Dumb-Bell had made that day. Later he could have had a fit in the front hall without my noticing it."

"That isn't so. Through it all he remembered his guest. At dinner he'd sit with a look on his face that made me want to scream, and talk hunting dogs and field trials and trout fishing with that old man, and laugh at his stories, too."

"Stuff. I simply wanted to forget during dinner that I owed a million."

"What!" I exclaimed.

"Oh, yes," said Gregory cheerfully. "Well over a million. I gave you the figures a while ago."

"It isn't possible!"

"That's what I said until Braithwaite got through. It's quite simple. Our contract was for three dollars and forty-five cents per shell for three million shells and it was costing us three eighty-five and a half to turn 'em out."

"But how could that be? Why were your estimates so far off?"

"New game. We didn't know the angles. And then things broke badly for us. For instance, we figured on three hundred lathes at eight hundred dollars. Well, everything went sky high and our lathes cost fifteen hundred each, and we had to get down on our knees and pray for 'em at that price. Same thing with our motors. They should have been a hundred and thirty-five; they were two hundred and fifty. We figured on seventeen-cent copper, which is high enough. We paid twenty-six cents a pound for every pound, and you could take it or leave it, they didn't care which; so every band on every shell cost forty-five cents instead of thirty-two. Then we got into a mess through improper heat treatment. The cases were annealed at too low a temperature, and they broke our machines and chewed up our tools and played the dickens generally. Same with the fuse sockets. We'd figured on free-cutting cold-rolled bar stock, point forty-five. Instead it was fifty-eight to sixty, and machine tools holler for help in that kind of going. Oh, it was a fine party, but expensive.

"To make everything perfect, the Russian inspector left the Hennessey long enough to wander from the office over to the plant and throw out the first batch of finished shells because the interiors weren't smooth.

"Of course anyone knows the exterior of a shell must be polished on account of air friction, but the inside—

"Braithwaite kept his temper somehow, so he told me, and asked in bad French if they wanted 'em polished just to be tidy, or what? And the inspector explained that the trinitrotoluol went into 'em under pressure and was extremely sensitive. Therefore a little roughness of the chamber wall might cause a spark if the shell were dropped, in which case—'Pouf!'

"'Oh, pouf! eh?' said Braithwaite. 'Well, we're a liberal crowd; at three forty-five we throw in a "pouf" with every shell.' But our Russian friend drew him gently to the office and got out the contract and it read: 'Surfaces must be polished.' One little s did the trick and Braithwaite beat the inspector to the Hennessey bottle.

"Of course we put it up to Midland at once, by letter, by wire, by long distance; then Braithwaite and I went on. After wrestling with 'em for two days and a night they agreed to allow us ten cents a shell, and that was final.

"I came home with two hands and the clothes on my back. I'm a good wing shot, throw a fairly accurate fly, and—I'll be forty next month.

"I sat in the smoker all night. I kept seeing the Chief in the rose garden. She had on a floppy pink sun hat and she cut roses, arm-loads of 'em—and sang."

Gregory stopped abruptly.

"Good Lord!" I said. I saw white fingers steal over and twine themselves about a lean brown hand clenched on the chair arm. I became absorbed in the fireplace with its bed of glowing ashes.

"Isn't it the deuce," said Gregory at last, "what just money will do! Just money. Think of it!"

I thought of it while the big clock tick-tocked in the hall, and something was done with an absurdly small handkerchief, and the pinched look left Gregory's face.

"I hadn't told the Chief anything," he began again. "I'd been hoping that Midland might see us through. Of course she knew something was in the wind, but she hadn't an idea how bad it was. On the train coming back I made up my mind to tell her as soon as I got in the house; so we walked in here as soon as we'd said hello.

"She asked me if I was tired, and I said 'A little,' and looked about the room. I'd forgotten old Mr. Parmalee was on earth, but I thought a servant might be about. I never looked in the bay window. There's nothing there but the chair and no one would be sitting in that.

"I sat down where you're sitting now, and I said, 'Come here, Chief,' and she came and sat in my lap, and then I told her.

"I got far enough along to mention Midland Iron, and then I heard a noise in the bay window as though someone had moved a foot on the floor. I said, 'Wait a moment,' to the Chief, and got up and went over to the chair.

"Old Mr. Parmalee was sitting there with Dumb-Bell asleep in his lap. The dog was wet and muddy and snoring—you know how he snores when he's tired.

"'Oh, hello!' I said, and the old chap looked as though I'd caught him stealing the silver.

"'I didn't want to wake him,' he said in a whisper; and I said, 'Won't he ruin your clothes?'

"He didn't answer—just looked down at the dog. 'We've had a wonderful day,' he said, 'wonderful!' And I said, 'That's good,' and took the Chief in the library, and finished telling her there.

"I had dinner alone with the old man that night. The Chief couldn't come down. You see she'd got both barrels at once, and it flattened her out for a few hours.

"I didn't say much, and neither did he. As soon as we'd had coffee I asked him to excuse me, and he said, 'Certainly,' but he fidgeted a bit and finally got out that he wanted to ask a favor, and I told him to go ahead.

"He said, 'You know I expected to leave tomorrow morning.' I said, 'Yes.' I hadn't known it, but I wanted to get rid of him, under the circumstances.

"'Would it be asking too much,' he said, 'if I stayed a day or so longer?' I told him to go ahead and stay. I wasn't very cordial, I'm afraid. I wanted to get up to the Chief, and I wanted him to go.

"I didn't see him at all next morning. The Chief wanted to look at the place and wanted me with her, so we wandered about and looked at everything as though we were seeing it for the first time."

"We were," Mrs. Gregory put in; "I saw things I'd never seen before."

"What with?" asked Gregory.

"Oh, I didn't cry all the time—just when things happened that would nearly kill you.... The cows, with their big kind eyes, all giving as much milk as they possibly could. And the work horses, the dear old work horses that would go away from the safe, warm stables. And the dogs, our own little doggies that were so glad to see us. And the grass and the trees and the fields, and Peter and Jerry and Felix—and all the men, so good and faithful, who had to be taken care of when they grew old. They were all so proud of what they were doing, even the man who was putting in tile, Jim, do you remember?"

"Yes," said Gregory.

"And then we came back to the house and in here and—there was the chair, all worn, and—" the ridiculous handkerchief was out again, "—and then I wanted to die before it all happened.... And just then —just then—You tell him, Jim!"

"Well," said Gregory, "just then old Mr. Parmalee came in, very much embarrassed, and asked if we were in trouble. And the Chief said yes, we were. And old Mr. Parmalee asked if he couldn't help. And I said no, and thanked him. Then he said—"

"And the way he said it, Jim! 'Sometimes people can help—other people.' That's what he said. Wasn't it, Jim?"

Gregory nodded. "Well, of course I said he couldn't help in this case, and he said, 'I heard you mention Midland Iron yesterday. Has that corporation anything to do with it?' I was surprised he even knew the name, but I said yes, and he said, 'If that's the case I think you'd better tell me about it.' He sat down then and folded his arms as though ready to listen, and for some reason, I don't know why, I sat down, too, and told him the whole business.

"When I got through he said, 'Yes, I see.' Then he got up and walked over and looked down at Dumb-Bell and said, 'He'd have to leave his chair as things are, wouldn't he?' Then he looked at the Chief, 'We can't have that, can we?' he said, and the Chief began to weep again.

"The old man said, 'There, there,' and picked up the phone and asked for long distance, and then for A. L. Warrington at Pittsburgh—he's president of Midland. I thought the old man had lost his mind. I sat there looking at him, wondering what the deuce Warrington would say when he found what he had on the wire.

"Nobody said anything while we waited for the connection. I patted the Chief while she sniffled, and the old man patted Dumb-Bell while he snored. It was quite a tableau. At last the bell rang.

"'Hello!' said the old man. 'Is that you, Alfred? This is Mr. Parmalee.' Think that over for a moment! The president of Midland Iron was Alfred and that old scarecrow was Mr. Parmalee! 'Alfred,' he said, 'do you know anything about a contract with the Gregory Furnace Company for machining three-inch shells?'

"Evidently Warrington said he did. If he didn't he had a poor memory; I'd spent sixteen hours with him over it. 'Well,' said the old man, 'have a new contract made out at three-ninety per shell, and mail it to Gregory tomorrow. Do you understand, Alfred?... All right.' Then he rang off.

"The Chief and I were sitting there gaping. I was wondering if I were crazy, too.

"The old man coughed nervously—we were both staring at him—then he said, 'You see, it just happens that I have an interest in—er—that is, I own a majority of stock in—er—the Midland Iron Company.' Then he sneaked out of the room. He was frightfully embarrassed."

Gregory tossed what was left of his cigar into the fire. We watched the small flame it made until it flickered into a wisp of smoke.

The sound of snoring in the bay window ceased. Dumb-Bell sat up in his chair, yawned tremendously, regarded us all for a moment—and grinned.

"Oh, yes," said Gregory, "It's very funny—*now*."

· VI ·

Ordered On

The wood fire leaped and crackled, and shot small embers out upon the bricks. The embers changed from white to red, from red to gray, from gray to sullen black. Their lives were short. One moment glowing, brilliant—dead smudges on the hearth the next. Dumb-Bell watched them.

It was the first time Dumb-Bell had noticed the embers. His chair had always stood in the bay window across the big room. That day they had moved it nearer the fire. He wondered why.

They had moved the leather-covered stool, too. He blinked down at it. The leather-covered stool had stood, for the past six months, just in front of his chair. He had disliked it at first because it was strange. He disliked strange things that interfered with his habits. It had been his habit, until the last year, to get into his chair by a single easy bound. Then he had found it better to put his forepaws in the chair seat, pull one hind leg up, and then the other.

One day he had hunted quail from a pink dawn to a red eve. They had taken out as his brace mate young Susan Whitestone, who was something of a flibbertigibbet. The perverse creature had insisted on flying to far dim thickets in her searchings, leaving nearer cover unexplored. It was that way with the young—success was always just over the hill. Dumb-Bell had humored the silly thing, had even been caught up by her infectious, sweeping flights. He had run without restraint, without dignity, with abandon.

Not as he had run in those all-conquering days when his sobriquet was the White Ghost; but he had held the flitting Susan, even, for a time, and there was this difference between them: now and then she would flash blithely past a bit of cover, without a thought, without a sign; and then he would come plunging by, weary in heels and heart, but with a champion's nose. One instant he was in his stride, the next moveless, high-headed, tense. Within the thicket, perhaps a hundred feet away, was a breathless huddle of brown feathers and close-held wings!

And then the airy Susan would come creeping back, awed by the splendor of his pose, vaguely troubled by the thought that, flit as she might for all her days, such miracles were not for her.

That night, when Dumb-Bell put his forepaws in the chair his hind legs, for some reason, refused to follow. He had tried to lift them up, his toes scratching on the slippery leather, until his mistress came and helped him into the chair.

Limping in from the garden next day Dumb-Bell had found the stool before his chair. He waited for someone to move it. No one did, and he decided to climb into the chair despite it. He found the stool was like a step. By using it he could walk right into his chair. He tried it several times to make sure. It worked perfectly every time. From then on he liked the stool.

And now they had moved his chair and his stool nearer the fire. It had seemed a little chilly in the bay window the last few nights. It must be a very cold fall. It was certainly nice and warm here by the fire. And then he could watch the embers.

He was alone with the fire and his thoughts. He could hear a faint murmur of voices coming from the dining-room. The people were about the pleasant, glistening table. It might be well to go in there and stand by his mistress. Then, just before Griggs took her plate away, her fork would come stealing down quite quietly with something delicious on the end. He would be careful not to let his teeth click on the silver tines. Not that it made any difference who heard, but they had done it that way for years.

It had begun when he was always hungry and inclined to beg, and perhaps annoy the guests, and rules had been made. Nowadays he was never very hungry and guests were never annoyed at anything he did. They were, as a matter of fact, quite flattered if he noticed them at all.

Dumb-Bell raised his head from his paws, stirred, and glanced at the door. It was a long way to the dining-room, and he was not in the least hungry. He had left three pieces of liver untouched on his plate in the butler's pantry....

He was still watching the embers when the people came in from dinner—his master and mistress and that old man named Parmalee. Dumb-Bell gave the two thumps on the chair seat that hospitality required, and Mr. Parmalee came and scratched him back of the ears.

It was pleasant, this scratching. He closed his eyes. The voices and the snapping of the fire grew fainter and fainter. At last they drifted away altogether, and he was in a queer thicket in which quail rose with a whir at every step he took but gave no scent, although he tried and tried to smell them. Why he, Champion Brookfield Dumb-Bell, was flushing birds! It was horrible. He twitched and whined in his sleep.

While he slept the people talked.

"Jim," said Mr. Parmalee, "I've come here this time to tell you something. I've discovered the Happy Hunting Ground. I want to take you there."

The master of Brookfield looked at him inquiringly.

"I not only discovered it, I made it," Mr. Parmalee went on. "No, I can't say that. Come to think of it, the Good Lord did most of the work. I just put on the finishing touches. It's in Minnesota."

"Are there quail up there?" asked Gregory doubtfully. "I've understood not. Nothing to speak of, at any rate."

"No, no," said Mr. Parmalee. "Bobwhite must have his comforts—his corn and his ragweed and his wheat. Some day, perhaps, he'll get there, but not now. The wilderness frightens him. We'll hunt a braver bird, king of them all."

"Ruffed grouse!" said the master of Brookfield quickly.

"Just so," said Mr. Parmalee, and then he explained. He owned, it seemed, a big tract of timberland in northern Minnesota. He coughed slightly as he admitted it—the things he owned embarrassed Mr. Parmalee. He had gone up there last year. He wanted to see the great pines tremble, sway, and crash down before the deep biting axes and snoring saws of the lumberjacks. He had seen this, and other things. In particular he had seen, or rather heard, the flight of innumerable ruffed grouse getting up before him in the thickets.

It was all but impenetrable cover, much too thick for wing shooting; and yet here was a country filled with the greatest of all game birds. He thought about it for several days.

In any direction he pushed his way through second-growth pine, silver birch, alders, and a riot of bushes and vines, a thrilling roar of wings was all about him.

One night he talked with the logging superintendent, who recommended and sent for one Red Harry, log boss extraordinary. He came, a big red man, as thick through the chest as one of the pines he smote, and stood in the doorway. Mr. Parmalee told him what he wanted. Could it be done?

"Sure, anything kin be done; but it'll cost—"

"That's my part of it," said Mr. Parmalee, who had taken stock of his man and was never embarrassed when it came to large affairs.

Red Harry turned and spat unhurriedly through the doorway. "I'll get a hundred rough-necks from Brainerd. You want some of the stuff left standin', an' brush heaps made every little bit. Have I got you right?"

"Exactly. If you thin it too much the birds will leave, and they like brush heaps."

"Twenty square miles?"

"About that," said Mr. Parmalee; "and a good, tight, four-room cabin."

"All set," said Red Harry and slouched into the night.

The master and mistress of Brookfield listened to further deeds of Red Harry and his rough-necks. The eyes of the mistress of Brookfield widened at this wholesale conversion of the wilderness into a shooting preserve.

"And so," Mr. Parmalee wound up, "the Happy Hunting Ground is ready." He turned to his hostess. "I hoped you would come, too. It will be a little rough, but— '

"I'd love it," said Mrs. Gregory. "And Jim will go quite mad."

"The trouble is," said Gregory, "I haven't a dog that will do. My stuff is all too fast for grouse. I'll talk to Peter tomorrow though and see what he's got."

But Peter tilted his hat over one eye and scratched the back of his head when asked, next morning, to produce a grouse dog. He let his eye rove down the line of runways and back to the master of Brookfield. A grouse dog must be a plodding, creeping, silent worker. A field trial kennel was not the place to look for one.

"Old Jane Aus'in, now, might do," said Peter at last. "She always was sly like, an' what with age an' whelpin' an' one thing an' other she might stay around where you could get a look at her now and then."

"All right" said the master of Brookfield promptly, "we'll take her along."

"Wait a minute," said Peter. "I ain't told you yet. She's 'eavy in whelp to Beau Brummell."

"Oh!" said the master of Brookfield. "Well, why didn't you say so at first?"

"'Ow can I say it all at once?" Peter wanted to know. "You come 'ere askin' me this an' askin' me that, an' I'm just tellin' you." He spent a moment in thought. "Ole Bang 'e's gone," he said meditatively. "Now the Beau 'imself might do. 'E's slowed down to nothin an' 'e's got a grand nose— "

"Just the thing," said the master of Brookfield. "We'll give him a trial at any rate. What else have you got?"

"'Old your 'orses a bit," said Peter. " 'Is rheumatism 'as been so bad 'ere lately 'e can't 'ardly get out of 'is kennel."

The master of Brookfield got out his cigarette case and seated himself on the kennel house doorstep. There followed a gloomy silence. It was broken by Peter at last.

"Lord!" he exploded suddenly, "I never thought." He folded his arms and directed a reproachful eye at the master of Brookfield. "You come 'ere askin' me for a grouse dog," he said. "Why didn't you look around afore you come?" He nodded toward the house. "What about '*im*?" he inquired. "With all the brains an' all the nose in the world, an' 'is speed gone from 'im. Take 'im with you up there, an' if 'e flushes a single bird, once 'e knows what they're like, you can 'ave my wages for a year."

"I believe you're right," said the master of Brookfield, brightening. "It's queer I didn't think of it. And yet, when you consider everything—" He broke off, overwhelmed by visions of the past in which a white speck swept distant horizons while horsemen cursed him lovingly and galloped after.

"It is funny now, ain't it?" said Peter. "'Untin' grouse with 'im. Lord save us!"

The pines had done it. At first Dumb-Bell had suspected the loons that laughed wildly from somewhere out on the black mystery of the lake. But it wasn't the loons; they, at least, were alive. It was the pines, the brooding pines—and the silence. Always before, wherever he had gone, there had been noises, reassuring noises. Early in the morning, like this, birds should chirp and roosters crow; dogs give tongue and cattle rumble a greeting to the dawn. Horses might nicker and stamp. Sheep quaver to one another. And, best of all, there would be human voices, or a laugh, or a song, or a whistle. And the trees, where these things happened, rustled comfortably and seemed to take an interest.

All this was far away, and Dumb-Bell had the shivers, and the pines had done it. He had heard them all night. When the wind blew, the pines made a noise. He did not like that noise. The silence in which, no matter how hard he listened, nothing could be heard was almost better.

Although the kitchen fire was banked and he lay on a shooting coat close to the stove he had begun to shiver as the noise went on. He had hoped that when it stopped he would stop shivering, but the wind had died out and the noise had stopped, and still he shivered. He could see the pines now through the cabin window, black and still against the sky, plainer every minute as the light grew. So many of them! There were a few pines at Brookfield. There had been a lot of them on one side of the course when he won the Continental. He had not shivered at them then. He had just run, with hundreds of men watching, and smashed into his bevy finds and gone on, while the men yelled.

But the pines down there were smaller and not so black and proud, and he had been wild with excitement, for of course he was winning, he always won, and he knew the men would crowd about him later and talk about him in hushed voices while he pretended not to hear what they said.

There had been so many people that day. Here there were so few. His master and mistress and Mr. Parmalee and the cook man. That was all. And millions of pines. Dumb-Bell shivered and watched them through the window, his head between his paws.

They called this place the Happy Hunting Ground; but Dumb-Bell was not happy as he lay there, although he had hunted every day since they came.

Of course it was not in the least like quail hunting—nothing was like that! You went as fast as you could when you hunted quail, and saw the country for miles and miles. It was glorious!

But they wouldn't let him do that any more, and these new birds were interesting. You must go very quietly, and at the first faint scent slow to a walk and then to a creep and then to a crawl, until something told you you could go no farther.

Dumb-Bell had flushed two grouse that first day before he had understood how they would burst out of the cover and roar off when he was fifty feet away. His master had said "Careful" to him reproachfully, and Dumb-Bell had grinned in an agony of remorse. After that no more birds were flushed. He just crept about and found them in every direction, while his master and Mr. Parmalee shot, and his mistress called him silly names and even hugged him, now and then, when he came back with the dead bird unruffled in his mouth.

He had disapproved of this hugging business. He was hunting, and even though he went slowly and was stiff for some reason, when night came he was still Champion Brookfield Dumb-Bell at his work and not a "precious lamb."

This was the dawn of their last day in the Happy Hunting Ground. Some of the things were packed already. The wagons would come tomorrow; and Dumb-Bell was glad.

The wagons would take them for miles through pines. But the train would come along, and after a while the pines would not stand in towering ranks on both sides of the track, and he would stop shivering.

He lay and watched the pines until the cook man came and gave the stove its breakfast. Dumb-Bell wondered why it always ate wood instead of the good-smelling things that were put on top of it.

Presently his mistress called good morning to Mr. Parmalee and came into the kitchen, and the last day in the Happy Hunting Ground had begun.

His mistress stayed at the cabin that day to finish packing, and he and his master and Mr. Parmalee started out. As they were leaving, his mistress gave him a hug and felt him shiver, and thought he was cold.

But his master said, "He'll warm up when he gets to moving. Won't you, old snoozer?"

Dumb-Bell grinned, and galloped stiffly to a small thicket. He skirted it with care to show that he was ready. ... It was much better to hunt and forget the pines.

He did forget them all morning long. Early in the day his master made a wonderful double, both of them cross shots, and soon after that Dumb-Bell pointed a live bird a long way off, with a dead bird in his mouth, and Mr. Parmalee—well, it wasn't exactly hugging, but it was near it.

They ate lunch in a small clearing where the low gray sky seemed to rest on the tops of the pine trees. Dumb-Bell ate his two sandwiches slowly, and stared at it.

There was something about the sky he did not like. As he watched it the shivers came back, and he was glad when lunch was over and he could go to work again.

Late in the afternoon, although he was working as hard as he could, he began to shiver worse than ever, and suddenly he knew....

It was not the pines that had made him shiver. It was something else. It was something that was coming. It would be here soon now.

It had been coming all night. The pines had been telling him. Why, perhaps they were not so proud, so aloof, as they had seemed! Perhaps they really cared like the friendly trees at Brookfield.

This thing that was coming was in the sky. In the gray sky that was growing dark now—and the pines were beginning to talk about it again.

Dumb-Bell stopped hunting, and stared into the north. As he stared his eyes changed, his soft, kindly, setter eyes. They filled with green lights. Those from which he sprang, centuries and centuries before, had fled and died before this thing, coming out of the north, and the sleeping wolf within him was awake and was afraid.

"Getting pretty dark, isn't it?" said the master of Brookfield. "Let's hunt this piece out and break for camp. We're going to have a storm I think. Dumb-Bell! Go on, old man!"

At the words Dumb-Bell turned. Rebellion was in his heart. He would not go on. He would put his tail between his legs and run. He would run to where the stove was that ate wood.

This tall man who said "Go on," who was he? Dumb-Bell looked at him wildly, and their eyes met... Dumb-Bell grinned, whined, and started—not for the stove and safety; he went carefully toward a distant brush heap. There might be a grouse in there, and the tall man, his man, in the old tan shooting coat which he had slept on so many times, had ordered him to find it.

Yes, there was a grouse in the brush heap. Dumb-Bell slowed to a creep and then to a crawl, until something told him he could go no farther. Then he stopped, his eyes no longer green and shifting. They were warm, faithful, eager—the eyes of Champion Brookfield Dumb-Bell on point.

And then, with one last wailing shriek from the pines, the thing that had been coming, that had made him shiver so, was there. Dumb-Bell did not move. His fear, the fear of slinking ancestors, was gone. What if there was a roar that deafened him! What if it was as dark as night! What if he could scarcely breathe for the smothering ice particles that stung his muzzle and filled his eyes and his nostrils! The years had thinned his blood and stiffened his limbs, but his nose, which was his soul, they could not touch. It was the nose of a champion still, and wind and dark and snow could not prevail against it—there was a grouse in the brush heap.

A blizzard was a terrible thing. The pines had moaned all night about it. It was here now, roaring and biting, all but lifting him off his feet. Still—there was a grouse in the brush heap. You couldn't change it.

The wind was the worst. It was so hard to hold himself erect, and he must do that, whatever happened. He was on point, and champions pointed with a high head and level tail.

If he moved, the grouse would flush, and he never flushed birds. Why, long ago, when he was a tiny puppy and they called him the runt and were ashamed of him, he never flushed birds. He had pointed sparrows when they kept him alone day after day in the runway. Of course no one knew he was pointing and no one came to flush the sparrows. They would hop about in the runway for a long time—so long that his legs would begin to tremble and his back would ache, and someone should have come—but no one ever did.

It was like that now, only worse. The wind was so cold. The winds were all much colder, lately. This one seemed to cut right into his chest as he held his head high against it. His hind legs were going back on him, too. They were beginning to let him down a little. He must straighten up somehow.

Why didn't they come? He was so cold, so very cold. If he could change his position it would help his legs. They felt numb and queer. He felt queer all over. But there was a grouse in the brush heap. They would come and flush it soon, now.

They had better hurry. He could not hold his head up much longer. It was not the wind, the wind was growing warmer, almost like summer, but he was sleepy. That was queer. He had never felt sleepy on point before. But then he had worked hard today and he had not slept well last night because of the shivers. He would sleep better tonight, much better. Why, he could go to sleep this minute. The wind wouldn't hurt him. The wind was his friend. It had blown the snow all over him, and it was nice warm snow. It packed itself under his chest. He could even rest a little weight on it and help his legs.

But they were gone away, his legs. Back to Brookfield, perhaps. He must go, too, back to Brookfield. It was bright and cheerful there, and always there were sounds that he knew, nice sounds — not like the pines and the loons.

He would come to the big gates first and then he would leave the drive and cut across the lawn toward the lights of the house shining through the trees. He would scratch on the front door and someone would let him in, and Peter would be glad to see him, and so would his chair, his own chair near the fire. And then — *But there was a grouse in the brush heap*! He had almost forgotten ... No, he couldn't leave just now. He must stay a little longer, alone in the dark in the nice warm snow.

The snow was getting higher about him all the time. Perhaps it would cover him up after a while. He was not very big. They had called him the runt long ago ... He had never flushed birds, though, even then. And now, although his master called him old snoozer, he was Champion Brookfield Dumb-Bell, with his picture in the papers, and there was a grouse in the brush heapl A grouse — in — the — brush — heap ...

The mistress of Brookfield raised her gun. "All ready, Tom." she said.

The cook put his shoulder to the door and let it swing open a scant foot. There was a whistling shriek, the room was filled with a vortex of snow, both lamps went out, and the cook threw his weight against the door until the latch clicked in its socket. It was done in five seconds, practice had made him perfect; but a tongue of flame had leaped out of the door as the twelve-gauge spoke in an abrupt yelp that just managed to rise above the voice of the storm.

The cook lit the lamps again. Mrs. Gregory dropped the gun butt to the floor and felt the muscles of her right arm. She was shooting three and a quarter drams of nitro. Her own little twenty-gauge could not have been heard to the edge of the clearing. Her arm and shoulder were bruised to a throbbing ache.

She stood at the door listening for a time, then she broke the gun and slipped a shell in the right barrel. "All ready, Tom?"

"Yes, ma'am."

This time the heavy charge made her stagger and forced an "Oh!" of pain through her clenched teeth.

The cook reached for the gun. "You can't do that no more," he said. "It'll tear the arm off of you."

"I must," she said. "I can't hold the door. If the lamp blows over again it might explode."

"I'll hold her or bust a lung," said the cook, "an' shoot with one hand."

Mrs. Gregory drew the gun away and gave the cook a white smile. "You're a good man," she said with a nod. "When this is over you must come back with us to—What was that?"

The cook listened intently. He heard what he had heard for the past hour, the shriek of the wind and the rattle of ice particles against the window.

But the mistress of Brookfield was a woman, and women listen with more than ears.

"Open the door!" she cried. "Quick, quick!"

The cook obeyed. For an instant the lamplight cut a yellow square a few yards into the blackness before the door. It was filled with a myriad of particles of hissing snow. These gave place to a staggering figure that carried another figure in its arms. Then the lamps blew out again.

When they were lighted a man of ice stood in the room. He crackled and tinkled when he moved, but he had the voice of the master of Brookfield.

"Glad you fired," he croaked. "I'd been hoping you would." He looked down at the quiet figure he carried. "Come and get him, Tom. I can't unbend my arms."

The mistress of Brookfield did not explain that she had been firing for an hour or more. She flew to the medicine case, then to the kitchen, then back with a steaming kettle. It was not until Mr. Parmalee stirred beneath the blankets a few moments later, then opened his eyes and muttered her name, that she flew to the master of Brookfield and asked a question.

"Where," she said, "is Dumb-Bell?"

The master of Brookfield sat in an unheated room with his hands in a dishpan filled with snow. His face, despite him, was twisted with pain. But the pain in his eyes as she met them was not physical. It was deeper and more lasting than the small agony of frozen fingers.

"I ordered him on," he said, "just before it hit us. I looked as long as I dared, and fired and whistled. I thought he'd come back here."

"Oh!" she said, with a sudden intaking of the breath. She returned to the main room and picked up the twelve-gauge. She picked the cook up bodily with her eyes and set him at the door, daring him with the same look to mention her arm and shoulder.

"All ready, Tom," she said. "He'll come to the gun if he hears it." She fired until her blue-black arm refused to lift the twelve-gauge any longer. Then she took a camp stool close to the door and sat there, waiting—listening for a whine or a scratch that never came.

When a grayness appeared at the windows at last, the outside world was still in a shrieking, whirling frenzy. But an hour later the storm swept away to the south as abruptly as it had come, and a red sun was climbing a salmon sky above the snow-bowed pines.

Beneath the pines the drifted snow was blue, but in the clearings it was a dazzling, shimmering pink that crept up the pines themselves, changing them to lavender plumes filled with violet shadows.

Not a breath of wind remained. The pines were only painted on a painted sky. The pink snow, too, was painted. The whole wilderness had become unreal. It was too scenic, too theatrical to be true, and Mrs. Gregory gasped as she stepped into it.

"Jim," she said, "this isn't the world, is it? There never were such colors in the world before."

The master of Brookfield squinted at the blushing snow, the unbelievable sky, and the still miracle of the pines with their impossible shadows.

"Why, no," he said, at last. "It isn't the world. It's—the Happy Hunting Ground, don't you remember?"

At this she looked at him.

"Ah, little Chief!" he said. And one of his bandaged hands fumbled for one of hers, and found it, and so they set out with Tom ahead breaking trail and Mr. Parmalee waving feebly from the doorway.

They floundered on, peering into thickets, eying small mounds of snow fearfully but passing them without examination. They would not admit, just yet, that one of those innocent mounds could have a dreadful secret. Now and then Tom would fire into the air, and they would stop and listen to the echoes of the shot crashing among the pines. They called, of course, and the master of Brookfield whistled, but the clearings were filled with snow and sunlight and the thickets with snow and shadows, and that was all.

At last they found something. It was a gun standing against a tree.

"It's mine," said Gregory. "Now I know where I am."

He broke open the gun, took out the shells, and blew the snow from the barrels. He slipped the shells into the breech automatically, closed the gun, and looked about him.

"We were standing in the middle of that clearing" he said, pointing, "and I ordered him on. He went toward the farther end—that's north, isn't it, Tom?—and then it hit us, and I never saw him after that. Chief, you stand here to give us our bearings and we'll make a circle around you. You go one way, Tom, and I'll go the other. We'll make the first circle to take in the edge of the clearing, and widen for the next when we meet."

The mistress of Brookfield stood and watched them go. Somehow it was a comfort to be here where the mannie had been. His blessed paws must have pattered by close to where she was standing. She knew exactly how he looked when he went by. He would be so earnest, so intent. He seemed to take on a remoteness when at work that shut her away almost completely from him. It was almost a sacrilege to hug him when he had to come in with a dead bird and could not avoid her. But who could help it when he looked like that, so proud and important!

If she had only been here yesterday. If she only had! If it was only now, this minute, that he was passing and she could call his name and see by the flicker of his eye that he heard!

She tried it. "Dumb-Bell!" she said softly. "Mannie! Oh, Mannie!".... She could not see whether he passed or not. She could see nothing until she found a handkerchief in her sweater pocket.

Then, when she could see again, her heart stopped beating, for Tom was waving to her and calling, and she ran toward him floundering, stumbling, falling in the snow.

When she had crossed the clearing and saw what Tom was looking at she gave a cry of thankfulness and joy.... There was the mannie—alive! He was standing deep in the snow. He was pointing with a high head and a level tail as he always did.

And then she saw a look of amazement in Tom's face. She came closer, and the light left her eyes as she sank down on a log and covered them with her hands.... She did not move when the master of Brookfield came and stood beside her.

Dumb-Bell was in a small glade, just beyond the shadow of a great black pine. He seemed to be carved in silver, for the sunlight flashed and twinkled on the sheath of ice that covered him from the tip of his outstretched nose to the tip of his outstretched tail. And if the ice had been enduring silver, the perfection, the certainty of his pose, could have served as a model for all the champions yet to come.

They wached him for awed moments in a vast silence. And then the silence was broken. From a white mound at which he pointed there came a sound, a scratching flutter.

The white mound, once a refuge, was now an icy prison. Its occupant was pecking and fluttering to be free. There was a grouse in the brush heap!

"Good God!" exclaimed Gregory, and then, "Let him out, Tom; kick the snow away!"

But the mistress of Brookfield put her hand on his arm. "No, no!" she said. "No, no! He's held it for you all this dreadful night—in this horrible land where he doesn't belong... my mannie, my own little mannie!"

"I see," said Gregory. "Good girl!" He waded to the white mound, kicked the snow away and swung his foot against the pile of brush, the ice tinkling in the dead branches.

The brush heap shivered. There was a drumming of wings, a shower of snow, and a big cock grouse shot for the blue above the pines. There was a staccato crash, a pungent breath of nitro powder, and still he went, like a bronze rocket, straight for that bit of sky.

The master of Brookfield winked the dimness from his eyes and set his jaw. The grouse topped the pines in a flashing curve. He was gone! No, not quite. He had spread his wings for his sail over the tree-tops when he crumpled suddenly in the air.

The master of Brookfield broke open his smoking gun and looked at the small white statue, banked in snow.

"Dead bird!" he said. "Dead bird, old snoozer!"

But Champion Brookfield Dumb-Bell gave no sign that he heard. He could no longer stoop to a ruffed grouse lying in the snow. His spirit was sweeping like the wind over Elysian Fields and flashing into point after point on celestial quail.

Allegheny

· I ·

Henderson's Thunder and Jake Lavan's White Rose first met at sea. It was a secret meeting, as far as the police were concerned, but two hundred gentlemen of the sporting underworld managed to be present. They withdrew quietly from the lights and babble of Manhattan, proceeded singly or in small groups through the dark and odorous warehouse district of the East River, and arrived at the steamer *Lucy Hammond*, made fast to Pier 19.

Each one who boarded the *Lucy Hammond* that night gave up the sum of ten dollars freely and without regret. For the comparatively small sum mentioned they were to have the privilege of observing whether or not the female bull-terrier was more deadly than the male. Henderson's Thunder had destroyed the pit dogs of Greater New York and suburbs like a devouring flame. Ten or more canine warriors of the Pittsburgh district had died hard in the iron jaws of White Rose.

At the stroke of ten the *Lucy Hammond* slipped from her pier, dropped silently down the river, and drew safely away from Manhattan Island and its minions of the law. Out to sea she stole, down the Jersey coast she crept, and presently Thunder and White Rose faced each other for a bristling instant upon her moon-bathed deck.

There were voices, suppressed voices, all about them.

"Two hundred on the Rose."

"You're on."

"A hundred more you've made a bad bet."

"Nope. I got enough."

"I'll bet five hundred to a thousand the dog stops her in thirty minutes."

"I've got that, pal. This guy can hold it."

"Back, gents! Everybody back! A match between Henderson's Thunder, champion of New York, and Lavan's White Rose, of Pittsburgh, at forty-five pounds, give or take three pounds—the dog gives a pound and a quarter. Back, gents, if you please, well back from the pit. Ready, Thunder? Ready, Rose? *Let 'em go!*"

An hour and forty minutes later the referee crossed the pit to where Jake Lavan was crouching, white-lipped and silent. For ten minutes or more Jake had ceased to whisper as though in prayer, "Come on, you Rose, come on."

"She's through," said the referee. "Don't you want to save her?"

Jake closed and unclosed his hands, and gave a last despairing look at the feeble efforts of White Rose to free herself from the abiding brindle jaws which held and shook her. He rose suddenly to his full height and flung up his hand at Tom Henderson. "Come on—break his hold!" he said hoarsely. "We quit!"

So ended the first encounter between Thunder and White Rose. In addition to disproving Mr. Kipling's poem, it led to a second and more amicable meeting.

As Jake Lavan stepped from the pit with White Rose, white no longer, in his arms, Tom Henderson called after him: "She's as game as they ever come. I'd like a pup from her and him. What do you say?"

Jake glanced down at the crimson head of White Rose, resting limp across his forearm, then at Thunder, still on his feet but swaying drunkenly.

"If she lives—you're on," he said.

The indomitable White Rose was pitted with Death that night, and won. She arrived at health and strength a month later, and the six greedy atoms that ultimately squirmed at her side were splotched with brindle on pinky white. Also, in an astonishingly short time, a bone must not be thrown among them. Little and soft and helpless they seemed, but each had a set of sharp puppy teeth, with which, over a bone, they would do instant, joyous, and bloody execution. It was not the snarling scuffle of other breeds, undertaken and ended lightly; it was the quiet and deadly warfare of the fighting bull-terrier, that goes, barring interference, to the finish.

White Rose, of course, adored them. Her remaining eye lost something of its bold assurance when she realized that six feet of steel chain limited the protection she could assure her offspring. Whenever one of them waddled beyond this safety zone, she became, for the first time in her heroic life, a prey to anxious fears.

She was confirmed in her anxiety one morning, when the puppies decided to investigate an ancient alley cat that chose a sunny spot at the corner of the house in which to brood upon his wrongs. The puppies advanced toward the dour and forbidding feline in column formation, the boldest at their head. The leader halted at a respectful distance from the cat and ventured an unimpressive puppy bark. Its effect was negligible, and he decided to assume a more intimate attitude. Drawing closer, he invited the silent stranger to a romp by executing a number of clumsy advances and retreats.

The tip of a long gray tall, lying moveless in the sunshine, began to twitch. It attracted the puppy's attention. It was a fascinating thing—

so long and still and furry, with just the end moving slightly. He felt a keen desire to pick it up and shake it with mock ferocity. Better not venture this at first, perhaps. Why not dab it lightly with his paw? The idea grew in his mind. It finally possessed him utterly and at last moved him to action. He drew closer to that fascinating tail. An instant later he was on his back, his round pink stomach exposed to two lightning claw strokes. When he regained his feet the cat was gone and his co-investigators had fled. He returned dazedly to his frenzied mother, who, from then on, would launch herself from the kennel like a bolt of destruction at the slightest sound or shadow.

This proved an effective method of securing the privacy she desired. Few visitors cared to remain in the vicinity of White Rose, silent, open-mouthed, lunging on the chain. It was a good, stout chain, to be sure, but chains have been known to break. The thought destroyed the morale of milkmen, icemen, children, dogs, and cats, impartially. The neighborhood learned that just to the rear of the Lavan house was a small kingdom ruled over by a white fury, entirely devoted to maternity, which they would do well to avoid.

Sol Litchenstein, however, was not of the neighborhood. He was not of any neighborhood. His goings and comings were bounded by the number of miles per day he could whack out of the forlorn thing of hide and bones that pulled his junk-piled wagon. He knew nothing of the hair-raising terror that was to be found in the Lavans' backyard.

White Rose was dozing in the kennel one afternoon. She had waived the responsibilities of motherhood for the moment, and was allowing herself the luxury of a dream. She was dreaming of the pit. She had broken the hold of her opponent, had wrestled him off his feet, and was about to fasten herself enduringly at the base of his neck, when she was rudely awakened.

"Ra-a-gs! Ra-a-gs! Papeer, Ra-a-gs!"

White Rose was up and out with one convulsive leap, scattering puppies in all directions. Sol Litchenstein missed his doom by a scant inch. He lost only a greasy corduroy cap and one trousers leg. As he fled blindly toward the alley and his wagon, as white as the whitest of the rags that it contained, there was a small wail of agony from the kennel. It did not continue long. It came from the leader in the cat investigation, who still bore two red scratches along his plump mid-section, and such as he are silent under pain.

When Jake Lavan returned from the rolling mill that evening he found White Rose licking a woebegone puppy that floundered and sprawled when she nosed him to his feet. When his mother had flung herself at the intruding Sol the chain had looped about one of the puppy's legs and crushed it, so Jake discovered, beyond repair.

Jake, although he could watch a pit dog take its punishment in a fair fight, was tender as a woman where animals were concerned. The puppy must bc destroyed—that was evident. Jake examined the damaged leg again and, holding the puppy under his coat to shield it from the winter wind, moved reluctantly toward the Allegheny River, two blocks away.

As he emerged from the alley that paralleled his domain, he encountered Mose Trimble shuffling disconsolately down Humboldt Street.

"Want to earn a dime, smoke?" asked Jake abruptly, as it came to him that another might relieve him of his dreaded business with the Allegheny.

Mose ceased his shuffle and rolled a yellowish eyeball at his questioner.

"What way?"

"Take this pup to the river and drown him."

"Whuffor?"

"He's through," explained Jake. "Broke his leg somehow."

Now Mose had looked upon bad gin when it is white until the early morning hours of the night before. He had slept all day and was just emerging in search of a drink with which to quench slightly the raging fires within him. He extended a shaking hand.

"Slip him to me, man," he said.

Jake placed the puppy in a huge chocolate-colored palm, produced a thin dime, parted with it, and retraced his steps up the alley. Mose, with more purpose in his shuffle than heretofore, moved on down Humboldt Street toward the river.

It had been snowing intermittently that afternoon; small flakes were falling even now; they showed white for an instant on Mose's face and neck before turning to moisture on his glistening black skin. The snow disturbed him not at all. He was anticipating the gulp of liquid consolation which he would presently tilt into his burning soul. As his small burden stirred uneasily he tightened his fingers about its body.

"Ain' no use gettin' fidgety, dawg," he told the puppy. "Come 'long wid Mose."

The puppy stirred again and began to shake. In addition to the pain of its broken leg it missed the soft straw of the kennel, the huddling bodies of its brothers and sisters, the soothing presence of White Rose. Its tremors increased until they distracted Mose.

"Whuffor you shake?" he inquired. "You ain' gonna shake long. That ol' river stop your shakin.' Allegheny git you soon, my frien'; no use to shake."

But the puppy continued to shiver, and presently it emitted a low cry of loneliness and despair.

"Wha's wrong wid you?" Mose demanded, lifting the puppy up for inspection. It was white except for a brindle splotch over one eye and a brindle saddle on its back. The tip of its muzzle and its nose were pink. Its eyes were the vague blue of the very young; but its head, as it moved it restlessly from side to side, expressed the qualities of its race. Unswerving tenacity, indomitable fortitude were stamped indelibly on that blocky little head. Here was purpose, determination, character. Mose, helpless drifter that he was, could see it. "Howdy, mistuh?" he said with a shade of uneasy respect. Still staring at the puppy, he arrived at the end of a small wharf and found dark water at his feet.

The Allegheny, inky black between its snow-covered banks, was broken here and there by floating cakes of ice. Mose shivered and felt cold for the first time that day. The fingers of his right hand were growing numb, he noticed, but his left hand, which held the puppy, was quite comfortable.

"Ain't you warm in the hand," said Mose; then added, after a pause, "Well, here we is." He looked at the river again. Lights were beginning to spring up on the farther shore. They sent yellow reflections along the surface, which wavered on the black water and glittered on the floating cakes of ice. They made the river seem more ominous, more forbidding if possible, than before.

Mose regarded the expanse of water and ice gloomily for a moment. He advanced to the edge of the wharf, stooped and dipped a finger in the river, clutching the puppy against the breast of his thin coat as he did so. Withdrawing the finger with some haste and a grunt of disapproval, he turned and climbed the bank.

"Too cold," he said.

· II ·

Christmas was coming. It was to be a wonderful Christmas that year. As evidence of the fact the drawers of the desk in the consulting-room of Herbert Bruce, M.D., contained many things that were not essential to the practice of medicine. Also, down in the darkest corner of the cellar stood an infant fir tree. Its hope of pointing majestically to the stars for a century or more was gone. It was to have a shorter and more brilliant career. It would assume an effulgent splendor for a day in accepting the principal part in the first Christmas of Herbert Lansmere Bruce, Jr.

Strictly speaking this would not be his first Christmas. It was, as a matter of fact, his second Christmas. But his hands had refused to close over a celluloid rattle the year before and a shiny silver mug had been completely ignored. Surely it was safe to assume that such a Christmas was no Christmas at all.

Arriving at the above conclusion, Herbert Bruce, M.D., looked at his watch and discovered that it was five minutes past office hours. He closed the consulting-room door, returned to the desk, and opened a lower drawer. As a miser gloats over his gold he hung above the contents of the drawer, seeing in his mind's eye the treasures that each box or package contained.

That knobby looking thing in the blue paper was the fire engine with its iron-gray team. That fat box was the fish pond. You fished with magnets for hooks. Each fish having a metal mouth, it was astonishing with what avidity they took the bait. Ah, what a pleasant world it would be if livelier fishes rose as promptly to the lure! The long package was an engine and the cars it pulled triumphantly around a circular track. That bit of roadbed would be the scene of many a calamitous wreck, no doubt. Soldiers were in the big flat box, both prancing cavalry and plodding troops afoot.

What was in the oblong box of gray cardboard? Bruce tried to remember, failed, and took the box from the drawer. Removing the cover he discovered a white rabbit with pink glass eyes and long pink-lined ears. Now, where did that come from? He hadn't bought it. "One of Julia's things," he thought, as he remembered that she had shopped with him one morning.

He lifted the rabbit from the box and examined it. From its furry stomach a key protruded unobtrusively. This key he proceeded to wind.

The effect on the white rabbit was electrical. It kicked madly until he set it on the desk and released it, whereupon it hopped briskly across the blotting pad, banged into a paper weight and caromed against the ink well.

"Hey, look out!" yelled Bruce. His warning was unheeded. The white rabbit plunged its head into the ink well, and kicked frantically.

Bruce rescued the rabbit and held it at arm's length until its kicking became a faint twitching of the limbs and at last ceased altogether. Then he bore it to a wash basin and let a water faucet remove the signs of its unfortunate experience. He dried the rabbit's head and whiskers with absorbent cotton and was replacing it in its box when someone knocked at the side door of the consulting-room, which led directly to the street. Bruce put the box on the desk, went to the door, and opened it.

Mose shuffled into the room. He removed his hat with one hand, the other hand he held within his half-opened coat.

"Evenin', Doctuh," said he.

"Good evening," said Bruce. "What's the matter, hurt your arm?"

"No, suh," said Mose, "nuthin' wrong wid me." He shuffled his feet and coughed uneasily.

"Well, what is it? What do you want?"

"Doctuh, please suh. Is you a animal doctuh?"

"You mean a veterinary. No, I'm not a veterinary."

"You don't nevah tend animals?"

"No; I never attend animals."

Mose blinked thoughtfully over this statement, moved toward the door, halted, and turned. "I looked in the window when I'm passin'," he said significantly. "That's how I happen in."

The look of accusation that accompanied the words could not be ignored. "What are you trying to get at, anyway?" asked the now puzzled Bruce.

Mose advanced a firm step. "If you ain' tendin' a rabbit when I look in that window jus' now, what is you doin'?"

The light of understanding broke upon Bruce. The corners of his mouth twitched, but the earnestness of his questioner restrained him from unseemly hilarity.

"I see," he said gravely. "Well, here's your rabbit." He took the white rabbit from its box and held it out for inspection. "It's a toy for my little son — Christmas, you know."

Mose blinked at the rabbit for a moment. "Sure fooled me," he admitted finally. "Thought I seen him a-kickin' and a-squirmin'...."

"You did," said Bruce, and gave the key a half turn.

At the first convulsive movement of the rabbit, there shot from Mose's coat a round little, fierce little head, its pink mouth wide, its eyes flaming, its forehead wrinkled with rage. It was apparent that the son of Thunder and White Rose disapproved of rabbits and would do battle with this one.

"Good Lord!" said Bruce. "How old is he?"

"Can't rightly say. I ain' had him long," Mose confessed. "Look like he's mighty young. If you be so kin' and lay dat rabbit away, Doctuh, please."

Bruce put the rabbit on the desk. The puppy grew quieter. The white furry thing was undoubtedly another of those creatures that scratch one on the stomach and then disappear. He watched it with smoldering eyes, growling softly, while Mose, holding him cupped in his hands, explained.

"I've heard of Lavan's dogs," said Bruce when Mose had finished. "He wouldn't tell you to drown a puppy, if there was a chance for it."

"It's jus' his laig, tha's all. Jus' his hin' laig."

"But I'm not a veterinary, I've told you once. Why didn't you drown him, as you were told?"

Mose looked down at the puppy, then raised his eyes and met Bruce's half-amused, half-impatient glance.

"He was so warm in the han'," he explained simply.

There was a moment's silence.

"I see," said Bruce at last. "Well, let's have a look at him."

"Thank you, Doctuh."

"H'mm, double fracture—poor little cuss. Just one thing to do for him."

"Yessuh," said Mose, brightening.

Bruce laid the puppy gently on the desk blotter, strode to a wall cabinet and returned with a small sponge and a glass-stoppered bottle filled with a colorless liquid,

"This is the best thing for him," he said.

"Yessuh." Mose's face was alight with the supreme confidence of his race in the medicine man. "Shall I rub it on the laig, Doctuh? Or give it internal."

"Neither. I'll hold it to his nose."

"Nose! What you got?"

"Chloroform," said Bruce briskly, saturating the sponge.

Moses face fell from the heights of expectancy to the depths of gloom. "Ain' nuthin' you can do, Doctuh?"

"Not a thing. You see, he— " The sentence remained unfinished as Bruce turned toward the sound of a thudding clatter on the desk and stared dumfounded at what he saw.

The son of Thunder and White Rose had never for an instant taken his eyes from the furry thing that scratched and disappeared. Suddenly he had found himself on the desk facing the creature. One leg refusing to aid him, he had found it hard to cross that broad expanse of green blotter, very hard; but he had finally succeeded in doing so.

He was now, with the silent intensity of his breed, shaking the life out of his enemy.

Bruce hastened to the rescue of the white rabbit for the second time. It was saved with difficulty and the loss of a tuft of fur, to which two small jaws were steadfastly attached. When it was safe in the drawer once more, the eyes of Bruce and Mose met.

"He's hell on wheels, ain't he, Doctuh?"

Bruce nodded. There followed a silence, in which the white man and the black stared at a small puppy with a broken leg ridding its mouth of a tuft of fur. In the eyes of both was the same shining look. Civilize him as you please, make his color what you like, man still will worship the born fighter.

Bruce spoke first. "I'll see what I can do with a splint and plaster of Paris."

Mose beamed, then sobered suddenly. "One thing mo,' Doctuh. I jus' don't happen to be financial right now."

"Oh, that's all right," said Bruce.

Two hours later Mose was again facing the snow-laden winter wind. His thirst, forgotten while he was absorbed in the wonders of surgery, was now raging once more. He felt for the reassuring dime in his pocket, located it, and headed for One-Eyed Johnson's place, an emporium devoted to serving members of his own race with food and drink. He was still a block from its warmth and hospitality when there came a whimper of distress from beneath his coat.

"Less noise from you," said Mose. "Ain' the doctuh fix you up all nice and good?"

But the whimper grew.

"Say, lay off me, dawg," Mose advised.

A sudden alarming thought left him so limp that his shuffle became a drag. "My Gawd—he's hongry!"

Grumbling, threatening, cursing the ever-growing whimper in his ears, Mose reached the haven that he sought. In he shuffled. He gave one look of supreme longing toward the bar, then slouched to the lunch counter. "Gimme some hambu'ger steak and a nickel's wuth of milk,' was his order.

The patrons of One-Eyed Johnson's place crowded about him a

moment later and watched interestedly as the whimper changed to a violent lapping and gobbling.

"Whose dawg?"

"Mine."

"Whar you git him?"

"Neveh min'."

"What's dat on his laig?"

"Plastuh Paris—he jus' been tended by a doctuh."

"Huh—look like a good one. What's his name?"

Mose hesitated for an instant, then straightened up and swept the attentive circle with an important eye. "I calls him Allegheny," he said.

· III ·

A year slipped by, as years do. It made no noticeable improvement in Mose or his fortunes. He was occupied with what he described as odd jobs, while looking for "regulah wuck with good people," and remained the same impecunious drifter as before.

The change in Allegheny, however, was startling. He grew into a forty-eight-pound, steel-muscled song of war, that ran, diminuendo, from a heavy chest and head to a neatly tapered tail.

That a slight swelling on his left hind leg did not trouble him was proved by the agility he displayed in treeing cats, or in romps and mock battles with playfully inclined dogs.

The latter amusement was frowned upon by Mose, after an interview with Jake Lavan, whom they met on the street one day.

"What'll you take for him," asked Jake, when he had been told how Alleheny had escaped a watery grave.

"He ain' for sale," said Mose promptly.

Jake's appraising eye lingered on Allegheny a moment longer. "I tell you what I'll do," he decided at last. "I'll train him and pit him, and see how good he is. It looks to me like it would take an awful dog to stop him. He might win some coin for us."

"When do I git him back?" Mose inquired.

"Oh, I dunno. If he's good we'll keep him workin'."

"Kin I have him when he ain' fightin'?"

"Why, sure, if you'll feed him right. What do you want with him?"

"Jus' comp'ny. Jus' to ramble aroun' wid me."

Jake gave way to ironical laughter. "Do you think you can pit him, and then let him sashey around town? Listen, nigger — that's a fightin' dog. He's by Thunder out of White Rose."

"Shuh," exclaimed Mose. "He don't bother nothin' 'cep' cats. He's a good-natured dawg."

"Oh, he is, ehl" said Jake grimly. "Well, I'll tell you what he'd do — after he learns what he's for — he'd kill every kioodle in Pittsburgh, as fast as he got to 'em."

"Huh," said Mose uneasily, as he visioned the unpleasant consequences that would follow the sudden taking off of white folks' dogs by Allegheny. "I'll keep my eye on that gen'leman."

"Well, lemme give him a whirl," urged Jake. "What do you say?"

"I don' say nuthin'," said Mose, getting abruptly under way. "Come on, dawg."

At the next street corner Allegheny was advised to sing small and watch his step. "If you git uppity," he was warned, "bad times goin' to ketch you by the short hairs." From then on he was heaped with reproaches if he so much as looked in the direction of a canine that assumed a belligerent attitude, and even polite exchanges with friendly strangers were discouraged. "Jus' ten' to your own business, and take no chances wid nobody," he was told. "Min' your p's and q's, an' some day you git a home."

The home referred to was the stately mansion of the "good people" of Mose's dreams, who would furnish ease and comfort to a handyman and a "splendid watch dawg," in exchange for a leisurely performance of light duties.

Good people, however, who desired to add a handyman and a watchdog to their establishment were rare. Mose was bitterly aware of this fact as he plodded homeward one evening after four hours with a post-hole digger under a beating sun. As he passed a brick and stucco dwelling with a sweep of lawn in front, he halted suddenly. His listless eye had taken in some gold letters on a black nameplate.

"Herbert Bruce, M.D.," he read. He repeated the name aloud and addressed Allegheny. "Come here, dawg." Allegheny reluctantly gave up sniffing a telephone post and approached.

"Look at dat sign," said Mose. "Look at it good. Dat's de vehy doctuh dat fix your laig. He move on away from whar he was and I ain' neveh seen him since. Now, here he is. You come on in along wid me an 'spress your thanks."

Allegheny, impressed, followed Mose sedately up the walk to the door beside the black and gold nameplate. A maid informed them that the doctor was in the backyard, but could be called.

"Thank you kindly," said Mose; "I'll jus' go roun' and speak to him."

When Allegheny realized that their business lay in the rear of the premises, his dignity fled. He had never forgotten a certain humiliating experience of puppyhood, and cats are found more frequently in backyards than anywhere else. He shot around the house like a brindle and white flash, his pads rasping crisply on the cement walk.

There was no cat in the back yard, he discovered. There were three people—a man, a woman, and a child. It was a boy child, with earnest blue eyes, pouting cherry lips, and tousled red-gold hair. He was digging a hole in a pile of sand with a very small shovel. The man and woman were standing with an arm about each other, watching.

Allegheny was interested at once. He knew something about digging holes himself. He promptly jumped the boards that confined the sandpile and confronted the child.

Several things happened in quick succession. The man sprang forward with a shout, the woman gasped and grew pale, the child stared round-eyed into Allegheny's wide red mouth for an instant, then—

"Oo-oo, doggie!" said he, and flung himself promiscuously on Allegheny's neck.

Allegheny decided to greet a brother hole-digger with proper cordiality. He turned his head and spread a wet tongue across the small face that had been pressed against his rolling jaw muscles.

"'At's all right, Doctuh," called Mose. "He won' hurt him."

"I see he won't," said Bruce huskily. "It's all right, Julia. It's all right, my dear." He turned in suppressed fury on Mose. "Why do you let a dog like that run into people's yards? You frightened us — you frightened my wife. What do you mean by it?"

"'Scuse me, Doctuh," said Mose abashed. "I was jus' bringin' him in to 'spress his thanks."

"To what?"

"I see your name as I wuz passin'. Don't you 'membah me? 'Membah how he shake the rabbit? 'Membah how you fix his laig?"

"Well, well!" said Bruce, his anger vanishing. "I wondered how that job turned out. And this is that puppy!"

"Dat's him. I take off de splint in fo' weeks, like you say, an' he's good as new."

"Well, well!" Bruce repeated, as he eyed the mighty Allegheny with a touch of professional pride. "Let's see, which leg was it?"

"The left, Doctuh. Got a little swellin' on it, dat's all."

Bruce bent over Allegheny and attempted to examine the leg. "Let go of the doggie, little son. Daddy wants to see him."

"Doggie mine," said Herbert Bruce, Junior, firmly, and tightened his arms about Allegheny's neck.

"No, no. Let Daddy see him. That's a good boy."

"Do away! Doggie mine."

"Let Daddy have him, do you hear me?"

"Doggie mine! Doggie mine! Doggie mi-i-ine!"

"Julia."

Mrs. Bruce moved quietly forward, and presently Allegheny was freed; but the son and heir of the house of Bruce was dancing up and down on his sandpile emitting sounds of utter woe.

"Bad Mudder — doggie mine."

"Baby! Baby dear! You mustn't! This isn't my great big boy. This isn't mother's man. Aren't you ashamed!"

"I want 'at doggie."

Allegheny saved the situation. He had kept his eye on the hole in the sandpile from the first. He now approached it, gave it a brief examination, and went to work with such enthusiasm that a cataract of sand shot from between his hind legs as his head and flying forepaws rapidly sank from view.

Herbert Bruce, Junior, grew suddenly quiet. His mouth closed as his eyes grew wide. So swift was his transition from rage to joy that huge tears were still rolling to the sand below via his cheeks and chin as he rewarded Allegheny's efforts with a shriek of appreciation.

"See a doggie! Oo, see a doggie!"

"Yes, darling, he's helping Junior. Isn't that nice of him?" And so the skies were cleared.

It developed a few moments later that the ordered contentment of the Bruce establishment was threatened by a dreaded and inevitable general house-cleaning. Mose, having mentioned the names of a multitude of housewives to whom he had proved a solace upon like occasions, was engaged to appear the following Monday morning and become a staff and comforter.

"I kin hep you out all nex' week, Miz Bruce," he confided. "Afteh that, can't say. I'm lookin' foh a regu luh place wid good people. Jus' how much wuck could a handyman do 'roun' here, Doctuh?"

"Oh, we haven't enough for all of a man's time, Mose. Some grass to cut, furnace looked after — that's about all."

"You got a shoffuh?"

The average human being is reasonably healthy; there are many young doctors in the world, and bills for their services are paid last of all.

"No," said Bruce, with something like a sigh. "I drive myself."

"I wash and polish in ga' age three weeks once," suggested Mose dreamily. "Well, I'll be gettin' on. I wuck on a B. & O. diner one time, when I relieve a sick frien', Miz Bruce. Yessum, I'll be here at eight o'clock, Monday mawnin', yessum."

He was as good as his word and, being a new broom, swept clean. But Allegheny, early in the day, committed an indiscretion. A heavy rug was hoisted to a clothesline and smitten thunderously despite its writhings. Convinced that the rug was alive, Allegheny rushed to Mose's aid and fastened himself to a corner of the thick Bokhara. Mose promptly turned the beater upon his assistant, who withdrew crestfallen and assumed the role of interested spectator. Mose addressed him through a cloud of dust.

"Wha's got into you?" he inquired. "If Miz Bruce ketch you a-shakin' her dinin'-room rug, you'll hit trouble. Look like you lef' your senses home to-day. I seen you walkin' stiff-legged by dat loud-mouth coal-yard dog when we come pass. You betta look out, mistuh if you start fightin, you know where you'll lan'? On de end of a chain, dat's what you will."

The coal-yard dog Mose referred to was Tiger, a huge striped and sullen Great Dane owned by the yard boss of the Pocahontas Coal Company.

It was Tiger's custom to lie in the doorway of the company's stables and indulge in watchful waiting. A dog might pass unchallenged if he kept steadfastly on his way, but if he lingered to investigate a tree or the fence, Tiger would gallop forth with a heart-shaking bellow that sent most loiterers flying down the street. Allegheny had not fled when he heard the foghorn voice of Tiger for the first time. He had waited motionless with raised head until the lumbering giant was upon him, looked him in the eye for an instant, exchanged sniffs with him, and trotted calmly on. Mose and he had passed the coal company's stables many times since then. Tiger's challenge and Allegheny's reception of it had always been the same. That morning there had been a change. At sight of Allegheny Tiger had appeared, as usual, but with this difference: he was growling, not barking, as he came. Then, as he drew near, Allegheny saw his eyes, and in those bloodshot eyes was an unknown something that Allegheny loathed and feared.

Ten feet away Tiger halted. He glared at Allegheny for a moment, then slouched past him to the horse trough at the curb. Plunging his muzzle deep in the water he lapped and gulped noisily, leaving streaks of slaver on the surface. Allegheny turned and left the spot, as though walking on eggs.

Mose had observed the formality of Allegheny's withdrawal. He now dwelt on the episode at such length that Allegheny, after scratching an ear thoughtfully for a time, yawned and laid down.

"You chase that wearisome look off your face," said Mose severely, "an' listen good. I carry some knickknacks up in the attic a while ago. You know what I fin' up there? Lot of ole fuhniture. Bed, washstan', chairs—jus' layin' there ketchin' dus', ain' doin' no good for itself or nobody. You know what's up oveh de ga'age? Nice big room, nothin' in it but a wuck-bench." Mose took the rug from the line, hoisted it to his shoulder, and started for the house. "You min' your p's and q's like I tell you," was his parting advice. "Can't neveh tell what's gonna happen."

Allegheny, left to his own devices, found them stale and unprofitable. He had resigned himself to complete boredom when a screened door banged and a small figure in blue rompers appeared with a pail and shovel.

"Oo-oo, doggie!"

Allegheny's pensive attitude vanished. There was a meeting that involved a passionate embrace and a wildly wagging tail. There were shrieks of rapture and deep barks of delight. There was a rush to the sandpile, where marvels of excavation were accomplished, under the command of a chief engineer who breathed hard and indicated with sandy fingers the spot where Allegheny was to dig "anozzer one."

The mother of the chief engineer was also fully occupied. Her problem was the removal of dirt, not its excavation; but she managed to glance out the window every moment or so at the scene of her son's endeavors.

Two busy hours fled by. Allegheny unearthed a piece of rubber hose half buried in the sand. It served as an excellent instrument for tug-of-war, and brought such shrieks of rapture from the chief engineer that his mother flew to a window. Her face cleared at what she saw.

"Careful, Junior!" she called. "Let go if he pulls too hard." She was turning from the window when she paused, listening.

From so far away that she had barely heard it had come a pistol shot. Others followed in rapid succession, until six shots were fired. She wondered vaguely what they meant, and again would have turned from the window, but now she heard, from somewhere down the street, faint shouts and screams, and as she listened they drew nearer.

Two painters were passing carrying buckets, brushes, and a ladder. One of them looked back over his shoulder and did a curious thing. He dropped his bucket and brush, jerked the ladder from the other painter, and set it against a tree. Then both painters climbed the ladder hastily just as a dog appeared, a huge dog, running in the middle of the street.

There was a horse hitched to a delivery wagon standing before the house next door. The dog sprang at the horse, snapping his great jaws. The horse reared, shook the dog off, and ran away, with the wagon bouncing along behind him. A wheel of the wagon struck the dog and knocked him down. He got to his feet again and broke into a heavy, lurching run. The mother of the chief engineer screamed as only mothers scream, for the dog turned at the Bruces' drive and came into the yard.

Allegheny heard the scream. He dropped his end of the piece of rubber hose, looked inquiringly toward the liouse, and suddenly became a statue.... Tiger was lumbering up the drive, his mouth dripping slaver, his head swayinc, from side to side.

"Oo-oo," said the chief engineer. "Anozzer doggie."

But the hair on Allegheny's back lifted into a stiff ridge, for the eyes of Tiger, far worse than in the morning, were the eyes of a dog no longer; they belonged in a devil from hell.

"Nice doggie," cooed the chief engineer, with outstretched dimpled arms. The distance between those arms and Tiger lessened, lessened!—then something shot between. It was a forty-eight-pound fighting machine that was going into action at last .... Tiger went down, with Allegheny fastened to his throat.

There followed a battle that seemed one-sided. In noise and weight Allegheny was outclassed. He appeared to have no chance against the huge demented beast that roared like a lion as he struggled; but Jake Lavan, or Bill Henderson, or any of the gentlemen who had spent an interesting evening on the *Lucy Hammond* two years before, would not have wagered on the Great Dane had they been present. Having noticed that the bull terrier had a throat hold, they would have bet their money on the silent-fighting son of Thunder and White Rose.

And Allegheny proved true to the blood that was in him, by holding on. He was flung against the fence, and held on. He was beaten like a flail on the cement walk, and held on. He was ground into the sand of the sandpile, and held on.

The weeping chief engineer was snatched to safety by his wild-eyed mother. Men gathered timidly in the street before the house.

Mose came running, and Herbert Bruce, M. D., and at last a sweating policeman, while Allegheny held on.

The policeman had fired six shots at Tiger some little time before. He now fired a seventh from a two-inch range and did not miss. He might have saved his powder had he cared to. Tiger's roars had sunk to a choking rattle when the bullet entered his brain. For, under his great carcass, half buried in the sand, was Alleheny—still holding on.

"There's no danger," Bruce told the policeman a few moments later. "There isn't a tooth mark on him. He hasn't the smallest scratch. Here, look for yourself."

"He's been fightin' wid a mad dog," insisted the policeman, flourishing his gun.

Bruce caught the weapon in his hand and forced the muzzle to the ground. "Put it up, Tim," he urged. "I'll send him to a veterinary hospital for thirty days. If he doesn't show hydrophobia in that time, he never will."

But the policeman shook his head. "Let go the gun, sohrr. I'm sorry, but it's got to be done."

Then Herbert Bruce, M.D., played his trump card. Having brought a small Irishman into the world the summer before, he now looked the proud father steadily in the eye.

"Tim,' said he, "he saved my boy. He saved my little son— "

The policeman shifted his glance. He took in the panting Allegheny, caught the pleading eyes of Mose, and looked down at the revolver in his hand.

"If ye could git a permit from the boord av health— " he began. And so a second battle was won.

As a result of it, Allegheny was taken to the hospital that afternoon, but seemed likely to return, for Mose spent the evening moving furniture from the attic to the room over the garage, and when the chief engineer wailed for his "doggie" at bedtime his mother took him in her arms and held him very close.

"He's gone away for just a little while," said she. "When he comes back, you'll have him every day."

Trub's Diary

· I ·

The Chewing of the Chow

November 7. Solitude. A puppy biscuit did it, part of a puppy biscuit. Maybe I should blame it on my loss of appetite. If I had been myself, I'd have eaten all the biscuit. Or maybe my great-grandfather is responsible. Mike said something about that when he shut me in here. Mike is the head kennel man. He has red hair. I like Mike!

There were seven of us together when it happened. Myself and my sister. Her name is Lass of Craycroft. I know because I heard a kennel man tell a visitor. Don't know my own name.

Besides us there were three Scotch terriers and two chows. One chow was red and one was blue. The chows were older than the rest of us. We were all in number twelve runway. I don't like the red chow. I never did!

It was nice in the runway. We played games. We played King-of-the-Kennel, and Wolf-at-Bay, and Look-Out-Behind, and Nip-Nip-Nippy-Legs. Those are all splendid games.

Then we had barking parties. We'd all learned to bark weeks before, but there is nothing like practice. At barking parties you try to bark down everyone else. It's glorious!

Our bad times were on washing days. They are terrible! Awful tasting soap and the most disgusting stuff in the water. Flea killer! I should think as much.

All this fuss about fleas makes me sick. If you are busy, you don't notice them. If you aren't, they give you something to do.

Where was I? Oh, yes! We played all afternoon in that runway. We'd held a few barking parties. We slept some. The fat kennel man who feeds us didn't come around with our supper. We had a long barking party. Nothing happened. We played Dig-the-Hole-Deep. We made the best hole yet. Then we had a perfectly marvelous barking party. Still they didn't bring our supper. Everybody else gave up in disgust and went into the kennel for a nap. I stayed outside. I was ravenous.

At last I heard Mike talking to the fat kennel man. He was calling him names. He said something about a stew. I was glad to hear that. I thought we were going to have it for supper. But when it came it was corn meal mush. The fat kennel man brought it. He smelled funny. He nearly fell down when he put the feeding pan inside the gate. I ate half of the mush before the others heard me and came rushing out. Delicious!

I did not sleep very well that night. It was on account of a feeling. It was an oppressive feeling. I am subject to attacks of this sort. First the appetite goes, then comes the feeling. It seems to be in the abdomen—mostly.

We all had puppy biscuits next morning. The fat kennel man brought them. I ate all of mine and one of sister's and half of one that a Scotty hadn't got to yet. Suddenly I lost my appetite. It worried me. I was afraid I was in for one of my attacks. I decided not to finish the biscuit just then. It was hard to know just what to do with it. I didn't care to lay it down—not with that red chow around. He has no conception of property rights—absolutely none. Well, some people are like that!

I went over quietly to where we played Dig-the-Hole-Deep. I dropped a piece of puppy biscuit in the hole and pushed dirt in on top of it. I went away from there and laid down—watching.

Can you believe it? That red chow sidled over to the hole and began to sniff.

I said, "I'll thank you to stop sniffing."

He said, "This is a free country. I'll sniff if I feel like it."

I got up. I walked over to him. I said, "Is that so?"

He said, "Yes, that's so."

I said, "Well, sniff somewhere else!"

He said, "I guess the sniffing is as good here as anywhere."

I said, "Maybe so; but just get away from that hole while you're doing it."

He said, "Let's see you make me, you little white shrimp!"

I am not clear about what happened next. Everything seemed to turn red in a most peculiar way. I noticed my mouth was full of fur—chow fur. I heard a shout and the gate banged. The fat kennel man was lifting me up by the hind legs. My mouth was still full of fur and some of what was underneath. I heard the kennel man calling to Mike. He yelled, "Come here quick. A bull terrier pup has a chow by the neck and I can't git him loose."

The next thing I remember is being out of the runway with Mike holding me.

Mike said, "Be aisy, be aisy now, or I'll give ye a clout on th' ear! Stand still, you little drop of TNT—It's advice yer naidin'."

I didn't want advice. I had business to attend to back where that chow was.

Mike said, "Now, listen, me son. Yer in wrong. Ructions is out of date. 'Tis th' she-men and he-women have charge of things now. Pacifism is all th' rage. If ye don't git in the bandwagon, ye'll be unpopular. Are ye listenin'?"

I was. I was wondering what pacifism meant.

Mike said, "There's that in yer blood will scandalize th' neighbors if it iver comes out. It's put there by yer father and yer mother and a lot that comes before thim. Yer great-grandfather especial—as I had good raison to know whin I bet tin pounds against him on th' Dublin Terror in Cross-eyed Rafferty's cellar. Stop lookin' so wistful at that chow, now, an' attind to me."

I licked Mike's chin. It prickled my tongue.

Mike said, "Ye have th' makin's av a hellion like I've told ye. Remimber and watch yer step. If some wan bangs ye in th' jaw give him a look av gintle reproach an' let him take a crack at th' other side av yer map. If some wan puts his heel in the pit av yer shtomich turn round till he boots ye in th' behind. In that way ye'll get along nowadays, and no other. Now, go back in there where ye come from an' lave th' chow alone."

I tried to do as Mike said. No use! The minute I was back where the chow was it all got red again. The next thing I knew Mike was carrying me down the line of runways.

He said, "'Tis too much of yer grandfather's in ye for this day and age. In ye go, now. Ther's nothin' in here to disthract ye. Think over th' beauties av pacifism."

He shut me in the end runway and left me there.

Solitude! I still have a few fleas, though. I wonder what pacifism means.

· II ·

A Singing Molecule

November 14. Still alone in the end runway! I can see the Boston Post Road from here. I can see automobiles going by. I can see a big sign at the gate. It says, "Craycroft Kennels. Prize Winning Stock. Take Home a Pet!"

Held a barking party by myself. Not much fun in it. Chased tail. No good. Played Dig-the-Hole-Deep. It needs a crowd... ! Solitude is awful!

November 16. Scratched at fleas carefully. I need them. Slept. Watched automobiles go by. If Mike would put me back with the others, the red chow could sniff his head off. Would I let him take my biscuit? I would not!

November 17. Scratched. Slept. Chased tail. Watched automobiles go by. I would let the red chow have the biscuit—maybe.

November 18. Solitude.

November 19. More solitude.

November 20. Solitude is killing me.

November 21. He could have the biscuit.

November 22. Much has happened. I know my name. It's perfectly sickening. "Craycroft Regent's Royal Boy." Royal Boy! Wouldn't that make you swallow up! I learned my name in this way. Many automobiles were going by. More than ever before. Some had blue flags and some had orange. I watched them for a while and then took a nap. The noise of an automobile waked me. It was coming up the drive. It had blue flags all over it. It stopped in front of the runway.

Mike came out of the kennel house. A young man in a fur coat tried to get out of the automobile. He fell down. Another young man in the automobile said:

"That stuff all around everywhere is the ground, Freshman."

He began to sing something about an undertaker. The other young men sang with him. It was nice. I joined in. It was almost as good as a barking party!

Mike said, "Whin yer through wid th' concert would ye mind tellin' me why yer ravishin' me ear wid yer byootchus melodies; or, are ye serenadin' th' dogs?"

The young man sitting on the ground stopped singing. He said, "Your words interest me strangely, but I don't know the answer."

Mike said, "Make an iffort. Why did ye wander off th' road into this? Ye had a grand raison now, if ye could only think av it."

The young man said, "It had something to do with my aunt."

Mike said, "'Tis as clear as crystal, but go on."

The young men in the car kept on singing.

The young man on the ground sat looking at Mike. At last he said, "I'll bet you a hundred even Princeton doesn't score."

Mike said. "Wan thing at a time. Let's stick to yer aunt till we git her settled."

The young man said, "She's settled now—terribly. It's sad. I can hardly bear to think of it. Just talking of it in this way to you is hard. You understand?"

Mike said, "'Tis a pitiful thing—I kin see that."

The young man took out a silver bottle. He said, "I think I'll try to cheer up a little."

Mike said, "'Twould take a heart av stone to deny ye what consolation ye kin find."

The young man drank out of the bottle. He held it out to Mike. He said, "Try it! You'd be surprised how refreshing it is."

Mike said, "I'll bet on that; but wid such a load av sorrow, ye'll be naidin' ivery dhrop. Supposin' I giv ye a bit av a lift till yer back among th' other canary birds and on yer way."

Mike helped the young man up. He helped him into the automobile. It turned and drove away. I was sorry. The singing was splendid. I watched the automobile. It passed the sign at the gate. It turned around and came in again. The young man that had sat on the ground got out. He did not fall down—just nearly. He went over to Mike in a zigzag way. He held on to Mike. He said:

"It all came back. Take home a pet! Now you know everything."

Mike said, "Th' wonder av it, and where does yer aunt come in?"

The young man said, "Birthday. 'Fectionate nephew. Sooble gift. Whasort you got?"

Mike said, "Is she a maiden lady, now?"

The young man said, "Very."

He looked at the runways and saw me. I wanted them to sing some more. I barked and wagged my tail. He said, "I'll take that one!"

Mike said, "'Tis not the wan I'd advise fer a maiden lady."

The young man said, "'Splain slowly."

Mike said, "'Tis a five months old bull terrier ye have yer eye on—or do ye see siveral?"

The young man walked over in a zigzag way and took hold of the gate. He looked at me hard through the wire. He said, "One—mostly."

Mike said, "Ye have a great gift av vision. 'Tis wan, an' I'll not deny it. But a maiden lady would think he was a dozen."

The young man said, "Meaning what—'f anything?"

Mike said, "Manin' this: Whin he gits a bit av age on him héll be composed av inja rubber, barbed wire, an' nitroglycerin. He'll fear nayther God, man, nor devil. His middle name will be Throuble."

The young man looked pleased. He said, "What's his name now?"

Mike said, "He's registered as..."

I won't repeat it. Once is enough.

The young man reached under his fur coat. He pulled out a roll of something. He said, "Take him. Stop on m' way back f'r um. How much?"

I could smell the young man through the gate. He smelled like the fat kennel man had when Mike talked about a stew. But his coat was so nice. It would be fun to get hold of it and shake. And then the solitude. Anything was better than that. I stood on my hind legs and pawed at the gate. I whined and barked and wiggled.

Mike said, "Put up yer money. This is only a dog. If ye give th' Princetons a batin' ye may want to buy yer aunt a hippopotamus."

The young men in the automobile began to yell. They called the young man in the fur coat names. They called him a damned freshman. They called him an infant worm. They called him a filthy little wart. One of them said, "Come and get in this car, you drunken Molecule...."

Mike said, "Run along now or yer boy friends'll be lavin' ye."

The young man said, "Have no fear—too subtle. Got starting key in pocket. Sooble present. Stop on way back New York. Head's clear as a bell. How much?"

Mike said, "Listen thin, wid yer fine clear head; this wan has all the makin's av a hellion."

The young man closed one eye at Mike. He said, "Subtle, subtle as hell. How much?"

Mike said, "Subtle is ut? I'm tellin' ye agin—his middle name will be Throuble."

The young man said, "Tha's point. Makes it subtle. Trouble's broadening. How much?"

Mike said, "Wan fifty, an' if ye think it's too subtle whin yer not so refrished I'll change him fer a Pekingese or a Scotty."

When the automobile had gone Mike looked at me. He looked a long time. At last he said, "Yer sold, me son. If he don't change his wonderful moind—God hilp his maiden aunt."

Sold! To a Molecule! I think I like Molecules. They sing. It's splendid.

· III ·

A Coughing Lothario

November 23. I am in New York. It's not like the Craycroft Kennels. Not at all. I do not understand much that happened.

It was beginning to get dark when an automobile drove in and stopped by the runways. I had had my supper. Bread and chopped meat. Not enough of it. There never is! The Molecule was in the car. He blew the horn. Mike came out of the kennel house.

Mike said, "An' did ye bate the Princetons now?"

The Molecule got out of the car. He walked over to Mike. He said, "In answer to your question, listen: A fair meadow lies before us under God's own sky. It is all marked out with nice white lines. Into the meadow come eleven little children. They are not in their prams. They are toddling along, alone. From the opposite direction come eleven bull elephants. They are traveling at a high rate of speed. The herd of elephants passes over the spot where the little children were last seen by the horrified spectators and continues on its way. The band plays 'Boola-boola.' The trembling multitude departs. Where's my dog?"

Mike said, "Do ye happen to remember the wan ye picked out?"

The Molecule said, "I do not, but I know his middle name."

Mike said, "An' what is that?"

The Molecule said, "Trouble.'"

Mike said, "Ye've grasped the main point. A chain goes with him."

The Molecule said, "Produce dog and chain. A pressing matter calls me elsewhere."

He got into the automobile.

Mike opened the gate. He picked me up and carried me to the car. He said, "Good-bye, me son. Kape thinkin' av th' beauties av pacifism." He opened the rear door of the automobile and shut me in. He handed a chain through the front window to a young man sitting beside the Molecule.

He said, "Ye'll understand he's kennel raised and not housebroken."

The Molecule said, "The plot thickens."

He started the car, we went out the drive. We went in a quick way. We turned into the Post Road.

The other young man said, "Step on it."

We went in a much quicker way. It was glorious! We passed many automobiles. I sat on the backseat and watched through the window. A dog came out of a yard and ran after us.

He yelled, "Get off my road, you dirty bum!"

Before I could think of anything to yell back we left bim behind. I was sorry. A man on a motorcycle came along very fast. He wore a uniform. He motioned to the Molecule. The Molecule said—I think I had better not repeat it. He stopped the car.

The man in uniform said, "What's the hurry?"

The Molecule said, "Late for a date."

The man in uniform was looking at me. He had blue eyes like Mike's. I liked him. I gave him some wags and a wiggle. He put his hand in the window. I licked his hand. He took hold of my nose and gave it a pinch. I pretended to bite his hand. He made a grab for my front legs. I bounced back and jumped at him and got his arm in my mouth. I gave it a shake. It was fun. He said, "You let go of that!"

I growled and kept on shaking.

He got his arm loose and rolled me over on the seat. When I got up he had taken his arm out of the car. I scratched at the door and dared him to put it in again. He didn't. He spoke to the Molecule. He said, "If you don't drive slower from now on, you'll keep a date at headquarters."

The Molecule said, "What town is this?"

The man in uniform said, "Pelham. You can do twenty through the parkway, not fifty-five."

The Molecule said, "Mail me ten tickets to the next field day and clambake of the United Pelham Firemen and Police. My name is Feitlebaum. I live in New York. Address the Bronx to be sure."

He handed something to the man in uniform.

The man in uniform grinned.

Then he looked at me again. He said, "He'll make a good one. I had one like him once."

He got on his motorcycle and went away from there. So did we. The Molecule said, "Atta boy, Trub." He seemed to be talking to me. I wondered if Trub was my new name. I hoped so. I liked it. Who wouldn't, after Royal Boy?

We did not go in such a quick way after that. I was sorry.

The young man said, "Have you seen the friend?" The Molecule said, "No, but Gladys says she's the alligator's elbow."

The other young man said, "They always do. I'll look her over. If I can't see her, I'll cough and we'll toddle along."

The Molecule said, "Check, Old Companion! And listen, I've mingled with the haughty Gladys twice. Both times she's done the eat and run. If she happens to mention another date, ere we foregather at the groaning board, we exit smiling. Gimme a cigarette."

My neck is still stiff. It is from turning my head so much. Driving down a road called Broadway did it. It was night when we got to this road. Then it was daytime again. If I looked out one window, something happened at the other. It was like that every second. We drove to a place called the Biltmore. It was a nice place. It was full of girls and young men. The girls all smelled delicious! We went over to two girls sitting on a couch. One was a dark-haired girl. One was a light-haired girl. The dark-haired girl had on pink stockings. She was frowning. She looked at the clock. She said, "We've been parked here twenty minutes. Who do you think you are? Valentino?"

The Molecule said, "Snap out of it, Glad, and meet my boyhood friend, Count Cuspidor."

The other young man shook hands with the girl in the pink stockings. She said, "This is Edith, and we're both starving."

The other young man looked at the blonde girl. He said, "Hello, Mary, does Doug know you're here?" Then he coughed.

The blonde girl said, "Help, I'm up against a kidder and I like his eyes."

She gave the other young man a look. It was a kind look.

The Molecule said, "The count's epiglottis won't click, or something. He's got to see a throat specialist, or he'll cough his head off. You wild women reel over to your apartment and we'll give you a jingle in half an hour."

The dark-haired girl said, "I wouldn't wait a half hour for Flo Ziegfeld. I've got a rehearsal at nine."

The other young man had sat down on the couch. He was holding the blonde girl by the hand. He said, "Forget it, Fishface—my cough's a lot better."

The Molecule said, "It seems to come and go."

The other young man said, "I'll tell the cockeyed world!" He gave the blonde girl a look. It was a kind look.

The Molecule said, "Listen carefully to what follows. You are going with me and say 'Ah' for the nice doctor." He gave the other young man a look. It was not a kind look.

The other young man got up from the couch. He said, "Sure thing, if you say so, old egg."

The lights had begun to hurt my eyes. I crawled under the couch and lay down. It was nice and dark like a cave. I began to play a new game: Wolf-in-His-Lair. When people walked past I could see their feet. I pretended the feet were going to attack the cave. I growled at them. It was splendid!

I could hear the Molecule and the black-haired girl talking. They were having an argument. She said, "Don't tell me he can't eat something before he sees the doctor."

The Molecule said, "I wish he could—I'm hungry myself, but he might have a paroxysm and they're awful."

No more feet were going by. I was sorry. It spoiled the new game. I saw a slipper and a nice shiny pink leg just outside the cave. The slipper began to tap on the floor. I growled at it and crouched for a spring.

The dark-haired girl said, "I'll tell you what to do; let Mr. Whatever-his-name-is go see the doctor alone and come back. We'll order dinner. I want guinea hen en casserole and mushrooms under glass."

The slipper stopped tapping. I attacked. It was fun. I missed the slipper, but I got the leg. I pretended to bite it. I heard a scream. The leg was snatched away. I still have some of my puppy teeth—quite sharp. One of them caught in the pink stocking. There was a ripping sound. The Molecule pulled me from under the couch.

The dark-haired girl's stocking was torn down to her slipper. I can't remember all she said—she talked too fast. She was calling the Molecule names. She called me names too. She called me a sneaky kioodle and a snapping little cur.

The Molecule said, "Here's the price of a new pair, and now go to hell."

We went away from there.

When we were outside the Molecule stood on the sidewalk and looked at me.

The other young man said, "There was something about the blonde I liked."

The Molecule said, "Guinea hen and mushrooms under glass—and then he bit her."

He began to laugh. The other young man began to laugh. They leaned against a building and laughed. They hung on to each other and did it.

I wonder why. I do not understand New York.

· IV ·

Toodles

November 24. Still in New York. I met a Pekingese today. I met him quite unexpectedly. It was in an elevator. I do not like elevators. Something happens to my stomach when they stop.

The elevator was in a high building. The Molecule and I went up in it to see a man. The man was in a big room. He was sitting at a big desk. He had gray hair. He did not smile with his mouth. He did it by crinkling the corner of his eyes. The Molecule said, "Greetings, guardian!"

The gray-haired man did not answer. He opened a drawer in his desk. He took out some sheets of paper fastened together.

The Molecule gave a horrible groan. He fell into a chair. I was worried. I licked his hand. He said, "Stick with me, Trub, he's going to read it! "

I chewed one of the legs of the chair. Too hard. I chewed a corner of the rug. Too fuzzy. I found a basket under the desk. It was full of paper. I chewed the basket until the side came out. Then I chewed the papers.

The gray-haired man began to talk. He spoke from one of the sheets of paper. He said:

"And further I direct under this bequest that my son, Robert Holmes Trescott, shall receive no sum in excess of the above-mentioned $10,000 per annum until he arrives at such discretion and judgment as may be his at the beginning of his twenty-fifth year."

The gray-haired man put down the sheet of paper. He said, "Is it perfectly clear or shall I read it again?"

The Molecule got up from his chair. He said, "Well, I'll be getting along to the East River."

The gray-haired man got up from the desk. He said, "So this is the end!"

The Molecule said, "What else is left?"

The gray-haired man said, "Perhaps you're right. Any last request?"

The Molecule said, "Yes, one. Read it aloud at the funeral."

The gray-haired man crinkled his eyes. He said, "I'll attend to it. Where did you get the bull pup?"

The Molecule said, "Bought him while in liquor. His name is Trouble. He has a mission. Ere we leave this tomb of my hopes allow me to nominate you for Perpetual President and Grand Master of the Sacred Order of Human Fish."

The gray-haired man bowed. He said "You overwhelm me!"

The Molecule said, "If you wish to decline the nomination, do it in writing."

The gray-haired man did more than crinkle his eyes. He chuckled out loud. He sat down at the desk. He scratched with a pen in a narrow black book. He started to hand it to the Molecule. He said, "Wait a minute. Why aren't you in New Haven?"

The Molecule said, "The authorities at Yale University have expressed a wish that I do not mingle with my happy, carefree schoolmates until after Christmas."

The gray-haired man said, "Suspended, eh? What will Aunt Caroline say to that?"

The Molecule said, "Nothing, I hope. Why bring the matter to her attention? Why burden a worthy woman with the tiresome details of my scholastic career? Why not remain here in New York in quiet retirement?"

The gray-haired man said, "Go out to Gray Gables and tell Aunt Caroline and you can have this. Otherwise not."

The Molecule said, "I spurn your gold, Jack Dalton. How much is it?"

The gray-haired man said, "A thousand."

The Molecule said "Who can resist you? I'll go out Monday."

The gray-haired man said, "All right, Monday." He handed the Molecule the slip of paper.

The Molecule put it in his pocket. He said, "By thus saving his boy friend he won the Carnegie Medal."

The gray-haired man said, "Look what that damn pup's done!"

We went away from there.

I saw nice marble stairs. I tried to go down them. The Molecule wouldn't let me. He pulled me to the elevator. When the door opened I was surprised. There was a Pekingese in the elevator. He was with a girl. She was a nice looking girl. She was holding the Peke on a little chain. I was glad to see him. Very! I tried to smell noses with him. He backed away. He said, "You leave me alone!"

I tried to give him a paw-poke. He ran around the girl. I ran after him. When we got to the end of our chains, they were all around the girl. Nobody could move. It was funny.

The Molecule said, "I never saw anyone so wrapped up in dogs."

The girl laughed. She said, "You had better unleash Toodles and give him to me."

The Molecule unchained the Peke. He gave him to the girl.

The Peke said, "Disgusting young ruffian."

I said, "Who, me?"

The Peke didn't answer. He just sniffed.

The Molecule said, "If you'll turn around slowly, now, he'll come unwound."

My stomach gave an awful flop. It was the elevator stopping. We all got out. The girl put the Peke down and snapped the chain on him. I gave him some wags. I said, "I'm sorry about your name."

The Peke sniffed again.

I said, "I had an awful name, too, but it's changed. My new name is Trouble. Trub for short. How does it strike you?"

The Peke said, "Insufferable!" He went to the other side of the girl.

I tried to go with him. The Molecule held me back. He was talking to the girl. He said, "Toodles seems upstage to me."

The girl didn't say anything.

The Molecule said, "I'll tell you the only fair thing to do—ride uptown in the same taxi and give them a chance to get acquainted."

The girl looked at the Molecule. She said, "Toodles never did such a thing in his life."

The Molecule said, "Of course not, but there comes a time when it's the only thing to do."

The girl said, "Perhaps, but this isn't the time."

The Molecule said, "How do you know?"

The girl said, "It just isn't."

The Molecule said, "It might be. How can you tell?"

The girl said, "You're perfectly crazy."

The Molecule gave the girl a look. It was a kind look. He said, "Of course—who wouldn't be?"

The girl said, "This is absurd, I'm going now."

The Molecule said, "Go ahead; Trub and I will sort of bring up the rear."

The girl said, "You'll do nothing of the kind."

The Molecule said, "I'll make you a little bet on it."

The girl said, "What earthly good will that do you?"

The Molecule said, "I'll find out where you live. Then I'll find out who you are. Then I'll find somebody who knows you."

The girl began to laugh. She stooped down. She said, "Good-bye, puppy. If you aren't busy tomorrow at one, and still want to get acquainted with Toodles, telephone Plaza 8744 and ask for Dacia Kendle."

The Molecule said, "Something tells me he won't be busy."

The girl didn't say anything. She stood up and nodded to the Molecule. She went down the street with the Peke.

The Molecule stood where he was. He had his hat off. He was looking in the direction the girl had gone. He stood and looked a long time. He still kept his hat off. Many people were passing. They looked at the Molecule.

I gave him a paw-poke. He put on his hat. He took out his watch.

He said, "All right, Trub. But what'll we do for the next 26 hours, 43 minutes, and 15 seconds?"

· V ·

Snow, Snow, Beautiful Snow

November 28. More solitude. The Molecule is not pleased with me. I think the new game had something to do with it.

Toodles and I played the game together. We played it in Toodles' home. It was a nice home. It is full of interesting things. It is called an apartment. The girl we met in the elevator lives there. Toodles lives with her. He calls her Muvver. The Molecule called her Miss Kendle at first. Now he calls her Old Party and Mrs. Mulligan.

Before we played the game something else happened. It was in a place that Miss Kendle goes to. She goes to this place to get bread and butter. I heard her tell the Molecule. I was glad when the Molecule took me into the place. I didn't see any bread and butter. Only a hall with a fat man standing in front of the door. It was an iron door. The Molecule wanted to go through the door.

The fat man said, "No chance, Bud, they're shooting right now."

The Molecule said, "Look this over, Old Timer."

He handed a piece of paper to the fat man. The fat man looked at the paper. He said, "That lets you in; but the dog is out."

I was worried. I gave the fat man some wags. He didn't notice them. The Molecule said, "Here's his pass." He gave something to the fat man.

The fat man said, "He can go anywhere in New York on that stuff, but don't say I let him in."

We went through the iron door. It was a big place inside. There was no bread and butter. Just people. Miss Kendle was there. The place was all dark except where she was standing.

A man was walking up and down. His coat was off. His collar was undone. His hair was sticking up on end. He was holding his head with both hands. He was making a groaning sound. He said:

"I could shoot 'The Covered Wagon' on the footage we've wasted on one lousy scene."

Two men were standing in the light with Miss Kendle. One had black hair and a black mustache. He was not a kind looking man. The other was a tall young man. He had on a white sweater with a big red "H" on the front of it. His hair was very slick and shiny. He said, "Why not have luncheon before the retake, old man? I'm absolutely faint!"

I liked what the young man said. I wondered where they kept the bread and butter.

The man with his hair sticking up spoiled everything. He said, "We'll put this scene across if it takes till midnight. If you want to eat—gimme something! Let's go, everybody! Remember, girl, you're fighting for what is dearer to you than life. And, remember, Joe, go after her! She won't break. Winston, don't forget you're captain of the Harvards. You've just run through them all for a goal. You've heard her scream. You run to the dressing room. The door is locked. You buck the door. It flies from its hinges. You come diving into the scene. This brute has your feeawnsay in his power. Crouch where you land, and then make the tackle like the football guy showed you.

Now, remember, every bit of this is big, people, BIG! All right. Abe, music! Ready, everybody! Lights! Action! Pick it up where you sneer and lock the door, Joe! That's good! CAMERA!"

I was surprised at what happened. The black-haired man started it. He grabbed Miss Kendle by the neck. Her tongue stuck out. It was awful! I barked in horror.

The man with his hair sticking up was yelling. He yelled, "Who the hell let that dog in? Atta boy, Joe! Bend her down over the sofa!"

The young man in the sweater came in where it was light. He came in on his head. He sat up and blinked.

The man with his hair sticking up yelled, "What are you sitting there for, you big stiff ?"

The young man in the sweater said, "I think my skull is fractured."

The man with his hair sticking up yelled, "No chance! It's solid ivory. Get up and nail him!"

The young man in the sweater got to his feet. He flew through the air. He knocked down the black-haired man and Miss Kendle and a table. It was terrible!

I pulled the chain from the Molecule's hand. I rushed into the light place, barking. The black-haired man and the young man in the sweater were rolling over and over.

I bit the one that came on top when I got there. It was the young man in the sweater. I bit him in the back of the trousers. It was not a fun bite. He yelled.

The Molecule pulled me away from the young man in the sweater. The man with his hair sticking up was saying many things. Not a single word he said can be repeated. I held a barking party. I don't know why.

The Molecule took me out through the iron door. He put me in a taxi. He said, "I don't blame you, Trub—after that tackle." He began to laugh. He lay down on the seat and did it.

Miss Kendle came out and got in the taxi. She gave me a hug. She said, "Bless his heart, he tried to rescue Muvver! We'll leave him at the apartment, Bobbie. I want to look at a wristwatch I'm crazy about before luncheon."

We drove to Toodles' home. Toodles was there. He was lying on a cushion on a couch. The Molecule and Miss Kendle went away and left us together. I said, "Well, what's the good word?"

Toodles didn't say anything. He just sniffed. Pekes are like that—poor mixers!

A flea disturbed me. I gave it some attention.

Toodles said, "Faugh! Infested with vermin."

I said, "How do you get that way?"

Toodles sniffed.

I found a pink box in a chair. The box was full of brown stones. They had a nice smell. I bit one. It was soft. I chewed it. Delicious!

Toodles said, "You let those chocolates alone!"

I said, "Go chase your tail."

I ate all the soft stones that were in the box. I began to have an oppressive feeling in the abdomen. I thought it would be best to swallow up. I did.

Toodles said, "Oh, my God!"

I felt better. I began to look around. I went into a closet. There was a big round pasteboard box in the closet. I chewed the box. The cover came off. There was something inside the box made of wire and mosquito netting and what-not. I chewed off all the what-not. Then I chewed the mosquito netting.

Toodles was watching me. His eyes were sticking out. He said, "That's Muvver's best hat!"

I said, "This is the life, Kid."

There was a row of slippers in the closet. I took a white one with a shiny buckle. I chewed off the buckle. Then I chewed the slipper.

Toodles said, "How does it taste?"

I said, "Delicious! Have one!"

Toodles got down off the couch. He came over to the closet. He said, "I've been repressed for years. I've just realized it. I think I'll try a black one."

We chewed all the slippers.

A yellow cushion had fallen off the couch. I chewed it. So did Toodles. White feathers came out. They flew about the room. We chewed more sofa cushions. They all had feathers in them.

I made up the new game, then. It was called, Snow, Snow, Beautiful Snow! It was a splendid game. We rolled in the feathers. We dug in them. We chased them. They stuck to everything. Especially Toodles.

He looked so funny. I thought Miss Kendle and the Molecule would laugh when they came back. They didn't laugh. Miss Kendle sat down and began to cry. She cried terribly. The Molecule was patting her and asking her to stop.

He said, "Listen, Old Party; I'm going out right now and get you that watch."

Miss Kendle kept on crying. The Molecule went away from there. When he was gone, Miss Kendle went to the dresser and looked in the glass. She put white stuff on her nose. She went back to the chair. When the Molecule came in she began to cry again.

The Molecule said, "Here it is, Old Party. Now cheer up!" He took a sparkle thing out of a box. He put it in her lap.

Miss Kendle stopped crying. She put the sparkle thing around her wrist. She said, "You're a darling." She got up from the chair. She gave the Molecule a hug. They put their faces together.

The Molecule and I went away from there. We went to a place called the Yale Club. The Molecule handed my chain to a man.

The Molecule said, "Put him down in the basement. He's just cost me eight hundred smackers!"

· VI ·

The Movie Queen's Move

November 29. I am in a place called Gray Gables. It is a nice place. It is in the country. The Molecule and I came here in an automobile.

Before we left New York we went for a ride with Toodles and Miss Kendle. Toodles and I sat on the back seat. I had not seen him since we chewed pillows together. He seemed low about something. I tried to cheer him up.

I said, "Not a bad game, that Snow, Snow, Beautiful Snow."

Toodles said, "Don't speak of it, I beg of you." He looked at Miss Kendle's back. Then he looked out of the window.

I said, "What's biting you, anyway?"

Toodles said, "I don't know what possessed me — I've thought and thought. I've always been self-repressed. It's the result of a shut-in life. Suddenly I felt that I must burst the bonds — if you know what I mean."

I said, "Sure — I've had that bursting feeling often. I had it when I ate the pan of cornmeal mush. I had it when I ate the soft stones. I always swallow up."

Toodles shuddered. He said, "Suppose we change the subject."

I said, "But wait a minute. You don't know how relieving it is. Just try it. Try it now."

Toodles gave a large shudder — very. I thought he was going to. He didn't. He said, "In an ill considered moment I joined you in a wanton and degrading exhibition, but we have nothing in common, nothing." He moved to his end of the seat. He looked out of the window.

I said, "Oh, very well." I moved to my end of the seat. I looked out the window.

We were going through a park. It was full of children and ponds and nurses and policemen. We passed several dogs. I barked at one or two of them. The only one that answered was a Scottie. He yelled, "Dinna blather at me, ye yelpin' tike."

The Molecule stopped the car. It was in a woods by a pond. Miss Kendle said, "Give me a light, Bobbie-Wobbie." She put a cigarette against the Molecule's cigarette. She made smoke come out of her mouth. She said:

"And you don't get anything until you're twenty-five?"

The Molecule said, "Nothing except ten thousand fish per fiscal year." He put his arm around Miss Kendle.

Miss Kendle said, "Wait, I want to talk."

The Molecule said, "Prattle on, Old Party."

Miss Kendle said, "Don't think I'm curious. It's just that, well — you've swept me off my feet. You know that."

The Molecule said, "With his slick city ways and his oily tongue."

Miss Kendle said, "Of course, I've had men friends before."

Toodles stopped looking out the window. He looked at me. He said, "How true!" He winked.

I wondered why he winked. I wanted to ask him, but he looked out the window again.

Miss Kendle said, "This is different, somehow. I knew it from the first. I actually felt it in the elevator. Something about you. I was—oh, you know—I don't have to tell you. And naturally I'm interested—just because it's you." She gave the Molecule a look. It was a kind look.

The Molecule put his arm around her again.

Miss Kendle said, "Not yet. Listen. How much was your father worth?"

The Molecule said, "You can search me. I went to sleep after the clause about me, naturally."

Miss Kendle said, "But you have an idea, haven't you?"

The Molecule said, "The matter is not of moment. It belongs in the far distant future. It comes to me vaguely that should I still be doddering about at the age of twenty-five, this shell of what was once a man will receive four quarterly payments per annum of twenty-five thousand each."

Miss Kendle said, "That's a hundred thousand a year!"

The Molecule said, "I cannot controvert your bold and startling deduction."

Miss Kendle said, "Income, not principal!"

The Molecule said, "Again you score heavily. Flips gets the same. We receive the principal when Aunt Caroline passes to her just reward. I shall now quote from the poets as follows, to wit: 'A little necking now and then is relished by the best of men!'" He put his arm around Miss Kendle.

Miss Kendle closed her eyes. She said, "Oh, Bobbie-Wobbie—what do you do to me?" They kissed.

Toodles said, "What a life!" He yawned. He lay down and went to sleep.

I lay down and went to sleep.

I woke up when the car started. We took Toodles and Miss Kendle to their home. Then we drove out of New York. We drove a long time. At last we came to some gates. We turned in through the gates. We went along a drive. We came to a house. It was a big house. It was made of stone. We went in the house. There was a man at the door. He was a little man. He had black hair. He had funny eyes. He grinned at the Molecule and bobbed his head. He said, "How-do you? Well? Yes? Mas' Rob?"

The Molecule said, "Hello, Saki! How's your codliverous spiloochum these days?"

The little man said, "No? Yes? Verree nice. Oh, my!"

The Molecule said, "Where's the well-known aunt, Saki?"

The little man said, "She read papeer, sun room, yes."

We went through the house. We came to a room made of glass. There were flowers in the room. There was a lady. She was an oldish lady.

The Molecule began to sing. He sang, "O Caroline, wilt thou be mine?"

It was a nice song. I liked it. I joined in.

The oldish lady stopped us. She looked at me. She said, "What have you got there, may I ask?"

The Molecule said, "You may, indeed—but you'll hardly believe me. I have here a dog."

The oldish lady said, "Whose dog is it?"

The Molecule said, "Your dog. I bought him for your birthday, as I remember. His name is Trouble. A chain goes with him—also love and kisses."

The oldish lady said, "My birthday is in August and I don't want a dog."

A girl came running into the glass room. She was a young, thin girl. She had cut off hair. It flopped when she moved her head. It flopped all over her face. She hugged the Molecule. She said, "Oh, the darling pupsums." She hugged me. I gave her some wags and a chin-lick. She said, "What are you doing home, Bobby?"

The Molecule said, "I've left Yale. I'll be here now until I'm married."

The young thin girl said, "Married, oh, gosh!"

The oldish lady got up from her chair. She said, "You're not by any chance serious?"

The Molecule took out a cigarette case. He said, "Want one, Flips?" The young thin girl took a cigarette from the case. She lighted it. The Molecule lighted one. He said, "Serious—I'll tell the cockeyed world!"

The oldish lady turned quite pale. She sat down in the chair again.

The Molecule said, "I've been knocked for the well-known platinum circle. Met her in New York. She's in pictures. You'll love her, Flips!"

The young thin girl said, "Pictures! Oh, gosh!"

The oldish lady sat very still. Tears began to come out of her eyes. They ran down her face. I was worried. I went over to her. I licked her hands.

The Molecule said, "Now listen, Aunt Caroline...."

The oldish lady said, "Not now—please go away."

The Molecule and the young thin girl went out of the glass place. I stayed with the oldish lady, I don't know why. I whined and gave her a paw-poke. She put her arms around my neck. She bowed her head. She said, "They're too much for me, little doggie. Too much!"

I wondered what she meant. I did not understand. I gave her a chin-lick.

· VII ·

Exit Ladies

December 1. I'm just learning about rules. It's terrible. There's a rule about everything. You think of a nice way to pass the time, and there's a rule in the way. Flips keeps saying, "Be yourself." She says it to everybody. A fine chance I've got to be myself. I'd break a million rules a minute.

I broke a rule today. It was on account of some cakes. It happened like this:

A lot of ladies came to see Aunt Caroline—fat ladies, and thin ladies, and middle-sized ladies. They all talked at the same time—very fast. It was nice. I liked it. I ran around barking.

Aunt Caroline called Saki. He came in. He took a cake from a dish on the table. He held it out to me. When I tried to take it he grabbed me by the collar. He dragged me to the front door. He put me outside. Stung!

I sniffed some trees. Then I played Dig-the-Hole-Deep on the front lawn. The gardener came around the house. He called me names. He tried to hit me with a rake. I suppose there's a rule about just digging. I went away from there. I went a far ways. I hoped I would find something interesting. At last I did. I found some bones and pieces of wool and things in a field. It had been an animal once. Now it was dead. Very.

A dog came across the field. He was sniffing the air. He was a slinky dog with yellow eyes. When he saw me he started to run.

I ran after the slinky dog. He ran faster. I stopped running. He stopped running. I said, "Hello!"

The slinky dog didn't say anything. He kept looking at me with his yellow eyes. I started toward him. He started to run. I stopped. He stopped.

I said, "Is it a game?"

The stinky dog said, "I haven't done nothin' to you."

I said, "Let's touch noses and then play."

The slinky dog said, "You let me alone." I ran at the slinky dog. He tried to run again. I caught him. He lay down on his back, with his feet in the air. He said, "Oh, please, Mister, please!"

I said, "Please what?"

The slinky dog said, "Please, don't bite me, Mister."

I said, "Why should I bite you? Let's play some games."

The slinky dog said, "On the level, you won't bite me?"

I said, "Only fun bites, maybe."

The slinky dog got on his feet. He said, "It's a bet. Let's do our rolling first."

I said, "What rolling?"

The slinky dog said, "You know. Over there."

I said, "Over where?",

The slinky dog said, "Your beezer needs fixing. I made it clear from the road." He went over to the wool and bones. He took a big sniff. He said, "Gosh, ain't it rich? Well, here goes!" He rolled around in the wool and bones. He got up. He said, "I'll tell the cockeyed world it's rich. Take a roll, Mister."

I said, "What for?"

The slinky dog said, "Say, you don't know nothin', do you? Take a sniff at me."

I did. It was wonderful!

The slinky dog said, "Got the idea? It'll stay with you for days."

I rolled in the wool and bones. Then I played with the slinky dog. We played Wrestle, Wrestle and Fun-Bite-the-Throat.

The slinky dog began to pant. He said, "I'm all in. Let's freshen up before we beat it."

He rolled in the wool and bones. I rolled in the wool and bones. The slinky dog went away from there.

I wondered what to do next. I began to feel hungry. I thought of the cakes on the table where all the ladies were. I started for home.

I thought of the cakes all the way. They were yellow cakes with white tops. The more I thought, the hungrier I got. I wondered if there was any rule about the cakes. I thought it over. There was. Never take anything from a plate until they put it on the floor. Can you beat that one?

When I got home I barked at the front door. I don't scratch at the door any more—there's a rule about that. Saki opened the door. I went in a quick way. I went to the drawing-room, where the ladies were.

The ladies weren't talking so much as before. They were sitting at a lot of tables. They were picking up papers and laying them down again. The cakes were on a bigger table in the center of the room.

I stood at the door and looked at the cakes. They were in a big silver dish. Nothing could be done about them, on account of the rule. It was sickening.

An idea came to me. I thought, "There must be a kind lady among so many. I'll go in and look for a kind lady." I did.

There was a lady at a table not far from the cakes. She was a fat lady. I thought, "I try that one."

The ladies at the table where the fat lady was stopped putting down papers. A thin lady gave the fat lady a look. It was not a kind look. She said, "I discarded the nine of spades, partner; you must have known I was out."

I went over to the fat lady. I put my head in her lap. I rolled up my eyes at her.

The fat lady said, "Oh, look at this precious lamb put his head in my ..."

I was surprised at what happened then. The fat lady stopped talking. She turned white. She put her handkerchief to her face. She got up from the table. She went away from there.

The thin lady said, "Well, what do you think of that? She lost a dozen tricks for us in one rubber, and when I just mentioned...." The thin lady stopped talking. She did just what the fat lady had done. So did the other ladies at the table. So did ladies at other tables. It was strange.

I went to the table where Aunt Caroline was sitting. All the ladies left the table in a quick way. Aunt Caroline said, "Merciful heavens!" She left the table in a quick way. She went out in the hall with the other ladies. Many of the ladies were coughing. I heard Aunt Caroline calling Saki between coughs.

I looked around the room for another kind lady. There were no ladies left in the room. I was afraid they'd taken the cakes with them. I looked. They hadn't.

I went over to the table where the cakes were. I stood on my hind legs and looked in the dish. I thought, "A kind lady might put it on the floor." But there were no kind ladies left—just chairs and tables and cakes and me. There were nine cakes in the dish. I broke the rule. I broke it nine times in a quick way.

Saki came in. He dragged me out of the room. He dragged me out to the garage. The shofer was there.

Saki said, "I request much water from hose quickly—soap also."

The shofer said, "Listen, fella, you can't pull that stuff in here. You'll spatter every car in the—" The shofer stopped talking. He made coughing noises. He said, "Great jumping polecats!" He went away from there. Saki made the water come out of the hose. He held me under it. He rubbed me with soap. He held me under the hose. He rubbed me with more soap. He kept on doing it for hours and hours. He got soap in my mouth. He got soap in my eyes. I don't know anything so disgusting as soap.

I am shut up in the storeroom now. It's for breaking a rule, I suppose. It's too much, I claim. The soap was enough. If the ladies had wanted the cakes, why didn't they stay and eat them?

The Molecule has given me another name. It's a long name. He calls me "Just a Sweet-Scented Nosegay from an Old-Fashioned Garden."

· VIII ·

Heroism Pure and Simple

December 2. I have a new name. It is a long name. The Molecule gave it to me. The name is Trub Trescott the Hero! I got the first part by coming to Gray Gables. As soon as you come here your name is Trescott. Like this: Aunt Caroline Trescott; Robert Trescott—that's the Molecule; Florence Trescott—that's his sister—Flips; Trub Trescott. Trub Trescott! Not bad, I claim.

I got the last part of the new name in a funny way. It was at night. I was all alone. I was in the storeroom. I must stay in the storeroom at night until I'm housebroken. I wonder what housebroken means!

The way they go on about unimportant things is ridiculous. Saki is the worst. The upstairs girl is nearly as bad. Aunt Caroline is perfectly silly, too.

It began the first day I was here. I was playing a new game. The game is called Sliding Rugs. You start down the front hall. You go fast. Sometimes you fall down, it's so slippery. When you are going as fast as you can you come to a rug. You jump on the rug. The rug goes with you. You come to another rug. It goes, too. You and the rugs end up at the front door. You wait until Saki puts the rugs back. You do it over again. That's all there is to it.

It is a good game, but warm. I got thirsty. I looked for some water. I found some in the library. It was in a glass bowl on a stand. Pink fish were sleeping in the bowl. I got up on a chair and drank a lot of water. I watched the fish. They were interesting. I wondered if I could get them out of the bowl. I paw-poked the bowl. The fish woke up. They went round and round, in a quick way. I barked at them to make them go in a quicker way.

Saki came in. He got excited, as usual. He pulled me down from the chair.

He said, "Bad dog, veree, Oh, my!"

I went back into the hall. I began to play Sliding Rugs again. I had to stop for a minute.

It was on account of drinking so much water I stopped in the hall by the front door. You'd be surprised the way Saki acted. He called Aunt Caroline. You'd be surprised the way she acted.

They put me outdoors. It was cold. I whined and scratched on the door. I made long scratches. Saki opened the door. He looked at the scratches. He got excited again. He let me in. I sat down and thought it over. I didn't like to be put outdoors. I came to a decision.

I said, "They can keep their old front hall."

You'd think that would settle it, wouldn't you? It didn't. I tried the living room. Saki put me outdoors. I tried under the dining-room table. Saki put me outdoors. I went up and tried Aunt Caroline's room. That's where the upstairs girl came in. She actually screamed. Well, I've done my best! I'm almost glad when night comes and they put me in the storeroom.

It's dark in the storeroom. Sometimes I feel the solitude. I felt it last night. I wished someone would come—even Saki. Some one did.

The storeroom window began to open. I was surprised. I watched it. It was a man opening the window. I was glad to see him. I gave him some wags.

The man made a light. It was a round light, very bright. It made me blink. I hoped he would come into the storeroom. He did. He came in through the window. He had left his shoes at home. He gave me some pats.

He said, "Nicea puppa. Gooda leetle dog!"

The quiet man opened the storeroom door. I was glad. I gave him some more wags. He started to close the door right in my face. I squeezed through before he could do it. He stood at the door and pretended he wanted to give me some pats. Old stuff!

I went away from there.

I went down the hall into the butler's pantry. The quiet man came after me. I went into the dining room. The quiet man came after me. He kept on pretending he wanted to give me pats. I wonder what kind of a boob he thought I was.

The quiet man went out into the front hall. He went to the front. door. He unlocked the door. He opened it. He left it open and went back into the dining room.

The quiet man did not bother me any more. I had the whole house to myself. It was glorious! I hardly knew what to do first. I started for the kitchen to take a good smell—for once. Guess what I found. I found a pair of rubbers by the hatrack! I could hardly believe it. When it comes to chewing, a rubber is in a class by itself. Absolutely!

I started for the kitchen again. I thought of something. I thought it would be a good time to play with the pink fish. I did.

I got up on the chair and paw-poked the bowl. The pink fish went round and round. I put my paw in the bowl. They went even faster. I put my head in the bowl to see better. It was a mistake. I saw that as soon as I tried to get it out again. It wouldn't come out. I tried to get off the stand. No use. Everything went, stand and bowl, and water and pink fish, and me. It was funny! And scaring, too, in a way.

Everything had been quiet and peaceful until then. Now it was all changed. Even the quiet man was changed. He came running down the hall very fast. I saw he was going to play Sliding Rugs. I ran barking to play it with him. We played it splendidly until we came to the second rug. Then the quiet man stumbled over me. He slipped and fell. I slipped and fell. We slid right through the front door into the vestibule together. So did the rugs.

The lights lighted in the hall. Saki came down the stairs. I was glad. I wanted him to put the rugs back, so the quiet man and I could play again.

The quiet man didn't wait to play. He got up and went down the front steps. He went in a quick way. He didn't come back. I guess he thought Saki would get excited about the rugs.

The Molecule came downstairs. So did Aunt Caroline. So did the cook. So did the upstairs girl. Everybody got excited.

Flips came and stood on the stairs.

She said, "Can't you let a person get her sleep? Have you all gone crazy?"

Aunt Caroline said, "Burglars! Inside the house! There must have been a dozen!"

Flips said, "Burglers! Oh, gosh!"

Aunt Caroline said, "Florence, dear, listen. This blessed puppy attacked them and drove them off!"

The Molecule looked at me. He began to laugh.

He said, "Trub Trescott, the Hero!"

He's called me that ever since. He always laughs. I wonder why.

· IX ·

To Become Unslippery

December 4. Saki is making my life a hell! It's his tagging around after me. And closing all the closet doors. The upstairs girl does it, too. Just the minute I come into a room she rushes to the closet and shuts the door.

She's done it since I found the bedroom slippers. I found them in Flip's room. They were in the closet. They were made of pink satin. Inside was fur. It was hard to get the pink satin off—but worth it.

I took the fur lining downstairs. I made up a new game. It was called Helpless Prey. To play it you simply growl and shake.

Saki saw me playing the new game. He got excited. You'd know he would. I took the fur lining and ran. Siki ran after me. I ran faster. Saki ran faster. We ran down the hall. We ran into the dining room. We ran around the dining-room table. It was fun!

We went out into the glass room. We went fast. Aunt Caroline and Flips and the Molecule were in the glass room. They were eating breakfast. I ran under the breakfast table.

The Molecule said, "If it's a race you lose, Saki."

Saki said, "Troobal have brought in outside animal of sorts."

I began to play the new game under the table. I changed the name. I called it The Battle-in-the-Den! To play it with that name you simply shake harder and growl louder.

Aunt Caroline looked under the table. The Molecule looked under the table. Flips looked under the table.

Flips said, "Oh, gosh!"

Aunt Caroline said, "Good heavens! What is it?"

The Molecule said, "It's all right. He's just brought in a little pole-cat friend for breakfast."

Flips screamed and got up on her chair. Aunt Caroline screamed and got up on her chair. The dining-room girl screamed and went away from there. Before she went she dropped a plate of scrambled eggs on the floor. Delicious!

I went back under the table when the eggs were gone. Saki had taken away the fur lining. I felt like being quiet for a while. I was.

Flips said, "When love comes to me I shan't require advice from anyone. Pass the toast, Bobby!"

Aunt Caroline said, "Will you be quiet, Florence!"

Flips said, "I will not be quiet. Just because Dacia is in pictures you go on this way."

Aunt Caroline said, "Dacia?"

Flips said, "Why not? She's going to be my sister-in-law, isn't she?"

Aunt Caroline said, "Suppose you wait until you meet this young woman before you begin calling her by her first name."

Flips said, "Well, suppose you let me meet her?"

The Molecule said, "She has you there, Aunt Caroline. Another cup of coffee from your fair and gracious hands."

Aunt Caroline said, "Florence, I've asked you to be quiet. Do you intend to obey me?"

Flips said, "Not when my own brother's happiness is..."

Aunt Caroline said, "Florence, leave the room!"

Flips said, "I shan't leave the room. Not if you cut me in pieces. My own brother's happiness is...."

Aunt Caroline said, "If you don't leave the room this instant I'll stop your allowance for three months."

Flips got up from her chair. She said, "I call that a dirty trick, when my own brother's happiness is...."

Aunt Caroline said, "Florence!"

Flips went away from there. I went with her. She put on a coat and hat. She said, "The old dud! Come on, Pupsums!"

We went outside. We went into the garage. The shofer was there. Aunt Caroline calls him William. He has light hair and a pink face and blue eyes. He was holding a big red hose without any ends in a pail of water.

Flips said, "H'lo, Bill!"

The shofer didn't say anything.

Flips said, "What are you doing?"

The shofer said, "Testing this tube."

Flips said, "How?"

The shofer said, "Watch the bubbles."

Flips said, "I don't see any bubbles."

The shofer said, "I'll say you don't. When I fix 'em they stay fixed."

He stood the red hose thing against the wall. He got a big tin pan. He put it under an automobile. He slid under the automobile on his back.

Flips said, "What are you going to do now?"

The shofer said, "Drain the crank case on this wagon."

Flips said, "What for?"

The shofer said, "Listen! Drop into high and give yourself the air."

Flips said, "Why are you so hateful to me, Billy?" Tears began to come out of her eyes. Black stuff began to come out of the automobile into the tin pan. The shofer came out from under the automobile. I went under the automobile. I smelled the black stuff in the pan. I tasted it. Terrible! I went over to the red hose thing standing against the wall. I began to chew the red hose thing. It chewed splendidly.

Flips and the shofer were talking. The shofer said, "Turn off the water. It don't get you a thing."

Flips said, "You'd better look out. You know what Shakespeare said—all about a woman scorned."

The shofer said, "Where do you get that woman stuff?"

Flips said, "A man should be ten years older than the girl."

The shofer said, "Say, lay off that, will you?" He pulled the pan of black stuff from under the automobile.

Flips said, "You're not twenty-seven."

The shofer didn't say anything.

Flips said, "I'll bet you're not anywhere near it. I'll bet you're not more than twenty."

The shofer said, "Twenty! Listen, I'll never see twenty-two again." Flips said, "Twenty-two. Why that only makes you five years older than...."

The shofer said, "Now get me right. You've gotta cut this out. If Miss Trescott gets wise to your cracks about ages and this and that, I'm out of a good job with no reference."

I was surprised at what happened. It would surprise any one. The red hose went off right in my mouth. It blew air down my throat. It was a queer feeling. I gave a big jump. I landed in the pan of black stuff. I rolled over in the black stuff. The smell was terrible.

I got out of the pan and went away from there. I ran out of the garage. I ran around the house. I felt very slippery. I tried rolling on the grass. I still felt slippery. I could hear Flips calling me. I did not respond. I was thinking. I wished to become unslippery.

An idea came to me. I went, and scratched on the front door. I went in the door quickly when Saki opened it. He tried to stop me. Couldn't—too slippery. I ran upstairs. The door to Aunt Caroline's room was open. Lucky for once.

I went in Aunt Caroline's room. I jumped upon the bed. I tried to become unslippery on the bed. I think I could have done it if they'd let me alone.

They didn't. I don't think I ever saw them get more excited. And then guess what? Three bathsl Three of them! One right after the other. Saki did it. He used up a whole cake of soap. Talk about awful.

I'm still just a little slippery.

· X ·

The Wild Hyena

December 5. I have been concentrating. I have been concentrating on how to get into the kitchen. You'd know why if you could smell the smells that come out of that place.

I wonder why no one lives in the kitchen except the dark woman. Aunt Caroline and Flips and the Molecule never go there. Something must be wrong with their noses.

The dark woman's name is Ruby. She is the color of the brown stones in the pink box at Toodles' home that made me swallow up. I watch her through the window. When she looks out I give her wags and wiggles. Nothing happens.

There are two ways of getting into the kitchen. One is through the door at the back porch. The other is through the butler's pantry.

I decided to try the butler's pantry way. It is a hard way on account of the door. It's a queer door. If you give it a paw-poke it swings open. Just as you start through it comes back and bangs you on the nose. I tried it three times to make sure. Every time I got a nose-bang. Then I sat down and concentrated.

The dining-room girl was going through the door quite often. She carried things on plates. The smell from the things on the plates was beyond words. I came to a decision. I said, "I shall accompany her quickly." I did.

I was surprised at what happened. I think the dining-room girl was, too. She was so surprised she sat down suddenly. What she was carrying on a platter slid along the floor. I slid after it through some gravy. Can you imagine! Sliding through gravy! It was the greatest moment of my life.

And I came to what had been on the platter. Will I ever forget the sensation? Just the size of it was breathtaking. And the smell—there is no way of giving you an idea of that smell. I closed my eyes at the first taste. That's why I didn't notice the dark woman. I just heard a swishing noise. Then something hit me. It was a broom. The dark woman had hit me with a broom.

She said, "Leggo 'at pot roas', dawg."

I growled at her. She hit me again. Things began to get red. It was like the time with the chow, when Mike shut me in the end runway.

Then I remembered what Mike had said about pacifism. I made an effort. I controlled myself. I just took another bite of what had been on the platter and ignored the dark woman.

She hit me again. I growled louder. Would you believe it—she hit me again!

I don't think Mike would have approved of what happened then. It had nothing to do with pacifism. When I came to myself I had something in my mouth. It wasn't what had been on the platter.

It was a piece of something the dark woman had been wearing. The dark woman was standing on a table. She was yelling. I don't think I ever heard anyone yell louder.

Aunt Caroline came into the kitchen. So did Flips. So did the Molecule.

Aunt Caroline said, "Ruby, Ruby, stop it this instant! Good heavens, Robert, she's gone crazy!"

The dark woman stopped yelling. She said, "Crazy, is I? Take 'at wile hyeenah out-a here an' lemme' pack."

The Molecule looked at me. He said, "Ah, collecting lingerie, are you, Trub?"

He dragged me out of the kitchen. He shut me in the storeroom. And then guess what! Gravy! All over me! I licked every place I could reach.

December 6. I have a new name. It is almost as nice as Trub Trescott, the Hero. The Molecule gave it to me. He calls me the Wild Hyena.

The dark woman is not in the kitchen any more. I don't know where she has gone.

December 7. The gray-haired man is here. I like him. He scratches me back of the ears. Aunt Caroline calls him Frederick. The Molecule calls him Worthy Guardian and Esteemed Sir. Flips calls him Freddy Darling and Ducky Daddles. It's confusing.

The gray-haired man came to have a talk with Aunt Caroline. I heard him say so. They had it in the library. I was there. Just we three. I chewed a book I found on the floor. Not bad after the cover came off.

Aunt Caroline said, "Well, have you seen her?"

The gray-haired man said, "Had her to luncheon."

Aunt Caroline said, "Impossible, of course."

The gray-haired man said, "Oh, I don't know."

Aunt Caroline sat up straight. She gave the gray-haired man a look. It was not a kind look. She said, "Just what do you mean?"

The gray-haired man said, "Well, she's quite easy to look at."

Aunt Caroline said, "Of course—that's her business."

The gray-haired man said, "It's the best business I know of for a woman."

Aunt Caroline said, "Motion pictures?"

The gray-haired man said, "No. Beauty. She has it. Why don't you ask her out here for a few days?"

Aunt Caroline sat up straighter than before. She said, "Have her here in this house?"

The gray-haired man said, "Exactly. I'd like to be here at the same time. Arrange it, will you?"

Aunt Caroline said, "I most certainly will not. That creature!"

The gray-haired man came and took my book. He looked at it. He said, "Marvelous pup, Caroline. He simply devours Emerson." He put the book on a shelf—what was left of it. I tried a magazine.

Aunt Caroline said, "Hmh! He also devours the servants."

The gray-haired man said, "So Bob tells me. Now Caroline, let's get down to cases. I have a little knowledge of just two things in this world—finance and human nature. Both enter into this affair, I think. The girl's motives are purely mercenary. The boy has fallen, temporarily, for a pretty face. Suppose you stop opposing him and let me run the show for a while. What do you say?"

I like to understand what people are talking about. I did not understand the gray-haired man. It made me yawny. I closed my eyes for a minute. And then guess what? Saki was giving me a bath in gravy. Aren't dreams wonderful!

Aunt Caroline and the gray-haired man woke me up. They were leaving the library. Aunt Caroline said:

"Very well, but you're responsible. If things go wrong..."

The gray-haired man called to me. He said, "Come on, you bookworm!" He put his arm around Aunt Caroline. He said, "They won't, Caroline, they won't."

Flips was in the hall when we came out of the library. She said, "I know what you've been gabbing about and you both make me sick. Just as though a person can't live their own life."

Aunt Caroline said, "Florence, I've heard quite enough from you on the subject."

Flips said, "Have you? Well, some day you'll find out."

She went out the front door. I went with her. She slammed the door. We went around the house to the garage. The shofer was there. He had on big black boots. He was rubbing the window of an automobile with a yellow cloth.

Flips said, "Kiss me, Billy!"

The shofer said, "Like hell I will."

There was a rubber hose that went from the wall to an iron thing with holes in it in the floor. Water was running out of the hose down the iron thing in the floor. I took a drink of the water. It was hard to drink, it ran so fast. Then I lay down and tried the hose.

Flips said, "Why won't you, Billy?"

The shofer went on rubbing the automobile window. He said, "Too busy."

Flips said, "All right; I am going to wait right here till you have more time."

The shofer stopped rubbing the window.

He said, "Aw, listen, Kid!"

Flips said, "Then kiss me!"

The shofer said, "Will you beat it if I do?"

Flips said, "Yes, Billy." She put her arms around the shofer's neck.

I thought of a new game just then. I began to play it with the hose. It is called Kill-the-Serpent. You do it by shaking the hose. It is a good game, only wet.

I played it only a second. Aunt Caroline spoiled everything. She started to come in the garage door. The water from the hose went right in her face. She screamed. It seemed best to stop the game and go away from there. I did.

December 8. Flips has given me three bones today. She hugs me a lot. She keeps calling me a darling, darling, darling, darling pupsums.

· XI ·

The Gentle Art of Chasing Cats

December 9. I have a new friend. His name is Ginger. He is a wire-haired fox terrier. He lives in a house with red chimneys. You can see the chimneys between the trees if you go upstairs and look out the windows in the Molecule's room.

The Molecule has a nice room. Everywhere you look is a picture of Miss Kendle. In one picture she is holding Toodles. I wonder how Toodles is getting along. Not that I care, really. I like Ginger much better.

I met Ginger at the front gate. We walked around each other. We exchanged sniffs. I jumped back and gave him some wags. He gave me some wags. Then we were acquainted.

It was not a cold day, but he was shivering. Every now and then he sneezed. His nose needed attending to, if you ask me.

He said, "By dabe's Gidger. What's yours?"

I said, "My regular name is Trub, but I have others. Trub Trescott, the Hero, is one, and the Wild Hyena is another. I got that lately."

He said, "And they shod Lincoln!"

I said, "Who's Lincoln?"

He said, "Debber bide. Trub'll do for me. You lib id here, Kid?"

I said, "What makes you talk so funny?"

He began to walk toward me—stiff-legged. He curled back his lip. He said, "Dode you lige the way I talg?"

I walked up to him. I curled back my lip. I said, "No, I don't think I do."

He walked away. He kicked dirt with his hind feet. He said, "Oh, well, led id go! What do you do to bass the tibe away?"

I said, "Chew things and play games."

He said, "What sort ob gabes?"

I named some games. I named Sliding Rugs and Helpless Prey and

Bark at the Enemy.

He said, "Kid, you're udcodshus. Did you eber chase cads?"

I said, "No, what's it like?"

He said, "Id's the kig ob outdoor spords."

I said, "What's a cad?"

He said, "Didn't you eber see a cad?"

I said, "Not that I know of. Where do you see them?"

He said, "Why, you boor fish, you see theb eberywhere. They drig milg."

I said, "Milk! You mean cats."

He said, "Ob course, I bede cads. Thad's whad I said three tibes—cads. You chase deb ub a tree ad drig the milg yourselb. I do id with my buddy. We'd be doig id now odly he's ad hobe. He can't cub oud. He's god disteber."

I said, "What's disteber?"

He said, "You'll fide out if you eber ged id. I thig I' b cubbig down with id byself. I'b subbosed to be in the house covered ub with blaggets. I sneaged oud. Let's fide a cad. What do you say?"

I said, "I don't care if I do. Where will we find one?"

He said, "Eddywhere. They're thig this year."

We went down the road. When we came to yards Ginger would go in and look around. He looked in many yards. Nothing happened. He said, "Thad's the way id is. If you go for a walg with your beople cads are just swarbig. Whed you're in shabe to hadle theb you'd thig they were extig."

We went farther down the road. We came to a house with a red barn. Ginger said, "Wade here!" He went in the gate and around the barn. I sat down by the gate. I waited a long time. I got sleepy. I was just going to take a nap when Ginger stuck his head from behind the barn. He said, "Pst!"

I said, "What is it?"

He said, "Duck soupl"

I wasn't sleepy any more. I said, "In a plate?"

He said, "You're still udcodshus. Cubbod and keeb quied."

I went with Ginger. We went behind the barn. We came to a shed. Under the shed was a man and a cow. The cow was making its mouth go sideways. The man was taking milk out of the cow. The milk was going into a bucket. All around the man and the cow were cats. One was rubbing itself against the man's leg.

Ginger said, "Led's go, Kid—ad mage id snabby." He started for the shed. I went with him. We went in a quick way. When we got to the shed things began to happen. They seemed to happen all at once. Everywhere you looked were cats going quickly. The one that was rubbing against the man went up the man's back on to the cow. It ran along the cow. It jumped from the cow to a post. It went up the post to the roof of the shed. The cow went out of the shed. It went suddenly. It kept kicking its hind feet in the air.

I couldn't think, it was so excitingl Cats were going up trees wherever you looked. The bucket was upside down. Milk was running everywhere. Ginger was barking. I was barking. The man was saying words. I was never so thrilled in my life.

The man kept on saying words. He said them in a loud voice. He began to pick up something. All the cats were in trees. I thought I'd try a little milk. But Ginger said, "Loog oud for rogs!" He went away from there. I went with him. We went out to the road. Stones came after us. We went down the road very fast.

I said, "Where was the duck soup? I only saw milk."

Ginger said, "You're a hard guy to suid. You bedder go hobe and play gabes. Gosh, I feel terrible! By head's as big as a ballood."

Ginger was shivering worse than ever. His eyes looked very bright and strange. He did not walk straight any more. He began to go zigzag. He kept bumping into me.

I was thinking over what had happened. I began to think of the milk running everywhere. The more I thought the hungrier I got. I said, "Listen, I've got to eat. Let's go home."

Ginger said, "If I go hobe they'll put blaggets on me. We'll go on a garbage raid. Then we'll fide sub bore cads."

I said, "How do you go on a garbage raid?"

Ginger said, "You push the lids off garbage cads with your nose ad thed ead whad you fide."

I said, "What's a garbage cat?"

Ginger said, "I didn't say cad. I said cad. Cubbod, I'll show you wud."

A girl came running along the road. Her hair was flapping about like Flips'. It was not light hair like Flips'. It was red.

Ginger said, "Holy backerel." He started to run.

The girl said, "Ginger Jessup, you come here."

Ginger stopped running. He gave the girl some wags. She went and picked him up. She said, "You're a bad, bad dog. If you weren't sick I'd give you an awful whipping." She gave him some hugs.

Ginger said, "Blaggets for be. So log, Kid. See you in Suddy school."

The girl stopped hugging Ginger and looked at me. She said, "Where do you live, puppy? You go straight home."

I was ravenous. I did what the red-haired girl said. When I got home Saki gave me a plate full of liver. There is nothing I am fonder of.

The end of a perfect day! What if I hadn't met Ginger! I suppose I should have gone on playing games. I might have gone for years never knowing. Imagine spending your life without chasing cats. I won't do much of anything else from now on.

· XII ·

A Visitation

December 18. It's been awful. I'm just beginning to be interested in things again. It started two days after I'd chased cats with Ginger. I'd been out looking for Ginger. I couldn't find him. I came home and tried playing games. I tried Sliding Rugs. No good! Nothing is any good after chasing cats! I only played it because I like to watch Saki put the rugs back.

The doorbell rang. Saki opened the door. There was a man there. He came in. He said:

"Please tell Miss Trescott the rector is calling."

Saki took off the man's overcoat. The man took off his own hat. He put it on a chair in the hall. I went over and sniffed his legs. The man said. "Nice doggy! Is he — er — dangerous?"

Saki said, "No, sar — not always."

The man went into the drawing-room. He went quickly. I went with him. The man sat down in a chair. I sniffed his legs. The man said, "Hello, Old Fellow. Nice, nice, Old Fellow." He kept wiggling his legs.

What do you suppose I smelled on the man's legs? Cats! I could hardly believe it. I took a long sniff to make sure. Yes, it was cats. The man said, "Goodness, gracious!" He took out a handkerchief. He wiped his face with it.

Sometimes I play a game with Flips. It's called Catch-It-If-You-Can. We play it with a handkerchief. I started to play it with the man. He was not quick with the handkerchief like Flips. I simply took it away from him. I played Helpless Prey with the handkerchief until it was quite dead. Then I went back and sniffed at the cat smell. The man said, "This is terrible!" I could hardly sniff his legs he moved them about so.

Aunt Caroline came in. She said, "Why, Doctor, you're white as a sheet!"

The man said, "Oh, my dear lady, oh, my dear lady."

Aunt Caroline said, "What is it, Doctor? You must be ill."

The man said, "No, not ill—just unstrung. Nerves, you know. Parish troubles. Splendid dog you have. Watchdog, I suppose. Shall we let him go out and run and play? And if I could have—er—just a small glass of er—"

Aunt Caroline put me out in the hall. She shut the door. I was sorry. I would rather have stayed and sniffed the cat smell. I saw the man's hat on the chair. It was a funny hat. I sniffed it. No cat smell! It fell off the chair and rolled on the floor. I pounced. It jumped away. I pounced again. It was not a bad game. I played it as long as the hat lasted. Saki found what was left of the hat on the floor. He got excited, of course. I went away from there.

I went out to the glass room and lay down. I began to feel queer. I felt very tired. I stayed in the glass room a long time. I kept feeling more and more queer. The glass room began to go around. The chairs and tables began to go up and down. There were cats on the chairs and tables. Hundreds of cats. I wanted to chase the cats, but I was too tired.

The Molecule came in. He had turned into three Molecules. I was too tired to give the three Molecules a tail thump. He said, "Ah, the Mad Hatter!" He sat down. He lit three cigarettes. He said, "Caroline is annoyed with you, Old Companion."

Flips came in. She said, "There's my darling Trubsywubsums. Come here, Lamby."

I made an effort. I gave her a tail thump.

The Molecule said, "He's a loathsome atheist. He's just made a dastardly attack on the church."

Flips said, "Talk like a human being. What do you mean?"

The Molecule said, "He totally masticated and devoured the Reverend What-you-may-callem's lid."

Flips said, "Oh, gosh!" She lay down on the window seat and made noises.

The Molecule rocked back and forth and made noises. He said, "Lord, how I suffer!"

Aunt Caroline came and stood in the doorway. She watched the Molecule and Flips. She said, "This is too much!"

The Molecule said, "Much too much." He slid out of his chair. He rolled on the floor. Flips put her face in the window-seat pillows. She made louder noises.

Saki came to the door. He said, "Animal physic have came."

Aunt Caroline said, "Tell him to come here!"

The Molecule stopped making noises. He sat up. He said, "Who's coming in here?"

Aunt Caroline said, "The Veterinary."

The Molecule said, "Veterinary! What for?"

Aunt Caroline said, "To take this dog away."

A man came in the glass room with Saki. He came over and looked at me. He stooped down and lifted up my had and looked in my eyes.

The Molecule and Aunt Caroline were arguing. Flips was crying.

The Molecule said, "If you do this I promise you'll regret it, Aunt Caroline."

The man stopped looking at me. He stood up. He said, "The young man is right. A chill might kill him."

Aunt Caroline looked at the man. Flips looked at the man.

Aunt Caroline said, "What on earth are you talking about? I sent for you to take him away from here."

The man said, "Well, I'll be—Then you didn't know he was sick, Lady?"

Aunt Caroline said, "Naturally not—since he's perfectly well."

The man said, "If he's well I'd hate to see a sick one. He's got a temperature of 104 or 105 this minute."

Aunt Caroline said, "I don't believe a word of it!"

The man stooped down. He lifted up my head. He said, "Come here, Lady."

Aunt Caroline came over to me. The man said, "Look at this puppy's eyes. Now listen to him breathe. Now watch his head drop when I let it go."

Aunt Caroline said, "Oh, the poor thingl The poor, dear puppy. He's trying at times, heaven knows—all young things are. Robert, Florence—I'm sorry."

The glass room began to spin worse than ever. Millions of cats were floating through the air. Aunt Caroline was rubbing my head. Flips was crying. The man was telling the Molecule about distemper.

Aunt Caroline said, "And he saved us all the night the burglars came!" She began to cry, too.

It's hard to remember anything after that. Everything was queer for days and days. I know this much. I like Aunt Caroline better. All the time things were queer she gave me soup and warm milk with a spoon. Flips or the Molecule would hold up my head. Flips always cried. Aunt Caroline only cried when I was too tired to swallow.

Things stopped being queer all of a sudden—except my legs. They were wobbly. They stayed wobbly for several days. Everyone says I had distemper. Except the Molecule. He says it was a visitation from God. He says, "Moral! Never touch a minister's lid."

They let me out of the house this afternoon for the first time. I was glad. I had a plan. It was a plan to show Aunt Caroline I appreciated the things she gave me in a spoon.

I had buried a bone under some dead leaves the day before the visitation from God came. I was afraid the bone wouldn't be there. It was. It had improved a lot with age. The smell was simply wonderful.

I wanted it myself, but I knew who was going to get that bone. I carried it straight upstairs to Aunt Caroline's room and laid it in the middle of her bed.

· XIII ·

Five Little Rolsey Polseys

December 19. Guess who's here? Toodles. He brought Miss Kendle with him. The gray-haired man is here, too. They all came together. They came in an automobile.

The Molecule kissed Miss Kendle when she came. Flips hugged the gray-haired man. Miss Kendle said, "So this is Gray Gables! And this must be Aunt Caroline."

Aunt Caroline said, "Yes, I am Miss Trescott. Miss Kendle will have the pink room, Saki."

When I said hello to Toodles he just sniffed.

I said, "This is my home. How do you like it?"

Toodles said, "Strange, strange!"

I said, "What's strange about this home?"

Toodles said, "Finding you in it. Do you do much 'swallowing up' around here?" He shuddered.

I said, "Oh, that was in the old days. I'm housebroken now—nearly."

Toodles said, "Nearly! Oh, my God!"

I said, "Say, how do you like to chase cats?"

Toodles shuddered again. He said, "Always the vulgarian."

He went upstairs with Flips and the Molecule and Miss Kendle.

The gray-haired man stayed downstairs. I hoped he had not forgotten how to scratch back of the ears. I gave him some wags. He hadn't.

Aunt Caroline said, "Well, you've had your way."

The gray-haired man said, "Why, yes, Caroline. And I suggest that you soften your attitude:"

Aunt Caroline said, "What did you expect me to do—embrace her?"

The gray-haired man said, "My dear Caroline, there's no fool like an old fool, is there?"

Aunt Caroline gave the gray-haired man a look. It was not a kind look. She said, "I'm afraid you are going to prove that to me, Frederick."

Toodles came downstairs again with Miss Kendle.

I said, "I want to tell you about this chasing cats."

Toodles said, "Go away—you annoy me."

He went into the library with the Molecule and Miss Kendle.

I went after him.

I said, "But listen, it's the king of outdoor sports."

Toodles said, "I have no interest—none whatever in outdoor sports." He got up on the couch with Miss Kendle. I lay down in front of the fire.

The Molecule was sitting on the couch with Miss Kendle. He gave her a long hug. He gave her some kisses.

Miss Kendle said, "You're mussing me up something scandalous, Bobsy-Wobsy. Isn't a Rolls too delicious? We just seemed to float along."

The Molecule said, "Tell it to the garage man, Old Party. The important thing is this: Why do I feel it in my toes when your hair tickles my ear?"

Miss Kendle said, "Imagine owning a heavenly thing like that,"

The Molecule said, "I have two. Let's try it on the other one."

Miss Kendle said, "I mean a Rolls, you nut."

The Molecule said, "My mistake. I thought you meant my ear. Not that it's pertinent or of the slightest interest, but the poor goof owns five."

Miss Kendle said, "Five what?"

The Molecule said, "Five little cute little Rolsey Polseys."

Miss Kendle said, "Your guardian?"

The Molecule said, "He has that honor."

Miss Kendle said, "Five!"

The Molecule said, "Five, Light of my Life. I counted them twice."

Miss Kendle said, "Heaven help the working girl. Just what is his wonderful name?"

The Molecule said, "The guy's moniker is Frederick Ogden Steele."

Miss Kendle said, "Don't tell me he's F.O. Steele—railroads and banks and everything?"

The Molecule said, "The head of the class for yours, Pansy. 'Everything' is right. The paupers will now toddle out and catch some free air. My arm, Lady Gwendolyn."

Toodles and Miss Kendle and the Molecule went for a walk. I went with them. Toodles stayed beside Miss Kendle.

I said, "Come on, let's run!"

Toodles said, "What for?"

I said, "Don't you ever run when you're out for a walk?"

Toodles said, "Why should I?"

I said, "You run ahead and sniff trees and telephone poles."

Toodles said, "Disgusting!" He went to the other side of Miss Kendle. I went with him.

The Molecule nearly stepped on Toodles. He said, "Here, you pups, get the hell out of here." He gave Toodles a shove with his foot. Toodles snarled. The Molecule laughed. He shoved Toodles again. Toodles snapped at the Molecule's foot. The Molecule picked Toodles up by the neck. He turned him over and gave him some spanks. They looked like fun spanks to me.

I was surprised at the way Toodles yelled. He kept on yelling when the spanks were over. I said, "Say, what's the matter with you?"

Toodles yelled, "He's killing me, the big bully!"

The Molecule said, "His middle register is a knock-out, but his high notes are a little sour."

Miss Kendle took Toodles from the Molecule. She took him in a quick way. She said, "Come to your own muvver, sugar lump." She gave Toodles some hugs. He stopped yelling.

The Molecule said, "Better see if any bones are broken."

Miss Kendle said, "I think I'll go back to the house."

The Molecule said, "Ruffled a bit?"

Miss Kendle said, "Certainly not. I'm just tired of walking."

The Molecule said, "You're not getting your feathers up because I gave the penwiper a few love pats, are you?"

Miss Kendle said, "I've told you I'm tired, Bobby. Please stop talking about it—I'm getting a headache."

The Molecule said, "Sure you're not steaming under the seams?"

Miss Kendle said, "Not in the least. I've simply got a headache coming on."

The Molecule said, "I'm sorry, Old Thing; can I do anything?"

Miss Kendle said, "Yes, stop talking."

We went back to the house. Miss Kendle carried Toodles. Nobody said anything. I sniffed a few trees. I looked for cats. I didn't see any. We went in the front door. Miss Kendle said, "I'm going up and lie down. I suppose all men have a streak of brutality?"

The Molecule whistled. I thought he wanted me. I went over to him. He said, "Wouldn't that jar your tonsils, Old Companion?" He went to his room. I went with him. He shut the door in my face. I came downstairs again.

Flips and the gray-haired man were in the living room. They were talking. Flips said, "But, if they love each other, Freddy darling, nothing else counts."

The gray-haired man said, "More or less correct, infant."

Flips said, "Then why don't you approve?"

The gray-haired man said, "I brought her here, didn't I? What more do you want?"

Flips went and sat in the gray-haired man's lap. She put her hands behind his head. She said, "Now, Ducky, look me straight in the eye. Do you, or don't you, approve?"

The gray-haired man said, "You are sitting on that corned-beef hash we had for luncheon."

Flips said, "Never mind your old tummy; answer my question."

The gray-haired man said, "First let me breathe."

Flips got off the gray-haired man's lap. She said, "Now, have you breathed?"

The gray-haired man said, "Sort of."

Flips said, "Well then... ?"

The gray-haired man said, "You hope to choke you'll never tell?"

Flips said, "May I be a dud when I'm a deb, if I do."

The gray-haired man said, "What a blood-curdling oath; all right, listen. If they really love each other—as you say—I approve."

Flips said, "Oh, goody!" She went away from there.

The gray-haired man kept looking at a book. I wanted him to scratch me back of the ears. I gave him a paw-poke. He went on looking at the book. I took a nap.

Toodles and Miss Kendle came in. The gray-haired man stopped looking at the book. He stood up.

Miss Kendle said, "Oh, Mr. Steele, I'm simply smitten."

The gray-haired man said, "Mutual, I assure you."

Miss Kendle said, "I mean with confusion. The way I chattered in the motor. Just as though you weren't anybody. Of course, I never dreamed. What did you think of me?"

The gray-haired man said, "I refuse to confess."

Miss Kendle said, "Please do; I deserve it."

The gray-haired man said, "It wouldn't do; imagine my becoming my ward's rival."

Miss Kendle said, "I don't dare imagine that—it would be too thrilling." She gave the gray-haired man a look. It was a kind look.

Toodles yawned. He said, "Another one, evidently."

I said, "Another what?"

Toodles said, "You wouldn't understand."

I said, "Why did you yell so about a little spanking?"

Toodles said, "You wouldn't understand that, either."

I said, "Don't tell me it hurt."

Toodles said, "I was hurt in my sensibilities."

I said, "What are sensibilities?"

Toodles said, "That's something you'll never know." He got up in Miss Kendle's lap.

The Molecule came in. He said, "Esteemed Sir and Lady Friend, I greet you. How's the head?"

Miss Kendle said, "I was talking to Mr. Steele, and suddenly it went away."

The Molecule looked at the gray-haired man. He said, "Some line! A few words, and she loses her head."

Saki came to the door. He said, "Dinnair is served."

Guess what happened! Toodles went into the dining room with the rest. I warned him. I said, "You're not allowed in there while eating's going on."

Toodles just sniffed.

I said, "All right, you'll find out."

I waited to see what would happen. Nothing did. He stayed in there during all the eating.

I call that a dirty trick!

· XIV ·

Toodles Gets Some Experience

December 20. Something has come between Toodles and me. Don't know what it is. He won't look in my direction. He just lies in Miss Kendle's lap. When I say something to him he doesn't even sniff. It happened like this.

Miss Kendle and the gray-haired man went away in an automobile. Toodles didn't go. He was having some crackers and cream. The dining-room girl was giving it to him. That's what he eats—crackers and cream. Imagine!

When the front door closed he came into the hall. He came in a quick way. There was cream on his nose. He said, "Where is Muvver?"

I tried to lick the cream off his nose. I couldn't. He didn't stand still long enough. He kept running from one room to another. He said, "She's not here. Oh, my God, she's left me behind!"

I said, "Stand still a minute—there's some cream on your nose."

He said, "What do I care—she's left me behind!" He licked the cream off his nose himself. He lay down by the front door. He began to cry.

Flips came into the hall. So did the Molecule.

The Molecule said, "What's wrong with the penwiper?"

Flips said, "Dacia has gone without him."

The Molecule held up two fingers, close together. He said, "He and I are like that. Where's she gone?"

Flips said, "She went for a drive with Freddy."

The Molecule said, "As usual."

Flips said, "Don't be a nut. How can he approve unless he knows her?"

The Molecule said, "Having heard you in respectful silence, I now repeat—as usual."

Flips said, "She's going to be with you all evening at the Country Club, isn't she?"

The Molecule said, "The thought has already occurred to me. What makes your paws so filthy?"

Flips said, "William was showing me how to put on a tire."

The Molecule said, "With a gentle smile, he replied, 'Anything in trousers.'"

Flips said, "You're a liar! A nasty, sneaky, little liar!"

The Molecule said, "Flips is mad and I'm sad and I know what'll please her. A dirty tire to make her perspire and a fair-haired shofer to squeeze her."

Flips said, "If you ever speak to me again I'll—I'll spit in your face."

The Molecule said, "Tut, tut, my dear Countess!"

Flips stamped her foot. She jumped up and down. She made her fingers go in front of the Molecule's face. She said, "I'd like to scratch your eyes out. You—you—"

She went upstairs in a quick way.

The Molecule went into the living room.

Toodles had stopped crying. He just lay by the door and sniffed.

I said, "Say, listen! Now would be a good time to chase cats."

Toodles said, "Have you no respect for grief?"

I said, "One cat—and you'll forget it."

Toodles stopped sniffing. He looked at me in a strange way. He said, "Mud puddles!"

I said, "I don't get you."

Toodles said, "How do we get out of here?"

I said, "Watch me!" I scratched the front door—good, long scratches. Saki came in a quick way. He opened the door. Toodles and I went out. I said, "Simple, when you know how!"

Toodles said, "But it makes marks all down the door!"

I said, "That's what does it. He'll try to rub them off with something in a bottle."

Toodles said, "Where is a mud puddle?"

I said, "We're not looking for mud puddles—we're looking for cats."

Toodles said, "First—mud puddles!"

I said, "What for?"

Toodles said, "You'll see!"

We found a mud puddle. Toodles walked into it. He lay down in it. He rolled over in it.

I said, "What's the big idea?"

Toodles said, "I'll show her! Where is a muddier one?"

I said, "We'll see plenty. Just look for cats." We did.

I saw the first cat. It was a small cat. It had a ribbon on its neck. A girl was with it. She was a small girl. They were sitting on the steps of a house.

I showed the cat to Toodles. I said, "Are you ready?"

Toodles said, "Ready for what?"

I said, "Ready to chase the cat!"

Toodles said, "Where do we chase it?"

I said, "Up a tree."

Toodles said, "What for?"

I said, "Then you drink the cat's milk."

Toodles said, "I don't like milk—only cream."

I said, "Are you going to stand there and argue all day?"

Toodles said, "No, I'm going to find more puddles."

I said, "Wait till I chase this cat."

Toodles said, "All right, but hurry."

I said, "Watch me and you'll get the idea."

I went toward the cat in a quick way. The cat did not go up a tree. The small girl picked it up. She said, "Go way from here, you nasty dog."

I barked. The small girl went in the house with the cat. She had dropped something on the steps when she picked up the cat. Guess what it was? A piece of chocolate cake! I ate the cake and went back to Toodles.

Toodles said, "What were you eating just now?"

I said, "Cake."

Toodles said, "What kind of cake?"

I said, "Chocolate cake!"

Toodles said, "I'm rather fond of chocolate cake. You told me milk."

I said, "Sometimes it's one thing and sometimes another."

Toodles said, "There's more in this than I thought."

I said, "You'll be wild about it in no time."

We found cats in the very next yard. Two of them. One was a black and white cat. It was sitting on a cellar door. The other was a yellow cat. It was sitting on a pile of wood. I said, "You take the yellow one."

Toodles said, "I'm beginning to like this. It gives one a feeling of power—if you know what I mean. Where do I take him?"

I said, "Just go for him lickity split. Don't bark till he starts to run."

I went for the black and white cat. It went off the cellar door very fast. We went around the house in a quick way. The cat went under a fence. I tried to go under the fence. My collar caught on the fence. Before it came loose the cat got away. Then I heard noises.

I listened. I had never heard such noises. I ran back around the house.

The yellow cat was not on the woodpile. It was not up a tree. It was playing a game with Toodles. They were rolling around everywhere. The cat was making its feet go in a quick way. Toodles was making the noises I had heard.

A man came out of the house. He said, "Scat, you!"

The cat went up on the pile of wood. The man looked at Toodles. He said, "The bell was all that saved you, Kid." He laughed. He went back in the house.

Toodles began to run. He ran out of the yard. He ran down the road. He was still making noises.

I ran after him. I said, "You're not supposed to play with cats. Just chase them up a tree."

Toodles stopped running. He stopped making noises. You would never have known him. The mud puddles and the game with the cat had done it. He gave me a look. It was not a kind look. He said, "Chocolate cake!" He hasn't spoken to me since.

When we got home Miss Kendle was there. When she saw Toodles she screamed. She said, "Muvver's darling, precious angel! What's happened to him, Bobby?"

The Molecule came and looked at Toodles. He said, "Let us approach our problem in a scientific manner. Let us summon deduction to our aid. You'll observe here five parallel abrasions on what, I presume, you call his nose. Now, note a similar condition on the outer surface of the aural flap, or ear. Let the eye rest for a moment on this distressing appearance of the entire fuzz or fur. Having tabulated our data, and established our premise, we now come to our conclusion: He tried to lick a rabbit."

Miss Kendle said, "You may think this is the time be funny—I don't." She took Toodles and went upstairs.

· XV ·

A Pearl and a Hop-Toad

December 21. More talk today. There always is—about everything. I wonder why.

The first talk was in the glass room. Just the Molecule, Miss Kendle, and I were there. Toodles had gone to eat crackers and cream—as usual. Miss Kendle said, "But it's so important to have him like me, Bobby."

The Molecule said, "It can be overdone."

Miss Kendle said, "You don't mean to insinuate that I...."

The Molecule said, "Back to the cross-word puzzle with INSINUATE. Are you going to the country club with me this afternoon or not?"

Miss Kendle said, "I'd love to. You know that. But what can I do? I've already promised to drive with him."

The Molecule said, "And I've promised Tibo Ethridge we'd shoot a foursome at three o'clock."

Miss Kendle said, "You can telephone."

The Molecule said, "Yes, I learned to do it as a child; but I won't."

Miss Kendle said, "But what am I to do about Mr. Steele?"

The Molecule said, "Approach him in a dignified manner and speak as follows, 'Listen, Bud; the goof who is about to smear up my fair name with his own disgusting moniker has just passed me the word that you're out of the picture. Therefore, and in consequence, my absence from your Rolls-Royce on this and other occasions will be complete. For further information, address the Boy Hero.'"

Toodles came in. He was licking cream off his nose. I tried not to watch him. I couldn't help it.

Miss Kendle went in the library. Toodles went with her. He was still at it. I went with him. The gray-haired man was in the library. He was looking at a book.

Miss Kendle said, "I must tell you something—Bobby is jealous."

The gray-haired man stood up. He said, "Of what?"

Miss Kendle said, "Of you."

The gray-haired man said, "Flattering, I'm sure."

Miss Kendle said, "Why flattering?"

The gray-haired man said, "When we pass forty—such things are."

Miss Kendle said, "The idea, you with all your power, you could sweep any girl off her—I'm talking too much."

The gray-haired man said, "Possibly; it's for you to decide."

Miss Kendle gave the gray-haired man a look. It was a long look. She said, "I've never met anyone like you before. It makes me feel so helpless—like being in the dark. I'd give anything to guess a little of what you think."

The gray-haired man said, "I think you're engaged to my ward."

Miss Kendle said, "Is that all you think?"

The gray-haired man said, "All I can tell you."

Miss Kendle said, "Why?"

The gray-haired man said, "Because you're engaged to my ward."

Miss Kendle said, "And if I weren't engaged to Bobby you could tell me more?"

The gray-haired man gave Miss Kendle a look. It was a kind look. He said, "Undoubtedly, my dear."

Miss Kendle said, "I'm so frightfully curious—you tempt me to go driving with you this afternoon."

The gray-haired man said, "I thought you were."

Miss Kendle said, "No, I can't. That's what I came to tell you. If I went I shouldn't be engaged to Bobby any more."

The gray-haired man said, "Then, of course, you're not going. I shall be disappointed." He sat down in the chair.

I wanted him to scratch me back of the ears. I went to the chair. I stood up on my hind legs. I paw-poked the gray-haired man. I paw-poked his chest. I paw-poked a pink marble out of his tie. It fell to the floor. It rolled toward Miss Kendle. She picked it up.

Miss Kendle said, "See what you've done, Trouble. What a wonderful pearl!" She looked at the pink marble.

The gray-haired man began to scratch me back of the ears. He said, "I didn't know it was loose. You like it?"

Miss Kendle said, "Who wouldn't?"

The gray-haired man said, "You may have it."

Miss Kendle said, "You're joking, of course."

The gray-haired man said, "No, I'm not joking, but I claim a reward."

Miss Kendle was looking at the pink marble. Her eyes were shiny. She said, "I couldn't reward you enough for anything like this."

The gray-haired man said, "Just our drive this afternoon will be ample."

Miss Kendle looked at the gray-haired man. She said, "I couldn't—you know why." She looked at the pink marble again. Her eyes were more shiny.

The gray-haired man said, "I'm sorry. It's worth ten thousand dollars."

Miss Kendle said, "Ten thousand—ten thousand—here, take it." She started to give the pink marble to the gray-haired man. She didn't. She said, "I could stay home with a headache; would that do?"

The gray-haired man stopped scratching me back of the ears. He looked at Miss Kendle. It was a long look. He said, "Yes, I think it would."

Miss Kendle said, "Then it's mine!"

The gray-haired man said, "Yes, it's yours."

Miss Kendle looked at the pink marble. She kissed it. She gave the gray-haired man a look. It was a kind look. She said, "I'm speechless. I'll come down here when he's gone to the Country Club." She went away from there. Toodles went with her. The cream was gone, but he was licking his chops. I wanted to ask him something. I followed him into the hall.

I said, "Listen, why do they talk so much?".

Toodles stopped licking his chops. He yawned. He scratched his left ear. He said, "It's the old army game." He went upstairs with Miss Kendle.

I barked at the front door. Saki let me out. I went around to the garden. The gardener wasn't there. I was glad. A gardener just ruins a garden!

There is a rule about hole digging. It goes like this:

"Holes may be dug in the field back of the garage, but never in the garden."

Wouldn't you know it would be like that? The garden is just perfect for hole digging.

I thought I would try just a small hole. I did. It was in a pansy bed. I thought I would make it just a little bigger. I did. I was surprised how big it got. It would not be a good thing to be near when the gardener came. I hid behind the syringa bushes. He didn't come. He didn't come all afternoon. I don't know how many holes I dug.

I was digging the biggest hole when I found the hop-toad. He was sitting by a stone. I barked. He blinked. I paw-poked him. He hopped. It was wonderful!

I thought of Toodles. I thought, "Why should I keep all this to myself?" I picked up the hop-toad. I went to find Toodles. I couldn't scratch on the front door on account of the rule. I couldn't bark on account of the hop-toad taking up so much room.

I was glad when a car came up the drive. It was the Molecule. He had on baggy pants and stockings. I went in the side door with him.

I went to look for Toodles. I went in a quick way. He was in the library. So was Miss Kendle. So was the gray-haired man. Toodles was sitting in Miss Kendle's lap. I put the hop-toad down by her feet for Toodles to see. I said, "Look it over, Old Companion."

The hop-toad hopped. It hopped on to Miss Kendle's feet. She stood up in a quick way. Toodles fell right on top of the hop-toad. Miss Kendle made a bigger hop than the hop-toad. She hopped over to the gray-haired man and hung on to him.

The gray-haired man had to hold her up. He was holding her up when the Molecule came in. The Molecule looked at the gray-haired man. He said, "You've cured another headache, I see. It's a gift." He went away from there.

I barked at the hop-toad. It wouldn't blink any more. I paw-poked it. It wouldn't hop any more. I gave Toodles a look. It was not a kind look. I said, "Now, you've done it."

Toodles said, "You mean you've done it."

I said, "Who sat on this hop-toad, you or I?"

Toodles said, "I wasn't speaking of that filthy reptile. Take it away!"

I said, "It will be a cold day when I'll let you in on anything again." I took the hop-toad and went away from there.

December 22. Toodles went away today. He took Miss Kendle with him. Miss Kendle and the gray-haired man talked some more

when she was leaving. Miss Kendle said, "Now you can tell me what you think."

The gray-haired man said, "About what?"

Miss Kendle gave the gray-haired man a look. It was a kind look. She said, "About me."

The gray-haired man said, "Do you want me to?"

Miss Kendle said, "I want you to — a lot."

The gray-haired man walked over to Miss Kendle. He gave her a look. It was a long look. He said, "I thought it of you the first time I met you in New York. I've thought it of you ever since. While there was a chance that you'd be Bobby's wife some day, I couldn't tell you. Now, since you've asked me, I will. I think you're an utterly mercenary little person."

Saki came in. He said, "Scoose, please; automobile have come at door."

The gray-haired man said, "Good-bye, my dear."

Miss Kendle didn't say anything. She picked up Toodles. She went out and got in the automobile. It went away from there.

· XVI ·

The Molecule Holes Out in One

December 23. If they don't look out my head will bust. Sometimes I think one more rule will do it. I had to learn two new ones today. The first one was easy:

"Do not pick up little white balls when they are hit with sticks."

Now there's a rule anyone can understand. It simply spoils a good time, which is what rules are for. But listen to this one:

"If you pick up one of the white balls when no one sees you, some like it and some don't." That's a tough one. You don't know where you stand exactly.

I was with the Molecule when I learned the two rules. I was with him all day except right after breakfast. Then I was in the glass room. Aunt Caroline and the gray-haired man were in the glass room.

Aunt Caroline said, "I shall never forgive you, Frederick."

The gray-haired man said, "My dear Caroline, isn't it exactly what you wanted?"

Aunt Caroline said, "Did you think I wanted the boy's heart broken? Did you think I wanted you to get involved with her yourself?"

The gray-haired man laughed. He said, "His pride's been hurt—that's all. As for my being involved—don't be silly."

Aunt Caroline said, "The engagement was broken because of you. If you're not involved, who is, may I ask?"

The gray-haired man laughed again. He said, "Come here, Trouble!"

I went to the gray-haired man. He pulled me up on his lap. He said, "This is the villain that blighted love's young dream. Don't be deceived by his innocent expression. He's a conjurer at the heart. He worked his spell with a jewel and a toad. Look at him and shudder."

Aunt Caroline said, "Have you lost your mind, Frederick?"

The gray-haired man said, "I think not, Caroline. My entire loss is trifling—one pearl, to be exact. May I ring for Saki? I must get back to New York."

More talk I couldn't understand. It's like that mostly. I went upstairs. I went to the Molecule's room. I paw-poked his door. It opened.

The Molecule was taking a picture of Miss Kendle from the mantel. He put the picture in a drawer. He kept on putting pictures of Miss Kendle in the drawer. When all the pictures were in the drawer he sat on the bed. I gave him a nose-poke and a hand-lick. He didn't notice it.

Flips came in. She said, "My darling, darling brother!" She tried to give the Molecule a hug.

The Molecule pushed Flips away. He got up from the bed. He said, "Do me a favor, will you, Countess?"

Flips said, "Oh, darling, what is it?"

The Molecule said, "Get the hell out of here."

Flips began to cry. She said, "You poor crushed thing, with your heart all mangled."

The Molecule made a sort of snorting noise.

He said, "Come on, Trub, we'll take our mangled heart with us and toddle."

We went away from there. We went to the garage. We got in a car. We drove to a place called the Country Club. It was a nice place. We went downstairs to a room with tables. The Molecule sat down at a table. A man in a white coat came and stood by the table. He said, "Good morning, Mr. Trescott. Do you want anything?"

The Molecule said, "I want an assistant, Felix. I want him to assist me in some grand and lofty drinking."

The man in the white coat said, "Yes, sir, may I have the key to your locker?"

The Molecule said, "Linger near me and you can have the keys to the city." He gave something to the man in the white coat. The man went away from there. He came back with things on a tray. He put the tray on the table.

I was glad I had come with the Molecule. I gave him some wags and a wiggle. The Molecule said, "Help yourself, Old Companion." I thought he had forgotten the rule about taking things from the table. I gave him a paw-poke to remind him. He said, "Here it is; go as far as you like."

I thought it over. I thought perhaps the rule was only for home. I thought perhaps at country clubs you can take things from tables. I made up my mind to try it. I jumped up on a chair by the table. Can you believe it? Not a thing worth smelling, even.

Nothing but bottles. I call that a dirty trick. I got off the chair and lay down under the table.

A young man came in. He looked at the Molecule. He said, "Felix, why do you let the underworld into the club grill?"

The Molecule said, "Don't speak until you're spoken to, and then remain utterly silent."

The young man said, "While I dislike your personality, I admire your occupation. More ice and another glass, Felix. I'll do a little slumming." He sat down at the table.

The Molecule said, "Lay off the so-called humor, and listen. Tibo, I've broken my engagement!"

The young man said, "You shock me. Gosh, how you shock me! Back at you — so have I!"

The Molecule said, "No!"

The young man said, "Yes!"

The Molecule said, "When?"

The young man said, "Last night."

The Molecule said, "Me, too. Here's looking at you without getting sick."

The young man said, "Here's staring right in your baby blues."

They drank out of glasses. They kept on drinking out of glasses. I went outside. I went around the clubhouse. I found a big can by the back door. It smelled delicious.

There was a cover on the can. I tried to nose-poke the cover off. A man came out of the door. He had a white cap on. He had on a white apron. He picked up a broom. I remembered what the dark woman had done with the broom. I went away from there.

I went back to the Molecule. He and the young man were still drinking out of glasses.

The Molecule said, "In addition to being a human wen, it occurs to me that you are also the world's worst golfer."

The young man said, "That being your idea, I'll shoot you syndicates for twenty-five a hole. Fifty first nine, fifty second nine, a hundred for the match."

The Molecule got up from the table. He said, "If the Society for the Prevention of Cruelty to Worms doesn't interfere, you are about to learn what life on a golf course is like."

We went out of the room with tables. We went out on a lot of green grass. The Molecule put a white ball on a little pile of sand. He took a stick from a bag. He wiggled the stick. He swung it around his neck. He hit the white ball. He said, "Laugh that one off, Pink Toes."

I looked for the white ball. I couldn't see it. Then I did. It was jumping along far away on the green grass. I ran after it. So did the boy with something full of sticks tied to him. I beat the boy. I picked up the white ball. I threw it up in the air. I picked it up again. It was fun. The boy with the sticks tied to him was yelling at me. I ran back to the Molecule. I took the white ball with me.

The Molecule was using language. He chased me. He took the ball from me. He took me by the neck and shook me. That's how I learned about the first rule.

The Molecule put the ball on another pile of sand. He started to wiggle the stick.

The young man said, "Playing three."

The Molecule stopped wiggling the stick. He used more language. He said, "You don't needs clubs—get a jimmy." When he hit the ball again I didn't chase it on account of the rule. I didn't chase the white ball the young man hit, either.

The Molecule and the young man and the boys with the sticks tied to them went a long way over the green grass. I went with them. The Molecule and the young man kept hitting the white balls. The boys with sticks tied to them were allowed to chase the white balls. I wondered why.

I began to get tired of watching them hit the white balls. I began to feel hungry. I thought about the can with the delicious smell. I thought, "What if they forgot to put the cover on!" I went to find out. I went in a quick way.

The cover was still on the can. The man in the white apron was sitting on the steps beside it. The broom was standing close to the man. I went away from there.

I went and lay down on the green grass. I felt sleepy. I started to take a nap. A noise woke me up. It was a thump. It was made by one of the white balls. It rolled past me to a place of very smooth grass. There was another thump. It was another white ball. It rolled on to the place of smooth grass, too.

I thought it would be fun to roll the white balls on the place of smooth grass. I thought it was too bad about the rule. I looked all around. There was no one else there. Just the white balls and me. I picked up the nearest white ball. I threw it up in the air. When it came down I pounced. It rolled along the place of smooth grass. I pounced again. It rolled again. It rolled to a flag on a long, thin stick. I couldn't see it any more.

I went to the long, thin stick. It was stuck in a hole. The white ball was down in the hole. I tried to get it out. I couldn't. I heard some voices over the hill. One of them was the Molecule's. I went away from the white ball in the hole. I went off the place of smooth grass. I lay down in a quick way.

The Molecule and the young man and the boys with the sticks tied to them came over the hill. I yawned. It's a good thing to yawn when you don't know what's going to happen.

The young man said, "One of us is on." He went to the white ball still on the place of smooth grass. He looked at the ball. He said, "Dear, dear, it's papa's own little private pill. Four syndicates, the last nine, and the match on this hole, Sweetheart, and we lie alike." He lay down on the smooth grass place. He said, "Give me air, men, I'm sinking fast."

The Molecule said, "Get up, you putrid mass of corruption. I've got to be close—I never hit a better shot."

The young man did not get up. He began to make noises. He said, "Fan me, caddy. Fan me until the end."

The Molecule said, "I'll fan you with a niblick, you lucky stiff. Where in hell is that ball, caddy?"

They all looked for the other white ball. They looked a long time. One of the boys with sticks said, "I guess you'll have to drop one, Mr. Trescott."

The Molecule said, "What would that get me, you myopic amoeba? This is what I'll drop!" He had a stick in his hand. He threw it over the top of the hill.

I ran over the hill. I looked for the stick. I couldn't find it. I looked some more. I found the stick in some long grass. I chewed it. Then I took it back to the Molecule.

When I got back the Molecule was lying on the place of smooth grass. He was making noises. The young man was looking in the hole. He was using language.

The Molecule said, "In the cup! In the cup! Tibo, darling, would you do me a favor?"

The young man used more language.

The Molecule said, "Just a little favor, Tibo. As my eyelids close for the last time, kiss me on the brow."

The young man threw his stick over the hill. I went and got it.

· XVII ·

A Wall Street Cough

December 28. The gray-haired man came last night. Flips gave him hugs and kisses.

Tile Molecule said, "Esteemed Sir and Guardian, I greet you." Aunt Caroline said, "Well, Frederick, what brings you here?"

The gray-haired man said, "Does a weekend with my wards call for an explanation?"

Aunt Caroline said, "Certainly not, but there generally is one."

The gray-haired man said, "Hmm!" He scratched me back of the ears. I like him. I like anyone who scratches back of the ears.

The gray-haired man looked at the Molecule. He said, "The authorities at Yale University shrink from attempting to impart further knowledge to you, it seems."

The Molecule made a groaning noise. He said, "I'm it! I saw it in his eye when he first came in."

The gray-haired man said, "While I hesitate at the thought of placing Wall Street at the mercy of a giant intellect, there will be an opening in our Bond Department February first."

The Molecule fell back in his chair. He said, "Oh, the horror of it!"

Aunt Caroline said, "You're quite right, Frederick; we'll talk it over later." She went to the dining room. The others went with her.

I found the gray-haired man's arctics in the vestibule. There is nothing like arctics to pass the time. Except rubbers. Rubbers are in a class by themselves.

December 29. The Molecule played the Hitting-White-Balls with-Sticks game today. He played it with a youngish man called Old Top. They pushed the little balls into holes with great care. The Molecule did all the talking. He kept talking about ohell and godamit.

The Molecule and Old Top went downstairs in the clubhouse. They took their clothes off. They let water come down from the ceiling on their heads.

The Molecule said, "Mother told me there would be days like this."

Old Top said, "Forget it. We all blow, now and then."

The Molecule said, "But why should such as you, with neither brains nor beauty, give me ten strokes and a beating?"

Old Top said, "I stay with it. Comes now the gentle snowflake and the running noses. While you're necking the steam radiator, I'm smacking 'em down the middle at Miami or Palm Beach."

The Molecule said, "You interest me strangely. If the worthy guardian and the esteemed aunt could understand the importance of breaking eighty, all would be jake. They now lean toward the marts of trade for little Egbert during the fast approaching season of chills and sneezes."

Old Top stopped the water running from the ceiling. He got a big towel. He began to rub himself with the towel. The Molecule stopped the water running from the ceiling. He got a towel. He began to rub himself.

Old Top said, "I have a thought."

The Molecule said, "Possible but not probable."

Old Top said, "Lung trouble!"

The Molecule said, "Lung trouble?"

Old Top said, "Lung trouble—with alarming symptoms." He looked at the Molecule.

The Molecule said, "Symptoms?" He looked at Old Top. He said, "My wonder man! Listen!" He made a coughing noise.

Old Top said, "Deeper and hoarser."

The Molecule made another coughing noise.

Old Top said, "Practice makes perfect." He picked up a glass. He said, "To your very bad health."

The Molecule picked up a glass. He said, "To a painless end."

They drank.

January 3. The Molecule is still making coughing noises. He does it whenever Aunt Caroline is there. He does it whenever Flips is there. It was like that today.

The Molecule was looking at a thing called a book. A book is something to chew, not to eat. People look at them. I don't know why.

Flips came in. The Molecule made a coughing noise. He made another coughing noise.

Flips sat in the Molecule's lap in a quick way. She put her arms around him. She said, "Oh, my darling, darling brother!"

The Molecule said, "Hey, look out! You've got a pin somewhere."

Flips said, "I haven't."

The Molecule said, "Would you mind taking your hair out of my face?"

Flips began to cry. She said, "I just can't bear it when you cough like that."

The Molecule said, "Don't be a pink ass."

Flips said, "I'm not. Whenever doctors talk about a warmer climate, it's terrible."

The Molecule said, "Take yourself off me, woman, and listen."

Flips went and sat in a chair.

The Molecule said, "First cross your heart."

Flips said, "I have — go ahead."

The Molecule made a coughing noise. He said, "Hear that voice from the tomb?"

Flips said, "Oh, don't, Bobby!"

The Molecule said, "Your ears deceive you, Countess. Notice the inflection on the last whoop? It's merely a Wall Street cough."

Flips said, "What are you driving at?"

The Molecule said, "Think of a word. The word is Bond Department. Think of Bond Department hard. That's enough — you'll be coughing yourself in a minute. Now think of Florida. Let your mind flow freely over Florida. Girls, golf, Gulf Stream. Note the instant improvement in the patient. Now do you get it? Listen." He made a coughing noise.

Flips said, "Robert Trescott!! Why, you nasty, dirty, deceiving thing! I'm going straight and tell Aunt Caroline!"

The Molecule said, "Not so fast, my proud beauty. Let me recall one little fact to what you call your mind — you crossed your heart."

Flips said, "But this is terrible!"

The Molecule said, "Again you are in error, Countess. List to me and keep on listing. Having journeyed to the land of warmth and promise, I shall take my pen in hand and write as follows, to wit:

"Dear Caroline, my health is swell, but, oh, the loneliness! I long for those near and dear to me. Gosh, how I long! Bring my fair sister,

Dumb Dora, down to my aching arms, and make it snappy. I remain, yours truly, Horace K. Fishball.'"

Flips got up from her chair in a quick way. She gave the Molecule hugs and kisses. She said, "Oh, Bobby, you promise?"

The Molecule said, "You have the word of a simple soldier."

Flips said, "Cross your heart?"

The Molecule said, "She's crossed."

Flips said, "If we all leave here, what about Trub?"

The Molecule said, "The child goes with me, Lady Cuthbert!"

Flips gave me hugs and kisses. She said, "Darling Trubsum Wubsum, we're all going to Florida. Isn't it too scrumptious?"

I gave her a chin-lick. I gave her some wiggles. I gave her some tail-wags. Flips started to dance. I started to bark. Aunt Caroline came in. The Molecule started to cough.

January 4. I saw Ginger today. He was sitting looking up into a tree. There was a cat in the tree. He said, "Hello, Kid!"

I said, "Hello." I sat down beside him. I said, "What's your plan?"

Ginger said, "Starve him out."

I said, "Old stuff. It never works."

Ginger said, "Some day it might."

We sat and looked up in the tree. We did it a long time.

I said, "Say, I'm going to Florida."

Ginger said, "Shut up!"

I said, "Why?"

Ginger said, "Keep your mind on your business."

We sat and looked up in the tree.

A man came out of a house. He picked up a stone.

Ginger said, "It's always like that!"

We went away from there.

I said, "Say, I'm going to Florida."

Ginger said, "Huh! I've been there."

I said, "What's it like?"

Ginner said, "Kid, it just misses being heaven."

I said, "Why?"

Ginger said, "The trees are so slick a cat can't climb 'em."

I said, "Why, that *is* heaven!"

Ginger said, "Nope!"

I said, "Why not?"

Ginger said, "There aren't any cats."

I don't think I want to go to Florida.

· XVIII ·

The Bone That Nobody Wanted

January 8. I am on my way to Florida. The Molecule is with me. We are on a boat. A boat is a thing for people to sit on in long chairs. There is water all around it. The water does not keep still. Neither does the boat.

I do not sit on the long chairs. Unless the Molecule is exercising me I stay in a room. There is a chain fastened to the side of the room. I am fastened to the chain. Disgusting!

There are other dogs in the room. Two of them. We can bark. We can growl. We can sleep. That is all. We can't touch noses to get acquainted. We can't play Wrestle, Wrestle. It is on account of the chains.

The other dogs are strange dogs. They are very thin dogs. Their faces are long. So are their legs. So are their tails. The Molecule calls them greyhounds.

One of the greyhounds is big. One is small. The small one is named Phantom. She told me so when the Molecule chained me in the room and went away.

I said, "My name is Trub. I am going to Florida."

Phantom said, "How fast can you run a quarter?"

I said, "Fast enough to catch it if it doesn't go up a tree."

The big greyhound laughed. He said, "Oh, I say, fancy a thing like that going to Florida."

I said, "I guess I've got as much right in Florida as you have."

The big greyhound said, "Do you happen to know who I am?"

I said, "I don't give a dead rat who you are!"

The big greyhound said, "Vulgar little beast!"

He yawned. He lay down. He went to sleep.

Phantom said, "You mustn't talk like that to him."

I said, "Why not?"

Phantom said, "That's imported Dashaway. He holds the world's record for three-sixteenths."

I said, "He gives me a pain in the neck."

Phantom said, "Hush—he might hear you. Don't you ever run?"

I said, "Sure. I run after cats. Do you like to chase cats?"

Phantom said, "Cats are too slow."

I said, "Slow! Quit your kidding."

Phantom said, "I only chase electric hares."

I said, "Never saw one. Where do you find 'em?"

Phantom said, "They go on a rail around the track."

I said, "Do they go up trees?"

Phantom said, "Of course not."

I said, "Me for them! Are there any in Florida?"

Phantom said, "Oh, my goodness!"

She lay down. She went to sleep.

I lay down. I went to sleep.

The Molecule woke me up. He came and unfastened the chain. He took me out of the little room. He took me up where I could see the water. People were sitting in the long chairs looking at the water.

The Molecule went to an empty chair. In the next chair was a girl. She had yellow hair. She was a nice-faced girl.

The Molecule sat down in the empty chair. He said, "Where is she now?"

The yellow-haired girl said, "Gone for a drink of water. What a darling pup!"

The Molecule said, "He's all of that—but, listen: is she your mother?"

The girl said, "Stepmother. I told her I'd met you before."

The Molecule said, "Certainly you have. Where was it?

The girl said, "At Edith Bramwell's."

The Molecule said, "Nice girl, Edith. Where does she live?"

The girl said, "Stamford, Connecticut."

T'he Molecule said, "Now it all comes back! Her father's a lawyer or something."

The girl said, "A doctor."

The Molecule said, "There you are—I knew it! Now, suppose we drift to a sheltered nook on the upper deck."

The girl said, "I wouldn't dare."

The Molecule said, "Well, how about a little dancing?"

The girl said, "She wouldn't stand for that either."

The Molecule said, "Not even dancing! At eight bells listen for a muffled shriek followed by a heavy splash. Splash will indicate that hero has pushed stepmother overboard."

The girl said, "She got seasick once. It was last year, going home. She stayed in bed all the way. I had a lovely trip. There was a man from—Here she comes!"

A fat lady sat down in a chair next to the girl. She gave me a look. It was not a kind look. She gave the Molecule a look. It was not a kind look.

The fat lady said, "Is that your dog, Young Man?"

The Molecule said, "Well, yes and no. As a matter of fact, he belongs to my aunt." He looked at the yellow-haired girl. He said, "You remember Aunt Caroline? She called on Edith's mother while you were there."

The fat lady said, "Edith's mother has been dead ten years."

The Molecule said, "Really? I didn't know. I don't know the family intimately."

The fat lady said, "I feel certain of that."

The Molecule said, "I remember, now—Aunt called in a professional way on the Doctor. It was about Trub here. He had something the matter with his stomach. He couldn't seem to keep a thing on his stomach. No matter what we fed him it would all—you know—come up."

The fat lady gave the Molecule a queer look. She opened and closed her eyes in a quick way. She said, "I am not interested in—"

The Molecule said, "We were awfully worried. We tried everything. We tried dog biscuits. We tried raw liver. We tried cooked liver. We tried milk. He'd eat it all. Oh, quantities. No use. In a few minutes it would all—come up."

The fat lady got up from her chair. She said, "I don't care to hear about your dog or his ailments. Come, Lucy!" She went away from there. The yellow-haired girl went with her.

January 9. We had bones with meat on them for breakfast. I ate mine. Phantom ate some of hers. The big greyhound only sniffed at his. It was the biggest bone of all.

I said, "Aren't you going to eat it?"

The big greyhound said, "How does that concern you?"

I said, "I just thought I'd ask."

The big greyhound lay down with his back to me. I watched the bone. I don't think I ever saw a better bone. There was a lot of meat on it. Some fat. Not too much. I like some fat on a bone. It helps the flavor.

The floor was not keeping still. First it would tip one way. Then the other. I thought, "If the floor tips enough, the bone might roll over here." It didn't.

The Molecule came for me. He said, "A bit of fresh air, Old Companion." He unfastened the chain from the wall. He started for the door. The floor gave a tip. I gave a pull. We went right over to where the bone was. I picked up the bone in a quiet way. I went away from there.

The big greyhound saw me going out with the bone. He jumped up. He pulled at his chain. He cursed and yelled. He said, "I'll get you for this, you dirty thief."

I didn't say anything. I couldn't, on account of the bone.

The Molecule took me to where the people were sitting in chairs. I looked at the water. The water was not keeping still. The boat was tipping and tipping. I couldn't walk in a straight way. Neither could the Molecule.

I was hoping the Molecule would sit in one of the long chairs. I wanted to lie down by the chair and eat the bone.

A funny thing happened. I began to think I didn't want the bone. I began to think so a lot. I didn't even want to carry the bone. I thought, "I am going to put this bone somewhere and go away from it."

We came to the place where the yellow-haired girl was. The fat lady was sitting in the chair beside her.

The Molecule said, "Good morning. Leaping from crag to crag a bit!"

The yellow-haired girl said, "I love it."

The fat lady didn't say anything. She just sat. She looked pale. She seemed worried about something.

I thought, "You don't want this bone. Why not do a kind act?" I did. I put the bone in the fat lady's lap.

I was surprised at what happened. The fat lady made a gurgling noise. She began to wave her hands in the air. She began to turn whiter. She got up from her chair in a quick way. She said, "Help me to get to my cabin!"

The yellow-haired girl put her arm around the fat lady. They went away from there. The Molecule picked up the bone. He threw it over into the water.

Nobody seemed to want that bone. I wonder why.

January 10. A sad thing has happened. Some one is going to die. I heard about it when the Molecule exercised me. He exercised me by standing looking at the water. He had his arm around the yellow-haired girl.

The Molecule said, "Do you think she'll get on deck today?"

The yellow-haired girl gave me a pat. She gave me a hug. She said, "When I went down just now she told me to go away and let her die."

I wonder what's become of the fat lady.

· XIX ·

A Dark Woman in a Dog's Life

January 15. Ginger was wrong. There are cats in Florida. The trees are slick, all right, but the cats *can* climb 'em.

I started to meet cats today. It was on account of the Molecule just sitting. I can't stand just sitting long.

The Molecule and I were walking along the beach. There were many people on the beach. Some were in the water. Most of them just sat.

I ran ahead of the Molecule. Then I ran back to him. Then I ran ahead again. Then I dug in the sand until he caught up to me.

I was running ahead of the Molecule. I saw a little child. The child was digging a hole in the sand. I thought, "I will help the child." I did.

I jumped into the hole and began to dig. The child opened its mouth. It began to make a loud noise. Some of the sand went in the child's mouth. The child stopped making the loud noise. It made a noise like barking.

The Molecule came in a quick way. He picked up the child. He hit it thumps on the back. I thought, "That'll teach it not to bark." But it didn't. The child kept on barking.

A girl came in a quick way. She grabbed the child from the Molecule. She put her finger in the child's mouth. She pulled sand out. The child stopped barking.

The Molecule said, "Awfully sorry. He's all right now, I think."

The child opened its mouth again. It began to make loud noises.

The girl said, "Hush, darling!"

The Molecule took out his watch. He said, "Listen to the tick-tick, Alphonso." He held the watch to the child's ear.

The child made loud noises.

T'he Molecule said, "Look at the nice doggy, Archibald! Listen to him! Speak, Trub!"

I barked. The child made loud noises.

The girl said, "Hush, darling! Where on earth is that nurse?"

The Molecule said, "Is there a nurse?"

The girl said, "There should be. She was here a moment ago."

The Molecule said, "If I could only find a policeman."

The girl said, "Why a policeman?"

The Molecule said, "The nurse would be talking to the policeman."

The girl said, "Oh, do hush, darling! Sometimes his father rides him on his back. Would you mind?"

The Molecule said, "Pleasure, I assure you. Want to go Pig-a-Back, Reginald?"

The child made loud noises.

The girl said, "Not Pig-a-Back; it's Whoa-Horsy—on your hands and knees."

The Molecule said, "Ah, he's in the Meadow Brook set!"

He got down on his hands and knees.

The girl held the child on the Molecule's back. The Molecule crawled around in the sand. He said, "Whoa-Horsy! Whoa-Horsy!"

The child made loud noises.

The girl said, "No use! Thanks a lot." She took the child from the Molecule's back. The Molecule stood up. He brushed the sand from his knees. He said, "May I make a quaint, old-fashioned suggestion, Madam?"

The girl said, "What is it?"

The Molecule said, "Spanky-spank!"

The girl said, "I'd have done it long ago if he were mine. I'm only his aunt."

The Molecule said, "Only his aunt! The sky brightens!"

The girl gave the child a shake. She said, "Stop this instantly—do you hear me?"

The child made loud noises.

A woman came in a quick way. She had on a white dress. She had on a white cap. She took the child from the girl. She said, "It's sorry, I am, Miss Eunice. Has he been this way long?"

The girl said, "Hours and hours, Maggie!"

The woman said, "'Tis not over ten minutes. I was exchanging the time of day with the lifeguard." She took the child away from there.

The Molecule said, "Lifeguard! I never thought! Stupid of me."

The girl laughed. She said, "I must run along too."

The Molecule said, "After what we've been through together?"

The girl said, "Oh, but I must!" She sat down on the sand.

The Molecule said, "Of course you must." He sat down on the sand. He said, "The subject of the meeting will be, 'Tiny Tots and When to Soak 'Em.'"

The Molecule and the girl just sat and talked. I dug a hole. I took a nap. I chased waves. I scratched. I yawned. I had an idea. It came to me suddenly.

Cats!

I went away from there.

I went along the beach. Then I went into the yards of the houses along the beach. Nothing happened. I thought, "Ginger was right. They don't have cats here."

A dog saw me passing through his yard. He was a police dog. He rushed at me, yelling. He yelled, "Get the hell out of here, you dirty bum!"

I stopped. The police dog stopped. I said, "Are you addressing me?"

The police dog didn't say anything.

I walked up to him. I put my face close to his.

The police dog backed away. He said, "I thought you were another guy."

"I said, "You're sure of that?"

The police dog said, "Absolutelyl Make yourself at home."

I said, "I was looking for something, but there aren't any."

The police dog said, "Aren't any what?"

I said, "Cats. They don't have them in Florida."

The police dog said, "How do you get that way?"

I said, "Ginger told me."

The police dog said, "Who's Ginger?"

I said, "A friend of mine."

The police dog said, "He's full of prunes."

I looked at the police dog. I said, "I said he was a friend of mine."

The police dog said, "I'll bet he's a good scout. But, listen—Do you see that green house down there?"

I said, "Yep."

The police dog said, "Go on down there and look around, and listen—keep an eye out for a dark woman."

I said, "All right. Want to come along?"

The police dog said, "Not me."

I went to the green house. There was a sign in front of it. It said, "White Angoras for Sale." I went in the yard. A window was open on the front porch. A cat was sitting in the window. It was asleep.

I went up the steps of the porch in a quiet way. No use. You can't walk up to a sleeping cat. The cat put up its back. It swelled up its tail. It jumped off the window sill into the house. I jumped over the window sill after the cat.

I was in a room of the house. In the room were two oldish ladies and cats. I had never seen so many cats. I thought, "I'll never make Ginger believe this!"

The oldish ladies were sitting in chairs. They were looking at books. The cats were lying around the room. They were sleeping. It was a quiet scene. But not for long.

The oldish ladies stopped looking at books. They began to scream. Cats began to go in every direction. They went up the backs of chairs. They went up the curtains. They went round and round the room. Everywhere I looked was a going cat. I thought, "This is the life!" But it wasn't. You can't chase ten or twelve cats at once.

I had an idea. It came to me in a quick way. The idea was — "Pick a cat!" I did.

The cat I picked went under a table. I went under the table. The table fell down.

I picked another cat. He went behind a stand-up thing for lights. The stand-up thing fell down. It fell on me. A round thing of paper went over my head.

I picked another cat. He went under one of the oldish ladies. I went under the oldish lady. The oldish lady fell down.

A dark woman came running. She was a big dark woman. She had a mop with her. She said, "Miss Ida, Miss Julia, for Lawd's sake git out of here! Gimme room to knock him cockeyed!"

The dark woman hit at me with the mop handle. I dodged. I thought, "I guess I'll go now." I did.

I went through the window. I went a long way from the green house. I don't think I'll go back there. Too many cats. It's confusing.

I started back to where the Molecule was. I came to a pink house with a wall around it. In the wall was a gate. I looked through the gate. One cat! It was a yellow cat. I went in the yard in a quick way.

The cat went for a tree. I hoped it was a slick tree. It was. I thought, "This is a great country!"

I was surprised at what happened. The cat went right up the slick tree. I could hardly believe it. I sat down to think. I looked at the slick tree. It was a funny tree. There was nothing on the sides of the tree but the cat. At the top of the tree were some big brown balls. I thought, "Nothing for him to sit on—I'll wait." I did.

A little girl was playing in some sand. She went to a window in the house. She said, "Daddy, a nasty dog has chased Pussy up the coconut tree."

A man came to the window. He said, "Where is the dog now?"

The little girl said, "He's sitting under the tree looking up at Pussy."

The man said, "Is he right under the tree?"

The little girl said, "Yes, Daddy, just ezackly under."

The man said, "Good."

The little girl said, "Why is it good, Daddy?"

The man said, "Wait and see."

We waited.

Suddenly something happened. It was a sort of thud. Everywhere I looked were stars. I couldn't see the tree. I couldn't see the cat. I could just see stars.

I found I was lying on the ground. One of the brown balls was on the ground beside me. I wondered how it got there.

I got to my feet. I couldn't see the little girl, but I could hear her. She was saying, "Goody-goody-goody!"

I went away from there.

· XX ·

Pertaining to a Bone

February 3. We are still in Florida. I do not like it here. The Molecule just sits. He sits on the beach in the sun. He does it with a girl called Eunice. He holds the girl called Eunice by the hand.

He was doing it today. He did it a long time. I began to get sleepy. I thought, "Better dig a hole." But I didn't. I just blinked and looked at the ocean.

A man came along the beach. He was a little man. A woman was with him. She was a big woman. A dog was with them. He was a little dog. He was all curly.

The little curly dog ran up to me. He said, "Want to fight?"

The big woman screamed. She said, "Look out, Pop! He's going to start another!"

I yawned. I said, "Nopel"

The little man said, "It's all right. They're not going to fight. Sit down and take a load off your feet."

The little man and the big woman sat down on the beach. The little curly dog said, "It's lucky for you you don't want to fight."

I said, "Why?"

The little curly dog said, "I can whip my weight in wildcats."

I said, "Yeh? How do you know?"

The little curly dog said, "Pop says so. Sure you don't want to fight?"

I yawned. I blinked. I said, "I'd sooner go to sleep." I started to do it.

The little curly dog said, "Gosh, I'm a terrible fighter!"

I said, "Yeh?"

The little curly dog said, "Pop calls me Jack Dempsey."

I said, "Yeh?"

The little curly dog said, "My real name is Wiggles. Mom gave it to me. I belong to Mom. Pop's dogs are all long dogs. That's why we're here. We're here so the long dogs can run."

I said, "Yes? Why do they have to come here to run?"

The little curly dog said, "They chase electric hares. The tracks are all here. It's a duinb business. I'd rather fight."

I said, "I heard about that on the boat coming down. There was a long dog on the boat. I took his bone."

The little curly dog said, "Well, I'll be a Mexican hairless! So you're the guy that took that bone?"

I said, "How did you hear about it?"

The little curly dog said, "That was Dashaway's bone. He's one of Pop's dogs. He's talked about it ever since."

I said, "Let him talk."

The little curly dog said, "You've said it. Gosh, but he hates himself. If you meet him and I'm there don't worry. I'll take care of the big stiff. I'll—look what's coming! Now you're going to see something! I'm going to show you how to fight!"

A dog was running down the beach. It was a police dog. It was the police dog that told me to get out of his yard on the day of many cats.

The little curly dog ran at the police dog in a quick way. He yelled, "Get off this beach or fight."

The police dog said, "Why you piece of dandruff! You cross between a diseased flea and a mangy mouse!"

The little curly dog flew at the police dog. The police dog picked him up and began to shake him. The big woman began to scream. The little man began to shout.

I wasn't sleepy any more. Things began to get red. They got redder. The next thing I knew I had the police dog down in the sand. I had hold of his neck.

The big woman snatched up the little curly dog, and held him in her arms. He began to wriggle and yell. He yelled, "Give him hell, Whitey! Oh, for the love of the trees, let me get in it!"

The Molecule came in a quick way. So did the little man. The Molecule got me by the collar. He said, "Will you be good enough to take hold of the other dog and pull a little?"

The little man said, "Sure, I know. I used to raise that kind myself." He took hold of the police dog. He pulled. The Molecule pulled on me. I tried to get a better grip. The Molecule gave a quick pull. I lost most of the grip I had. I tried again. The Molecule gave another quick pull. I gave a quick grab. Too late! All I got was hair.

The little man swung the police dog away from me. He set him on the beach. The police dog went away from there. He seemed to be in a hurry.

The big woman came and gave me a pat. She said, "Thank the nice bulldog for saving you, Precious." She put the little curly dog down beside me on the beach.

The little curly dog stopped yelling. He said, "What did you butt in for, Whitey?" He made a rush at me.

The little man grabbed him and gave him to the big woman. He said, "Can you beat that? Take him home, Mom, and keep him there."

February 6. The Molecule and the girl called Eunice were sitting on the beach again today. The little man came along the beach.

The Molecule said, "Good morning, where's the pup?"

The little man said, "I couldn't talk Mom into leaving him home, so they're both at the cottage. Speaking of dogs, do you ever bet on them?"

The Molecule said, "Once. Just once."

The little man laughed. He said, "Well now, that's my business. I've got a string of dogs down here and one of them starts this afternoon. I wouldn't tell many people, but I'm telling you—you could tie the kitchen stove to him and he'd still win."

The girl called Eunice said, "Oh, Bobby, let's!"

The Molecule said, "Let's what, Sugar?"

The girl called Eunice said, "Bet on the gentleman's dog."

The Molecule said, "What makes you think your dog will win?"

The little man said, "This is an imported dog. He can beat anything in the world at three-sixteenths. I started him once down here in a long race when he was just off the boat. He stopped to a walk. He runs his distance this afternoon and he's right. The bad race will make the price right, too. Now you do just as you like, but I'm telling you."

The girl called Eunice said, "Imagine that! It's too wonderful!"

The Molecule said, "Listen, Saccharine, I spent one day at the dog track. Having wired home for financial assistance that night I swore a dreadful oath as follows, to wit, 'No, not any more.'"

The girl called Eunice said, "But this is different. If you don't want to do it I will."

The little man said, "Is this lady your wife?"

The Molecule said, "Not yet."

The little man said, "Well, what she says is right. This is different. If you go out and bet 'em blind you haven't a chance. If you go out there this afternoon don't bet a nickel on anything else. Wait for the one race, play it, and come home."

The girl called Eunice said, "Thanks a lot. We'll do it just that way. What's the name of your dog?"

The little man said, "Dashaway. Third race. See you at the track."

The girl called Eunice got up from the beach. She said, "Come on, Bobby!"

The Molecule said, "Come on where?"

The girl called Eunice said, "We must have lunch and get money, and I'm too excited to sit still anyway! How much do you think we'll win? I've got fifty dollars at home and I'll get more at the bank. How much are you going, to bet? We'll take Trub, the lamb. He's responsible for everything. The man wouldn't have told except for Trub saving his funny dog. Oh, Trub, you're just a darling. Bobby, for heaven's sake, why do you sit there like a great lump?"

The Molecule got up from the beach. He said, "Allow me to make a modest suggestion, Fair Lady."

The girl called Eunice said, "What is it?"

The Molecule said, "Keep your shirt on." He looked at me. He said, "Guilty as charged, Your Honor, but I was led astray." He went away from there. I went with him. So did the girl called Eunice.

We went to a place on the beach. The place had chairs and tables. We had things to eat. We had bread and butter and cold chicken, and things called avocados, and ice cream. Delicious! Except the avocados. They were terrible!

We drove in a motor car. We stopped at a place called The Bank. I didn't go in. They wouldn't let me. I sat in the motor car.

A dog came by. He started to smell the wheel of the motor car.

I said, "Here! Cut that out!"

The dog stopped smelling. He looked at me. He said, "Holding down the seat, are you, Useless?"

He went on down the street. He stopped at a lamppost.

I thought, "The idea!"

The Molecule and the girl called Eunice came out of The Bank. We rode some more in the motor car. We came to a place of many people. There was a round road with white fences. The many people were sitting in a big house with only a roof and standing along the white fences.

We went to a square hole in a wall. It was under the house with only a roof. A man was looking through the hole.

The Molecule said, "Dashaway to win." He gave the man something.

The man gave something to the Molecule.

We went to the round road with white fences. The Molecule and the girl called Eunice looked at the round road. Nothing happened. They kept on looking at the round road. I wondered why.

There was a tooting noise. The Molecule said, "Hark to the well-known bugle. It won't be long now."

The girl called Eunice said, "I don't see how you can be so calm. I'm shaking in every limb!"

The Molecule said, "Limb? How Victorian! Here they come! He's number seven."

The girl called Eunice said, "Trub must see too. Here, Darling, see the racing dogs!" She picked me up. She held me on top of the fence.

I looked over into the round road. Men were walking along it. They had on white coats. Each man led a dog on a strap. They were long dogs like the ones on the boat.

The men and dogs came along the round road to where we were standing. I yelled at the long dogs. I yelled, "Hello, Boys! What's going on?"

The long dogs looked at me. The third one in the line stopped. He said, "You!" It was the dog whose bone I took on the boat.

I said, "Yep, it's me."

The long dog whose bone I took started for the fence. He said, "Why, you dirty bone snatcher, I'll— " The man who held him pulled him back by the strap. He pulled him into the line. He began to pull him along with the others.

The dog whose bone I took kept looking back at me. He kept yelling remarks. I shall not repeat the remarks he yelled. I yelled a few myself. I yelled them until he was out of hearing.

I was surprised at what happened next. A cat came out on the round road. It was a long-eared cat.

I thought, "Fences on both sides. Not a tree in sight. Pretty soft." I tried to jump down into the round road. The girl called Eunice held me by the collar. The long-eared cat began to make a funny noise. It began to make a noise like a motor car. It began to run. I didn't try to get down into the round road any more. There was no use. I just watched that long-eared cat run. I yelled right out. I yelled, "He don't need trees! Merciful dogcatchers, look at him go!"

The long-eared cat went all the way around the round road. It was all alone. Suddenly it wasn't. Suddenly a lot of long dogs were after it. I thought, "Not a chance!" But there was.

I've always thought I could run. I never knew what running was. The long dogs went as fast as the long-eared cat. They made me dizzy.

There was one long dog ahead of the others. The farther they went the farther ahead he was. The many people were making noises. I never heard so many peoples' noises. It was deafening.

The girl called Eunice was screaming. She was screaming, "Dashaway's in front! Dashaway's in front!" right in my ear. I never saw anyone so excited.

I was excited myself. I got more excited when the long-eared cat came down our side of the round road. Just behind the long-eared cat was the long dog whose bone I took. He was much nearer the long-eared cat than the other dogs. I forgot all about taking his bone. I forgot all the remarks he had made to me. I leaned out over the fence. I yelled, "Catch him, Big Boy!"

The dog whose bone I took did a funny thing. He tried to stop. He couldn't. He slid along with his feet together for a long way. The other dogs kept after the long-eared cat.

The girl called Eunice made a groaning sound. She went all limp. She let go of my collar.

The long dog whose bone I took stopped sliding. He came back to me. He said, "Now, you bone-stealing worm, get down on this track!"

I jumped down on the round road. I said, "Here I am, you long-legged, sour-bellied stiff!"

Men grabbed the long dog. The Molecule jumped over the fence and grabbed me. We went away from there. The girl called Eunice went with us. The Molecule said, "Good old Western Union!"

The girl called Eunice didn't say anything.

February 7. The Molecule is not pleased with me. I give him tail-wags. I give him wiggles. I give him paw-pokes. He says I give him a pain in the neck. I wonder why.

· XXI ·

Rat-Catchin'Fool

May 15. Home again from Florida. Glad of it. Guess who I've seen? Ginger! I was out looking for cats all by myself. I went in a yard. Ginger. was sitting by a shed. He was looking at a hole that went under the shed.

I said, "Hello."

Ginger kept on looking at the hole. He said, "Listen, whoever you are, just slide on by."

I said, "What for?"

Ginger kept on looking at the hole. He said, "Never mind what for; hit the grit."

I said, "I thought we were friends, but I guess I was wrong."

Ginger took his eye from the hole in a quick way. He gave me one look. He looked right back at the hole. He said, "It's the game-playin' kid! Didn't recognize you! Thought it was some nosey bozo tryin' to horn in."

I said, "Horn in on what?"

Ginger said, "Horn in on this hole."

I said, "What's in the hole?"

Ginger said, "The godamdest rat you ever saw!"

I said, "I never saw a rat."

Ginger said, "Well, anyway, you're in."

I said, "In what?"

Ginger said, "In on the rat."

I said, "All right—what do I do?"

Ginger said, "Watch the hole."

I said, "I'm watching it now."

Ginger said, "Atta kid, keep on watchin' it."

I watched the hole. Ginger watched the hole. We did it for a long time. Nothing happened.

I said, "I don't see anything to this."

Ginger said, "You wait."

I said, "For what?"

Ginger said, "For the rat, you poor simp."

I said, "Where is the rat now?"

Ginger said, "In the hole; but he'll come out."

I said, "When?"

Ginger said, "How the hell do I know?"

I said, "Maybe he won't come out."

Ginger said, "He's gotta eat, ain't he?"

I said, "Maybe he has, but so have I—I'm hungry right now."

Ginger said, "You're always hungry. Shut up and watch the hole."

I watched the hole. Ginger watched the hole. We did it a longer time than before. Nothing happened.

I said, "Listen, I've got an idea."

Ginger said, "Shoot!"

I said, "Let's dig in the hole 'til we come to the rat."

Ginger said, "No use; I've done it before."

I said, "With two of us digging, you'll be surprised."

Ginger looked at me. He looked at the hole. He said, "Well, it can't hurt to try—let's go!"

We started digging. We dug and dug. I got dirt in my eyes. I got dirt in my mouth. I looked at Ginger. I had to laugh.

He said, "What's funny?"

I said, "Your face—it's the dirtiest thing I ever saw."

Ginger looked at me. He said, "My face? Listen, your map makes a coal hole look like a snow bank." He stopped digging. He sat and panted.

I said, "What are you stopping for?"

Ginger said, "I'm through."

I stopped digging. I said. "Why?"

Ginger said, "We've dug our paws off and we haven't got anywhere. Lemme think."

I sat and panted. Ginger sat and panted. He thought. I waited.

Ginger said, "Maybe we can scare him out."

I said, "How?"

Ginger said, "Bark—both together—what do you say?"

I said, "Suits me—here goes."

I barked. Ginger barked. He kept on barking.

A man came around the shed. He was a black man. He had white teeth. I liked him.

The black man said, "What you got, boys?"

Ginger whined. He looked at the hole. He barked. I barked.

The black man said, "Rats, huh?"

Ginger barked. I barked.

The black man went over to the fence. He said, "Hey, Eeph!"

Another black man stuck his head over the fence. He said, "What you want?"

The first black man said. "Jessup's dawg wid a hole-up rat—lemme have 'at fer't 'bout a minute."

The other black man said, "I ain' goin' loan you no fer't."

The first black man said, "Come on, Eeph, git lib'ril."

The other black man said, "Not me—you lose 'at fer't, maybe, an' den whar is I at?"

The first black man said, "Fetch de fer't ovah heah an' op'rate him yo'self, den."

The other black man said, "I ain' got no time fo' rat catchin'. I'se got two rows-a tomatoes to set out."

The first black man said, "Listen, Eeph, heah's a ten-case note. You han' de fer't ovah de fence. When I han's him back, safe an' soun', you slips me back de ten."

The second man said, "Han' me 'at ten, boy—I'll get de fer't!"

I was still barking. Ginger had stopped. He said, "Lay off the noise, Kid, now you're gonna see somethin'."

I said, "What?"

Ginger said, "Never mind what—just stick around."

The black man came back to the hole. He had something in a bag. It was alive. I could see the bag wiggling. He put the something in the hole. It went down the hole.

I said, "What's the idea?"

Ginger said, "You'll know in a minute—work fast when they come."

A gray thing with a long pink tail ran from under the shed. It ran in a quick way. The black man said, "Howdy, Mistuh Rat—catch 'im, dawgs!"

I didn't know anything could move in such a quick way as Ginger did. It was so quick you couldn't see him. He said, "Yip, yip," and then he wasn't where he had been. He was where the rat was. The rat went up in the air. While it was still in the air Ginger was back at the shed. When the rat came down it didn't move any more.

The black man said, "'At's work, boy—git movin', bulldawg."

Another rat came from under the shed. I started for the rat. When I got to where the rat was it wasn't moving any more. Ginger had been there and was back at the shed.

The black man said, "'At bulldawg's standin' in molasses, Ginguh."

I said, "How do you do it so quick?"

Ginger said, "It's, a gift."

I said, "Aw, listen, let me catch one."

Ginger said, "You couldn't catch a cold at the north pole!"

A rat came from under the shed. Another rat came. Many rats came. They went in all directions. I didn't get a single one. It was on account of Ginger. The air seemed full of rats. All I did was sniff them when they came down.

I said, "I call this a dirty trick." I saw a rat. I started for it in a quick way.

Ginger was after another rat. He said, "What's on"—he put a rat in the air—"your mind"—he put my rat in the air—"Kid?"

I said, "That's what I mean—that was my rat."

Ginger said, "These are"—he put a rat in the air—"free rats"—he put another rat in the air—"help yourself"—he put another rat in the air—"Kid."

The black man said, "A rat-catchin' fool, 'at's what I mean. G'wan home, bulldawg"

I sat down and thought. Ginger kept putting rats in the air. I had an idea. I went close to the shed. I put my nose under the shed. I waited right there for a rat. When it came it was a big one. It was a yellow rat. It had a bushy tail. It was not moving in so quick a way as the other rats. I reached under the shed. I got the bushy-tailed rat. I pulled it out from under the shed. I gave it a shake. I put it in the air. When it came down it lay still.

Ginger yelled, "Beat it, Kid!" He started to run.

I started to run with Ginger. I didn't know why we were running. I said, "Don't let's go yet—I just got a big one."

Ginger kept on running. He said, "You got a big one, all right—you got the ferret!"

· XXII ·

The Eternal Feminine

May 18. A terrible thing nearly happened. I nearly saw red with Ginger. It would have been the end of our friendship. It's a lucky thing the Airedale came along.

I met Ginger in the road. It was in front of my house. He said, "Hello, Kid, what's on your mind?"

I said, "Rats or cats. I don't care which."

Ginger said, "It's out. I've got a date with the girlfriend."

I said, "What's a girlfriend?"

Ginger gave me a look. He said, "Well, I'll be a—Didn't you ever have a girlfriend?"

I said, "Not that I remember."

Ginger began to grin. He said, "Not that you remember.." He grinned some more. He said, "Listen, Kid, if you ever get mixed up with a broad you'll remember. Come on, I'll let you give this one the once over."

Ginger started up the road, I went with him. He went in a yard. There was a brick house in the yard. There was a dog looking out of the window of the brick house. It was a wire-haired fox terrier like Ginger.

Ginger said, "There she is. She sees me. She'll be out in a minute."

I said, "How do you know?"

Ginger said, "How do I know? Say, this frail falls for me like porterhouse steak. She don't notice fleas when I'm around."

Ginger sat down in the grass. I sat down in the grass. We waited. We waited a long time. Nothing happened.

I said, "Let's make it cats."

Ginger said, "Sit still. Sit still. This don't mean a thing."

I said, "I'm tired of waiting."

Ginger said, "Lemme put you wise, Kid. You'll do a lot of waiting at this game."

I said, "Why?"

Ginger said, "Frails always stall. No matter how cuckoo they are about you they make you wait."

I said, "What for?"

Ginger said, "Nobody knows. It's just the way they are."

I said, "What if you don't wait?"

Ginger said, "You'll wait, all right. Here she is now."

The fox terrier that had been in the window came out of the back door of the house. It was a girl fox terrier. She had a spot over one eye. She had a short, stick-up tail. She didn't seem to see us.

Ginger said, "Hello, Trix. Thought I'd drop over."

The girl fox terrier gave a little jump. She said, "Goodness, how you startled me. I didn't know you were within a mile of here."

Ginger said, "Tie that outside and touch noses with my friend, Trub Trescott. Kid, meet the red-hot mamma, Miss Trixie Warner."

Miss Trixie said, "Charmed, I'm sure, Mr. Trub." We touched noses.

I was surprised at what happened. I had the funniest feeling. It went all through me. It was a nice feeling.

I said, "Let's do it again."

Miss Trixie said, "You work fast, don't you?"

I said, "No, I'd rather do it slowly."

Miss Trixie said, "Go on, you probably say that to everyone you meet."

I said, "I never said that to anyone before — did I, Ginger?"

Ginger said, "How the hell do I know what you say? Listen, I thought you never chased a frail."

I said, "What do you mean, chased a frail?"

Ginger said, "I should tell you what I mean. I didn't bring you up here to shoot your line. Save it for your own frails. Get me?"

I said, "Save what?"

Ginger said, "Now don't you try to kid me. It's all right. I'm not sore, understand, but don't try to kid me."

I said, "I'm not trying to kid you. What's the matter with you, anyway?"

Miss Trixie said, "He's like that half the time. Don't let it worry you, Mr. Trub."

I said, "Never mind the Mister. Call me Trub."

Miss Trixie said, "All right, Trub, and you can call me Trix. I'll bet you can't catch me."

I said, "Trix! Say, I like your name. I like it a lot. I'll bet I can catch you."

Trixie started around the house in a quick way. I ran after her. She ran across the lawn. She ran out in the road. Whenever I nearly caught her she dodged. At last she didn't dodge. I caught her. I played Wrestle, Wrestle with her, and Fun-Bite-the-Neck. I liked it. I was surprised how much I liked it.

Trixie said, "My, but you're strong. You're the strongest thing I ever saw."

I said, "I must tell you something. I would rather play with you than with anyone."

Ginger came out of the gate. He came out in the road to where we were.

Trixie said, "He's the strongest thing, Ginger. I'm perfectly helpless with him."

Ginger said, "Oh, is that so?" He walked up to me. He curled back his lip. He snapped his teeth. He said, "Give yourself the air, and do it quick." He pushed me with his shoulder.

Everything began to get red. I didn't know why. I noticed Ginger's neck. I noticed his throat just above the collar. I tried to look away. I couldn't. I couldn't look away from Ginger's throat just above the collar.

Trixie gave a yelp. She said, "Look out. Look out. Here comes Rowdy." She ran into the yard. Ginger ran into the yard. I was surprised.

I was more surprised right after that. Something ran into me. It knocked me down. When I got on my feet there was a dog. He was an Airedale. He was a big Airedale. His eyes were green, with red lights in them.

I heard a lady scream. She screamed, "Rowdy, Rowdy, come here, Rowdy."

The Airedale said, "I'm going to kill you, you white louse."

I didn't say anything. I can't make a sound when things turn as red as they did then. I just hear a Voice. It comes from inside of me somewhere. It says, "Hold on and shake. Hold on and shake." It keeps on saying it. I don't know why. I only know I must do what the Voice says.

I did what the Voice said after the Airedale jumped on me again. We rolled over and over. When we stopped rolling I remembered the place I had noticed above Ginger's collar. I found the same place above the Airedale's collar. Then the Voice began.

The Airedale had been making snarling noises. He began to make choking noises. Very choking noises.

People came. Many people. They yelled and screamed. They kicked me. They hit me with sticks. I didn't feel it. You don't feel anything when you're listening to the Voice.

A man rode up on a thing with wheels. It made a noise like an automobile, only louder.

Another man said, "Here's a motor cop. You'll have to shoot the bulldog, officer."

The man got off the thing with wheels. He came through the people. He stood beside me. He said, "Shoot nothin'. And he's not a bulldog."

The other man said, "He's killing the Trent dog."

The man who had come on the thing with wheels said, "And a damn good riddance if you ask me." He took hold of me by the shoulders. He lifted me off the ground. He said, "Now someone take hold of the big hairy mutt like I've got this one. That's it. Now we'll give a bit of pull on them till the terrier tries for a better hold. Now—whisk! That's it. Now again. Whisk! There's your dog, Mrs. Trent—what's left of him. He jumped on the wrong one this day."

A lady took the Airedale and went away from there. Most of the other people went away from there. The man who had come on the thing with wheels didn't. He held me by the collar. He rubbed me back of the ears. He rubbed me along the back. He said, "Cool down, young fellah, it's all over." He rubbed me a long time. He rubbed me until things weren't red any more. I gave him a hand-lick and a chin-lick. I liked him.

Trixie came out in the road. So did Ginger.

Trixie said, "Oh, Trub, you were wonderful! Wasn't he wonderful, Ginger?"

Ginger said, "Listen, Kid, if you happen to take a fancy to any frail of mine, hop to it."

I was glad things weren't red any more. I was glad to be friends with Ginger. I wonder what made him get so cross—I was very nice to his girlfriend.

· XXIII ·

A Fortune-Teller's Misfortune

June 3. The Molecule and I have made a new game. It is called Hang-on-and-Swing. You play it with a piece of cloth. The Molecule holds the piece of cloth over his shoulder. I grab it. He pulls me off the ground. I walk up his back. He goes round and round. I swing out in the air. It is fun.

We had been playing the new game. We were playing it in the garden. The Molecule stopped playing. He went to the garage. He got in an automobile. I asked to go with him. I did it with tail-wags and wiggles.

The Molecule said, "Sorry, Old Companion. You're out of the picture." He went away from there.

I went back to the garage. The shofer was squirting water on an automobile with a hose. I wondered if he would play Hang-on-and-Swing with me. I grabbed the hose. He didn't. He turned the water right in my face. I went away from there.

I laid down in the sun to take a nap. Before I could start taking a nap I saw a big blue fly. I snapped at it. It got away. I began to snap at other flies. Some got away. Some didn't. The biggest fly of all came along. It was black with yellow stripes. It made a humming sound. I snapped at it. It didn't get away. I wish it had. It was like the time I picked up the red thing that jumped out of the living-room fire, only worse.

Sometimes the Molecule says, "Live and learn, Old Companion."

He said it when I picked up the red thing out of the fire.

Well, I've learned that there are hot flies. Very. This one made my mouth burn and burn. I couldn't rub it with my paw. I thought of the nice, cool water coming out of the hose. I went to the garage in a quick way. I drank some of the water running on the floor. My mouth felt better, but not much. I wonder why some flies are hot. I wonder how you can tell the hot ones from the other kind.

Flips was in the garage. She was talking to the shofer. She said, "Guess what? Ted Martin is back from St. Paul's!"

The shofer went on squirting water out of a hose.

Flips said, "I suppose he'll be over here a lot."

The shofer went on squirting water out of a hose.

Flips said, "He gave me a frightful rush Easter vacation."

The shofer went on squirting water out of a hose.

Flips said, "He's not afraid of anything."

The shofer said, "Is that so?"

Flips said, "Yes, and you are."

The shofer said, "Is that so?"

Flips said, "You're afraid of Aunt Caroline."

The shofer put the hose down on the floor. He walked over to Flips. He said, "Listen, you're a nice kid, but you're a nut. You're a bug on this love stuff. You'll get over it. In a couple of years you wouldn't look at me no more'n if I was transmission grease. If this Martin kid has fell for you, fly at it. They can't fire him without a reference."

Flips put her arm through the shofer's. She said, "I'll never get over you, Bill. Never. You're my first, last, and only love. I was just kidding you about Ted! He hasn't really..."

Flips stopped talking. She stepped away from the shofer. A woman came to the garage door. She was a queer woman. She had a yellow face. She wore a red cloth around her head. She had a yellow cloth around her neck. The ends of the yellow cloth hung down to her waist. She was carrying a basket. It was a round basket with a cover. I wondered what was in the basket.

The queer woman said, "Good day to you, my Pretty."

Flips said, "Oh, gosh; she's a gypsy."

I went to the queer woman. I smelled her basket. There was something to eat in the basket. I couldn't tell what.

The queer woman said, "I fear dogs. Will this one harm me?"

Flips said, "Goodness, no. He's just a lamb."

The queer woman said, "If you would know the future, cross my palm with silver."

Flips said, "You mean tell my fortune?"

The queer woman said, "Yes, my Pretty."

Flips said, "Lend me a quarter, Bill."

The queer woman said, "A borrowed coin brings no luck."

Flips said, "I have some money in my room. I'll get it."

The queer woman said, "I will go with you. If I can touch your pillow with my fingers your dreams will help me."

Flips and the queer woman went in the house. I went with them. Going upstairs I smelled the basket. I said, " I think it's ham, but I'm not certain."

We went in Flips' room. Flips gave something to the queer woman. The queer woman said, "Do you want a full reading, my Pretty?"

Flips said, "What do you mean, full reading?"

The queer woman said, "Everything the future holds for you?"

Flips said, "Gosh, yes."

The queer woman said, "Then I must have a cup of tea."

Flips said, "I know why; you look at the tea leaves in the cup.

The queer woman said, "Yes, my Pretty."

Flips said, "All right; I'll get it."

The queer woman said, "Take the white dog with you; he frightens me, my Pretty."

Flips laughed. She gave me a hug. She said, "He's just a precious pupsums that wouldn't hurt a fly." She went away from there.

I stayed with the queer woman. I smelled the basket again. I said, "Yes, it's ham or maybe bacon."

The queer woman went out of Flips' room. She took the basket with her. I went along. We went in Aunt Caroline's room. I hoped the queer woman would put down the basket. She didn't. She stood in front of the thing you can see yourself in.

The queer woman went back in Flips' room. Flips came in with something in a cup. The queer woman looked in the cup. She talked a long time. She talked about light men and dark men. I looked at the basket.

The queer woman stopped talking about light men and dark men. She and Flips went downstairs. I went with them. They went to the side door.

The queer woman said, "Power and riches are dust and ashes. Follow your heart, my Pretty. And now, farewell."

Flips said, "Good-bye; thanks a lot."

The queer woman went outside. She still had the basket. I went with her. She started for the gate. I thought I would give the basket one more smell. The queer woman took hold of the cloth that was around her neck. She said, "Shoo!" She waved the cloth in my face.

I was surprised. I hadn't thought of playing Hang-on-and-Swing with the queer woman. I didn't know she knew the game. I grabbed the cloth. I was surprised again. It was on account of the queer way the woman screamed. I tried to walk up her back. I couldn't. She kept turning around too fast. And screaming. I have never heard anyone scream so much.

Saki came in a quick way. Flips came in a quick way. Aunt Caroline came in a quick way.

Aunt Caroline began to scream, too. She said, "Oh, the poor thing! Get hold of him, Saki."

Saki tried to take me by the collar. He couldn't on account of the queer woman turning round and round. She kept on turning round and round until she fell down. The Molecule never falls down when he plays the game. I wish he would. You land all in a heap. It's fun.

Guess what happened when the queer woman fell down! She dropped the basket! The cover came off. Things fell out of the basket.

Aunt Caroline was helping the queer woman up. She said, "That settles it, Florence; we'll have to get rid of him."

I went to the basket in a quick way. I said, "Yes, it's ham." It was quite a big piece. Delicious!

Saki came to pick up the basket. He looked at the things that had come out of the basket. His eyes stuck out. He said, "Oh, my! Honorable Missus, come quick, please!"

Aunt Caroline came and looked at the things that had come out of the basket. She said, "My emerald necklace! Agatha's sunburst! Good God!"

I went away from there. I was looking for more cool water.

The place in my mouth from the hot fly had begun to burn again. Eating the ham did it. It burned for a long time. It didn't burn when Aunt Caroline gave me that big piece of steak. She gave me the piece of steak that evening. Also many hugs. I wonder why!

· XXIV ·

No Admittance

June 9. There are two kinds of rules. One kind comes from the Molecule or Saki or Aunt Caroline. The rules that come from them all begin with "don't." Don't scratch on the front door. Don't dig in the garden. Don't bring bones in the house. Don't swallow-up in the front hall. No sense in any of them.

The other kind of rules is my own kind. I don't know where they come from. They just seem to be inside of me. I don't know how they get there. Here's my latest one: Never let strangers in a house unless someone you know is there!

I follow this rule every day. I do it with men who bring things in wagons to the back door. I just stand there and look at one of them. He stands and looks at me. He starts for the door. I growl. He stands still. He looks at me some more. He calls to the cook. The cook opens the kitchen door. She says, "You, Trub!" I stop looking at the man. He goes in the kitchen.

There is one person I don't follow the rule with. It is the butcher's boy. He smells delicious. So does his wagon. So does what he brings. On account of the smells I forget to follow the rule.

I followed the rule in a new way last night. It was not in my own house. It was in the house of the young man who came in an automobile. I'm not sure you should follow the rule when it isn't your own house.

The Molecule and I were playing a game. The game is like this: The Molecule lies down in the swing thing on the porch. He takes out a handkerchief. He snaps the handkerchief at my nose. I grab it. I pull. The Molecule holds on to the handkerchief. The swing thing goes back and forth as I pull. The Molecule calls the game One Dog Power.

A young man came in an automobile. He stopped the automobile in front of the porch. He said, "Hello, Old Cough-and-Spit."

The Molecule looked at the young man. He did not get up from the swing thing. He said, "Drive on, drive on; you're all wet."

The young man said, "Uncle William is dead."

The Molecule said, "The shock is more than I can bear. Who is Uncle William?"

The young man said, "It doesn't matter. He croaked in Des Moines. Parents absent from hearth and home attending funeral. I need cheering."

The Molecule said, "All right, I'll cheer." He closed his eyes. He spoke in a faint, high voice. He said, "Hurrah!"

The young man said. "You don't get me. I mean sympathetic companions. I know where the male parent put the key to the wine cellar."

The Molecule said, "When do the mourners gather?"

The young man said, "Nine o'clock or thereabouts."

The Molecule said, "I shall be with you in your hour of sorrow. Stud or deuces wild?"

The young man said, "I thought strip poker might be soothing. The low hand to pay a dollar all around, take off something, and inhale three fingers of Scotch. See you later." He went away from there.

I went to the house of the young man who had come in the automobile that night. I went with the Molecule. There were many young men at the house. They all sat around a table. There was nothing to eat on the table. Only round red, white, and blue things and bottles and glasses.

A young man held some square papers in his hand. He gave all the other young men some of the papers.

The Molecule said, "My eagle eye detects nothing whatever in the hand. I shall be pleased to distribute one smacker to each sad-eyed member of our little circle! I am also prepared to gargle the required amount of Scotch; but before removing a garment from the person I wish to give voice to a thought: All these doors seem to be open. Should I fail to prosper in this game of chance what is to prevent some dimpled housemaid bursting in upon my seminudity?"

The young man who had come in the automobile said, "Fear not, Little One—the servants had instructions not to come in this part of the house. Here's three fingers—down the hatch!"

The Molecule drank out of a glass. He gave each of the other young men a blue round thing. He took off his necktie and dropped it on the floor. He said, "Let the good work go on!"

The young men and the Molecule sat at the table a long time. They kept taking off things and dropping them on the floor. I took a nap. It was a long nap.

A noise woke me up. It was the noise of an automobile. The young man whose house it was got up from the table. He had on a white shirt without any sleeves and one sock. He went to the door. He looked out in the hall. He came back in a quick way.

He said, "My God, the parents! Start dressing! Shove those bottles under the couch! Leave the ginger ale! Somebody start the radio! Where in hell are my pants?"

The automobile was coming to the front door. I went to the front door to see who was in the automobile. Nobody came with me. I began to hear music. It was a nice music.

A man and a lady got out of the automobile. It was an oldish man with glasses on. It was an oldish lady. They came up the front steps. They stopped when they saw me.

The oldish lady said, "Look at that dog! What's he doing here, do you suppose?"

The oldish man said, "How do I know what he's doing here?" He started to come into the house.

I followed the rule. The oldish man stopped. He looked at me. I looked at him.

The oldish lady said, "Good heavens, whose dog is it, do you suppose?"

The oldish man said, "Don't ask so many foolish questions. Ring the bell!"

The oldish lady started for the door.

I followed the rule.

The oldish lady stopped. She said, "Ring it yourself! The idea!"

The oldish man spoke to me. He said, "Here, you, get out of here!"

I didn't say anything. I just looked at the oldish man.

The oldish lady said, "John Giddings, are you afraid to walk into your own house on account of a dog?"

The oldish man said, "Don't you see what kind of a dog it is?"

The oldish lady said, "Of course I see what kind of a dog it is. It's a white dog."

The oldish man said, "A white dogl What do you think of that? Let me inform you it's a bulldog."

The oldish lady said, "You're mistaken, George. Cousin Eustace had a bulldog once, and its nose was all squashed in. Besides, Cousin Eustace's dog had a..."

The oldish man said, "Never mind, never mind! Jack must be here. I hear the radio. I'll call him."

The oldish lady said, "You always change the subject when you're wrong. Cousin Eustace's dog had the funniest tail you ever saw—twisted like a pretzel. I remember distinctly because I..."

The oldish man began to shout. He shouted, "Jack! Oh, Jack!" He kept on shouting it.

Nothing happened.

The oldish lady said, "Another thing about Cousin Eustace's dog was its legs. They bowed out in the most extraordinary way. They reminded me of a Chippendale chair that used to stand in the..."

The oldish man said, "I want to ask you one thing, Lucy—just one: Are you going to stand there and talk about Cousin Eustace's dog all night?"

The oldish lady said, "What else am I to do? You're afraid to walk into your own house. If I were a man I'd..."

The oldish man began to shout again. He shouted, "Jack, dammit, where are you?"

The young man whose house it was came out in the hall. He had his clothes on again. He said, "Who's that? Why, Dad, Mother! Didn't expect you till tomorrow. Gosh, I'm glad to see you! What are you standing out here for?"

The oldish man said, "Are you deaf? Where have you been? What's going on here? Whose dog is that?"

The young man said, "It's Bob Trescott's dog. Some of the fellows came over to spend the evening with me. We've been listening to the radio."

The Molecule came out in the hall. So did the other young men. I gave them some tail-wags. They gave me pats. The oldish man came in the house. So did the oldish lady. I gave the oldish man some tail-wags. He didn't notice them.

June 10. I have a new name. The Molecule gave it to me. He calls me Horatius. I wonder why?

· XXV ·

A Bearer of Gifts

June 11. I have seen the rat-man again. He is still black. It was in a garden. I went in the garden to do a little digging. It is better to do your digging in gardens that aren't yours.

The Rat-man was squirting something from a barrel on wheels. He was squirting it on a rosebush. I decided not to do any digging. I hoped the Rat-man would come and hunt rats. I gave him a tail-wag. I gave him some barks.

The Rat-man said, "On your way, fer't killer." He stopped squirting the rosebush. He squirted me. It went in my face. I went behind a rosebush. I went in a quick way. I sneezed and sneezed.

The Rat-man said, "How you like 'at insec' 'stirminator, Pink Eye?"

I sneezed.

The Rat-man said, "Killed any mo' fer'ts lately, has you?"

I sneezed.

The Rat-man said, "Cost me a ten-dollah bill, an' try to git frien'ly, eh?"

I sneezed.

The Rat-man said, "I s'pose you forgot 'at little matteh. I ain' forgot her. Time foh you to come roun' here making your wags is when I totally disremember 'at tranzacshun."

I sneezed.

The Rat-man said, "Yes, suh, when she passes fum my min' complete, you come roun'."

I sneezed.

The Rat-man said, "At'll be quite a while yet, Pink Eye; you ain' goin' live long enough to see it happen."

I sneezed.

The black man said, "Just pass on out 'at gate an' push on down th' road." He picked up a big stick.

I went away from there.

I looked for Ginger. I couldn't find him. I looked for cats. I found one. It was a white cat. It went up a tree. I sat on the ground and looked up at the cat. The cat sat in the tree and looked down at me. Nothing else happened for a long time.

A man came out of the house where the white cat lived. The white cat made a cat sound. The man looked up in the tree. He looked at me. He picked up a stone. I went away from there.

I went to my home. I went up on the porch. I saw something in the swing thing. It was the black bag Aunt Caroline takes with her when she goes in stores.

I took the black bag out of the swing thing. I took it out on the lawn. I played Helpless Prey with it. I ran round and round the drive with it. I took it under the back porch. I lay down under the back porch and chewed the black bag. Then I just thought.

I thought about cats. I wondered how they can climb trees. I wondered what it would be like if they couldn't climb trees.

I thought about rats. I wondered why there is always a hole close to every rat. I wondered what it would be like if there were no holes for rats.

I thought about the Rat-man. I wondered why he had squirted stuff in my face. I wondered why he had picked up a stick. I wondered if he would ever go rat hunting with me again. I thought I would go and see.

I went to the garden where the Rat-man had been. I took along the black bag. I thought I would chew it some more if the Rat-man had gone away.

The Rat-man had not gone away. He was in a little house with one window. The house was full of things men dig in gardens with. There was a nice smell in the little house. It came from a tin pail with a cover on it that the Rat-man was holding in his lap. I gave him some wags and a wiggle.

The Rat-man said, "Back again, is you? Want me to take 'at tenspot out of yoh hide wid a hoe han'le?"

I gave the Rat-man some more wags.

The Rat-man said, "What you got in yoh mouth, Pink Eye?"

I gave the Rat-man a wiggle.

The Rat-man came and took the black bag from me. He said, "Lemme look, Pink Eye!" He opened the black bag. His eyes came popping out. He sat down in a quick way.

He said, "Hush, people, hush!"

The Rat-man took something from the black bag. He looked at it. He looked at it a long time. He said, "Is I settin' here or is I ain't? Is dis jack or is it a optical loosion? Is you Pink Eye or is you de tail en' of las' night's white mule? Look like you come in here an' han' me fo'ty-eight dollahs an' fi-ty-cents. 'At's what it look like."

I gave the Rat-man some wags.

The Rat-man said, "Pink Eye, is you real, me an'you is fas' frien's. Le's fin' out is you real."

The Rat-man went away from there. I went with him. We went to a store. It was a small store. There were black men in the store.

The Rat-man said, "Wait where you is, Pink Eye. Here's where we put the acid tes' on 'at dream jack whut you bring. If I come out steppin' slow I got me a bottle on my hip an' we is fas' frien's. If I come a-runnin', you ain' neveh goin' to ketch me else you got wings."

The Rat-man went in the store. I waited. He came out of the store. He said, "Pink Eye, I is proud to name you as my fastes' frien'. Le's go."

The Rat-man went back to the little house in the garden. I went with him. He sat down on a wooden bench. He picked up the tin pail. He took the cover off. He said, "Two poke chops, Pink Eye—one foh you an' one foh me." He gave me a pork chop. I ate it. Delicious!

The Rat-man said, "Two ham san'wiches, Pink Eye—one foh you an' one foh me." He gave me a sandwich. I ate it. Delicious!

The Rat-man took a bottle from his pocket. He said, "Is you got use foh dis I splits her wid you, Pink Eye. Nex' bes' thing I kin do is name you as my fastes' frien'. Here's lookin'." He drank out of the bottle. He kept on drinking out of the bottle. He stretched out on the wooden bench. He pulled his hat over his face. He made snoring noises. He did it for a long time.

I went out in the garden. I did a little digging. I saw something under a bush. It was a wiggly thing. I barked at the wiggly thing. It stuck out its tongue at me. I paw-poked the wiggly thing. It went away from there. It went all along the ground. It went in a quick way.

I ran after the wiggly thing. I caught it. I threw it up in the air. When it came down I paw-poked it. The wiggly thing just wiggled. It kept on wiggling. I played with the wiggly thing a long time. It was fun!

It began to get all dark. The rain began to come down. I thought I would take the wiggly thing somewhere out of the rain. I took the wiggly thing into the little house. It was still wiggling.

It was dark in the little house. The Rat-man was still on the wooden bench. I thought I would let him play with the wiggly thing, too. I gave him a paw-poke.

The Rat-man sat up on the wooden bench. He said, "Here comes my frien' bearin' gif's. What gif' you got now, Pink Eye? Le's look." He put out his hand. He took hold of the wiggly thing. It gave a good wiggle.

I was surprised at what happened then. The Rat-man gave an awful yell. He jumped in the air. He gave another awful yell. He went away from there. He went in a quick way. He kept on giving awful yells. He went through the garden doing it. He ran into the fence. He gave another awful yell. He fell over the fence. He went down the road in a very quick way. Hc didn't take the wiggly thing with him.

· XXVI ·

All Grows Dark

June 12. I have met a new thing. It is called a Baby. It makes strange noises. It smells like people, but isn't. I heard about it first at breakfast.

Aunt Caroline mentioned it. She said, "Robert, I want you to be here for luncheon."

The Molecule said, "Why, Light of my Life?"

Aunt Caroline said, "Your cousin Jane is coming over from White Plains to show us the baby."

Flips said, "That will be sweet."

The Molecule said, "The following information is yours without the asking: I shall be far away o'er hill and dale when Jane and infant arrive. I shall continue to lurk in the wildwood until mother and child have departed. Pass the muffins, Flips!"

Flips said, "Meaning he'd rather hang around the Country Club than see Cousin Jane's baby."

The Molecule said, "Countess, you said a faceful."

Flips said, "I call that mean."

The Molecule said, "You go too far—human is the word. May I again call your attention to my crying need of muffins?"

Flips gave the Molecule a plate. It was full of brown-and-yellow things. I gave him a paw-poke. He gave me half of a brown-and-yellow thing. Delicious!

Aunt Caroline said, "I shall expect you here for luncheon. You will remain as long as she stays."

The Molecule said, "Admire little Pink-Toes all afternoon? You're simply brutal, Caroline. Now, listen...."

Aunt Caroline said, "We won't discuss it. A young mother is driving thirty miles to show her first-born to those who *should* be most interested. I won't have her hurt by your indifference."

The Molecule said, "He seen his duty and he done it. Why do you say first-born?"

Aunt Caroline said, "Because it happens to be a fact."

The Molecule said, "Despite my youth and innocence, I have wisecracked, now and then, with the modern matron. If you wish to stick to facts, say first, last, and only born."

Aunt Caroline said, "You're disgusting!"

The Molecule got up from his chair. He picked up Aunt Caroline's eyeglasses from the table. He put them on the end of his nose. He looked down over the top of them. He said, "Aren't we all?" He went away from there.

Flips made giggling noises.

Aunt Caroline said, "You think him funny?"

Flips said, "I can't help it—he's *such* a fool."

Aunt Caroline said, "True; but why laugh? If my brother were a jackanapes I should grieve."

I began to feel wild. When a wild spell comes on, I can't keep still. I gave three barks and a spin-around. Then I ran round and round the breakfast table. Aunt Caroline had dropped her napkin. I pounced on it. I ran round and round the table with the napkin.

Saki came in. He said, "Bed dog, hi, hi, whoa!"

I ran out in the hall. Saki chased me. I played Sliding Rugs going down the hall. A rug and I ended at the front door. I stood on the rug and played Helpless Prey with the napkin.

Saki came down the hall. He tried to grab me. I dodged him. He grabbed the napkin. I pulled. He played Sliding Rugs. He sat down in a quick way. Hc said, "Darn, damn, oh, my!"

I went away from there.

I went through the long window to the porch. I was still feeling wild. I ran round and round the house some more. I played Helpless Prey with the napkin till there wasn't any napkin. I lay down and panted.

Guess what? A rat came from under the garage! I went for the rat in a very quick way. It ran down the cellar steps in an even quicker way. It ran into the cellar. I was just behind it. I thought, "Good-bye, Mr. Rat"—but it wasn't so. Before you could wink, it jumped into the coal bin. I jumped in too. I thought, "This is soft"—but it wasn't. The rat went down between the coal and the side of the bin.

There was only one thing to do—dig. I dug. I dug the coal all away from that side of the bin. The rat wasn't there! I dug the coal all away from the other side of the bin. The rat wasn't there! Can you beat it?

It seemed best to let the rat go. I did. I went up into the yard. It was past noon already. I could hardly believe it. I had been in the coal bin since right after breakfast. It's funny how the time goes when you're interested.

I went in the house. I saw the Molecule go in the dining room. I went in the dining-room door. Aunt Caroline was in the dining room. Flips was the dining room. A strange lady was in the dining room.

The Molecule kissed the strange lady. He said, "Great to see you. Jane old thing. Where's the bouncing baby boy?"

The strange lady said, "You'll see him after luncheon, Bobby. He's having a nap in the library."

The Molecule said, "Couldn't I just steal in for a peek at the little darling?"

Aunt Caroline gave the Molecule a look. It was not a kind look. She said, "Sit down and eat your luncheon, Robert!"

I wondered what a baby was. I wondered why there was so much talk about it. I wondered why the Molecule wanted to see it. I thought I would find out.

I started for the library. I saw black marks along the hall floor where I had come in. I looked behind me. I saw black marks from the dining-room door to where I was. Everywhere I went, black marks happened. It was strange.

I went in the library. There was something on the library couch. It had on a white dress. It had on white shoes. It had on white stockings. It had on a white cap with white ribbons. It was very still. It looked like one of the pretend-people little girls carry. I thought, "So this is a baby! It smells alive. Why doesn't it move?"

I gave the baby a nose-poke. Nothing happened. I gave it a face-lick. Its fingers began to go. I thought, "It can move, all right—but not much." I gave it another face-lick. I was surprised at what happened.

It began to wave its arms. It began to kick its feet. It said, "Wug gluggle da." It put its fingers around my nose.

When the Molecule wants to play he grabs me by the nose. I thought, "It wants to play. I suppose I'd better play with it." I did.

I gave the baby paw-pokes. It waved its arms harder. I gave it nose-pokes and fun-bites and pretend-shakes. It made giggling sounds and noises like a rooster.

I jumped back to make a pounce. I didn't pounce. I was too surprised. I was never so surprised in my life.

The baby had turned black! Face, cap, ribbons, dress, shoes, stockings—all black. I could hardly believe it. I thought, "There's something wrong somewhere. I know it."

I sat down to think. I thought a long time. It came to me. *Coal bin*! I started to go away from there. Too late! The strange lady was coming in the library door. So was Aunt Caroline. So was Flips. So was the Molecule.

The strange lady said, "Here's the Lambkin of the Skies, Bobby. Isn't he a pretty fine— "

She gave a shriek. So did Aunt Caroline. So did Flips. The strange lady went to the couch. She picked up the baby. She said, "My God! My child!"

The Molecule looked at the baby. He looked at me. He said, "Bless his little heart—he's been having a romp with Trouble."

I went away from there. I went out the front door. There is a hole under the front porch. I went in the hole. I lay down under the front porch. I thought I would stay there for a while and rest.

A motor car came round the house. The strange lady got in the motor car with the baby. Aunt Caroline stood on the porch. So did Flips. So did the Molecule.

Aunt Caroline said, "But just a little while, Jane dear. It won't hurt him."

The strange lady said, "Do you think I'd let a child of mine look like this one second longer than was necessary?" The motor car went away from there.

Aunt Caroline said, "And now, where's that dog? Call him this instant!"

The Molecule whistled. I came out from under the porch.

Aunt Caroline said, "Take him round the house and give him what he deserves!"

The Molecule said, "Leave it to me. Come, Snowdrift!"

The Molecule went to the back of the house. He went to the ice box. He got out a lamb chop. He said, "Take that, Foul Fiend!"

I ate the lamp chop. He said, "And that!" He gave me another lamb chop. I ate it. He said, "And that!" He gave me another lamb chop. He said, "I guess *that* will teach you a lesson!"

He went away from there.

· XXVII ·

A Different Kind of Cat

June 13. I'm down in the cellar. I've been here for days and days. I sleep and scratch. I only scratch to be doing something. I have no fleas. The fleas have gone long ago.

No flea could stand the baths I've had. Every day a bath. Think of it! It's a wonder I'm alive myself.

It began with a new game. Ginger made up the game. It is a good game. It is called Chasing Chickens.

You go out in the country to play the game. You go along the road. You come to a house. In the yard around the house will be chickens. The more chickens there are the better.

You go into the yard in a quiet way. You go for the place where the chickens are the thickest. The chickens go in every direction. Some of them run. Some of them fly. You grab a running chicken. You pull feathers out of it. You grab another chicken. You pull feathers out. If the chickens are white, you would think it was snowing. That's the way the game goes.

It is not quiet while the game is going on. You bark. The chickens make noises. A woman comes out of the house. Generally she brings a broom. She makes noises, too. It is glorious!

The game ends when all the chickens have got up on the roof. If a man comes out of the house instead of a woman, the game ends then. That is on account of the man picking up stones. When this happens you go away from there.

Ginger and I had played the chicken game all morning. At the last house a man came out. He did not pick up stones. He had a stick in his hand.

Ginger said, "Snap out of here, Kid!" He went away from there.

I went with him. I said, "He hasn't picked up stones."

Ginger said, "Don't talk—run!"

A loud noise came out of the man's stick. I had a stinging feeling where I sit down. I gave a jump. I said, "Bees are biting me!"

Ginger kept on running. I kept on running. He said, "Every time you open your face you hand me a laugh."

I said, "If it isn't bees, what is it?"

Ginger said, "If he'd been a little closer you'd have thought it was alligators."

Ginger kept on running. I kept on running. I said, "Why did the stick make a noise?"

Ginger said, "That was a shotgun, you poor simp."

I said, "What's a shotgun?"

Ginger said, "Never mind what it is; when you see one, step on the gas."

He stopped running. I stopped running.

I said, "Let's go home."

Ginger said, "Home was never like this."

I said, "I'm famished."

Ginger said, "Don't you ever think of anything but your stomach?" He went on down the road. I went on down the road. I stopped. He stopped.

I said, "Something's got to be done."

He said, "About what ?"

I said, "I've got gnawing pains."

Ginger said, "Oh, all right, we'll go grab a lunch."

I said, "Where?"

Ginger said, "Listen!"

I listened. I heard voices. They were high voices. They were screaming, and laughing and yelling.

I said, "What's that?"

Ginger said, "Eats — come on!" He went on down the road. I went with him.

We came to a white house. The house had a bell on it. All round the house were boy children and girl children. Some were running. Some were eating out of boxes. Ginger went to a girl child who was eating out of a box. He gave her tail-wags. She gave him a piece of cake. I went to a boy child who was eating out of a box. I gave him tail-wags. Nothing happened. I gave him a paw-poke. He gave me a piece of ham. Delicious!

We kept on going to different children. Everyone gave us something. You never knew what it would be. I got brown bread and butter. I got white bread and jelly. I got pie. I got hard-boiled eggs. I got tongue. I got chicken. Once I got a bone from a pork chop. I love children!

I was feeling better. Not full exactly, but the gnawing pains had stopped. The bell on the white house began to go back and forth. It made a noise.

All the children went into the white house. I was going in with them.

Ginger said, "Not in there, Bozo."

I said, "Why not?"

Ginger said, "A woman with spectacles will knock you for a loop."

I said, "What with?"

Ginger said, "A ruler."

I said, "What for?"

Ginger said, "I dunno—she just does."

We went down the road. A small furry thing ran out in the road. We went after it in a quick way. It went into a stone fence. Ginger sat down where it went in.

I said, "What is it?"

Ginger said, "Chipmunk."

I said, "What do we do now?"

Ginger said, "Keep quiet—it might come out."

We did. Nothing happened for a long time.

I said, "I think I could dodge the ruler."

Ginger said: "Will you close your face?"

I did.

Nothing happened for a long time. I got to thinking about the children. Once a lady asked Flips if I was fond of children. Who wouldn't be fond of a dear little child with a lunch box? I thought I would go to the door of the white house and look in.

I started to go. I went in a quiet way. I went along the stone wall. I saw something move. It was in the ditch along the road. I went over to the ditch.

It was a cat. It was a different kind of cat. It had a white stripe on its back. It had a bushy tail.

I went for it in a quick way. It went up the ditch. It did not go in as quick a way as is usual with cats.

I thought, "My cat, all right!" But it wasn't. It went in an iron pipe.

I could get my head in the iron pipe, but that was all.

I barked for Ginger. He came running.

He said, "What's the big idea?"

I said, "Cat in here. Too small for me. You can make it."

Ginger said, "Atta boy! Watch at the other end!"

I said, "It's a different kind of cat. Wait till I get there!"

I went to the other end of the pipe.

Ginger started in. He backed out in a quick way.

He said, "I'll say it's different! Come on, Kid."

I said, "What's the matter? What are you going to do?"

Ginger said, "Just fade away while the fading's good."

I said, "Are you going to leave this cat?"

Ginger said, "I'll tell the cockeyed world I'm going to leave him!"

I said, "I believe you're afraid to go in after him!"

Ginger said, "Boy, you ain't said the half of it!"

I said, "Go, if you want to. I'll stay here."

Ginger said, "You're in wrong, Kid. When they pack too big a wallop, leave 'em lay."

I said, "I'm not afraid of any cat."

Ginger said, "No? Well, maybe he won't come out. If he does—don't blame me!"

He went away from there.

I put my head in the pipe. I could see the different kind of cat half-way up the pipe. I barked. He didn't move. I went to the other end of the pipe. I put my head in. I barked. He didn't move. I kept on barking. Nothing happened.

A man came along the road. He was an oldish man. He had white whiskers. He stopped. I barked and whined at the pipe.

The oldish man said, "Got a rabbit there, hev ye, pup? Mebbe we kin git him out if we try!"

The oldish man took out a knife. He cut a long stick from a tree. He poked the stick in one end of the pipe. I stayed at the other end.

The different kind of cat came down the pipe toward me. He was coming backward.

I thought he would turn round when he got to the end of the pipe. He didn't.

Something happened. I don't know what it was exactly. I didn't seem to know anything for a minute. When I did I was lying on the ground trying to catch my breath.

I looked for the different kind of cat. It was gone. I looked for the oldish man. He was gone, too. I saw him going. He was going down the road. I would not have thought such an oldish man could be going in such a quick way.

I thought, "Well, that is that!"

I thought I would go to the white house and see the children. I did.

I went to the door of the white house.

The children were sitting behind little tables. The tables were in rows.

The woman with the spectacles was sitting behind a bigger table at the end of the room.

I went in the door.

I was surprised at what happened.

The children began to cough. They jumped up from the little tables. The girl children began to scream. The boy children began to go out the windows.

The woman with the spectacles got up from the table. I wondered if she would get a ruler. She didn't.

She said, "Children, children—the back door!" She went out the back door in a quick way. So did the girl children. I was the only one left in the white house. It was strange.

I thought I would go home. I did.

It was strange there, too. I barked at the front door. Saki opened the door. He turned pale. He shut the door in my face.

I went to the back door. I barked. The cook started to open the door.

She said, "The mercy of God be upon us!" She shut the door in my face.

The first bath happened just after that. Saki and the shofer did it. They did it in the garage with a hose. Saki put me in the cellar. I've been here ever since. I've been thinking over things. I've come to a conclusion: Ginger was right!

June 14. The Molecule just came down in the cellar. I thought he was going to let me out. He didn't. He sniffed.

He said, "The flavor lasts!" He went away from there.

· XXXVIII ·

A Change of Mind

June 16. I have seen the visitation-from-God man again. He was at the home of a girl named Polly. I met a wave at the home of the girl named Polly. It was like this:

The Molecule and I were at the Country Club. He was sitting in a chair on the porch. He was drinking out of a glass. I was lying at the top of the steps. I was watching ants go in and out of a crack in the steps.

A girl came out on the porch. She said, "Hello, Bob."

The Molecule said, "Hello, Polly."

The girl said, "Always drinking."

The Molecule said, "Not always—one must sleep."

The girl said, "What about a little tennis?"

The Molecule said, "Your suggestion pains me deeply."

The girl said, "Well, give me a stroke a hole and I'll play you nine holes."

The Molecule said, "The thought makes me shudder."

The girl sat down on the steps by me. I stopped looking at the ants. I looked at the girl. She was a nice girl. I gave her a paw-poke. She put her arm around my neck. She gave me a nose-pinch. I sneezed.

The girl said, "Why are you such a flat tire?"

The Molecule said, "I am as God made me."

The girl said, "Always lopping around and acting bored."

The Molecule said, "Do not reproach me, my child. You see but the shell of what was once a man. Sorrow has brought these silver locks, these palsied arms, this withered form—sorrow and bum hooch."

The girl got up from the steps. She gave the Molecule a look. It was not a kind look. She said, "You gripe me terribly. I'm going home and take a swim."

The Molecule got up from his chair. He said, "Swim! Now, there's a thought. Make it the Beach Club and I'm with you."

The girl said, "My suit is at home. Why drive out there?"

The Molecule said, "Allow me to recall to you the nose-dive I did in the lap of your lady mother at your coming-out party."

The girl said, "She's forgotten a little thing like that. Come on—it's high tide right now."

We went away from there. We went in an automobile. It was a long automobile with only one seat. The girl drove. She drove in a very quick way. It was fun. I barked. I could not hear the barks. The wind took them back of me too fast. I had never felt such a wind.

The Molecule said, "How much is the purse?"

The girl said, "I don't want to lose high tide."

The Molecule said, "If you don't slow for this corner you'll lose more than the tide."

The automobile tipped up on one side. I fell against the girl. The Molecule fell against me. It was fun. I barked some more. We went through some gates. We went up a long drive. We went around a big house. We stopped. I was sorry.

We got out of the automobile. We went through a garden. A lady was sitting in the garden. She was sitting on a bench by a table. She said, "Is that you, Polly?"

The girl said, "Herself in person."

The lady said, "Who is that with you?"

The girl said, "Bob Trescott, Mother; we're going to take a dip."

The lady said, "Come here a moment, will you, Polly?"

The girl said, "Be with you in a minute, Bob. Go on down the beach."

The Molecule went down a path in the garden. The girl went to the lady. I wanted to see what was on the table by the lady. I went with the girl. There were dishes and cups on the table. They were empty. Can you beat it?

The lady said, "Isn't that the boy who fell over me at your— "

The girl said, "Yes, what of it?"

The lady said, "I don't think I approve of that young man, Polly."

The girl said, "Will you ever get over these mildewed ideas of yours? I'm embarrassed for you, Mother—honestly, I am. For the love of Mike, snap out of it."

The lady gave a sigh. She said, "Well, if you think he's all right, I suppose there's nothing more to be said. But please don't go bathing alone with him just now."

The girl said, "And why not?"

The lady said, "The rector is coming for tea. You know how conservative he is, and your bathing suit is so—so—Why not wait and go in after he has gone?"

The girl said, "Miss high tide for that prehistoric mammal? Keep him here by the tea table and let him babble."

The girl went away from there. I went with her. We went down the path after the Molecule. At the end of the path were two little houses. They were standing by a lot of water. I had never seen so much water in my life except in Florida.

Close to the water was a lot of sand.

There was a dog lying in the sand. He was a little black dog. He had long, black hair and soft eyes and very long ears. He was lying by a stick. When he saw the girl he barked.

The girl said, "I'll throw it for you when I come out."

She went in one of the little houses. The Molecule went into the other one. I went over to the dog with the long ears.

I said, "What's the rule about digging in this sand?"

The long-eared dog said, "I retrieve from land and water. I like water best. I don't dig in sand."

I said, "We could make this sand simply fly."

The long-eared dog said, "Have you ever retrieved a dead duck?"

I said, "No. Why should I?"

The long-eared dog said, "Why should you? My God, what is your specialty?"

I said, "What do you mean—specialty?"

The long-eared dog said, "What do you like to do best?"

I said, "Eat and chase cats."

The long-eared dog said, "One must eat, of course. As for chasing cats—a strange vocation."

I said, "A live cat beats a dead duck, if you ask me."

The long-eared dog said, "I don't ask you. I don't ask you anything. What would be the use?"

The girl came out of the little house. She looked queer—mostly legs and arms. She picked up the stick by the long-eared dog. She said, "All right, precious, here it goes."

The long-eared dog said, "Observe what follows, closely."

The girl threw the stick out into the water. The long-eared dog ran into the water. He went out to the stick. You could only see his head. Sometimes you couldn't see that on account of the waves.

He came back with the stick in his mouth. He put it down on the sand by the girl. The girl gave him a hug.

The Molecule came out of his little house. He was all arms and legs, too.

He and the girl went into the water.

The long-eared dog said, "That is retrieving. How does it strikes you?"

I said, "I like cats better."

The long-eared dog said, "Try a swim and you'll change your mind."

I said, "Is it fun?"

The long-eared dog said, "It's gorgeous."

I said, "Well, I'll give it a whirl."

I walked into the water. It came up to my chest. Then it came up to my neck. Then a wave came. I will never forget what happened next.

I went over and over. I couldn't see. I couldn't breathe. It was terrible.

I found myself lying on the sand. I don't know how I got there.

I know this much—I was never so glad to be any place in my life.

The long-eared dog said, "It's that way sometimes at first."

I coughed.

The long-eared dog said, "Swallowed a little water, eh?"

I coughed.

The long-eared dog said, "Don't wait for the waves—just meet them."

I coughed some more. I made an effort.

I said, "Let me tell you about that. I've met all the waves I am ever going to."

I went away from there. I went to see if anything had been put in the dishes where the lady was sitting. There hadn't.

A man was sitting with the lady. It was the Visitation-from-God Man. I recognized him by the same kind of funny hat. I wondered if he still smelled of cats. I sniffed his legs. He wiggled them. He did.

The lady said, "Just what is the idea of this meeting at the Parish House, Doctor?"

The Visitation-from-God Man said, "It is to be a Mothers' Meeting, my dear lady. I am convinced that the girl of today, who will be the woman of tomorrow, is not sufficiently restrained. Left to her own devices she is losing her sense of decorum, of maiden modesty. The present tendency in dress, or rather, er—undress, if you will allow me my little joke, is sufficient evidence of this fact. I feel that, er—something should be done. I am therefore asking the mothers of my parish to meet me, er—Thursday afternoon—for an informal discussion of the matter. I am anxious, needless to say, that you be with us, my dear lady."

The lady said, "I'm afraid I shall have to decline, Doctor. I try to be a companion to my child. If I cling to the customs of my girlhood I cannot hold her confidence, her respect for my judgment. Whether we like it or not, the world moves. A healthy frankness, a greater freedom is claimed by our daughters today and we must grant it. They may seem brazen to you, Doctor—that is only on the surface. At heart they are as shy, as modest as their grandmothers."

I began to hear a noise. It was a loud noise. It was a dog. He was in trouble. It came from down by the water. I thought, "Aha—he's met a wave." I hurried down to the water.

The long-eared dog was just coming from the water. He was coming in a quick way. There was something hanging to his tail. It was a big stone with legs on it.

The long-eared dog ran over the sand. He kept making the noises I had heard. He ran into the little house where the girl was. She screamed. She screamed some more. She came out of the little house. So did the long-eared dog. He kept on making noises.

The girl was in another kind of clothes. It was a pink clothes — very thin. The Molecule came out of his little house. He had on little white pants — only.

He said, "Hold him. It's a crab."

The girl took hold of the long-eared dog. The Molecule took the flat stone from his tail. He threw the stone into the water. The long-eared dog stopped making noises. He sat down and tried to lick his tail.

The lady and the Visitation-from-God Man came around the corner of the little houses. They were running. They stopped suddenly. The lady's mouth came open. It stayed that way.

The Molecule went into his little house. He went in a quick way. The girl went into her little house. She went in a quick way.

The lady said, "Doctor, I shall attend the meeting Thursday."

· XXIX ·

A Double-Barreled Lesson in Love

June 26. I have a new friend. Her name is Bridget. She is not a close friend. I saw her first at the Beach Club. There is a long row of little rooms at the Beach Club. The Molecule went into one of the little rooms. He took the things he wears in the water with him. He tried to shut me outside. I squeezed through the door in a quick way.

The Molecule took off his coat. He took off his shirt. I grabbed the shirt. I played Helpless Prey with it. The Molecule said, "Exit, smiling!" He pushed me outside. He shut the door in my face.

I scratched on the door.

The Molecule said, "Positively no admittance."

I lay down in front of the little rooms. I thought I would take a nap. I didn't on account of a girl. She came along the row of little rooms. She was a wet girl, but nice in the face.

She had a towel over her arm. She put a key in the door of a little room. When she opened the door she dropped the towel. I picked it up. I ran with it. I ran up and down in front of the little rooms.

The girl ran after me. I dodged. She stopped running. She called out loud. She said, "Does anyone in here own this dog?"

The Molecule answered from the little room. He said, "Describe dog!"

The girl said, "White bull terrier without a ray of sense."

The Molecule said, "Description perfect. What's he doing now?"

The girl said, "He's got my towel!"

The Molecule said, "Hold his nose and say 'Drop it!'"

The girl said, "He runs when I try to get near him."

The Molecule said, "Fancy that—the poor nut. Be with you in a moment."

A dog came in a quick way. It was a Boston terrier with a crinky tail

The girl said, "Oh, Bridget, he's got my towel."

I said, "Is your name Bridget? My name is Trub. Take hold here and we will run down the beach with it."

Bridget said, "You let go of that!"

I said, "What for?"

Bridget said, "If you don't let go, I'll give you a bite you'll remember."

I said, "Oh, you will, will you? Let's see you try it!"

Bridget started over to where I was. Things began to get red. The girl said, "Bridget! Come here, Bridget! Oh, won't you come out, whoever you are?"

The Molecule said, "I blush at the thought."

The girl said, "I'm afraid they'll fight."

The Molecule said, "How many dogs have you out there?"

The girl said, "One."

The Molecule said, "The name is Bridget?"

The girl said, "Yes. Please hurry,"

The Molecule said, "Calm yourself, fair stranger—there will be no fight."

A queer thing happened. It happencd when Bridget got close to me. I didn't see red any more. I liked Bridget in a sudden way. I liked her a lot. She clicked her teeth at me. I gave her a tail-wag. She snarled right in my face. I gave her a wiggle. She snapped at me. I gave her a paw-poke.

She said, "You let go that towel!"

I let go of the towel.

Bridget said, "Take your dirty paws off it!"

I took my paws off the towel.

Bridget said, "I've a notion to give you a bite you'll not forget in a hurry."

I said, "You can if you want to."

Bridget said, "I'll say I can."

I said, "I'll say so too."

Bridget said, "You needn't say anything."

I said, "All right, I won't."

Bridget said, "Get away from that towel."

I did.

The girl who was wet picked up the towel. She went in a little room. Bridget went with her.

I scratched on the door.

Bridget said, "Get away from that door!"

I did.

The Molecule came out of his little room. He went to the bcach. The girl called Polly was sitting on the beach. The Molecule said, "Not disporting in the billows?"

The girl called Polly said, "Got a cold."

The Molecule went in the water. I dug a hole in the beach.

The girl who was wet came along the beach. She had on a dress. She sat down by the girl called Polly. She said, "Who owns that dog?"

The girl called Polly said, "Bob Trescott."

The girl who had been wet said, "What's he like?"

The girl called Polly said, "Frightfully good-looking. Terribly indifferent."

The girl who had been wet said, "Sounds interesting. You'd be surprised how indifferent I can be myself."

Two youngish men came along the beach. Each youngish man had a youngish girl with him. They all sat down by the girl called Polly.

Bridget came running along the beach. I ran to meet her. I said, "Say, this is great! I've got a dandy hole started."

Bridget said, "Well, what of it?"

I said, "You can help me dig it."

Bridget said, "Dig it yourself."

She sat down in the sand. She looked out over the water.

The Molecule came out of the water. The girl called Polly said, "Oh, Bobby, come and meet Adelaide Price, from California. She is staying with me a whole month. Aren't I the lucky one?"

The Molecule looked at the girl called Adelaide. He said, "So nice to see you again."

The girl called Polly said, "Why, you've never seen her before!"

The Molecule said, "Yes, once before. Ah, well, boys will be boys—it was through a keyhole."

The girl called Polly said, "Keyhole?"

The Molecule said, "Yes—a bathhouse keyhole."

The youngish men laughed.

The girl called Polly said, "Are you being funny?"

The Molecule said, "Not very."

He sat down in the sand beside the girl called Adelaide.

The Molecule said, "So you're from California?"

The girl called Adelaide didn't say anything.

The Molecule said, "It must seem awful to you here where men are just rotten golfers."

The girl called Adelaide didn't say anything.

The Molecule said, "Tell me one thing. How do your boyfriends keep their hair so slick? If I so much as mingle in the foxtrot I look as though I'd just seen a headless woman in a graveyard at midnight. It's so different where you come from. Out there they swandive over precipices or knock low characters for a loop, and not a hair moves. I've watched them do it hour after hour, sick at heart. It's discouraging, if you know what I mean."

The girl called Adelaide got up from the beach. She said, "Polly darling, what about lunch?"

The girl called Polly got up from the beach. She said, "Are you hungry, darling? We'll trot along. By-by, everybody. Drop in this evening, Bobby!"

The Molecule got up from the beach. He said, "Thanks. I've asked Miss Price a serious question about the home talent. I'll toddle over for the answer."

The girl called Adelaide looked at the Molecule. She said, "I can tell you one thing about the men I know—they don't make misleading, suggestive remarks about a new girl the first time they meet her."

She went away from there with the girl called Polly.

Bridget got up from the beach. I said, "Let's run along the sand together."

Bridget said, "Go chase your tail!" She went away from there with the girl called Adelaide.

July 1. I am seeing Bridget every day. It is at the house of the girl called Polly. I try to make Bridget play Wrestle, Wrestle. She never does. Sometimes she snarls at me. Sometimes she tells me to chase my tail. Sometimes she doesn't say anything.

The Molecule talks to the girl called Adelaide. He doesn't talk long. Sometimes the girl called Adelaide says she has to write letters. Sometimes she says she has a headache. She goes in the house. The Molecule sits on the porch. He smokes a cigarette. He smokes another one. Then we go home.

It happened like that today. The Molecule was talking to the girl called Adelaide. I tried to make Bridget play Wrestle, Wrestle.

Bridget said, "Oh, for heaven's sake, let me alone!"

She went and lay down in the corner of the porch. I lay down by the Molecule.

The Molecule said, "Well, then, how about the Country Club dance? That's Thursday night."

The girl called Adelaide said, "I think Polly's planned something for Thursday. Now, if you'll excuse me, I must finish my letters."

She went in the house.

The Molecule laughed. He said, "We're a warm pair of sheiks, Old Companion!"

He lit a cigarette. He smoked it. He smoked another one. Then we went home.

July 2. We were at the house of the girl called Polly again today. The Molecule was waiting on the porch for the girl called Adelaide. Bridget was lying in the front hall.

I said, "Come on out."

Bridget didn't say anything.

I said, "I'll bet you can't catch me twice around the house."

Bridget said, "Hmph." She stayed in the front hall.

A dog came through the hedge in a quick way. It came from the place next door. It ran up to the porch steps. It was a little silky dog, It wiggled all over.

The silky dog said, "I'm Princess Woo. I win ribbons and sometimes cups. I was best in the show at Bar Harbor. What's your name? Don't you loathe cats? My, it's nice to be home. Let's touch noses."

I went down the steps. I touched noses with Princess Woo. I said, "My name is — "

Princess Woo said, "I think you're just splendid. Let's have a romp.

I said, "You're on. We'll play — "

Princess Woo said, "We'll play Chase and Worry. No fair off the grass. If I get in the dirt Mumsum won't like it. Don't you loathe being brushed?"

Somebody gave me a paw-poke. It was Bridget. She said, "Come on, Trubsy — twice around the house."

Bridget ran one way; Princess Woo ran another. I ran after Princess Woo. She dodged. I dodged. I caught her. I gave her a neck-chew.

Somebody gave me a paw-poke. It was Bridget. She said, "Let the wiggling little fool go home. I want to show you something in the garden."

A voice called from the other side of the hedge.

Princess Woo said, "That's Mumsum. Is there any dirt on my coat? Good-bye, everybody. Delightful time." She went through the hedge in a quick way.

I went up on the porch. Bridget came after me. She said, "Good riddance, I think." She gave me an ear-lick. She gave me a paw-poke. She gave me some wiggles.

The Molecule was watching us. He laughed. He said, "A light is dawning, Old Companion. Ain't nature grand!"

He went to the end of the porch. He called out loud. He said, "Moira! Oh, Moira! Come on over!"

A girl came through the hedge. She was carrying Princess Woo. She said, "Can't; my mother won't let me." She saw the Molecule. She said, "Hello, Thug!"

The Molecule said, "Hello, chased woman! Listen, how are you at drama?"

The girl that had come through the hedge said, "I'm good at everything."

The Molecule said, "Come and sit with me in yon porch swing!"

The girl said, "And then what happens?"

The Molecule said, "I want to make love to you for a special purpose.

The girl said, "They always do—with their slick city ways."

The Molecule said, "This is a new sort of purpose."

The girl said, "You intrigue me." She came up the porch steps. She sat in the porch swing. She held Princess Woo in her lap. The Molecule sat in the porch swing. The girl said, "Shoot the works, Don Juan."

The Molecule said, "Remain in neutral, Sappho. When the audience appears, drop into high and step on it."

The girl said, "The plot sickens. Is it Polly or the guest?"

The Molecule said, "From the Sunkist Slopes of California direct to you."

The girl said, "Has the hussy been ritzing you, Robert?"

The Molecule said, "I'll tell the cockeyed—Here she comes! A bit of love light in the baby blues!" He took the girl by the hand.

The girl gave the Molecule a look. It was a very kind look. She said, "It's simply thrilling to see you again, Darling. You haven't been playing about, have you, while mamma was away?"

The girl called Adelaide came through the front door. She gave the girl a look. She gave the Molecule a look. The Molecule jumped up from the porch swing. I jumped up from the porch. Bridget jumped up from the porch.

Bridget gave me a nose-lick. She said, "Guess what?"

I said, "What?"

Bridget said, "I've got a perfectly huge bone buried in the garden."

I said, "Don't care if I do."

We went away from there.

July 3. I have a new name. The Molecule gave it to me. It was at night. We were at the girl called Polly's. The Molecule had been sitting in the porch swing with the girl called Adelaide. They had been sitting there a long time without talking.

The girl called Adelaide said, "I'm afraid you'll have to go, dear; it's frightfully late."

The Molecule said, "One more and we'll call it a day."

He put his face to the face of the girl called Adelaide. He got up from the porch swing. He said, "Come on, Columbus!"

The girl said, "Why do you call him Columbus?"

The Molecule said, "Through him a new world was discovered."

JING

Yes-sirree, this is bird country. Real bird country, is what I mean. Why, there ain't a field of straw or a piney woods nowheres around but what there belongs to be a covey or two usin' close about. And that ain't all. It's flat country—ain't a pimple on it—you can see a dog a mile off if you're up on a hoss. I trained for Cass Meredith over in Alabama for a while. Plenty of birds—mebbe more than we got here—but the country was rollin'. Turn a wide-going dog loose and he was over a hill and gone before you could spit, and you spent an hour, mebbe, tryin' to find out which way he went. You'll have a right nice hunt down here, if you got the right kind of dogs for South Georgia—big-goin' dogs I meant—covey finders. Ain't no use to monkey with single birds around here. The birds go right spang into thick cover when they're flushed. It ain't hardly worth your while to root 'em out. Just find you another bunch out feedin', is what you aim to do....

No, sir, I cain't go with you, much as I'd like it. I got the misery in my back and shoulder so bad I cain't hardly set in a chair. If I was to straddle a hoss from sunup till dark, you might just as well shove me down out of sight in a gum swamp when you call the dogs in, and save the buzzards the trouble....

Yes, sir, I trained Jake Kate's Jingo. Who was tellin' you? ... Well, he tole you right. I trained the big fella and handled him as a Derby and in the All Age stakes and the National.... No, I never owned him. Sam Kepland owned him until he sold him up North. Sam lives just t'other side of town on the Americus Road.... Oh, you've seen Sam? I don't get to see much of him no more.... No, we never had a real fallin' out. We had a few words right after the National was run, or rather I made a remark or so; but that was some years back and nothin' to speak of. What did he tell you? ... Talked about ole Kate, did he? I might of knowed. He'll never have the sense that God give a shoat if he lives till cotton's a dollar a pound....

Why, yes, I'll tell you about Jake Kate's Jingo. Le's cross over and set down on that bench by the Jackson Memorial, or don't you feel like settin' so close to old Stonewall? You bein' a Yankee, I reckon.... Right nice here, ain't it? It's about the sociablist spot in town. You can set here on a Sataday and pass a word with about everybody in the county. This square'll have mebbe two hundred cars parked all around it on a Sataday. They'll be plenty of mule teams drove in, too, but mostly they hitch 'em down the side streets and leave the square for the automobiles.

To tell you rightly about the big dog, I reckon I'll start with ole Kate herself. I don't have to tell you Sam Kepland owned her—not after you've so much as passed the time of day with Sam. I don't know what notions you may have about her, after hearin' him go on, so I'll give you the facts. Ole Kate was owned first by Sam's brother-in-law, named Ernie Chevers, from up above Athens, that Sam's sister Eda married. When Ernie died, Sam's sister gives this Kate to Sam, and he brings her down here. She was mebbe a year and a half old then. I was trainin' a fair string of dogs at the time, knowin' that some of 'em would make good gun dogs and hopin' that one or two might train on to be field-trailers. Sam meets me one night and shows me Kate's papers and asks me would I work her a few weeks and kind of see what she was like.

Well, after I looked at them papers, I said to send her over. She was bred good enough to do anything—John Proctor out of Lady Ferris. We didn't know as much about that nick then as we've learned since, but I knowed it was plenty good. I give her a month's work just on her breedin'. Fact is, I'd have quit on her the first day I set her down, but the John Proctor blood with a good dam kep' me foolin' with her longer than I should of.

Then one evenin' I drove over with her to Sam's and told him she would hold a covey when she found one and was steady to shot and wing, and he owed me thirty dollars. He said that was a hell of a price to charge a neighbor just for takin' a dog out with those I was working for big money. I didn't say nothin' and pretty soon he hands me over twenty-five dollars and five boxes of sixteen-gauge shells that his sister had give him along with Kate—him shootin' a twelve gauge—and I took the money and shells and drove back home.

And now I'll tell you what ole Kate was like when I turned her back to Sam. She was one of them frog dogs, and that's what she stayed till the day she died.... What's a frog dog? Well, this country is full of kind of pothole swamps and the swamps is full of cat briers. A dog that's got his mind took up with findin' birds will hit one of them cat-brier swamps like a train of cars and bust his way right on in.

Then there's a kind of dog that will sort of work along the edge, lookin' at them cat briers. And right soon a frog will go kerplunk into the water and the dog will stop and cock his ears and tilt his head to one side, lookin' at where the frog has hit the water, and that's a frog dog. I don't crave to own one.

Far as Kate went, you could kill some birds over her. She'd hold a covey when she found one, like I told you, but the trouble was she'd do a lot of runnin' and not find much. There's some dogs that'll find a covey here and go right yonder and find another without hardly any fuss about it. That's bird sense. They just size up their country and work the birdy places and, man dear, when you get one of them bee-line bird finders, you're got yourself a shootin' dog.

Well, Kate wasn't nothin' like that. She had plenty of speed, and she'd sail out there and go skippin' back and forth and stumble on birds now and then, but she'd just as soon work a bare cotton field as a good patch of straw—sooner I reckon—the footin' being nice and easy between the cotton rows. She shore liked easy footin'.

'Nother thing about her! She could steal a point from a brace mate slick as you ever seen it done. Why, I've saw ole Kate backin' another dog like a rock maybe five or six rod from where the birds were. Next thing you knew, when you rode up to shoot, there'd be Katy ten feet, mebbe, ahead of the dog that made the find, and you'd have swore she's nailed the covey herself and the other dog had crep' in on her.

While she didn't have bird sense, she was plenty smart other ways. She'd manage to get the coolest place or the warmest in the kennel yard or the dog wagon, dependin' on the weather. She'd false-point and then road on like birds had been there and gone, just to get some attention. If a covey went into briers, she'd skirt round 'em or find a road to take her through, so she could edge in at the other side to make you think she'd worked through the patch and was just comin' out of it. 'Course she was a fine-haired bitch that briers raked plenty, but a good game pointer will be brier-slashed from his nose to the end of his tail when the season's over, and you never saw a scratch on Katy—you ain't apt to on a frog dog....

I'm tellin' you all this because it leads up to somethin' else. I reckon you've noticed that a lot of men can give you a fair line on anybody's dog but their own. Let 'em watch a dog work for a day or so, and they'll just about know where he belongs—so long as he's nothin' to them. Now let 'em buy a dog, and right there he's a different sort of dog from what he was before the money changed hands. Startin' right there, that dog improves 200 per cent. If he pops a covey, the wind was wrong. If he can't find scattered singles right where they went, it's too dry. If he don't give you much shootin', it's just one of them days when the birds don't give out scent like they'd ought.

Well, sir, that's what happened to Sam over this Kate. She just couldn't do nothin' wrong. If she false-pointed, Sam would say, "Looks like that dog of yours went through this way and popped 'em." If she sneaked up and stole a point, you'd hear Sam let out a whoop when you got there. "Ole Kate's got 'em," he'd say. "That dog of yours is backin' her nice, ain't he?"

It got to be a joke all through this section. The boys used to call Sam "ole Katy-did, Katy-didn't." If it was findin' the covey, she did; if it was flushin' 'em, she didn't—was what they meant.

It never fazed Sam. He went right ahead on braggin' over Kate and lyin' about her and makin' excuses for her, when everybody from here to Macon knowed she was just a road-pickin', point stealin', cotton-row-runnin' frog dog that was hardly worth a good panful of grits and gravy.

One evenin', when Sam has had Kate six years or so, I run into him down to Werner's, where he'd come to buy hisself some eatin' tobacco, and he draws me out in front of the store and asks me what is the best stud pointer in the country, to my notion. I ask him why he wants to know, and he says he reckons it's a shame to let the blood of ole Kate die out, and he's thinkin' of raisin' him a nice litter of puppies by some class pointer somewheres.

I tell him there's plenty dogs right around here that's bred good, but he says he wants somethin' as good as Kate herself, and that means the best there is. Well, when it comes to bloodlines and leavin' out what she can do in the field, he's right. So I tell him that right then I kind of liked Wide Valley Jake up in Tennessee over any dog I knowed of. I told Sam he was a young dog that hadn't had a chance to show what he could do as a sire. "But," I says, "he was a ball of fire at the trials, the biggest-goin' dog that's been put down in years, and I'll bet a nice ripe persimmon," I says, "that he gets pups that'll go places and do things."

Well, Sam says he'll think it over, and first thing you know, they tell me he's sent Kate up into Tennessee, and pretty soon here she comes back in whelp to Wide Valley Jake.

The boys around here like to kill themselves over it. The shippin' expenses and the stud fee have set Sam back plenty, and they kid Sam something wicked, but not so much to his face as you might

expect; it bein' well-known by then that if you want to pass remarks about ole Kate, Sam bein' present, you've got to lick him first....

Me, I don't say much. Fact is, I don't know. A man's chances of gettin' anything special out of any one litter is about one in ten thousand, but when you got right down to it, ole Kate was bred as good as they come, and I don't have to tell you about Wide Valley Jake—you being a bird-dog man. He didn't win the National—I know that—but he won a lot of other stakes and he'd make a two-mile cast and kill a calf or a pig or anything that crossed his path and go right ahead on and find his birds, and do it all day. All dog, that's what he was. All dog! A smashin', killin', ground-coverin', bird-huntin' fool.

Well, ole Kate has her pups—a nice litter—four bitches and three dogs. I go over to Sam's to have a look at 'em just after they've got their eyes open. Six of 'em were nice pups, that any man would like, but there was one that took my eye especial. He was about the biggest pup for his age I remember seein', and, man, was he rugged! He was black and white, with a black patch over one eye. Later he ticked out till they weren't no white on him. He was just enough undershot to remind you of a little old bulldog, and that, with the patch over his eye, made him look like you wouldn't want to fool with him none. I watched him squirmin' around in the straw for a while, and pretty soon ole Kate come in, and what that black-eyed pup done to the others was shameful. He just says, "Dinner-time! Hot damn!" and he plowed through the rest of the litter, throwin' 'em every which-away out of his road till he got where he wanted.

Sam got the litter raised up to be six months old when here comes the distemper and cleaned him out of five of 'em. He had two pups left—both dogs. One of 'em was the big pup I'd liked.

He took the two pups out a time or two with ole Kate. Then he begun to leave the big black-eyed fella in the runway and just hunt Kate and the other up. I met him workin' 'em over some nice birdy land I'd leased, one day, and he tells me this is the only pup he's got left. I asked him what's become of the big pup.

"He ain't worth the powder to blow him to hell," he says. "But come along for a piece and watch this one work. Looks like I got something' here."

Well, I rode along with him like he said, and watched the puppy work, and pretty soon I wouldn't have gave a cotton seed for him. Durned if he wasn't ole Kate over again. I saw him hit a cotton row and go down it and come to a cat-brier swamp and cock his head at a frog, and that was plenty for me. I told Sam I had to be gettin' back.

"What do you think of him?" he says. "Kind of reminds me of the ole girl," he says. "Not that he'll ever make anything like her," he says; "that's too much to expect."

"He's got some of her ways," I says. "What's wrong with the other pup?"

"Him!" says Sam. "Why, that big so-and-so'll run right out of the state every time you turn him loose."

"Is that so?" I says, and he had my attention. I'm here to remark. "What else does he do?"

"Kill turkeys," says Sam, "and pigs and calves and anything else that gets in his road while he's poppin' every covey from here to Atlanta."

"Well, well, well," I says. "Supposin' you bring him over to my place Friday mornin' and we'll put him down and watch him at it."

"Not me," says Sam. "I've paid for all the pigs and turkeys I'm goin' to. He can stay in that kennel and rot, for all of me. If he wasn't ole Kate's pup, and bred like he is, I'd of knocked him in the head long ago. I spent two dollars to have him registered as Jake Kate's Jingo," he says. "Ain't that sump'n?"

Well, I talked Sam into bringin' the big pup over by sayin' I'd be responsible for any damage he done, and on Friday here Sam comes with him, and we rode out and set him down. I caught him that evenin' over on the Thomasville road. I had wore out two horses an' a mule gettin' to him. I trailed him fur a while by seein' coveys go into the air that he'd popped. He never even hesitated at a covey; he'd just burst into it and watch 'em fly, and then go find him another. I'll bet he flushed fifty coveys that day. I saw him pop seven in twenty minutes. That was as long as I could keep in sight of him with the best saddle mare I owned. He didn't massacre much—just a Dominick rooster and couple of guineas.

That night Sam agreed to lettin' me handle him at twenty dollars a month, me to pay for what stock and poultry he killed in passin'. I didn't figure it'd be much after I'd worked on him some, and I was right about that. He kept too busy poppin' coveys to bother with killin' stuff. Seemed like he regarded puttin' a nice bunch of birds in the air as the king of outdoor sports.

First I worked him with a thirty-foot rope fastened on his collar. He went away with that and on out of the country. Next I tried dog chain. I put two lengths of it on him before I got through, an' that slowed him enough so I could stay with him on a hoss. It just give me a good view of him poppin' coveys. Man, he'd go from one covey right on to another like he had a date with 'em. A bird finder, if there ever was one! I figgered if he ever took to pointin' and I could keep him on a course, he'd out-bird anybody's dog.

But I couldn't handle him. A whistle meant nothin' in his young life. When you'd set him down, he'd just go hog-wild and stone deaf. His one idea was to get to birds. He didn't have room in his mind for nothin' else. I tried blowin' the long to-o-o-t, to come in on my trainin' whistle and then givin' him a dose of No. 8 shot at a hundred yards, but it didn't make him even hesitate. It burned him some, I reckon, but it was so far off, he didn't tie it up with me or the whistle. He just shook hisself and went on. I didn't dare shoot him any closer. No. 8's'll go into a dog at eighty yards.

I use to set up nights studyin' how I could get him to mind a whistle and begin to handle, without sawin' one of his legs off, but nothin' come to me. It looked like he was just too much dog for any man.

One day I'm drivin' down the road, and just at the edge of town I see Lafe Saunder's boy Ralph sneaking along the road fence with a little ole shiny gun. They was a sparrow hawk settin' on a telegraph wire, and the boy was tryin' to get a shot at it. I stopped the car so's to give him a chance, and right soon that little ole gun went "pht" and down come the hawk.

I called to young Ralph, and he come to the car and showed me the hawk and tol' me about his gun. It had been gave to him on his tenth birthday by his pappy. It was a repeatin' air rifle and he showed me what he could do with it, which was plenty. That boy was just naturally poison with that little old gun. He cut a straw in two at thirty yards for me and shot a dead leaf off a pin oak and hit a tobacco can that I th'owed up in the air for him.

Right then I got the idea I'd been mullin' around for.

I asked Ralph how he'd like to jump in my car and drive on back to my place with his gun and earn hisself four bits. He said that would be just fine with him, and he hopped in and I drove back to my place and put the big puppy on a leash and took him and the boy and a trainin' whistle over to a nice big open field.

"Now, Ralphy," I says, "I'm goin' to turn this here dog loose, and he'll start leavin' here in a hurry, the minute I do. Well, I'll blow this whistle when he's made mebbe a dozen jumps. The minute you hear the whistle, I want you should pop it to him with that little ole gun of yours, and keep on doin' it till I tell you to quit. Do you reckon you can hit him runnin'?"

"I've hit rabbits hoppin' along pretty good," he says.

"Well, he won't be hoppin'," I says. "He'll be flyin'."

"I can hit him right enough, I reckon," he says, "but I don't aim to do it. I don't aim to shoot no dog. That's a nice un. What's his name?"

"His name is Jake Kate's Jingo," I says, "and mebbe he'll be a whole lot nicer dog after you've worked on him some with that little ole gun of yours."

"But it'll sting him," said Ralph. "It'll sting him plenty."

"Le's hope so, Ralphy," I says. "Now you be a good boy and do like I tell you if you want to earn that four bits."

"Ain't you got a cat around somewheres I could shoot at instead?" says Ralph. "I'd a heap sight rather shoot at a cat."

"Listen," I says. "I'm trainin' this dog for to go to the field trials and beat a lot of other dogs that is mostly owned by Yankees. Now, if you can hit him after he gets goin'," I says, "it'll do him good and help him too. You just gotta take my word and four bits for that. Well, how about it?"

The boys studies some, a-lookin' at the dog.

"Do you reckon it'll make him beat them Yankee dogs?" he says after a while.

"I'm hoping so, Ralphy," I says.

"All right," he says. "Turn him loose."

I slipped the leash and the big pup went away from there. I yelled, "Whoah, Jing!" and blowed the long toot when he'd made ten jumps or so, and Ralphy's gun goes "pht."

Well, Jing slammed on the brakes and slid a rod or so, and then set down and started to go round and round, still a-settin'. It looked like Ralphy had made a bull's-eye!

I blowed the long toot and Ralphy hit him in the ribs. He got up instanter and started to leave. I yelled, "Whoah, Jing," and tooted, and Ralphy hit him in the seat of the pants again. He stopped and turned and looked at me. I says, "Come here, you Jing," and blowed the long toot. Ralphy didn't have to hit him again. He come in, lookin' puzzled and sort of mournful.

Well, that's what made Jake Kate's Jingo. He had plenty of brains—a great dog always has. He wanted to find birds and not be bothered by me and my whistle. He knowed I couldn't catch him with a hoss, but when he found out he couldn't outrun a BB shot from that little ole gun, he saw the light.

'Course it wasn't done in a day. Me and Ralphy and him had quite a lot of sessions. Before it was settled, I reckon that boy shot a pound of BB's at that pup. In a few weeks, though, I could stop him with the whistle and wave him to the right or the left and bring him in if I wanted to.

Then one day he was going hellity clatter along a sorghum patch and he put on the brakes like he'd done the first time Ralph had cut loose on him. He slid a ways and ended up with his head turned sideways and his tail like a flagpole, just froze solid on a bevy. I reckon he winded 'em so sudden he didn't have time to think about flushin'. I rode over and steadied him, thinkin' any minute he'd pop 'em, but he never moved. I got down and walked in and flushed a nice bunch of birds and killed two on the rise. I knowed right then it was going to take one awful puppy to beat me in the trials that season. As it turned out, there wasn't one good enough to do it. I expect you know what he done, if you read the sportin' magazines or the newspapers at the time.

One funny thing happened before I went away with him to the trials. I had Sam come over to watch him work a time or two, and one day he fetched Jing's litter brother along for a brace mate. We put 'em down and they went to it. Jing just sailed out to a piece of cover and banged into a covey point. By now he'd hold his find as good as a meat dog, so we rode over nice and easy to kill us some quail.

This litter brother of Jing's had swung after him at the breakaway, and he backed the point all proper as long as we were watchin'. But when we were busy gettin' off our hosses, he pulled one of his mammy's best tricks. He slid up quick and started to edge past Jing to steal the point. Well, sir, I kind of think he was cured of point-stealin' for good and all, right there. Jing made a jump into the middle of that covey and busted it wide open. Next thing we knew, he had the other pup by the neck, and it looked like he was going to start in at that end of him and eat his way clean through. He give that pup one awful trimmin' before we could choke him off. Sam had to take the pup home and doctor him for quite a spell.

I do believe, when he got his full growth, Jing could of cleaned up on any dog I ever saw. I know one night we was coon huntin' with a passel of hounds, and we treed not far from my house, right along the edge of the branch. It was a ole he-coon as big as a cub bear. One of the niggers clumb up and poked him out, and down he come right sprang in the middle of the branch.

I reckon you know a coon's all a dog wants to tackle on land. Well, in the water he's one of the best things I know of for a dog to let alone. The hounds jumped in and swum out to this one, and pretty soon here they come back,. That ole coon had liked to drown the lot of 'em.

Jing had been kind of runnin' at the eyes and nose for a day or so, and that mornin' I'd seen him shiverin' when he come out of the kennel, so when night come, I'd took him to the house so he could lay by the fire. Well, somebody goes out for wood and forgets to shut the door, so just while we're yellin' for the hounds to go back and stay with it, here comes Jing, bustin' through the brush to get to me.

He just stops long enough to say, "Howdy, boss; nice night!" and into the branch he goes, and out to the coon. Far as we could tell, he takes holt of the coon and shakes the waddin' out of him right in the water. Leastways when he brung him to the bank, pretty soon, that coon was plenty dead.

Well, Jing made his first start in the Dixie puppy stake at Union Springs, Alabama. Them other puppies didn't know which way he went. He outpaced 'em and outranged 'em and out-birded 'em. Then he went on through the Derbys like a hot poker through a can of lard. I believe that he could of won a All Age stake right in his Derby year.

Sam saw Jing run just one trial that year. He come over to Crawford, Mississippi, for the Derby championship. Jing won it like breakin' sticks—down once—the judges never called him out again.

That night at the hotel a lot of the boys were shakin' hands with Sam as the owner of the best Derby that had been put down as long as anybody could remember. I'm standin' there not thinkin' about much of anything except what me and Jing'll do in the All Age stakes next season if we both live and nothin' happens.

Right then Sam rares back on his hind legs and sticks his thumbs under his galluses and lets off a kind of oration.

"Boys," he says, "this is a nice-goin' puppy, but he'll never see the day when he's as good as his mammy. Ole Kate was his mammy, boys

—ole Kate, by John Proctor out of Lady Ferris—and them two never got a better one. Unless you've seen ole Kate handle birds," he says, "you ain't seen nothin'. Now, I've got a jug of good corn licker up in my room," he says, "and I'm going up there right now and take a little drink to ole Kate, dam of today's winner. If any of you all want to join me, you'll be shore-to-God welcome."

Well, there's a sort of stampede to Sam's room. I don't go. I just stand there and cuss for mebbe ten minutes.

My share of Jing's winnin's wasn't so bad for down here, but the main thing was the publicity. They begun to offer me dogs from here to Canada. They come in on every train. My barn was full of dog crates. I built me a lot of yards and a dog wagon and bought a couple mules to haul it and a couple more trainin' ponies aad hired me two assistants and a dog-wagon driver. Nigger named Joe. Best hand to nuss a wagon through soft ground and over down timber I ever saw.

I kep' Jing over to my uncle's brother's place by hisself. I didn't want him pickin' up nothin' some dogs might bring in to spread through the kennels. I'd drive over and hold court with him every day, and he got along fine all summer, except he got out once and sashayed off and killed him two pigs and a calf as he passed through. I didn't dare leave him with Sam. Him and his wife was a pair when it come to feedin' dogs too much and lettin' 'em lay back of the kitchen stove. That's where ole Kate stayed, mostly. I reckon that helped to keep her nose uncertain.

I worked Jing some, every day. I had to put the polish on him. I thought he could out-bird any dog in the world, and he was nothin' but style and class, but I was aimin' for the National championship, and they have to read and write in there. I had so much on my hands I thought I'd let the chicken trials go that year, aim for the National, then next season take him up to Saskatchewan or Manitoba, and work him on prairie chicken a spell; after that I'd win the chicken stakes, wind up with the All-American championship in Manitoba, and get on back to the quail trials in time to grab the National for the second time. I shore had a nice schedule laid out for the dog, and I'm sayin' now, he could of pulled it off if he'd had a break.

'Long the last of August they held the opening chicken trial up in

Saskatchewan, and that was the first anybody ever heard of Pride's Shot. He won that stake and the Manitoba Field Trial Club stake and the All-America at Pierson, one-two-three. The gun-dog writers went crazy over him. It didn't worry me none. We'd been beatin' the setters so regular these last years that I kind of thought the boys had overdone it when a fair sort of setter did come along. Then I run into Kirk Mellish up in Atlanta, where I'd went to have a talk with him about takin' a couple of Derby prospects he'd raised. Kirk had went and seen some of the chicken trials, aimin' to buy a young dog that was runnin', if he liked him. I asked him if he liked the dog.

"Not the one they wanted to sell me," he says, "but I liked this Pride's Shot dog extra plenty. He's all they say he is, and don't you forget it!"

"Do you think he can beat my dog?" I says.

"I dunno," says Kirk, "but listen, when you put Jake Kate's Jingo down with that setter, you better have him right."

Well, that didn't worry me, neither. Kirk knows a dog when he sees one, but I knew Jing, and I didn't think the setter ever lived that could beat him in the shape he was in right then. I could just forget the go-on signal when I put that gentleman down. All I had to do was keep him on the course and hope he didn't take a notion to kill a bull between covey finds.

I took him out to the Southern Illinois trials, and you'll recall he won the open for me, and done it easy. A kind of funny thing happened in the runnin' of the stake, I remember.

Jing went down for his first heat with Lulu Girl, a right nice pointer bitch. He outraced her at the breakaway and swung left to a hedge with some high ragweed along it. Just as he's through the ragweed a shoat popped out of the hedge right in front of him. I blowed the toot-toot, toot-toot, to go on, quick as I seen that shoat, and listen, that's the first and last time I ever tooted at Jake Kate's Jing in any stake he ever run in. I could just as well let the whistle hang, that time, because the next thing we saw was that shoat goin' up in the air as high as the hedge. He had time for one squeal, but that was all. Jing had just shook him once and tossed him and gone on. He hardly missed a stride.

Well, sir, out of the hedge pops another shoat, and up in the air he went, and then here comes out another one and he rose on high. And then there was Jing, fifty yards beyond, solid on point. He'd nailed that covey quicker than he'd killed one of them shoats. I was some dumbfounded. I didn't know what the judges would think about a field-trailer handlin' livestock. I looked back at 'em when I called "Point," and they was kind of grinnin' at each other. The whole gallery was hollerin' and laughin' too. I took a nice long breath and rode over and flushed the covey when they gave me the word, and shot my pistol.

One of the judges watched Jing stand nice and steady to wing and shot, then he spoke to me.

"Kind of a chip off the ole block," he says. "All right, send him on."

I led Jing back to the dog truck after the heat.

"Killin' pigs, you big bum," I says to him. "Don't you know you're runnin' in the Southern Illinois Open?"

Jing just panted. He didn't act worried about nothin'. He was right, at that. He had the stake already won. They give him first next day without puttin' him down again.

Well, I've talked a heap sight more than I aimed to when I set down here, and I won't go into the other stakes he won, except to kind of recall the National championship. Of course, a man would rather win that than all the other stakes combined. It seemed made to order for Jing. Them short sprints in the other stakes don't take much except nose and speed and style. It's the three hours down, in the National, that stops a class dog. A gun dog can go three or four hours easy, but look how he goes. If you was to make one of them hunt his country at the speed a dog must go in the National, your ordinary gun dog would slow to a trot in thirty minutes. When you ask a dog to go three hours at a field-trial clip and keep fresh enough so his nose will let him smash into his covey finds and snap up his singles, you're askin' him to do somethin', brother, and don't you think you ain't.

I've seen dogs that would go through the motions, but all during the last hour they didn't find nothin'. I'll tell you why. They was just runnin'. Their noses was gone. First thing that goes when a dog gets tired is his nose. A dog that can stay birdy for three hours at top speed has got to be all dog. And that's where I lived. I'd never seen Jing shorten stride; I'd never seen his nose go dull, and I'd worked him five hours just to search him.

He could of licked a covey of wildcats the day I shipped him to Grand Junction for the National, and I just naturally knew the championship was in the bag.

They told me, when I got there, that Pride's Shot had been shipped East for the National.

"That's good," I says, and as true as I set here, I meant it. I'd heard enough about that setter by then to want Jake Kate's Jingo to take him. He'd begun to get in my hair.

Sam had come up to see the National, of course, but I kep' away from him. I was afraid he might begin to talk about ole Kate, and right then I didn't want to listen to him.

I run into Kirk Mellish the night before the opening day.

"Well," I says, "your hotcha setter is here with the rest."

"So they tell me," he says.

Now, he had seen Jing win a couple of stakes by then, in his All Age form, which he hadn't at Atlanta.

"Well, what do you think?" I says.

I just asked to make conversation. I thought he'd say there was nothin' to it but my dog, but he surprised me.

"Just like I told you before," he says; "you'd better be good."

I kind of laughed, and begun to look forward to seein' the Western setter go. It looked like Jing and him in the final, sure. I thought maybe he could give Jing some real competition for a change.

I saw the setter go the next afternoon. He went down with Gladstone Pat, another setter, and a good one. When the pair was ordered up, I wasn't laughin'. I'm here to say that Western dog was all Kirk said, and more. He was just one awful dog to try and beat—that's what he was. He wasn't as powerful a goin' dog as mine, but he was streamlined. That baby split the wind. And did he know the birdy places, and did he spot 'em, and did he go to 'em? He had a choke-bore nose and it stayed that way. He moved so easy he finished the three hours rarin' to go.

I went back to the kennels that evenin' and had a word or two with Jing.

"You got somethin' to beat," I says. "How do you like that?"

Jing hit the kennel straw a thump or two with his tail and went to sleep on me. So I went back to the hotel and borrowed a bottle for a minute and looked at the ceilin' with it, and pretty soon I knowed there wasn't a setter alive or dead that had any business foolin' with Jake Kate's Jingo.

My dog run his first heat the next afternoon, and went on away from Lilly Lucas that Clem Hardwick was handlin' that season. She looked so bad against him that Clem drew her after two hours and took her up. The judges had me go on and finish out the heat alone. I kind of think they enjoyed seein' Jing go, and they knowed the gallery wanted to watch him, too, from the way they were yellin' over some of his smash finds.

I wasn't lettin' the Western setter bother me after that race. Jing was right and that was all it took. But I got a jolt when I went to put him in his kennel. As I started to leave, I seen a bloody paw mark on the boards of the kennel-house floor. It was right fresh, and I went back and turned Jing up to look at his feet and legs.

Well, sir, he'd cut a three-cornered chunk right out of his left fore pad as big as a two-bit piece. By next day that ugly cut would be sore as a boil. A lion couldn't have run on it and stayed game, I figured.

I set there holdin' the paw and studyin'. I had the most dog I'd ever seen and this was his big chance. I wouldn't have fooled away a minute on a ordinary field-trailer. I'd of just drawn him and cussed the luck and let it go at that. But Jake Kate's Jingo was somethin' else again. So I set and studied.

Pretty soon I went up to my room and cut me a leather dog boot out of a pair of high-topped huntin' shoes I had. I cut the full length of the tops for a pair of leather thongs to hold the boot on with. Then I got me a box of absorbent cotton and some adhesive tape from the drugstore, and I was all set as far as I could be with a foot like that and a race against that Western setter ahead of me.

They went down Thursday afternoon in the final, just like everybody figured. I had absorbent cotton taped on the cut pad and the boot over that, tied on as tight as I could without cuttin' off the circulation in his foreleg.

At the breakaway they left us like a pair of bullets, but Jing didn't go more than a hundred yards like that. He slowed up and hopped along on three legs for a piece and then he set down and sort of shook his left paw.

"He's wavin' good-by to that setter!" some clown yells, but it don't get a laugh out of nobody.

Next thing I knew, Jing was down workin' on that nice boot of mine with his teeth. He worried it off before I could get to him, and then he went from there with strips of adhesive flappin' like little white flags every time he took a jump.

The Western setter had banged into a covey by this time, and Jing froze into an honor point as he got to him, and there they stood.

After the flush, I held my dog long enough to get the adhesive strips off him, and that let the setter go out there and find him another covey, and Jing had to honor him again.

And then the real race started, with Jing two coveys down, and man, it was a dog race. That setter had never been held even in speed or range in his life before, but he was held, all right, from then on. It was a find for the setter and a find for my dog for the first two hours. And then it looked like Jing begun to step on the gas and really go places. He begun to get outside of the setter, a little more each cast. You'd of thought he'd increased his stride, but you'd of been wrong. He'd given all he had right along, and kept the setter strung to the limit to hold him, and that had took enough edge off the other dog, for all his slick goin', to make Jing look like he'd turned on somethin' extra special for the last hour. He got his two coveys back and then some. In the last thirty minutes he just birded Pride's Shot to death.

"He wasn't wavin' good-by, back there!" I heard somebody holler. "He was just pattin' the sod down on that setter's grave!"

They laughed at that one.

Now I'm goin' to tell you something, and I want you to think about it whenever somebody starts talkin' about such and such a bird dog bein' the greatest that ever lived because, accordin' to the records, he won this and that. Jake Kate's Jingo never took a lame step in them three hours. He showed as much as I'd ever seen him have. I led him off, after it was over, on three legs, mostly. Once in a while he'd go on four for a step or two, and whenever he done it, the grass was smeared with blood. That left front pad of his was just blood raw.

The judges give it to him right on the course. Naturally, the gallery ganged us to have a good look at the new National champion. Sam had got to me, and he stood lookin' at Jing, standin' there shakin', with his paw held up, waitin' till I could get him through the crowd and back to his kennel.

"Lemme tell you somethin,' boys," says Sam to the crowd. "He's as good as his mammy—every bit as good—and I don't care who hears me say it."

I don't say nothin' for a minute. I can't seem to find me any words. Then God give me speech.

"Why, you mule-faced, egg-suckin' polecat!" I says. "There ain't a hair on this dog's tail that ain't worth more than that frog-pointin' road-runnin' counterfeit you've been wastin' grits on for the last ten years, and I'll throw you in with her for good measure."

"Gimme my dog," says Sam, grabbin' for the leash.

I let go of it, and he led Jing off on three legs. I ain't never seen him from that day to this.

Speakin' up like that to Sam was a piece of foolishness. It didn't do no good. He's still talkin' about ole Kate—you heard him yourself. All it done was to lose me my dog. Sam owned him, right enough, but he was my dog just the same. Jing knowed it, and I knowed it.

Bein' around a great dog like that does things to a man. There's somethin' about a world beater that takes a awful hold of you. Jing never tried to get friendly with me. He never craved pattin' or bein' rubbed back of the ears or havin' his back scratched, or none of them things. He kind of kep' to hisself. But just the look in his eyes, the way he held his head, every move he made, kep' me feelin'—well, humble's the word, I reckon.

And that ain't all he done to me. When you've had as much dog as that, no other kind of dog will ever please you again. I tell folks I quit trainin' on account of the misery—arthritis, or some such a name, Doc Weaver calls it—but that wasn't it. I just couldn't get interested in no other dog, when I come back here without Jing—so, afterwhile, I quit tryin'.

Jake Kate's Jingo never won again. Sam sold him up North for five thousand dollars, and they turned him over to Tom Manning. Tom's a right good handler, but Jing went on off the course and out of sight whenever he put him down. Just too much dog for Tom—it seems like.

Well, the air's getting kind of sharp, now that the sun's dropped below them buildin's. Reckon I'll get on home. Hope you kill yourself a nice mess of birds tomorrow.

Dog Upon The Waters

Myrtle is dead, poor funny little snipe-nosed Myrtle. I left her, bored to extinction, at a gun club in Maryland. Between shooting seasons, life to her was a void. It consisted of yawns, the languid pursuit of an occasional flea, the indifferent toying with bones and dog biscuits, and a mournful, lackluster gazing at fields and thickets nearby.

During these dreary months she was never chained or confined in any way. Self hunting, which spoils so many gun dogs, did not affect Myrtle. Occasionally, when the dragging days became more than she could bear, she would betake herself listlessly to quail cover, find a covey, point it for a moment, flush it, and watch the birds whir off into the pines. She would then return, sighing heavily, to a twitching nap somewhat around the clubhouse.

She must have perished during one of these efforts to break the monotony of existence in a gunless world, because a letter from the club steward tells me that she was caught in a muskrat trap in the big marsh and drowned. The big marsh is perhaps a half mile from the clubhouse.

Drowned! Except for Chesapeake and a spaniel or two, I never saw a better swimmer. And yet, in preventing a similar tragedy, she became my dog, body and soul. Also I learned to sniff audibly when scientific fellows announce in my presence that animals cannot reason.

And now, I fear me, I shall have to divulge a secret that has been closely kept for many a day. I am about to spread reluctantly on the printed page the one formula for securing the kind of quail dog that

fills an owner with unspeakable joy from dawn to dark, year in, year out, come heat or cold, or drought or rain.

It has nothing to do with sending a check to a professional breeder and then waiting, all expectant, for a shipping crate to be delivered at one's door. It has nothing to do with raising endless litters of distemper-ridden puppies. If you want the rarest, the most perfect instrument for sport in all the world, and not the average plodder and flusher of commerce or home industry, stick to my formula. I set it down exactly as it was given to me by a wise man of the South many years ago.

Here it is: "A Georgia cracker will sell anything—his land, his mule, his house, his wife. By God, he'll sell a bird dog—a real one, I mean. Just show him cash money and he'll reach for it."

These words—after I had learned their true significance—accounted, some years ago, for my spending a winter in Atlanta. My string of gun dogs, so my handler told me, had petered out. I was looking for another string, and Atlanta is the clearinghouse for information about noteworthy setters and pointers located in various counties of south and central Georgia where the most quail and, ipso facto, the most good gun dogs are found. Working out from Atlanta by motorcar, as rumors of dogs that knew their business drifted into town, I had secured four pointers. I had shot over perhaps fifty dogs in selecting them. The four were all fast, wide-going, covey finders. Class dogs are good for about three hours at top speed. I, therefore, had a pair for mornings and a pair for afternoons, but I needed something that would stay in closer and go slower and find singles—an all-day dog—to back up my four whirlwinds.

One evening a voice spoke over the telephone—a voice that I knew well. The voice said: "Listen. The foreman of our bottling plant was down below Macon last week. He got plenty birds. He's been telling me about a little setter bitch he saw work that sounds like what you're after. He says he can fix it for us to go down and shoot over her next Saturday. What say?"

"How far is it?"

"'Bout a hundred and twenty miles."

"Does your foreman know a good dog when he sees one?"

"Yep!"

"What does he say she's like?"

"He says she's a ball of fire."

"Doing what?"

"Finding singles—coveys too."

"All right, have him fix it."

Thanks to that telephone conversation, my glance rested upon Myrtle for the first time about eight o'clock the following Saturday morning. She came cat-footing from somewhere behind a paintless shack, set in three or four acres of cotton stalks, at her master's whistle.

I took one look at her. Then my eyes swung reproachfully to the bottling-plant foreman who was responsible for, and had accompanied us on, a one-hundred-and-twenty-mile drive to see her.

"Never you mind," said he stoutly. "You want a bird dog, don't you?"

I did want a bird dog. I have ever been contemptuous of him who goes gunning with a silky-coated, bench-show type of setter calculated to drive a sportsman to undreamed-of heights of profanity with one hour's work in the field. But this specimen before me was—well, I felt that I could never bring myself to admitting the ownership of such a dog.

I had been told she was little. She was. She did not weigh much more than twenty pounds. She had a wavy black-white-and-ticked coat that gave her a claim on the setter family. Her muzzle was so pointed that her head suggested the head of a fox—a black fox—except for a pair of drooping bird-dog ears. Her tail was short, clubby, and without any flag. She carried it drooping and a bit to one side. Her eyes were the yellow fox eyes that belonged in such a head. Her gait, as she had come loping to us, seemed more cat than fox, but it reminded me of both.

Delicacy made me omit the opening of the ritual expected at such a time. "How's she bred?" was never spoken. I inquired without interest about her age.

"Comin' three. Reckon me an' you better stay together, an' yoh friends hunt their dogs."

"All right," I agreed feebly. I was in for it! A-hunting we must go!

And a-hunting we did go. My friend and the bottling-plant man with two of the former's dogs in one direction; my hapless self, with the unspeakable little setter and her lanky owner, in another. She had been named Myrtle, he told me, after his old woman. I had caught a glimpse of the "old woman" through the door of the shack ere we set forth. She was all of sixteen.

We walked in silence up a lane, and so came to fields and promising cover. "Get along, Myrt," said my companion, in a conversational tone, and Myrt drifted to our left into some high grass and disappeared. We found her presently, perfectly still, looking without particular interest straight before her. "She's got birds," I heard. And this, indeed, was true, if our finding a covey twenty yards ahead of her proved it. Accustomed to the tense rigidity on point of more orthodox shooting dogs, Myrt's method was disconcerting.

I shall not attempt to describe that day—my first day afield with Myrtle. She found, in her cat-fox fashion, twelve coveys, as I remember. After each covey find, she proceeded to point and promptly retrieve, when killed, every scattered bird of every covey—or so it seemed to me. And the day was hot, and the day was dry. Incidentally her master shot rings around me.

Her final exhibition that evening would have settled my desire to call her mine if she had not already won me completely hours before. We had joined my friend and the bottling-plant foreman. They had found two coveys and a few singles, had killed four birds, and my friend's pair of pointers were the apple of his eye.

"There just weren't birds in the country we worked over," my friend explained.

I saw the owner of Myrtle open his mouth to speak, then close it resolutely. We started down the lane to the house, my friend, with his dogs at heel, in the lead; Myrtle, cat-footing behind her master, in the rear.

The dusk had closed in softly about us. It was already too dark for decent shooting. The lane down which we plodded had a high wire fence on either side, with pine woods to the left and a flat, close-cropped field to the right.

Suddenly I heard a whine behind me. I stopped and turned. Myrtle was trying to squeeze through the right-hand wire fence to get into the field beyond.

"Birds out yonder," said Myrtle's owner.

I called to my friend and explained.

Now his dogs had just passed that way without a sign. Also, the field was almost as bare of cover as a billiard table.

"Out there!" he snorted. "Wait till we get back to Atlanta. Maybe we'll find a covey in the middle of Five Points."

Perhaps I should say here that Five Points is to Atlanta what Trafalgar Square is to London.

Myrtle's owner met the insult by picking her up and dropping her over the fence. She went straight out into the field and stopped. There followed an exhibition of fence climbing against the watch by my friend and the bottling-plant foreman. They managed to scratch down two birds from the covey that roared up in the gloom somewhere out ahead of Myrtle.

Thirty minutes later she was stretched out on the backseat of the car on her way to Atlanta, too tired to wonder where she was going or with whom.

She cost me—steady, gentlemen, don't throw anything; just observe the workings of the formula—forty dollars. The amount was simply spread carelessly before her owner. The result was inevitable.

And so I became the owner of Myrtle. But that was all. I made a point of feeding her myself. I brought her into the house and begged her to accept my favorite overstuffed chair. I petted her fondly. She accepted food and chair without enthusiasm. She barely submitted to the caresses. She was not interested in a mere owner. She wanted a master. She wanted the lanky cracker—that was clear. As to the matter of forty dollars changing hands, she completely ignored the transaction.

Having endured a few days of this, I accepted an invitation to go down with one of the best quail shots in the South to shoot with friends of his near Americus. I wanted birds smacked right and left over Myrtle. I wanted her to see shooting that was shooting, with the lanky cracker far, far away. This, I felt, might aid her perception of property rights. I loaded her into the car then, among a reassuring welter of gun cases, shell boxes, and shooting coats, and, lest she be distracted while learning that forty dollars is forty dollars, I left the four whirlwinds straining at their chains, yelping prayers and curses after me, as we drove off.

Eventually we reached a plantation house and its broad acres, over which we were to shoot, to be greeted by two tall brothers who owned it all. A mincing, high-tailed pointer, who seemed to be walking on eggs, and a deep-muzzled, well-feathered setter helped to welcome us. They were a fine-looking pair of dogs. I opened the rear door of the car and Myrtle came forth.

Now our hosts were true gentlemen of the South. After a look at Myrtle, they spoke earnestly of the weather and the crops and of how hard it was to get hold of good corn liquor. The crack shot from Atlanta became absorbed in assembling his gun. All in all, the moment passed off well.

In due time we marched out over the fields, four guns in line. We had planned to separate into pairs when we reached wider country. This we never did. I do not like to shoot with more than one other gun. I wanted the crack shot to help me kill birds instantly and stone dead when Myrtle found them; but, in a surprisingly short time, the brothers showed little desire to leave us, despite their pair of dogs ranging splendidly through the cover.

Myrtle, as we started, had run whining from one man to another for some moments. At last she stopped to stand and watch the other dogs quartering out ahead. She turned and looked deliberately at, or rather through, each of the gunners, myself included. Then with a last small whimper, she got to work. It became clearer and clearer from then on that the place to kill birds that day was in the vicinity of Myrtle.

That miniature, misbegotten what-not found covey after covey and heaven knows how many singles. Her work was marred, however. When a bird fell, she would find it at once and pick it up. She would stand uncertain for a moment and whimper, then start with the bird in her mouth for the nearest man. Having visited all four of us, she would begin to move in a vague circle, whining and looking about. Once she dashed for a high black stump in a field, to return dejectedly with the bird still in her mouth.

I blew my whistle at such times. She never seemed to hear it. I would go toward her, calling her name, and ordering her to "Bring it here!" She only retreated from me, whimpering as I advanced. Getting to her at last, I would take hold of the bird and persuade her to let go of it. All this took time. It was also, to me, her legal owner, somewhat mortifying.

I shared my lunch with Myrtle. She accepted a sandwich, then withdrew a little from the rest of us, to stand looking off into the distance. Suddenly she was away like a shot. I looked in the direction she was going and saw a Negro field hand working along the bottoms, gun in hand, looking for rabbits. I blew and blew my whistle. She rushed on. When close to the Negro, she stopped, looked at him, and came slowly back to where we sat. I rubbed her behind the ears and along the back. She submitted, gazing off into space.

Later that afternoon a covey scattered in a narrow thicket along the bank of the river. The river was in flood—a wide, tawny plain with hummocks of fast water in the middle and still reaches of backwater at its edges.

Myrtle pointed a single within inches of the water. The bird, when flushed, swung out over the river. The deadly gun from Atlanta cracked. The bird came down in the backwater just at the edge of the current. Myrtle was in the river swimming for the bird the moment it fell. She got to it quickly, but an eddy or the wind had carried it out into the current. As she turned to come back with the bird in her mouth, the force of the river took her, and downstream she went.

There was a bend just there, curving away from our side. We four stood helpless on its outer rim and watched her work slowly shoreward, going downstream ten feet for every foot she gained toward the backwater and safety. I remember yelling "Drop it, Myrt—drop it!" knowing that she could make a better fight without that wretched bird. She did not obey. She struggled on until she came at last to the backwater with the bird still in her mouth.

We all breathed sighs of relief and watched her swim swiftly toward us when free from the drag of the current. "Good girl! Bring it here!" I called, and got out a cigarette with shaking fingers. I began to bask in exclamations I heard along the bank: "Hot damn! That's the baby!" And "Come on home with the bacon, gal!" At least I was her owner.

But trouble swiftly met that small swimmer. There were cat briers growing below her in the flooded ground. One of the longer of these through which she swam fastened in her collar—the new collar I had bought her only the day before. Swim as she might, it held her fast. Her stroke became less smooth. She began to paw the water with her front feet—splashing as she did so.

My shooting coat, filled with shells, came off and in I went. No swimming, I found, was required. I was no more than up to my armpits in icy water when I reached Myrtle. For this I was duly thankful.

Myrtle was showing fright and exhaustion by now. She was no longer swimming. She was dog-paddling frantically to keep her head above water. The quail was still in her mouth.

I disengaged the brier from her collar and carried her to shore. Then I sat down to empty my hunting boots. I thought I felt the rasp of a pink tongue on the back of my hand as I did so. I can't be sure, for I was pretty cold.

The day was well along and my bedraggled state demanded the plantation house and a fire. We started toward both, hunting as we went.

I was at the left end of the line. Myrtle stopped on point, out in front and to the right. It was evidently a single, since flushed birds had gone that way. I called, "Go in and kill it!" And stood to watch the shot.

The bird fell at the report of the gun. Myrtle went into some brambles to retrieve. She emerged with the bird in her mouth. "Bring it here!" I heard from the man to whom it rightfully belonged. If Myrtle heard him, she gave no sign. Nor did she give that whimper of uncertainty that I had heard throughout the day, as she had stood with a recovered bird in her mouth. She came to me on a straight line, running eagerly, to lay the dead quail in my extended palm. Her eyes had that look—half pride in work well done, half love and faith and companionship—that is characteristic of a shooting dog as a bird is brought to the master's hand. "Here it is, boss!" that look seemed to say. "It's yours. And I am yours—to slave for you, to adore you, as long as I shall live."

Although my teeth were chattering, I was warmed suddenly from within.

Myrtle rode back to Atlanta that night, curled in my lap, a weary but contented little dog.

The White Grouse

·I·

A lonely cabin in the hills occupied by a he and a she suggests romance; but the interior of such, a cabin—although so occupied—was altogether free from things romantic on a certain star-filled October night.

Gladstone's Nellie, undeniably feminine, was staring with dreamy indifference into the fire. John Jones, indubitably masculine, happened to be staring at Gladstone's Nellie. It is to be doubted whether in all the land, there was a creature more worthy of inspection than Champion Gladstone's Nellie; yet John Jones saw her not at all. He had just harked back along a tunnel of dead years and come suddenly on a dun mare hitched to a yellow-wheeled buckboard, trotting briskly along a winding thicket-flanked road.

Startlingly clear, after the dimness of the tunnel, was the high-headed, ear-flicking mare and mud-splashed buckboard; startlingly clear was the man with the iron-gray mustache in the woods-smelling, sweat-stained, weather-beaten shooting coat who was driving the mare; clear also was the gawky, towheaded boy, perched beside the man, with a shiny new, single-barreled, twenty-gauge clasped in his arms. But clearest of all was the black, white, and ticked setter, shaking with suppressed desire as he crowded against the boy's knee and stretched his long, deep muzzle above a clicking wheel to read the autumn air.

Yes, clearer than mare and buckboard, clearer than his father, clearer than himself, was the stretching neck and head of old Don. Thanks to the brain within that head and the miracle called a nose at

its end, John Jones could exchange the vision of mare and buckboard and winding road for another. He could watch the towheaded boy follow a creeping black, white, and ticked shadow, through a thicket, down a gulch, along a watercourse, up a hillside, and so at last to a small jungle of blackberry vines. The shadow moved slower, slower; it ceased to move.

"Are you ready?" asked a quiet voice.

The boy found it impossible to speak. Even a whisper was beyond him. He nodded faintly.

"All right, Don. Go on!"

A roar of wings beating up from the briers, a hurtling bombshell all black and bronze and gold, the boy swung his gun and pulled the trigger, not knowing he had done so. A puff of floating feathers in the air, empty.of all else except blue sky and flaming branches; a heart-shaking thump and rustle in the dead leaves below. John Jones had killed his first ruffed grouse on the wing!

One night during the winter that followed, old Don came to the bedside of the father of John Jones and whined a yearning whine that the man could not understand. He laid a hand on the old dog's head and asked him what was the matter. Don whined again, stuck a cold nose against his master's cheek, and returned stiffly to the shooting coat in the corner, on which he slept. In the morning the man heard no thump of a tail against the floor when he sat up in bed. A moment later he knew that the whines and that cold nose in the night had been a last farewell.

When the next shooting season arrived the father of John Jones began to take long drives through the country with John Jones' mother. When they passed a flaming thicket he would shift the reins to his left hand and put his arm about his wife. John Jones wondered why his father never hunted any more. One day his father explained.

"A man is entitled to one good woman and one good dog during a lifetime. He'll never be happy until he gets them. You're going to be a man and a grouse shot some day, you're going to know a lot of women and think a heap of some of them—until you find the good one. You're going to own a lot of dogs and think a heap of them, too; but when you get the good one—you'll hunt him till he dies, and then—well, then you'll be glad you've got the woman."

"Yes sir," said John Jones, as though he quite understood.

Fifteen years had passed since then, passed like the landscape at the window of a train. In those fifteen years John Jones had learned to cut a grouse down with the precision of a machine. But that was all, and it was not enough. He must have the complement of perfect shooting—a perfect shooting dog. For ten of the fifteen years he had been looking for such a dog; for the one good dog to which he was entitled—a grouse dog like old Don.

As for the one good woman to which he was also entitled—there was a certain girl.... Sitting on a ribbon of white beach that edged a purple ocean, he had told her many things that summer. He had explained the lack of ambition of which he was accused. Happiness, he had told her, was what the bewildered human race was stretching and yearning toward. He had found it in woods and thickets, on little lakes and streams. He had found abiding tranquillity so long as he remained in the environment from which it sprang. A few days in the city and it was gone. In its place would come a growing restlessness, mental at first, physical later, like a gnawing, deep-seated pain.

The girl had drawn in her breath sharply and touched his sleeve.

"I know," she had said; "I know."

John Jones went on to tell about his shooting. In doing so he had tried to describe the indescribable—a ruffed grouse roaring up in the brooding hush of a thicket.

"But it can't be told," said he at last; "you'll just have to see for yourself."

That fall he had contrived to have them both members of the same house party in the Connecticut hills. On the opening day of the grouse season they had set forth together. She had exclaimed rapturously at the sight of Gladstone's Nellie, moving like music, through bowers of scarlet and gold.

But John Jones had recalled for her the black, white, and ticked shadow of his boyhood, that could follow a grouse through any cover and point him out again and again, like the finger of fate. He was looking, always looking for another like him, he had told her. He admitted—cautiously, lest she think the matter trivial—that he could never be wholly contented until he found such a dog. Mildred—that was the girl's name—regarding him with cool gray eyes, had seemed to understand.

It had rained the night before. The woods, when they plunged into them, were filled with the patter of silver drops and smoking with mist. The leaves and branches on which they stole along were too sodden to protest at alien footsteps. It was a day on which a dog with any sort of nose could find birds. Gladstone's Nellie had done surprisingly well. As for John Jones—with those cool gray eyes upon him he had shot as if inspired. Grouse after grouse, glimpsed through steaming vistas, had crumpled up at the pull of his magic trigger and thumped down on the wet leaves.

John Jones had come to a halt at last and laid the dead birds in a row on a fallen log, smoothing the feathers of each as he did so. "Nine," he counted, and looked up at the girl in triumph. He found her regarding the dead grouse with a strange white look.

"You told me you gave the birds a chance," said she.

"Of course. They were killed on the wing. A lot got away."

"None that you shot at."

"But the dog flushed a dozen or more ahead of us; you heard them get up."

"Yes, I heard them." She looked again at the row of grouse on the log. "And that's why you want the kind of dog you told me about—so that none would get up ahead." She had spoken softly, half to herself. Now her lips contracted to a thin red line, her eyes became gray agates. "I hope," she cried, "you never, never find him!"

That was the beginning of the breach between them. John Jones might have explained that it had been an extraordinary day; that had the woods been dry nine out of ten birds would have flushed wild before the beauteous but uncertain Gladstone's Nellie.

But why explain? Why explain anything to a girl who thought her feeling for wild things was deeper than his own? A girl who had brought a little silly sentimentality into his beloved woods and been shocked by what he did therein. Give the birds a chance! She seemed to think one poked a gun at a grouse going like a flash of light through thick cover, and down he came.

So John Jones had not explained. The breach between them had widened that evening. The next day she was gone.

He would never try to close the breach, he now reflected. Never! He had found the one good woman, apparently, only to have her think he lacked in sportsmanship. Well, the one good dog remained to be looked for. Some day he would find him; another like old Don.

What if he failed to do so? What if such a nose and such uncanny bird sense should never be combined again? John Jones stirred uneasily at the thought.

Gladstone's Nellie stirred also and lifted her head from her paws. John Jones snapped his fingers; she rose unhurriedly from before the fire and came to him with a slight wave of her tail. He put out his hand. Her muzzle sank into it. He covered her nose with his other hand and tightened his fingers until her nostrils were closed. For a moment breath was denied her. When he released her she sneezed. He smiled down into her amber eyes, into which came a gleam of amusement.

She adored him openly for a moment, not failing to come to a statuesque pose while so doing.

"You're a fraud," said John Jones. "Go and lie down!"

She obeyed the command with the carriage of a stag and the grace of a fawn. Yes, she was a fraud, he thought—self-conscious, vain, a born poser. A champion on the bench, she was only a fair bitch in the field and somewhat less than that when pitted against a wily old cock grouse. Her nose would do if the day was not too dry. She was quiet, steady, and obeyed his lightest word. But she lacked the quenchless passion of a great gun dog—old Don, for instance. He would go all day through briers or over stubble, gasping with the heat or shaking with the cold, lost in a frenzy of concentration on the finding and pointing of birds.

Gladstone's Nellie was not like that. Slush and mud distressed her. Burrs she abhorred. Always a lady in fine raiment, she shirked too-briery thickets, she skirted the edges of swamps. But oh, the wonder of her poses! The sheer breathtaking beauty of everything she did! At the first scent of birds she became a duchess. On point she dimmed the glory of a queen.

Perhaps, being feminine, this satisfied her soul. Perhaps she simply lacked in nose. At any rate, in solid bird-finding qualities she did not improve. John Jones knew she would never make the grouse dog that some day must be his. It was too bad. Just to watch her gave a man a thrill and, damn it all, she was a sweet old thing.

He watched her now as she sank down and resumed her contemplation of the birch logs pouring an inverted cascade of flame up the black mouth of the chimney. The chimney was a haphazard affair of stones and mortar. At one time the stones had been scattered on the surface of a timber-crested hill, rising like a threatening wave above the valley of the Neversink. The four-room shack that huddled against the chimney was borne up a hundred feet above the valley by the first swell of this wave. Across and farther down the valley was Slide Mountain, its rounded top the highest point in the Catskill Range. The shack belonged to a friend indeed, who was held in New York at present by the anxieties of a falling market.

John Jones had never hunted the Catskills before, but during the previous June he had spent a week with a fly rod anywhere from ankle to waist deep in the rushing Neversink. Above the noise of the stream there had come to him again and again the mysterious hollow drumming that a cock grouse achieves when he beats his love-racked body with ecstatic wings.

Finding the woods and thickets of the Connecticut hills curiously haunted by a pair of cool gray eyes, John Jones had recalled those feathered drums along the Neversink. Good! The grouse would be in the hills above the stream at this season. New country. Nothing to remind him of—He plunged into his packing.

That was on Monday. It was now Tuesday. John Jones and Gladstone's Nellie had dropped out of the stage from Big Indian that afternoon to find themselves just beyond the five-mile shadow of Slide Mountain. John Jones had a bag full of hunting clothes and shells in one hand, and a gun case in the other. In his pocket was a key to the shack—its roof a blank gray square among lemon-colored maple leaves well above the road.

Five hours had passed since then. A Flemish-oak clock gesticulated the fact from the mantel with thin brass hands. John Jones decided on a sniff of the night air, a look at the stars, and so to bed. Gladstone's Nellie accompanied him to the door and slipped out into the night when he opened it. At his whistle a moment later she seemed to float from the darkness into the light from the open door. She, too, stood and raised her eyes to the heavens. Her nostrils worked delicately as she sniffed the portent of a myriad blazing stars. Her tail moved in faint approval.

"Correct," said John Jones; "it's going to be a nice day. A little dry for you, Susan Jane."

He bent his knee against her silken side and gave her a push. Robbed of a marvelous pose she took her injured dignity with her and stalked into the shack.

"Good night," said John Jones, when he was ready for bed.

She only stared into the dying fire.

He chuckled and blew out the light.

· II ·

It was clear and warm next morning; it became hot as the sun rose with enviable ease above the hills that John Jones was climbing doggedly, the sweat running into his eyes. The sun drained each fern and fallen leaf, the briers and the laurels of every trace of melted hoar frost. It began to crack and rustle and snap under foot.

Gladstone's Nellie roaded like a spring song past a thicket and paused vaguely her head lifted. From the thicket came a sudden b-r-r-r-mph of strong wings beating among leaves and slender twigs, followed by th-r-r-r-rh to the left and below her, and then from somewhere ahead another th-r-r-rrh.

"Three of 'em," counted John Jones, deep in a tangle of wild grapevines, with a spider web pasted over one eye. "She was right on top of them," he reflected. "Well, it's pretty dry."

He struggled on and came in sight of what had been a stone fence. Beyond this was a semiclearing of matted briers and wild grass. A dozen wizened apple trees clung to the hillside, despite the overpowering advance of an army of birch, already swarming among them.

Once more Gladstone's Nellie paused, exquisite but vague. She began to move in her most royal manner up the hill along the stone fence. John Jones crept behind her—ready. The bird rose on all but silent wing, as they sometimes do. It was an instinct only that turned John Jones' head to see a flash of brown directly behind him a hundred feet down the hill. He whirled to fire but there was nothing to fire at by then.

"Susan Jane, Susan Jane!" he said reproachfully.

Gladstone's Nellie, somewhat abashed, leaped gracefillly to the top of the stone fence. Realizing that she was silhouetted against the sky above the clearing she poised there for an instant in an attitude. A lichen-covered stone rolled sullenly from beneath her feet. She disappeared from view and John Jones heard a yelp. When he reached the wall and peered over she was on three legs. He examined her crushed forepaw and realized that rough miles of steep hillside were not for her for several days.

Words escaped from John Jones for some moments thereafter. They were spoken softly but with extraordinary fervor. He returned to the shack with Gladstone's Nellie, bathed her forepaw with hot water and witch hazel, sympathized with her for a half hour or so, and set forth, gun in hand, alone.

For the rest of that day he fought his way through tinder-dry thickets, with a snapping and crackling as brazen in those silent hillsides as a brass band. When evening came he was thorn scratched, soaked with perspiration, and birdless. He looked about him and wondered where he was. The world just there was made up of birch, sumac, laurel, wild rose, wintergreen, and nothing more except a glimpse of pale green sky with the evening star hanging like a lantern between two dusky hemlocks.

To his left was a towering cliff which seemed to sway toward him as he looked up its unscalable side and caught its topmost pinnacle, dark against the sky. Ahead was thicket, thicket without end, apparently. To the right was thicket also, but he knew the road through the valley must be below somewhere in that direction.

He lit a cigarette before working down to the road, and watched the first puff of smoke hang in the still air. A hermit thrush poured out a throatful of rich contralto notes. A whippoorwill spoke thrice from the leaning gloom of the cliff. As the last syllable of his entreaty died away, another sound rose crescendo on the hush of evening. It came from no discernible point. It was as though the muffled heart of the hillside was beating; but John Jones felt that it was somewhere below him.

Making each slow footstep a matter of careful consideration so that not a twig should snap, not a leaf rustle, he stole in the direction from which the sound had seemed to come. Three times more it rose and throbbed through the thicket, a little closer each time.

A gray rock gloomed ahead. Bending low, he moved catlike to the rock and raised his head by inches above its moss-crowned top. Not ten feet away on his drumming log was a great cock grouse. All about him was purple shadow; but he was bathed from crest to toe in a last rosy beam flung across the valley by a red sun just sinking behind Slide Mountain.

John Jones, tense as a panther about to spring, quivered to his finger-tips. He had never seen a live grouse so clearly before. He had never seen, alive or dead, a grouse like this; for his feathers, from his spread tail to his lifted crest, were white as forest snow; or, rather, heliotrope, for such was their amazing color in that shaft of rosy light.

John Jones, staring, ceased to breathe. For an instant he seemed to hear a strain of fairy music that swelled his heart and dimmed his eyes. For an instant only, this lasted, then the hunter's instinct seized him again. He stepped from behind his concealing rock.

One look of horror that was like a scream the white grouse gave him, then sprang into the air in wild unheedful flight. John Jones glanced along the brown tubes of his twenty-gauge and pulled the trigger.

He found the bird, beak down, wings spread, in a bed of fern, fifty feet below. A drop of blood hung like a ruby from the tip of his bill. Blue gray eyelids had curtained forever his jeweled gaze, for no matter how swift his end, a ruffed grouse closes his eyes in death.

John Jones stroked the plumage of the unbelievable bird, still shaking from the tenseness of his stalk and the thrill that had followed. Now and then during a lifetime the eyes will receive an impression that is developed in the darkroom of the mind into a memory picture that will never fade. John Jones had one such picture—the vision of his boyhood that contained his father in his shooting coat and the never-to-be-forgotten old Don. Now he felt that the white grouse, strutting on his drumming log in the hushed mystery of evening-lighted thicket, would also remain with him for the full length of his days.

He reached the shack in the last of the twilight, received a passionate welcome from Gladstone's Nellie, and promptly moved kitchenward.

He was ravenously hungry. He had promised himself a grouse for dinner. He was just able to fulfill that promise. Having taken the white grouse from his shooting coat he hesitated. Was it Lucullus who had dined on nightingales' tongues? To eat the bird he held in his hand seemed almost as barbaric as that. What else was there to do—have it mounted? He shuddered. He always shuddered at wild things stuffed and molded to a dreadful parody of life. It was nearly as bad as seeing them alive in cages. Creatures in dying served other creatures; that was Nature's plan, and he never quarreled with Nature. He had no hesitancy in killing fish and game; but part of his creed was "Kill no more than will be used." Having killed this bird on the wing by fair woodcraft, it should not be wasted.

John Jones proceeded to pick and clean the white grouse. He also prepare a rabbit he had shot for Gladstone's Nellie. Next he poked about among the pantry shelves for a culinary accompaniment of some sort to broiled grouse. He was hoping for currant jelly, which he did not find. He did find some canned asparagus. He had no idea how long it had been on the shelf where he found it, but he opened the can and sniffed at the contents. It smelled all right. He examined a stalk—it looked all right.

Thirty minutes later he pulled a chair to the oilcloth-covered kitchen table and sat down with something of a gleam in his eye. He ate every morsel of the grouse. He ate the asparagus to the last stalk, despite a faintly bitter flavor that he could not account for. He topped off with canned cherries—more loot from the pantry. He consumed all the juice the can contained, and most of the cherries. At last he sighed deeply and regarded a scattering of well-picked grouse bones and an astonishing pile of cherry pits with a touch of disfavor. He rose, yawned, and lit a pipe; then sauntered into the living room, dispossessed the reproachful Gladstone's Nellie from the couch, and stretched himself upon it.

For a time he smoked languidly, watching the fire and thinking of that look of horror in the eye of the white grouse as he had roared up hopelessly from his drumming log. He was recalled to Gladstone's Nellie by the steady plop, plop, plop of her tongue as she resumed a patient licking of her injured paw. He would not hunt her another season, he decided. He would send her back to the bench, where her matchless poses would avail her more. Between the close of this season and the next he would comb the country for a setter with a chokebore nose and an uncanny ability to guess the destination of a grouse in flight—a setter like old Don. Surely somewhere there must be—

John Jones became aware of a peculiar numbness in his arms and legs and a weight across his body. He became aware that the light of the fire had grown dimmer. It was as though a veil had been drawn between the flames and his eyes. For a moment he remained motionless, wondering. In that moment the numbness of his limbs increased and a thicker veil was drawn across the fire. He made an effort to sit up. The weight had increased to such an extent that he found it impossible to do so. As he gathered his muscles for a final effort a black curtain cut off the last faint gleams of the firelight. The now tremendous weight across his body seemed to press him down into a faintly humming darkness. At last the humming ceased.

· III ·

Less than light, more than mist, a faint grayness, here and there was breaking through the smothering void of dark that surrounded him, changing it into irregular fantastic patches. This was his first realization of space and form, his first consciousness of being. On its heels came a feeling of unutterable loneliness and then indefinable horror. Horror of what? He did not know. He only knew that he was alone in some place of infinite danger, where help would never come.

Cowering, fearful, he eyed the dark patches, striving to understand them, wondering if they contained the nameless pressing danger with which the very air seemed filled.

The grayness slowly intensified. The dark patches became less vague. They were taking noticeable forms. He strained his eyes at them. They were trees. Trees! Towering above him on every side, enormous trees—the largest he had ever seen.

The grayness was—yes, it was the sky. The earliest sky of morning, unwarmed by a hint of the coming sun, still deep below the rim of a gloomy earth.

He was out of doors then, somewhere. But where? And why was it such a place of horror, so fraught with fear, so filled with peril? Why should trees—even astoundingly large trees, with the sky above them, shout "Danger!" to his soul? There was nothing to be afraid of in the woods. The woods meant a friendly all-pervading, quiet and—tranquillity. These woods in which he crouched now meant nothing like that. They filled him with a hair-trigger watchfulness that he dared not for an instant abate.

That watchfulness made him suddenly aware of a tangible and immediate danger. It took the form of a pair of blazing, greenish-yellow eyes fastened upon him with unwavering intensity. Instantly, with no thought whatever, he acted. He seemed to be shot, as though by a released spring, into the air. Straight up he went with no apparent effort. He found himself upon a lower branch of one of the enormous trees. It was a hemlock; in some unaccountable way the feel of the bark of the branch on which he sat told him so.

He stared down at the spot where he had been crouching an instant before and saw a tremendous creature. It sniffed longingly at the place where he had been, glanced upward with a soundless snarl, and melted into the undergrowth. Watching it as it went he discovered that it was a cat—a bobcat—larger than an elephant.

As he sat with surprising ease on the hemlock branch his nameless horror lessened somewhat. For a time a multitude of thoughts scudded through his brain like wind-driven clouds. He was able to grasp none of them. It was a feeling, not a thought, that told him he was not as he had been. He had been—he had been—He could not tell what.

And what was he now? That question, too, he found unanswerable. He only knew that he was alive, sitting in a tree, with innumerable dangers below him. It seemed best to remain in the tree.

He sat on the hemlock bough for some time while the cloudlike thoughts continued to drift through his brain. Merged with the thoughts, and at last overpowering them, was a craving, a bodily craving that grew until his whole mind surrendered to it. Hunger! He had never known such hunger before. He had been hungry, somewhere in that past that he could not recall. That is, he had had a pleasing appetite. Now his hunger was all-pervading. Every atom of his being demanded that it be sustained by food.

He moved anxiously back and forth along the hemlock bough, peering at the earth far down below. Danger was there, ceaseless danger on every side; but there was no food in the tree. He must have food.

He examined the ground in every direction. Each bush was scrutinized—each fallen tree trunk, rock, hollow, tangle, and fern bed. He pierced each shadow with his eyes until he read its heart and found it guileless. Lower and lower sank his head, stretching earthward until at last he tilted suddenly from the limb. To his surprise the earth did not rush up to shatter him. It swam along, rising gradually until he settled down upon a mossy slope, without shock, without harm.

For a long minute he remained immovable, giving a strained attention to the silence about him, ready for another instantaneous spring into the safety of the air. At last he relaxed a trifle and became conscious of the soft moss underfoot. He took a soundless step forward and listened. He took another step, and another, and another. He came to a hollow filled with great dead leaves that rustled, despite him, as he passed through them. He felt something hard below a leaf under one of his feet. He kicked the leaf cautiously aside with a peculiar backward thrust of his foot and beheld a beechnut, large, ripe, sound. He gobbled it like a flash, kicked more leaves aside, and more, and more, to be rewarded now and then by a beechnut.

As he became absorbed in his searching he tossed the leaves aside with growing eagerness. An almost constant rustle was the result. A faint little rustle it was, when the clamor of a world is considered, yet he knew somehow that the law of the place he was now in was silence. Hunger was driving him to break the law. It was also detracting from his watchfulness.

He found himself relying on an indescribable new sense that was more than hearing, more than seeing. It was as though there extended from him in all directions invisible antennae that felt the atmosphere for currents of danger. Suddenly these feelers warned him. He froze into immobility. His eyes fastened on a fallen beech tree, the leafless branches of its top smothered in a thicket of rhododendron. He saw nothing alarming for a time. He had almost decided to continue his feeding when something moved. It was an ear—a delicate pointed ear. It had moved along the trunk of the beech tree that angled toward the spot where he stood, rigid, among the scattered leaves.

Again he was shot upward. On a smooth limb of the beech tree that had furnished him food he found safety. From where he sat he could took down upon the fallen beech and see behind it. A great red fox, his coat gleaming like new copper in the growing light, rose from a belly-flat crouch, stretched, yawned, and stood listening. Somewhere in the distance a gray squirrel broke the silence and the law with a low staccato barking. Ears pricked, head raised, the fox stood as though painted. Presently a twig snapped faintly; dead leaves rustled. He watched the fox flatten down and steal toward the sound. Five minutes passed in deathlike quiet. There was a crash, a terror-stricken chatter ending in a scream, a pat, pat, pat of careless padded feet trotting triumphantly away.

Again he sat on his branch, fearful, dismayed. Again his hunger resumed its insistent demand that it be satisfied. It was not hunger, however, that drove him at last from his supposed point of safety. It was a winged shadow that dropped upon him from somewhere higher in the beech tree. With the tail of his eye he saw it coming and sprang from his limb. The talons of a gigantic horned owl clutched the empty air behind him.

Again the brown floor of the woods sped below him—much more rapidly than before. It was only a level blur as he tilted in and out among the trees, going like a bullet. Despite his sudden knowledge that the horror that filled this place reached well above the ground, he thrilled at this hurtling through the air and continued it until a sudden fatigue brought him slanting down.

Into his instinctive rigid listening at the end of his sweep through the air came the tinkle of running water. He pushed thirstily toward the sound through giant ferns and towering laurel. He emerged from the undergrowth at last and came upon a quiet pool, cradled in gray boulders.

Water! Cold, clear, as pure as the skies. His craving for it at the moment was even greater than his desire for food.

Slipping between two boulders to the edge of the pool he looked on all sides before stooping to drink. At last his eyes dropped to the still surface of the pool, in which gray rocks, an ancient bending pine, a far and fading crescent moon were mirrored. He did not drink. He remained as motionless as the boulders that flanked him. Something else was reflected in the pool; something at which he stared with a new and greater horror—his own reflection.

But was it his own reflection? He moved his head to be certain. He lifted his wings and was doubly certain. Wings? Yes, wings—the snowy wings of a white grouse.

So that was what he was—now. And he had been—It was no use! It would not come back. But there was a peculiar horror for some reason in being a grouse—a white grouse. He knew that. It was more than the fact that he was ringed by swift destruction with no single place of refuge, no smallest moment that did not hold a threat. He felt that some dark and terrible purpose must be fulfilled, and he therefore was a white grouse. What that purpose was he could not even guess.

At last his thirst rose above his shuddering thoughts, his trembling fears. He drank, dipping his bill in the pool and lifting his head until the water ran down his throat. Never had he tasted such water, so cool, so pure, so satisfying.

His thirst marvelously quenched, hunger took command of him once more. He turned from the pool to seek food in the silent scented woods and thickets of which he was now a part.

And the woods and thickets yielded him food—indescribably delicious, unbelievably sustaining. He found and ate the creamy-colored meat of scrub-oak acorns, withered purple raisins of the wild grape; bittersweet, brilliant red partridge berries, berries of the mountain ash and wintergreen and thorn; black haws, high bush cranberries and dried wild cherries, chestnuts in dull mahogany, he found; hemlock and pitch-pine seeds, and the crisp fronds of ferns; beggar-ticks, chickweed, frostweed, live-forever—all were to be found for a little seeking. He sought and found them all.

As his crop grew full his fears lessened, his courage increased. The sun rose and swept the thickets clear of shadows with a thousand glinting brooms. It swept the shadow of horror from his soul; he all but strutted through a sunlit glade.

Far up in the sky above the glade was a tiny speck, dark against that dome of blue, but flashing into silver now and then as it rocked and tilted in the sun. His new sixth sense lifted his eyes quickly to that remote dot in the heavens, which seemed as aloof from things of earth as a star. The dot was growing larger, it was falling down the wall of the sky with tremendous velocity. He took wing and flashed toward the cover at the edge of the glade. Through the thickest of the cover he shot—between maple saplings, slender popple, and the white wands of young birch. The thorny interlacings of a blackberry thicket swung into view. He curved to its edge, lit, and scuttled into it. The dot, which had become four feet of spreading wings, a rending beak, and talons of curved destruction, zoomed out of the glade, sailed across the blackberry patch, and came to rest on a weather-smooth, ash-colored limb of a dead tree.

Safe in his stronghold of briers he watched the hawk until it sprang, with a screaming whistle, into the air and spiraled up, up, until it was again a dot.

A curious exultation filled him. He no longer felt helpless or afraid. Each danger could be triumphantly offset, he had discovered, by choosing the proper safeguard from among the many that had been placed about him. It was good to feel the exquisite surge and throb of life within him; it was good to maintain it with pure water and abundant food in the warm, bright world. It was even good to be forced to guard it always with quick hearing, clear seeing, and instant wing stroke. It was good, good, good to be alive! Good to be a white grouse—capable of eluding every possible danger in sure and dazzling flight. He lifted his crest and spread his great white tail. A fallen log caught his eye. He strutted to it.

With a single stroke of his wings he was on the log. The spread of his tail grew more and more fanlike. His breast swelled with a desire that consumed all thought, all other instincts, like a flame. He beat at his throbbing body with his wings, his breath hard-held with a longing that was like a pain. He became engulfed in a hollow booming that filled the air about him with a muffled mystery of sound. It died away as he rested, listening. Again he smote his swelling breast, again the thicket pulsed with sound. Just one living thing could trace it surely to its source. Just one living thing. And so he beat his breast and waited, listening, and beat his breast and waited, listening, until at last she came—slowly, timidly, with shy reluctance dragging at her feet.

He had meant to strut before her when she came, letting the sunlight glisten on his plumage. He had selected the very shaft of sunlight in which his feathers would show to best advantage. In the red sun of evening he could have turned to heliotrope before her—he knew that. Under the blazing sun of high noon he could only gleam and shimmer; but she would be less striking, more modest in coloring, he felt sure. Having dazzled her with his snowy whiteness he would brush her softly with his wings and claim her for his own.

Yes, she was more modest in her coloring; he saw that when she stood shrinkingly before him. Her back and the upper surface of her wings were a sunlit pool of amber water in which were depths and shallows. About her throat was the rich dark of brooding pines at evening. Her breast was a scattering of small brown leaves against ghostly gleaming birches.

He did not strut as he had planned; nor did he brush her with his wings. It was not her loveliness that kept him marblelike upon his log. It was a rush of cloudy fleeting thoughts at which he grasped in vain. For her eyes were cool and gray, cool and gray; and this was strange, strange!

As he stared at her there came a faint crackling and snapping from the far edge of the thicket. The sound grew nearer. Something was moving toward them, its stealth frustrated by sun-baked leaves and twigs. Something else followed it with a rhythmic clumsy tread; but he knew that this clumsy something was more horrifying, more terrible than cat or fox or owl or hawk, and looking into her frightened eyes he saw that she knew too.

Through the thicket, straight toward them, came the first something, followed, always followed by the clumsy but more dreadful second something. At last the first something reached the thorny rampart of blackberry briers and hesitated; but it was dry, dry, and the briers were thick, and neither he nor she breathed or stirred a feather. The first something skirted the blackberry patch, vague and uncertain. Through a vista he caught sight of a glistening silk-coated creature, with the carriage of a stag and the grace of a fawn, moving like music along the edge of the blackberry briers, and so away.

And now he breathed again, deeply, thankfully. A name swam dimly through the depths of his mind. He reassured her in a soundless language of their own.

"It's Gladstone's Nellie," he said.

The fear went out of her eyes. He waited until the second something had stumped off after the first something, then moved to her side. But he did not brush her with his wings. Her eyes were cool and gray once more, and this troubled him. It seemed to hold him away from her for some reason.

He moved off through the briers with a masterful cluck. She followed meekly behind. He came to what had been a tree stump years before. It was now a reddish brown hillock, filled with holes, in and out of which busy black ants were hurrying. He gobbled an ant or so, and she, coming to his side, did likewise. Then he dug into the hillock, scattering it in all directions until he disclosed a small chamber filled with pearl-like larvae, delicious beyond words.

They ate these eagerly for a time, their heads only inches apart. He thrilled as she pressed against him, but always, even while eating, her eyes were cool and gray.

Full fed at last, they drifted on. He darted forward and caught a grasshopper, which he offered her. She thanked him with a warmer look, but partook languidly of only a wing and a leg. He disposed of the rest with some difficulty.

They moved ahead to where a one-time lumber road still struggled to force an uncertain curving way through the ever-crowding thicket. The road was choked with vines and briers. Now and then, however, it freed itself of all except dead grass. Surrounded, half hidden by this waving grass, were bare patches of sun-washed clay and sand. One of these patches they found. Into it they flung themselves and settled down.

With ruffling feathers and clawing feet they burrowed in the sandy soil, letting the warm grains sift along their skins. A fine dust rose and hung about them, dimming the trees and thicket, shutting them in together behind a translucent golden curtain.

At last they rested side by side in the snug hollow they had dug, the sun beating on them in pulselike waves. Closer she pressed against him in a sort of swooning lassitude, closer and closer until he could no longer feel the beating sun. It was less, far less, than his own internal fire.

And now he found her eyes. Soft they were, and dark and shining —no longer cold and gray. His own eyes swam into them while their world of woodland stole away and time was not. Slowly she rose from his side, her eyes on his. As she melted into the thicket she spoke one word of their soundless language.

"Come!"

He, following, found her in a bed of ferns, canopied and curtained with trembling scarlet leaves.

Still as death grew the thicket, wrapped in a breathless hush. He took one forward step on the carpet of moss that lay between them. He took no more. His triumphant spread of tail closed like the white fan it had resembled; his lifted crest went down. A faint rustle and snapping and cracking was drawing toward the leaf-walled bower of her selection. Through that red-and-yellow wall a head appeared. It grew motionless, rigid, except for its slightly working nostrils at the end of its long deep muzzle. White, black, and ticked were that head and muzzle. White, black, and ticked! The soul within him seemed to scream, "Old Don!"

And then he screamed to her in their wordless silent tongue.

"Fly! Oh, fly!"

He himself burst with a roar through the wall of leaves and, swinging low, shot down the edge of the thicket along the lumber road.

He heard another roar of wings beating up through leaves and branches. He heard a stunning crash, followed by a sickening thump. Downy feathers were floating in the air above the thicket. A wisp of thin blue smoke drifted across the road behind him.

Another crash just as he turned an angle in the road. A tuft of dead grass close beside him was cut down by the stroke of an invisible scythe. Three snowy feathers, sheared from his right wing whirled in the wake of his flight. Unbalanced by their loss, he beat his way with unaccustomed effort on and on, until he could fly no farther. He swung clumsily to the left, managed to reach a wilderness of briers, worked his way to the center of it on foot, and crouched there panting.

Ten minutes passed in which the leaves whispered in a timid breeze; a chipmunk ticked like a tired clock; a downy woodpecker tested his bill on a chestnut limb. Listening, listening, that was all he heard.

But now a bluejay screamed a warning. The chipmunk clock ran down. The woodpecker ceased his knocking at the limb. The whisper of the leaves remained, and something else — the faint swish of briers as they were forced aside by a black, white, and ticked shadow, stealing infallibly toward him.

He did not take wing at once. He ran to the far edge of the briers and sprang into the air, beating up as high as he could, then sailing without a sound across a deep ravine to glide down into the center of a chaos of dead timber, half sunk in water and muck.

It was longer this time than before. The faintest of hopes had begun to stir within him, when the black, white, and ticked shadow came plowing through the swamp up to its belly in muck, but struggling straight for him. He could not run, he dared not wait. He rose on floundering wing, rose and flew — blindly, wildly on. Through groves of pine and hemlock, across a rushing stream, over a wide valley to the high ridge beyond. Up the ridge he hammered, beating desperately at the hard air. Flaming hardwoods swung to meet him. By a stupendous effort he lifted above their tops and pounded on. An immense dark mass loomed before him, obscuring the sun. It was a cliff that seemed to scrape the sky. Half falling, half fluttering, he zigzagged to its base, dragged himself under the loam-caked roots of a fallen tree, and collapsed.

He was still shaking to the beat of his pounding heart when the black, white, and ticked shadow appeared. It came up the ridge, through the hardwoods across some broken scattered rocks, scrambling, panting, closer, closer, closer. It slowed to a careful walk, to a creep, to a flat crawl. It stopped—its body quivering, its eyes bulging with the suppressed frenzy of its pursuit. It would go no farther. Nothing would move it from where it stood; for it had found what it was seeking. The long deep muzzle with its vibrating nostrils was pointed, like the finger of fate, at him.

He, too, remained without movement, waiting helpless for what must come. He remembered his exultation when he had discovered that the forces of destruction all about him could be offset by vigilance and glorious flight. He had not known about this Nemesis then—this resistless, ever-pursuing, unbaffled creature that was somehow familiar, that he had known somewhere in the past. Its name had flamed through his brain in letters of fire when it had first appeared. He could not remember the name now. He only knew that the dreadful reason for his being a white grouse was about to be made clear. And so with crippled wing and shattered strength he waited for—he knew not what.

It came at last, up the ridge, over the scattered rocks. He heard it coming, step by step and then at last he learned in a blinding flash that it was infinitely more horrible than he could have conceived. He caught a glimpse of an iron-gray mustache above a faded, weather-beaten, sweat-stained shooting coat, he heard a quiet voice say, "All right, Don; go on," and he knew what he had been.

He had been John Jones, who could shoot even better than his father, for his father sometimes missed.

His father could not miss a crippled grouse out in the open with a great cliff to scale—that was sure. And the grouse, the white grouse under the tree roots, must try to take wing, must try to prevent an unspeakable horror, knowing that he had no chance.

No chance, no chance! He stepped from the sheltering tree roots and hurled himself into the air. A pair of brown gun barrels came up with the swift yet easy swing that a towheaded boy had copied long ago.

A shattering crash and a streak of flame. All was flame. Flames danced in his eyes. They were rushing upwards like an inverted cascade of molten gold. Their light was playing on a shining figure stretched before them, a wonderful, a marvelous, an adorable figure.

"Susan Jane, Susan Jane," whispered John Jones.

It was a timid unbelieving whisper, but the figure rose from before the fire, and despite a painful limp came, with the carriage of a stag and the grace of a fawn, to the couch on which he lay.

John Jones sat up and stared down into a pair of adoring amber eyes.

"I guess it was the asparagus," he said. Then he wrapped the head of Gladstone's Nellie in his arms. "Susan Jane, oh, Susan Jane!" he cried. You're the dog for me!"

He smoked one pipe after that; not a whole pipe; half of what came out of the bowl when he knocked it a trifle wildly against the fireplace was good unburned tobacco. This waste was caused by his pressing need to write a telegram, that would jolt by stage down the valley of the Neversink next morning, and at noon would go singing along the wires from Big Indian to New York. It would be addressed to a girl named Mildred. John Jones ran it over in his mind. as he looked for paper and pencil:

"Can you, will you save Friday night for me? I have something important to tell you."

Pocono Shot

· I ·

I wanted a certain long-barreled, full-choked twelve-gauge. It was one of five guns of mine somewhere in the club storeroom. Since the porter's somewhat ancient eye did not seem equal to penetrating sole-leather cases, and would not have recognized a twelve-gauge in any event, I descended an iron stairway that wound down the elevator shaft into the bowels of the earth.

I gasped as my lungs rejected the air of this lower region. It was a lifeless mixture that seemed to have hung for ages among sweating pipes, hot steam, and dank cement. A human creature—a man, God help him—sat on a stool before the fiery slits of a furnace door and directed me to the storeroom.

Having found what I thought was the right gun case, I opened it to make sure, and put the gun together to see that all was well with those velvet-brown barrels and polished walnut stock. At the crisp click of the gun locking shut I heard the scrape of stool legs and the shuffle of feet along cement. The furnace man stood in the storeroom door. He was a lanky, cinnamon-haired individual, whose face, I noticed at once, was an unusual color—a sort of milky yellow. He said nothing; he simply stood in the doorway and devoured the twelve-gauge with wistful half-shut eyes.

I handed him the gun without a word. Without a word he took it, snapped it to his shoulder, and swept it along in an imaginary cross shot. I noticed that his hands were the same color as his face, and suddenly I accounted for their peculiar shade. At one time he had been weather tanned, layer upon layer. The process of substituting a sickly white for his deep coating of wind and sun had not been completed by his present molelike occupation.

"You shoot, I see."

He gave me back the gun.

"Used to," he said. He stood uncertain for a moment, seemed about to speak, but at last muttered: "Much obliged," and went back to his furnace.

"Poor devil," I thought as I climbed toward better air. "But why does a man who likes a gun take such a job as that?"

I left New York next morning for a week with the ducks on Great South Bay. Those seven soul-filling days passed like a dream. I returned to the club at ten o'clock one night with the whistle of wings still in my ears, the vision of storming clouds above gray white-crested water still in my eyes, the tonic smell of mud flat and marsh still in my nostrils.

The club was drained of members and would remain so, I knew, until the theaters let out. I was in the dismal position of a proud hunter with no one—colored bellboys and a listless desk clerk excepted—to whom he can show his spoils. In my extremity I recalled the furnace man and plunged down the iron stairway with a bunch of black duck, mallards, and broadbills in either hand. I found him leaning on a shovel before the open doors of the furnace, staring in at the seething flames.

"How do these look to you?" I inquired.

He seemed more ruddy as he stood there, but as he came toward me I saw that his warmer coloring had been borrowed from the fire. He examined the ducks, said "Nice" with a nod; then, conscious perhaps that more was expected of him, he added, "Never shot ducks myself."

"It's great sport," I told him. "Cold work, but you forget that. What have you shot?"

He hesitated as he had before, shifted his feet, glanced at his furnace, but at last said, "Pa'tridge—mostly."

"Partridge!" I exclaimed. "The finest bird that flies! The greatest of all shooting—if you have the right kind of a dog."

His yellow hands slowly closed. A shadow swept his face and was gone like a squall at sea.

"I guess that's right," he said as he turned away.

I heard his shovel rasp in the coal bin as I put my ducks in the storeroom. I heard the clang of the furnace door as I went up the iron stairs.

Early spring had come before I saw him again. The last of his tan was gone. By now he matched the unwholesome dirty white of the cellar walls. This time I wanted a duffel bag, a tackle box, and rods.

"Well," I said, "I'm after trout tomorrow."

He nodded.

"I expect it's flies with you, ain't it?"

"Yes," I said; "dry."

"Never got to them," he told me. "I ain't wormed for ten years; but I always fished wet."

"Whereabouts?" I inquired.

He was seized by a sudden uncertainty, or uneasiness, or whatever it was, that seemed habitual with him.

"Oh, where I was raised," he said vaguely, and became absorbed in shaking down the furnace.

I took my plunder up to my room, inspected, sorted, and added to my tackle, and packed the duffel bag and a suitcase. It was late enough for bed when I had finished; but the feel of rods, the click of reels, the sight of neat compartments of tiny somber-colored flies had proved too stimulating. I decided to go down to the library and substitute the back numbers of *Punch* for the vision of a great trout shattering the mystery of a quiet pool at the drift of a Number 10 Fan Wing.

The library was like a cave—an empty cave, I supposed—its mouth a high window through which a rain-shrouded streetlight sent a pallid gleam. A desolation of ashes and the stone arch of the fireplace were painted dimly in gray and rose against utter blackness by staring blood-red embers.

There came the creak of leather and a rumble.

"Who's that?"

I felt among switches and pressed at random. The lights above the fireplace happened to click into being.

"Oh, you!" It was a growl—a relieved growl; some of his fellow club members do not appeal to Gregory Trane. He was sprawled hugely in a red-leather chair with a volume of some sort lying neglected in his lap. He scowled at me for a moment; then, his eyes falling by chance on the book, he brushed it from him as though he'd found it crawling there.

"Rotten!" he said.

Trane is an extraordinary person. He will plow up eight miles of fast water in a single day, whipping a nine-foot rod that would paralyze my arm in an hour; and the average man would drop in his tracks if he attempted to follow Greg, stride for stride, on "a fair day's hunt." Relaxed, he is as stolid, almost as moveless, as a mountain. He talks without the slightest gesture in a lazy mutter that comes rumbling from the great bellows of his chest, to fill a room to its farthest corners. He has quite a reputation as a special writer. You find his name in American and English sporting magazines, attached to articles about exploration, big game and wing shooting, salt water and fly fishing.

With all his passion for the out-of-doors, his wandering over continents, he has found time somehow to do a lot of reading, and to poke curiously about among the women-ridden, logrolling groups of publicity seekers that have turned New York into an asylum for literary and artistic fakers. How he can be welcome in such circles I do not know. Perhaps he trims his sails to the feverish airs in which he finds himself. Ordinarily the give and take of what he calls gabble drives him into a complete detachment that he maintains against all attacks by a series of grunts. During such an interval, however, an array of thoughts, almost sure to be colorful, is apt to well slowly to the surface of his mind. At the appointed time it rumbles forth and is spread before you.

Knowing this, and feeling that the result of an hour or so of undisturbed reflection by Trane might equal Mr. Punch as a sedative, I chose a mate to his red-leather chair and prodded the geyser.

"Why, who wrote it?"

"It doesn't matter," said Trane. "It's called a devastating novel. That'll tell you all you need to know about it. But I wasn't referring specifically to this book."

"Well, what is rotten then?"

Trane checked a bellboy on midskip at the head of the stairs beyond the library door.

"Go up to my room and get a bottle of Scotch you'll find on the table. Bring it here with some ice water and two glasses.... It's rotten that a lot of neurotics, a generation or so from the steerage, who know nothing of the reticence acquired through Anglo-Saxon culture, and the wisdom of that reticence, are spilling their thoughts on clean white paper. It's still more rotten that anaemia and horned spectacles—the chief requirements for modern reviewing—allow any unhealthy ex-sophomore to tell the cockeyed world that this pornography is not only literature but a true reflection of life.

"Now we"—the massive head turned my way—"are little better than imbeciles. If you don't believe it go to the unaired coffeehouses and studios where the modernists hang out and mention hunting or fishing or golf. They won't scream at you through the cigarette smoke as they will if you speak of America for Americans or the Nordic race, but you have no further chance to intrigue them. They draw away from you. You don't belong. You are interested in the childish diversions of the hopeless moron.

"And there you have it. It's at the bottom of the whole mess, as I see it. These people tell you their attitude toward outdoor sports and other traditional things involving competition is arrived at through a superior mentality. Well, let's consider the physical for a minute."

The boy appeared with the required bottle and its complements. Trane was presently musing above a glass.

"I broke through a seal hole once on a trip after musk ox. I've sometimes wished Mr. Volstead might duplicate that performance." The glass was tilted; its golden contents disappeared. "Where was I?"

"We were about to consider the physical."

"Right! Well, let's go ahead and consider it. Let's look over the intelligentzia from that angle. You'll notice a distinct type. You can observe it en masse at any morbid, dreary Russian play. Eyes staring and too bright. Hands pawing at the face. Gestures continuous and fluttering. The speech is filled with artificial inflections. The females strike you as bone-dry. The males are vaguely feminine. The expression of the face is characteristic. It is harassed. There is something in the eyes that tells of a driven, bewildered mind behind them. Don't expect these people to have a sense of humor. The joke is steadily on them—a diabolical joke, a soul-destroying joke. It's this: they're physical weaklings tossed into a world of competing human animals. In earlier ages they would have perished. Civilization keeps them alive. No wonder they jump at the promise of any new scheme of things. No wonder they hate tradition and try to circumvent logic. So long as two and two make four they haven't a chance.

"I spoke of seeing them at Russian plays. After sitting through one or two of these plays, you wonder how in God's name even the intelligentzia can chatter and flutter over such stuff. But these people are sick, primarily in body and consequently in mind. The Russians are sick men writing about sick people. They make the vagaries of sickness seem important. That's why the intelligentzia eat it up. That's why they adored Ibsen. That's why their favorite American playwright is a gloomy lad whose characters are apt to be tubercular.

"Just what has all this got to do with a lot of present-day novels and their glorification by modern reviewers, you ask. Why, this, as I see it: the intelligentzia sniff at outdoor sports, not, as they would have you believe, from a superior mental standpoint, but because as human machines they aren't equal to controlled intensive effort. Take a future member of the intelligentzia and put him in school. He's a highly nervous, frail kid. He hasn't the stamina for athletics and he doesn't go in for that sort of thing. He hasn't as good—that is, he hasn't as well balanced—a mind as sturdier boys but he's more mental, because, being out of athletics, he's apt to become the reading type.

"Now hard exercise in the open is tremendously important to male creatures during adolescence. It's a safety valve. Ask any trainer of trotters or runners what happens to a colt if you keep him shut up and don't race him or work him like the devil. Well, the same thing happens to boys. They're at the mercy of their natural instincts during their formative period and they aren't apt to get over it. Sex becomes to them not only the most important thing in life—which perhaps it is—but the only important thing in life—which it certainly isn't.

"They get through college and have to select a career. They're introspective, highly sensitive, womanish creatures who shrink from the grind of business competition just as they shrank from athletics. Well, what to do? Literary work, either critical or creative, seems alluringly soft and unduly important, and they hop to it. A few of them have the gift for yarn spinning, which is the fiction writer's biggest asset. Most of them have only a knowledge of words and an unworkmanlike method of getting them on paper in an affected precious order.

"It seems to be enough these days; the duller, the more muddled the stuff is, the better from the standpoint of the intelligentzia. And there's a reason for that—two reasons, in fact. First, no sane individual can enjoy it and the nuts and nutesses can seem superior in affecting to do so. Second, it lets so many into the game. Almost any humorless, self-absorbed mediocrity can hope to be called a genius.

"To get back to the erstwhile bookish college or high-school lad—now a man of letters—who attempts creative work. He, of course, lacks the skill of the finished or born writer in selecting and rejecting material. Not comprehending the twists and turns and lights and shadows that make a thing a joy to read, he falls back on a sort of uninspired journalism. He pounds doggedly along, describing just what he sees and feels. A fly on a dirty windowpane, greasy dishwater, any detail of the daily round that gets commonplace people from the cradle to the grave is as important as a cha——no, I won't say charming; charm is beyond him—as an interesting or dramatic episode. You see, being a supreme egoist—all unhealthy minds arrive at that—he can't get away from himself long enough to do imaginative work, and he hasn't the ability to handle it if he could. He's restricted to muddy autobiography. Having been in a sort of fever ward of desire, through adolescence and after, the result is exactly what you might expect.

"For some time I didn't believe that regular human beings could be impressed by the gang who are peddling and advertising this mournful, modernistic rot. But part of the propaganda of the bunkier-the-better crowd is that nothing in which there is any humor is to be taken seriously, and I'm damned if they haven't sold the idea pretty generally. You'll find it followed out in the prize awards for literature of one sort or another. You'll find it in lists of best stories or best plays or best novels prepared by the hopeless jackasses who do that sort of thing. Now the most difficult thing in the world to fish out of an ink bottle is genuine humor. I'd rather undertake to write three serious plays than one comedy. The ability to write humorously is a pure gift, almost invariably backed by a philosophic mind. That's why it's beyond most women and nearly all of the male modernists.

"Life is made up of smiles and tears. If you can't handle both, start an art theater or run a laundry wagon or teach aesthetic dancing, but don't write. If some of these tensely earnest souls think that unrelieved dreariness and the shibboleth of the unpleasant ending make for a better world, let 'em read the *Christimas Carol* once or twice and then tear up their latest drab effusions.

"They call an uninspired recital of unpleasant or commonplace happenings art. What is art? Is it an instrument of torture? Is it a method for dousing the human race in boredom or slime or anguish? The Russians think so; but if one well-rounded piece of literature ever came out of Russia I never read it—and that goes for Tolstoy.

"I've been wandering; I'll get back to my point. If humorless Zanies can put over the idea that anything humorous is trivial, they can put over other ideas. You may have noticed that the males of the intelligentzia are all a-twitter over equality for women. The explanation, as I see it, is this:

"This physically inferior type of man is apt to feel more comfortable with women than he does with his own sex. He has more in common with them. He has the acute sensibility, softness of fiber, and intuitive impulses of women. He can be as mental as he pleases with them—they adore it. He can act any part he chooses—they'll match it with another. He swaps introspections with them for hours at a time and comes fairly close to their point of view. He feels the injustice of their handicap and, of course, he can't fathom their compensations. He'd have to be all female to do that. Only an indeterminable percentage of him is female—just enough to tinge his face or figure or gestures with effeminacy and set him on fire for The Cause.

"The result is that in their semiautobiographical novels and what-not these young—some of 'em are middle-aged—weaklings dress up the shabby affairs they may have had with unprotected females by raising the mentality of the poor creatures and describing them as intellectual pioneers in the new and glorious freedom for women.

"Now the human animal is instinctively polygamous. It's taken a good many centuries to substitute an ideal for the overwhelming instincts of a species. If you reverse the process by blending idealism and nonrestriction, you've got an insidious mixture. Youngsters all over the country—who seem to read everything these days—are gulping it down in regular and copious doses.... Damn this pipe!"

I offered my cigarette case.

"Thanks, no. I'll get it cleaned out in a minute."

Trane alternately dug in the bowl of his brier and blew tremendously at its stem. Presently its guttural purr returned. His formidable torso sank back once more and became wreathed in tobacco smoke.

"All this philosophizing or moralizing or whatever it is I've been afflicting you with has probably bored you, because you think the condition I've indicated isn't worth getting excited about. Family trees are bound to grow nuts now and then, you say. True. It's also true that most native Americans have a fair amount of horse sense. But bear in mind that in this country today public discussion of artistic endeavor comes largely from the mouths and typewriters of an illogical minority. What philosopher was it who said that if he could make the songs of a nation he didn't care who made its laws? There's a lot in that thought when you consider it. This much is certain: if you let the type of mind that is blind to the laws of Nature—I'm thinking in particular of this freedom-for-women business—and can't comprehend that social laws are the result of half a million or more years of human experience, start indicating what plays shall be seen and what books shall be read, you're going to produce some sort of an effect, and don't you forget it."

Trane's arms rose like pillars in a Gargantuan stretch. His mouth became a cavern.

"What do you want—censorship?"

The cavern snapped shut with an audible click.

"Don't be an idiot! That would mean political dumb-bells throwing the occasional fine thing out with the swill. But this censorship discussion gives you another little angle on the marvelous minds of the intelligentzia. They're howling for paternalistic government. They want to substitute it for economic competition. Then they shriek to heaven if you talk about applying it to the arts."

"Well, what have you got to suggest?"

"Why not substitute sanity and real literary judgment for aestheticism or modernism or whatever they call it in book and play reviewing? It could be done by the publishers of the country in thirty days. Without the free advertising of their fellow neurotics, all the little geniuses would either get behind a ribbon counter or starve to death, and that would be that."

"You've explained to me why a certain type takes to bookish ways," I said. "If I accept the explanation, I'll have to ask you a question. Where will the army of sane, normal, thoroughly competent reviewers come from to supplant the new school now scratching away?"

Trane remained silent for a moment.

"God knows—now that you mention it," he said at last, then chuckled at a thought. "We might pass a law that no man can go into print with a criticism of anything until he's fifty." The cavern again opened hugely and again clicked shut. "Hi-hum—I think I'll stick to Kipling or go back to *Davy and the Goblin*. If I don't I'll be told by some reviewer that *Such-and-Such* by So-and-So is a masterpiece, and I'll discover in the first chapter that the plodding paranoiac who wrote it must have been in the same thought circle in high school with the reviewer.... Let's go to bed."

We got to our feet. It was my turn to stretch.

"I haven't heard you rave like this since the *Lusitania*," I said, when I had accomplished a miniature of Trane's yawn. "You're taking a lot of forlorn egomaniacs too seriously. Come and go fishing with me tomorrow."

"Like to—can't," said Trane. "I'm going up after salmon later and I'm after South American trade right now. Luck to you! And let me say one thing more—they're egomaniacs all right, but if you could see some of the effects of their outpourings they wouldn't strike you as so damned forlorn."

· II ·

I was to try a new stream. This might easily prove disastrous, but it allowed almost anything in the way of delightful speculations and filled me with impatience at the best efforts of a locomotive snorting up a mountain grade.

I had been told to get off at Emmetville. Eventually the train clanked away through a dripping rock-walled cut and left me confronted by a station bearing that magic name. It was a weather-beaten frame station with fleecy clouds on azure distantly above it, a road wandering off and down, and nothing else; no living soul; no vehicle of any sort.

Among busy telegraph instruments I found a man who explained that only mail trains were met. Having told me that they looked after fishermen at Gaylord's, he suggested that I leave my duffel bag and suitcase in the waiting room until they could be sent for, and pointed out a sort of goat trail that, he said, was quicker than the road. This, as I peered down it through the almost parallel trunks of standing hemlock, I could easily believe. Encouraged by what I guessed to be the roofs of buildings far below, and the steady roar of the stream that scaled even these heights, I followed the station man's parting advice to take it kind of careful, and presently slid into Emmetville, accompanied by detached fragments of shale rock.

Gaylord's, when I found it, was a white house with many windows staring in blindless amazement at a—to my pavement-weary eyes—great expanse of matted grass broken by scattered maples.

Having tugged intermittently at a bellpull set between the front door and a panel of etched red-and-white glass, I wandered along the porch around the house and came upon a squat figure spading in a garden. It was a man. He had a bright yellow handkerchief knotted at his bronze throat and gold earrings gleamed below the dark thatch of his closely curling hair. He came slowly erect when I spoke to him, showing a friendly row of teeth and passing the back of his hand across his brow. I explained that no one answered the bell.

"She gawn. She cawm back bam-by," he informed me. "You lack stay here?"

I told him yes.

"Feesh-mebbe?"

I nodded.

His eyes roamed over the chocolate-colored loam of the garden with a speculative gleam.

"A'right, I feex you nice for feesh," he promised. "She feex you nice"—he indicated the house with a flat thumb—"when she cawm."

He was stooping to his work when I told him of my things at the station. Once more he straightened up.

"A'right," he said, and shambled toward the rear of the house on a pair of stumpy legs bowed past all believing.

By the time I had regained the front porch a soul-jarring screech arose, drew nearer, hove in view. It was the protestations of a wheelbarrow as my friend of the garden urged it around the house, down a flagged walk, between the square rotting posts of the front gate, and so away. I allowed the blessed distance to take the sound into its quiet bosom before I followed through the gate for a look at Emmetville in the last of that day's sun.

Emmetville lay—or rather huddled—in little better than a gorge. Already it was in shadow. Except for an hour or so at noon, some or all of it was sure to be in shadow. The town pressed close to the edge of the stream; the main street bent like a half-drawn bow by a curve of rushing water. In the center of this curve, on a mound of jutting granite, was a planing mill with a grumbling turbine and shrieking circular saws.

The mill, obviously, accounted for the town. A few miles farther down, the train had hung for a moment above a comfortable valley, but the stream had ambled through those pleasant meadows in a series of contented pools. It takes a fretting river to drive a wheel.

Fretting? It did more than fret past Emmetville. It seethed and raged and roared and dashed itself to foam. I did not go down to the edge of that maddened froth of water—the stream would come tomorrow. Now I looked at the town and the great hills above and ruminated over the incredible difference a railroad train and a few hours can make.

Yesterday New York. Last night the rumbling voice of Trane discussing the aesthetes. The aesthetes! Forlorn, I'd call them. Futile was what I should have said—here in Emmetville. And so much of this great land was Emmetville; thousands of Emmetvilles. My eyes dropped from the sides of the gorge to what the gorge contained. Fifty years ago fox and bobcat had claimed this for their own—a sublime magnificence; but set a driven saw between walls of spruce and hemlock, with hardwood ridges just beyond, and a lot of things happen.

Comes a freight siding; and then a railroad station; a blacksmith shop; a general store; a schoolhouse; a church without a steeple; another general store; another church with a sprouting steeple; more stores; a lot of talk about a bond issue to pave Main Street that never reaches the point of action; a grist mill; another church with a sure-enough steeple; a high-school; an actual bond issue to put up a brick courthouse and jail. Mix in with and crowd around all this a lot of yellow or white frame houses and red barns; add plenty of paintless outhouses and chicken coops and woodsheds; cut through it all, here and there, with muddy alleyways—and there you had it! From a majesty of white water flanked by brooding tree-capped palisades to Emmetville; from—Trane's tirade now reacted—*Huckleberry Finn* to *Many Marriages*, all in fifty years. Progress was a wonderful thing! Upon which cynicism I wandered back to Gaylord's.

"She" had returned—a gaunt woman in black, blasted by toil, but with an unwrinkled shining brow. Her name was Firth, not Gaylord.

Her expression was contradictory, hard to define. The lower half of her face was set in hopelessness—the woman was undone. And then came her eyes, fever-bright with—it seemed like hope; and above, the serenity of brow.

Her manner was detached. Although she met my eyes, I could not feel that she took me in. It was something beyond me, not in the room—not, perhaps, on this earth—that was apparently stealing her attention. She admitted vaguely that she thought she could take care of me, and showed me to a corner room on the second floor of the house.

"It's on the west side," she explained as she opened the door; "but you'll be gone two hours before the sun strikes us here, and this"—she waved her hand at a black cylinder running from the floor to the ceiling—"is the pipe to the kitchen range."

It was like an introduction, and knowing something of April in the high hills, I bowed agreeably to the stovepipe and murmured, "Pleased to meet you."

She gave my lighter note no attention whatever. She peered about the room with her unseeing—or rather farseeing—eyes, went to the washstand, touched the folded towels lying upon it with the tips of her fingers, took the cover from the soap dish, replaced it, glanced into the water pitcher, and turned to leave the room. Before she had crossed the threshold she began to sing, or rather hum. I am not certain whether it was the closing of the door or the screech of the returning wheelbarrow that cut off her song. At any rate, the squat Sicilian was at my door a moment later with my suitcase and duffel bag. A dollar having changed hands, I learned that his name was Joe, and was again assured that he would feex me for feesh.

As I unpacked, the humming again grew clear—astonishingly clear. I discovered that the stovepipe as it came through the floor of my room acted as a sound conductor from below. I could have heard a whisper in the kitchen by standing close to the pipe.... The humming continued. I listened until its cadenced, droning melodies struck home. Hymns! Methodist or Baptist surely. Hymns—one after another, and the clatter of cooking utensils. But not, fortunately, the odors of cooking. Hymns only came up the stovepipe. They were pleasantly soothing and old-timey. They were the last thing I heard that night as, having turned out the acetylene gaslight and contemplated the stars above the crowding hills for a moment, I felt my way from the window past the stovepipe to my bed.

Getting into my waders on the side porch next morning, I saw Joe waiting in the offing. As I clumped down the steps in my wading shoes he sidled up and pushed a tomato can at me with something of a flourish. The can was filled with the largest night crawlers I had ever seen. They looked like an entanglement of pink boa constrictors.

That can of giant worms had meant an hour or more of searching and stooping after a hard day's work. It was not the time for a dissertation on the ethics of trout fishing. I accepted the tomato can beamingly. Ten minutes later its contents plopped into swift water. I watched it disintegrate and whirl downstream in wriggling spirals and loops before I assembled my rod.

By noon I knew that my venture to strange waters had been fortunate. The stream was magnificent. It and its rocky tree-hung banks did unexpected things it every bend. It was thrilling, rugged water that needed study and the careful placing of well-gripping hobnails. Trout could be taken almost in the heart of the town, I found; but not too many. Joe's "feexing" explaining what that stream had been standing for years from natives and city sports. I more than earned what fish I took—lusty gentlemen, however, in olive and brown who knew exactly where the swiftest current ran and what it was put there for. Never a one who accepted the quick challenge of the little rod failed to make that airy wand bow deeply, again and again, to the might of a worthy antagonist.

The sun was in the middle of that other river of blue above the gorge when a fallen hemlock just below a bend suggested a seat where I might lunch to the music of the stream. However thunderous that music may be, it dies to a faint accompaniment as line and leader straighten out to drop a fly on chosen water.

Tense no longer, as I munched a sandwich the blended voices of the stream claimed me for their own. I was immersed in, flooded with, became part of ceaseless, all-pervading sound; drugged by it, drowned in it, as though it were the water that was its cause and I had sunk beneath its surface.

I wondered dreamily why nothing of man's devising could so massage the heart and mind. An orchestra? I curled my lip. Strings and reeds and brasses, prodding at the senses, poking at the nerves, but leaving the ache of the mind, the yearning in the breast, the kinks in the soul, untouched. Orchestras would have to do in New York; but not two miles upstream from Emmetville.

New York! It was inconceivable. And yet there it was, a few hours away, with its shut-in millions; many of them, like the furnace man, down below the pavements, as forgotten as the dead. And those above ground, in the clatter and chatter of the surface, were struggling to be noticed—most of them. Aesthetes, modernists, intelligentzia, and what not. According to Trane, they were sick. If they could all be made to sit along a stretch of fast water like this, perhaps it would cure them! It would take a long stream to do it, though, because—I grinned—each one would have to be beyond shouting distance from the next.

I finished my lunch and lit a pipe. Gazing upstream and wondering what lay ahead of me beyond the bend, I saw a rod flash in the sunshine. The wielder of the rod, when he came in sight, was not worming. He was fishing downstream, wet, and making thirty feet of line behave. I had watched him make a dozen casts when a dog appeared—a setter—following along the bank about fifty feet in the rear of the man. When the man stopped to work a piece of water the setter stood still until the angler moved ahead again. The dog was absolutely absorbed by the fishing. His head would turn with each back-cast, his eyes following the line. As it whipped forward his head swung with it. When the cast reached the water he became rigid, with his jaws working slightly and his eyes riveted on the leader.

At last—just above me—there came a swirl as the flies took the water. The setter shook like an aspen. On the next cast the fish came again and was hooked. I forgot the dog for the next ten minutes. From the way the fish fought he was a good one. When he began to tire and come to the top he proved it beyond a doubt, and I noticed that his captor was without a landing-net. Getting to my feet, I asked him if he wanted mine. He looked in my direction, shook his head, and went on playing the fish. He played it until the fish was flat on its side, utterly exhausted, then worked it into some quiet water near shore and nodded to the dog.

"All right, Buddy," he said.

The setter waded in, picked up the fish by the middle, waded out, and laid it on the bank. The man got out of the stream to unhook and creel it.

I stood there frankly gaping for a moment, then procured my rod and worked up to the scene of this extraordinary exhibition.

I had seen the best setters of the world. I had seen one or two bench champions that in extreme refinement might have equaled this one; but one thing was sure—no other dog of any breed had impressed me as this fellow did when I got close to him. He was big for a setter; he was black and white, with tan markings; he was—words won't do it. He was as beyond description as a sunset—a living, breathing glory.

He had, of course, a magificent head, which he carried superbly; but this became mere detail when he looked at me. Most setters have that proud yet eager, friendly yet reserved, expression of eye that tells of the calm, fine, gentle spirit within. This dog had more of that shining look than I had ever seen, and with it a serene, assured, almost godlike beam of intelligence. It was as though his understanding far surpassed my own; as though it brushed aside all mysteries to get at the riddle of life and gravely solve it. Staring at the dog, I addressed the man:

"Does he always retrieve your trout like that?"

The man creeled his fish, said, "Yep," and stooped to rinse his hands. "It's a nuisance, having to wade out every time you land one," he told me; "but—well, he likes to be in things."

I took my eyes from the dog and turned them to the man. He had looked up over his shoulder after his explanation, wondering, no doubt, whether I was the sort of creature who could comprehend it. I was—quite. But something else was not so clear.

"I should think you'd be afraid he'd hook himself with a fly."

The man chuckled. There was good-natured tolerance of me in that chuckle.

"Oh, he knows about that," he said.

I thrilled at a sudden idea and asked a question:

"Is he broken to gun?"

The man stood up, shook the water from his hands, and began to wipe them on his trousers.

"I expect you'd call him broken," he drawled.

I was again staring at the dog—it was almost impossible not to do so—but there was something disconcerting in that drawl—my idea considered—and I turned definitely to the man.

He was of medium height and slightly inclined toward rotundity. His face was ruddy. His eyes, behind thick-lensed spectacles, would twinkle easily, I thought. Instead of waders and wading shoes, he wore hip boots with homemade leather sandals studded with hobnails, strapped about the feet. Above the boots were army breeches, an army shirt, and a worn canvas shooting coat. I guessed him to be a native despite an expression—half shrewd, half smiling, and quite sophisticated—that did not suggest Emmetville. It did not suggest dog selling, for that matter; but my idea had by now become a passion.

"He's very handsome," I said. "I'd like to own him. Is he, by any chance, for sale?"

The man stooped deliberately for his rod, reeled in his line, and examined the flies.

"You're a stranger here," he said at last.

It was not a question—it was a statement, but I nodded. His eyes swung to the dog. They regarded each other gravely for a moment, and then came the twinkle I had foreseen, and a single fanlike wave of the setter's tail.

"You for sale?" inquired the man.

Into the soft assurance of the setter's eyes came a flicker of—surely it was amusement. There followed a languid pink-and-black yawn. The man turned and began to wade out into the stream.

"I'm afraid he's giving you the laugh," he said.

Until the man was far enough downstream to be short of the dog with any possible back cast, the setter waited where he was, then took up his watchful trailing along the bank. He passed within five feet of me, exposing to my view the side of him that, until now, had been turned away. Running from the top of his neck where it joined his body down to the foreleg was a tremendous scar. His shining coat strove to conceal it in vain. I wondered what ghastly wound had made that scar. Perhaps a shotgun at close range, or the teeth of a mowing machine. At any rate, he did not limp from it—his prideful stalk was beautiful to see—and scar or no scar, I would have given a pretty penny for him. I watched him out of sight.

· III ·

During many a dreamy hour in warm pastel-like spring days that followed, I thought about the setter with the fearful scar. I could bring back the vision of his proud head and carriage, but his ineffably benignant look would not return.

I found that Emmetville and the country close about was full of his kind, or rather his species. As the hills had been robbed of their ancient covering of hemlock and hardwood, they had hidden their bareness as quickly as possible with thickets and briers. In such cover the partridge confounds most of his enemies, lives in plenty, and gives himself wholeheartedly to lovemaking. Little brown puffballs inevitably chip forth. They mature in a season and are ready for similar proceedings. Bird dogs in consequence were as numerous in those hills as mongrels in the average country district. They were chained to kennels in the yards in town. I'd meet them on the roads, running with flivvers and buggies and wagons. I'd see them curled up asleep on the sunny side of farmhouses or snuffing along a furrow behind a plow looking for field mice. Splendid dogs—some of them—arrived at in the only way a competent race can be built. I wanted none of them. I had been spoiled.

Meanwhile I fished and smoked and dreamed and was—barring twinges of desire to own that dog—thoroughly contented. My hostess, after saying that she thought she could take care of me, had quite expertly lived up to her surmise, in the silent, absentminded way that never for a moment left her. It was as though her mind, her whole inner being, were utterly absorbed by a problem or a vision that had nothing whatever to do with conducting Gaylord's.

"Conducting" was not the word. Conducting suggests leadership. There was no one to lead through wearing days of cleaning and cooking and serving. Later, during the summer season, she would have help, she told me. Now there was no one except the zealous purveyor of worms—I had persuaded him to neglect me in this particular—who looked after a cow and the garden. Automatically, or with the fringes of her mind, she made that barely furnished, hard-worn house a clean, comfortable abode. Nothing escaped her, nothing was forgotten. My pitcher of shaving water was as certain to be steaming on the scrubbed-smelling boards of the hall floor as that another day had come, bringing two brisk raps on my door. If I wanted to lunch on the stream, it required only that I put my head in the kitchen when I came down. She would stop humming and nod

vaguely. I would find my lunch, done up deftly in tissue paper, on the lid of my creel when I had finished breakfast.

There were few other guests. A scattering of traveling salesmen and now and then anglers, who came in pairs. These last were talkative at breakfast, extremely quiet by evening, and left that night or early the following day. The stream required nice judgment and a very delicate fly.

Bright days flowed shining, one after the other, across the hills to feather the second growth with a breath of green and soak down warmly into the gorge along the sparkling stream. I was enjoying Emmetville.

And then one night the wind changed. It got into the west and came moaning down the gorge, bearing scattered, hard-driven pellets of snow. About ten o'clock next morning the big trout—the one that had made me seek the library and Trane's tirade instead of bed—materialized.

He did not come up with my fancied smash, nor did he take a Fan Wing drifting serenely on the surface of a pool. His advent was not at all spectacular. He rose like a shadow from somewhere in an oily runnel of pitching water and seemed to inhale a coasting Woodruff.

Now that place was full of snags and the water was full-bodied and in a hurry. I have little recollection of subsequent proceedings. Eventually I realized that the monster was—in all probability—still going downstream with the Woodruff and the end of a nicely tapered leader. I also discovered that my right leg was in an ice pack up to the hip. I squelched ashore, removed the snag-ripped wader, and mended it with a patching kit; but I had to sit there on the frost-covered ground until the cement hardened, and that icy wind was still blowing and, of course, my leg stayed damp all day.

When I attempted to jump out of bed next morning someone stuck a knife in my back. I found I could not look over my shoulder to discover my assailant. I found I could not straighten up or raise my arms above my head. Crouching on the edge of the bed, I wondered whether I could perform the miracle of getting into shirt, trousers, and shoes. I decided to attempt it, and with what struck me as the strength of the dying, and an ability as a contortionist unsuspected until now, I achieved the impossible. If, as I feared, this was the end, New York was the place for me.

I managed to get downstairs and to the breakfast table, and to remain so erect in consuming poached eggs, bacon, and coffee as not to attract the far-away yet attentive eyes of the silent woman who set these things before me.

I had in mind the sign of an M.D. four or five houses down. Thither I expected to drag myself before being driven—or carried, if my malady progressed—to the first possible train. But the mere effort of rising from my chair after breakfast was so preposterous that I shut my teeth on a groan, called my hostess, told her I had an attack of some sort, and asked her to send for the nearest doctor.

For the first time during the ten days I had been in her house her glance concerned itself, instantly and intently, with me.

"Why did you get up? Go straight back to bed!"

She fled through the front door without hat or wrap.

Bed I wished to avoid. I would take to it temporarily, since standing or sitting was agony; but I would not undress for two reasons: first, it was now a physical impossibility; and second, I would not have thus acknowledged, even if I could have done so, the possibility of being persuaded to expire dolefully in Emmetville.

In some unaccountable manner I climbed the stairs, stretched myself out, and waited. Presently came footsteps on those creaking, uncarpeted stairs, and voices along the hall and a presence beside me in the room. I looked up into a ruddy face and a pair of thick-lensed spectacles.

"Oh, hello!" I said.

"Hello," replied the twinkling man of the stream who fished with the glorious setter. He set a black bag on a chair.

"If you want anything, doctor—hot water—" came from the doorway.

"Yes, I'll call. Thank you, Mrs. Firth."

The door was closed.

I described the attempted assassination and its subsequent harrowing results.

"This is the point," I wound up. "If I'm in for anything serious I must get back to New York."

A thermometer leveled at my mouth was backed, to my extreme relief, by a twinkle.

"Oh I don't know. Emmetville's a splendid place—to die in."

I gave those light and cheering words a joyous though impeded grin.

The diagnosis, after due thumpings and listenings, was as follows:

"If you were twenty years older, I'd say you had lumbago. As it is, I'll say you have—lumbago."

"Well, what does that mean?"

"Adhesive tape for the muscles of your back and a day or so in bed, and—yes, you might have your teeth X-rayed when you get back to town and you might take two of these tablets every four hours."

"Many thanks," said I, when I had been undressed, bound in adhesive tape, and assisted into bed. "And now tell me, where did you get that dog?"

The reverse of a twinkle appeared in the eyes behind the thick spectacles. They clouded with gravity and glanced quickly toward the door.

"That was Pocono Shot," said the doctor in an undertone, but with the air of making an extraordinary announcement.

"Pocono Shot?" I repeated, unenlightened. "Do you own him?"

"No," he said in the same low tone. "I don't own him." Suddenly, at a thought, astonishment grew in his face. "You've never heard of Pocono Shot?"

"Not that I know of," I said. "How did he get that scar?"

He stared at me, bewildered.

"Good heavens!" he said under his breath. Then aloud. "Why, we met you on the stream nearly two weeks ago!"

"Just about—what of it?"

He regarded me speculatively for a moment.

"I wouldn't have thought it possible," he said at last. "Right here in Emmetville for two weeks and—why, I wouldn't have thought it possible anywhere in the country after—" He broke off and became the victim of an unaccountable alarm. "You haven't mentioned him to—" He nodded significantly toward the door.

I attempted to sit up, was stricken as though by the kick of a mule, and collapsed.

"What the devil are you talking about?" I demanded, when I could again catch my breath. "Do you mean that setter and Mrs. Firth?"

"Sh-h-h," he said with another glance at the door. Then he came to the bed and leaned down, looking into my face. "You'll be out in a day or so," he told me hurriedly. "Drop around to my office about eight o'clock some evening. In the meantime don't mention the dog where Mrs. Firth can hear you."

He started to go. I seized him wildly by the arm.

"But listen, doctor!" I pleaded.

He disengaged his arm and moved to the door.

"I'll tell you at the office," he said, and left me flat on my back, a prey to lumbago and hopeless, raging curiosity.

· IV ·

My malady abated swiftly. I arose a well man two mornings later. My other affliction, on the contrary, had steadily increased. During a full half of the forty-eight hours in which I lay supine I wondered about Pocono Shot and his scar, and why I must not mention him to the silent woman of Gaylord's. Whether the doctor's tablets had anything, to do with my rapid release from lumbago I did not know; but one thing was certain—he could and must relieve my curiosity.

Warm weather had returned. I decided to fish that day, and set out with little enthusiasm. I looked upon the stream and the taking of trout as stop-gaps until evening should arrive, to find me knocking at the stroke of eight upon that doctor's door.

I fished a pool or two listlessly, came to swirling water, and was captured by the magic of the stream. The mystery of Pocono Shot ceased to be of moment. I was entirely concerned with placing well-cocked-up fly where it would join the dance, on amber depth, of bubbles and sunlight and foam.

The sun had begun to redden with the efforts required to finish a good day's work when I turned the jagged corner of a huge gray rock at an angle of the stream and came upon the swish of a rod, the gleam of spectacles on a blushing, peeling nose, and a high-headed, plume-tailed statue fifty feet beyond. This latter I eyed for a moment before I spoke:

"Get out of that stream! I was coming around tonight, but this is better. Get out of the stream! That bank over there is the place, I think.... Now call him here and sit down."

The doctor grinned and obeyed.

"So you're up and at 'em again, are you?"

"Yes," said I; "but no more today if it's a long tale."

"It's long enough," said the doctor, his grin departing. He motioned to the setter, who had stately joined us and now sank down on the bright spring grass. So you never heard of—" He nodded at the dog. "It's extraordinary!"

"So you implied the other day. Why?"

"Well, you've been here for two weeks. No citizen of Emmetville could meet a stranger and not—"

"I've met no one," I interrupted. "I've passed people on the road or along the stream, and that's all."

"H-m-m! Well, the newspapers."

"I didn't know you had any newspapers."

"We haven't. I meant the New York papers."

I smiled.

"The New York papers don't give much space to hunting dogs."

"They did to this one," said the doctor dryly.

Pocono Shot lay with his head between his paws. I turned involuntarily to survey him. He lifted his fine, deep muzzle and calmly returned my gaze. Having inspected me, he approved. A big paw came from the grass and was poked solemnly in my direction. I extended my hand and felt the rasp of pads against my palm. I was duly flattered, but my imagination had fed on hinted mysteries for two long days and I knew the New York papers.

"Did he pull a child from the stream or bark at a fire?" I jeered.

There was no answer. I found the doctor gazing at a vast tangle of briers and second growth, rising from where we sat to the blue of the sky six hundred feet above.

"This is a shooting country," he said suddenly, and indicated the slope with a wave of his hand. "That's why I'm here—that and the stream. I grew up in country like this, only on a smaller scale. There was a smaller stream and smaller hills, and I fished the stream and hunted the hills as a boy.

"Of course, a man must specialize to get anywhere in my profession, and the city is the place for that. I was ambitious—after Johns Hopkins—so I went to New York. I was an intern at Bellevue for a while, and then set up an office on Twelfth Street, not far from Washington Square. Do you know the neighborhood?"

"Greenwich Village!"

"Yes," said the doctor. "I did general practice—had to, to keep alive; but was working toward nervous diseases and—well, there was more of that sort of thing than money in the village those days."

He twinkled at me and went on:

"Then the war came and I went over. I did amputations and bone work and learned the Carrel techniqne with Dakin's fluid and came home. What practice I had was gone, and so was my ambition. Everything seemed silly after the mess over there. It seemed silly to try to get ahead. I had a longing for quiet and streams and hills. I ached to have a gun over my shoulder or a rod in my hand. I went back to my old stamping ground up in Connecticut, but the hills and streams were shot and fished out and the practice was sewed up by men who'd been there since Plymouth Rock.

"I had a few thousand saved up and I began to look for a practice for sale in the kind of country I was sick for. I spent three months at it, and finally came across this place and a man who wanted to go to Philadelphia. The minute I saw the stream and the hills, I felt as though I'd come home. I gave what I had for the practice and notes for as much more, and that accounts for me in Emmetville."

A large fly of some sort, with wings a-flutter, was borne past us on the current. It was swept over a miniature waterfall between two boulders and bobbed up on the pool below. The quiet of that pool was instantly shattered. There was a heave of water, a swirl—the fly was gone. Pocono Shot was on his feet like a flash, his eyes blazing at the widening ripples.

"My God!" said the doctor, and reached for his rod. My hand got to the rod ahead of his. I placed it well behind me. "But did you see him?" he pleaded.

"Yes, I saw him.... Go right ahead!"

The doctor sighed. Pocono Shot tore his eyes from the ripples and whined softly.

"It's plain cruelty to animals," said the doctor.

"Yes," said I; "and what was it when you left me helpless to wonder about your shushes and your psts and what not. Go right ahead!"

"Come and lie down," the doctor ordered. "We're ruined!"

With one last whine of regret the setter obeyed. He was almost instantly asleep—if a closed-eyed, dream-filled, hair-trigger watchfulness can be called sleep.

We regarded him in silence for a moment.

"You've noticed the number of shooting dogs around here?" said the doctor.

I nodded.

"Well, for years every man claimed his dog was the best. There was so much talk and wrangling about it that ten or twelve years ago they began holding a sort of amateur field trial each fall. The winner was supposed to be the best dog in the Poconos for that year, and for a month or so before each meet they couldn't get the crops in or timber to the mill or much of anything done around here. Then, after it had been decided, it took weeks to get over the decision. I wouldn't have been a judge at best-dog day for the practice of a New York specialist. The only man satisfied was the owner of the winner.

"The summer of the first year I was here there began to be some talk about a pup Bill Trimble had raised. Bill lived in a shack on a small piece of half-cultivated ground stuck like a postage stamp on the side of Bobcat Mountain, three miles north of town. He raised a little corn and a few vegetables; but he got his living mostly from taking city sportsmen out after partridge and woodcock, and trapping during the winter. A man from Scranton had come in to shoot with Bill one fall and brought with him an ex-field-trialer—a great dog in his day that had slowed down with age.

"Bill had a Llewellyn bitch that another sportsman had given him. She was a nice thing, bred in the purple—not what you'd call class in the field, but she knew partridge and had a good nose. Well, the two stole a mating that fall and she had a small litter that was wiped out by distemper except one dog pup. The man who owned the field-trialer wrote Bill to keep the pup, and that was the one the talk was about.

"Bill didn't know the bitch was in whelp at first and he didn't pay much attention to her when he did find it out. She was given to hunting on her own—which didn't spoil her, for some reason—and she hunted by herself, all day long, right up to the day she had her puppies. I've wondered about that. We don't know as much about prenatal influence as we'd like to. At any rate, those puppies were whelped pointing. Bill said the whole litter would nail a bird and back each other at three months. He said there was no choice among them until distemper got all but the biggest one, who came through on his vitality. He had the worst dose of all, but just wouldn't die." The doctor's hand dropped to a broad, well-domed satin head gleaming against the new grass. "You're hard to kill, aren't you, old man?"

One closed eye opened slightly. The tip of a silky plume twitched. The eye closed again.

"There was talk about this pup of Bill's, as I say; but somebody was always raising a world beater in those days, to hear them tell it, and the Poconos weren't prepared for anything astounding until it happened, publicly, for everyone to see. It happened on best-dog day when the pup was sixteen months old. I was there."

The doctor nodded at the sweep of briars lifting up to a feather of white clouds hanging like a puff of steam at its crest.

"See that hill? The one just in front of us, I mean. Would you believe it if I told you that a dog could turn in his tracks at the bottom of it, go straight to the top with his head in the air, and creep to a smashing point?"

"No," said I, with my eyes on that six hundred feet of brown tangle lanced by slim white birch.

"Well, this one can do it—twenty times a day. He did it, and other things, the first time he appeared at best-dog day; and kept on doing them until we sent the other dogs back to the wagons and followed him as though we were at church. If anyone got so excited that he exclaimed aloud, we frowned at him and said, 'Sh-h-h!' And many of us owned dogs that we thought would win, at nine o'clock that morning.

"That's what he did to us that day—Pocono Shot. There he lies at your feet. He's an economic factor in these parts."

I lifted my eyes from the sleeping setter to the doctor, who twinkled at my inquiring look.

"Why," said he, "we don't spend any more time arguing about who's got the best dog! We're now a fairly industrious people—the community, I mean. It wasn't true of Bill. The dog cut into his earning capacity in this way: you can imagine what a do like that would mean to a lonely man. Bill never stirred without him. He would have cut off his trigger finger sooner than go hunting and leave the dog behind to grieve. The sportsmen who came here to shoot with Bill each fall had always paid a good price to do so. Bill knew the cover blindfolded, could shoot like a fiend, and his guests took home the birds he killed. After this fellow showed up, Bill was in clover for a while. Almost any man would sell his soul to shoot over the dog. Bill doubled the tariff, took out two men at a time, and had a waiting list.

"Well, some man fired at a partridge one day in thick cover and nearly got Bill. That ended Bill's sinecure. He hunted alone after that. He caught his hand in a bear trap that winter and it became infected. When he came in to have it treated I asked him about the shooting business and this is what he said: 'He weren't over twenty feet from me when he pulled. I got to thinkin', after that load went by, that a little more and I'd of took it in the head. Then I figgered that if it could happen to me, it could happen to Shot, and I told him to keep his ten dollars a day and went home.'"

The doctor paused to chuckle. I offered a cigarette.

"Thanks," he said; "I'll roll one, if you don't mind. I never got over my corn-silk days."

He produced a sack of tobacco and papers, made a cigarette with deft, slightly pudgy fingers, lighted it, and went on:

"Bill's loss was my gain. His hand was pretty bad when I first saw it, but I hadn't been to France for nothing. I rigged up some Carrel tubes, went at it with Dakin's, and checked the infection. Bill said I'd saved his hand. I had, for that matter. His life, too, perhaps, if he'd known it.

"He was grateful of course. When spring came I began to meet him fishing. Shot had picked up the trick you saw and Bill fished as much to amuse the dog as himself. We'd get together now and then on the stream and talk and smoke and spit and cuss. I got to liking Bill a lot. He was as shy as a wood marten and as straight as a good piece of pine. He hadn't a relative in the world that he knew of. He was raised in the orphan's home at Stroudsburg, and how he did love these hills! I don't know whether he'd ever cared about any woman. If he had, the chances are he never got to the point of mentioning it to her. At any rate, there was no wife or child on Bobcat Mountain. That's why every bit of the affection corked up in Bill's system for twenty years went to this fellow lying here. There was a lot of it. Bill was a quiet, slow-speaking citizen who took his time about deciding to like you, and then—liked you.

"He liked me before that summer was over. Of course, there was the hand business, to begin with; but it was our talks on the stream that really did it. I was driving out to a confinement case one day and I met Bill hiking for town with a jug and the dog. I stopped the flivver and said 'Hello,' and he stood by the car and scratched his head and grinned—a sort of embarrassed grin he had. The dog was standing in the road with the sunshine blazing on his coat.

"'Well, he looks like he'd last till the guns begin to crack,' I said.

"There was a young maple at the side of the road that had started to turn yellow. Bill pointed to the tree and said, 'He ain't got long to go from the looks of that.' I started to let in the clutch, but Bill put his hand on the car and said, 'What's your hurry?'

"I told him Andy Slocum expected a son and heir that day.

"'Oh, I guess Mrs. Slocum'll wait a few minutes on you,' said Bill. He stood and shuffled his feet and grinned again, and looked still more embarrassed.

"'What are you fussing about?' I said, looking at the jug. 'I'm no prohibition agent.'

"'She's empty,' said Bill. 'She'll have molasses in her pretty quick now. Say, listen—' He stopped right there.

"'Still listening,' I said.

"'Say,' he said, 'I was wondering if you could see your way clear to be at my place with that sixteen-gauge you been braggin' on, about seven o'clock openin' day.'

"I nearly fell out of the machine. 'You mean that, Bill?' I said.

"'I sure do,' he said. Then he looked me in the eye and said, 'I' m thinkin', whenever you pull a trigger you'll know just where the dog is.'"

The doctor broke off and seemed to reflect for a moment.

"Have you done much partridge shooting?" he asked suddenly.

"A lot," I told him.

"Well," said he "until you've killed partridge over this dog you'll never know what real shooting is."

"My father owned a great partiridge dog," I said. "I shot over him when I was a boy."

The doctor waved his hand, palm outward, as though wiping out the memory of that dog of bygone days.

"Forget him," he said. "I don't care how good he was—forget him. Listen! Imagine the brain of a man, plus the cunning of a fox and the tread of a cat. Now put a nose on the combination that can stay up in the air and outtrail a hound and you'll get a faint idea of this dog."

"A setter outtrail a hound?" I protested.

"Any hound that ever lived," the doctor declared. "The first time I saw it was one day that fall. We'd killed our limit on partridge by ten o'clock. That's what you do when he takes you out. Get that straight, too—you don't take him—he takes you. You just follow him and kill birds—that's all you've got to do.... We'd stopped at a spring for a drink before working down to some woodcock ground. Somewhere along the opposite hill a hound had a fox going and we listened for a minute. He had a good big voice on him and it echoed and reëchoed between the hills. I said, 'Bill, what if that was a bloodhound on your trail with a posse right behind him? How would you feel?'

"'Well,' said Bill, 'I'd rather have the hound after me than Shot here.'

"I started the sort of argument about hounds and setters that you did just now, and Bill told me to work on down to the woodcock ground alone and take any trail I liked. 'Wade the stream a couple of times and wade in it,' he said, 'Get up on the big rock this side of the glen so you can look back over your trail for a ways. I'll give you half an hour and then tell him to go find you.'

"'But, Bill,' I said, 'that'll send me right through the woodcock cover. If he does happen to follow me he'll strike a woodcock sure.'

"'Well, what of it?' said Bill.

"'Why he'll go on point,' said I, 'and that will end the trailing business.'

"'Don't worry,' said Bill. 'If I tell him to find you he'll walk right over a woodcock, if it's on your trail, and never notice it.'

"I left Bill and the dog, sitting there. When I got out of sight I zigzagged and circled. I backtracked my own trail and milled around in one spot and jumped up and caught a hazel limb and went out it hand over hand for twenty feet and dropped to the ground. Then I waded across the stream twice and walked up it a hundred yards, and whenever I struck a big log I walked on that.

"I'd been up on the rock about twenty minutes when here came Shot on a lope, with his head up. He was coming through the woodcock cover on my trail, when he stopped as though hit by lightning and stiffened. 'There's a woodcock,' I thought, 'and he hasn't walked over it!' He didn't walk over it. I'll tell you what he did. He backed out like a cat, swung wide of the bird so as not to flush it, picked up my trail on the other side, and came loping to the rock. He looked up, saw me, wagged his tail, and began to bark. Bill whoo-whooed back in the woods and Shot barked direction signals to him until he showed up. What do you think of that?"

"Wonderful, of course—especially the woodcock," I said. "But that was a fresh trail."

"Wait!" said the doctor. "You see this ridge back of us? All of it from here to town, and for two miles below, and the opposite ridge, beginning at that dip there and running a mile and a half north, was owned at the time of his death by Emmet Mulhauser. The town was named for him. He came into this section sixty years ago and bought those ridges for about a nickel an acre. His father was a German who had married an American wife. His German blood gave him thrift, his Yankee blood shrewdness. The land cost him every cent he had, but he dammed the stream, put up a sawmill, and hacked a road out from the mill up to the new railroad just going through. He slaved and saved, and the timber on the ridges and the lumber he cut got more and more valuable until he died, thirty years ago, worth over a hundred thousand in cash and half the timber still standing.

"He left a son, a timid, overworked, browbeaten daughter, and no will. The son had looked after things more and more as the old man gave out, and people thought it strange that no will was found. The son—his name was Emmet, too—told his sister that since he was a man—a generous man, willing to work, she could have the hundred thousand and he'd be satisfied with the standing timber and the mill. It's hard for a woman to resist cash, and she was a spineless thing, deathly afraid of her brother. She took the money and pulled out, leaving the second Emmet with timber worth half a million, just as it stood, and twice that when his mill got through with it.

"When his sister left, Emmet went down to New York and brought back a dazed immigrant woman—a Russian Jewess, with a sickly girl child about twelve years old. Emmet's little deal with the immigrant woman was so simple that even she could understand it. She was to do Emmet's housework, look after two cows, pigs and chickens, and prepare the noon meal for a timber crew of twenty men. For this, Emmet would give her and her child a home. It was a good deal—both parties were satisfied. Any place where Cossacks couldn't drop in for a little visit seemed like heaven to the woman, and the only cash required of Emmet was for a little cheap clothing for the woman and her child.

"The last deal didn't turn out quite so well as Emmet expected. The immigrant woman had looked like a good animal with a sound constitution, but four years of Emmet's work was all she stood. She got out of the bargain by dying. Emmet was disappointed in her, naturally. He thought it all over and hit on a plan that looked good. The woman's child had picked up amazingly in this altitude. She matured early, as the women of her race do. Emmet married her two months after her mother's death. She was sixteen and big for her age and—poor Emmet!—looked capable of any amount of hard work for years to come.

"Well, I'm darned if she hadn't learned her mother's tricks. She did Emmet's work for three years and then, as we say in the Poconos, up and died on him. She'd taken an hour or so off to have a child one day—or perhaps it was at night after the work was done. At any rate, the baby was two years old when she died—a boy—and a pretty poor specimen.

"But that made no difference to Emmet. He had no friends and the child filled a big gap in his life. He gave him everything on earth he asked for from infancy on. Emmet's mother had been a Russian. This boy then was one-eighth Yankee, one-eighth German, one-quarter Slav, and one-half Jew. That's quite a mixture; and he was raised on coffee, doughnuts, pies, candy, and such truck from the day he learned to yell if he didn't get what he wanted.

"Emmet planned to make a gentleman of leisure out of him. He allowed him to go to school in town for a while and then imported a tutor for him who had been educated in Europe—mostly in France, I believe. The tutor stayed for several years. He filled Emmet's house and the boy's head with decadent French literature, and then had to get out to escape one of Emmet's lumberjacks who had a good-looking daughter. Emmet then sent the boy—he also was named Emmet—to a first-class boarding school and later to college, with summers abroad. After graduating, the boy spent a winter in New York and came up here for July and August; not that he liked it here, but in this one thing he didn't get what he wanted. Emmet Senior was determined to have him with him for those two months at least, and stuck it out.

"I saw Emmet Junior for the first time that summer. It was the third year I'd been here. I was standing on the post-office steps when a high-powered, single-seated roadster pulled up to the curb. It was painted in three colors — queer colors that didn't belong together; that didn't belong anywhere except in a nightmare. The car was as startling on the streets of Emmetville as a pink monkey or a sky-blue elephant. The driver got out and passed me on his way into the post office, and he didn't belong in Emmetville any more than his car. I knew exactly where he belonged the minute I looked at him. He belonged back in Greenwich Village. I'd seen hundreds like him when I was practicing on Twelfth Street. It's extraordinary how that sort run to type. I never realized it so strongly as when I got this first look at Emmet Junior, with the streets of Emmetville and pine ridges as a background. He was — "

"I'm going to interrupt you, doctor," I broke in. "It's curious but a friend of mine gave me a long dissertation on the type you seem to mean the night before I left New York. I'd like to ask you a question or two. In the first place, how would you define this type? Have you a specific name for it?"

"Well, no, not exactly. They call themselves bohemians or radicals around Washington Square. They're called a lot of things by other people. Parlor Bolsheviks, for one thing, when they get so enthusiastic over the Russian insanity."

"'Sophisticates' is popular just now," I said. "My friend seemed to prefer 'intelligentzia.' He says their sickness of mind is due to anaemia."

"M-m-m," mused the doctor. "True in some cases, I should say."

"He thinks lack of outdoor exercise in adolescent youths of this type warps them permanently."

"They're warped, all right, and lack of exercise gives them a further twist; but how does he account for the women?"

"He didn't account for them, as I remember," I admitted.

"Well, I think it happens before birth."

"You mean heredity?"

"No," said the doctor. "I think it happens at the moment — if it is a moment — or during the period when sex is determined. These people are the result of malfunctioning in the process of sex determination. In extreme cases we have the hermaphrodite. Less complete results are the effeminate man and the masculine woman. There's your warp, mental and physical, for life."

"That does account for a great deal," said I, thinking it over.

"It accounts for it all," said the doctor promptly. "I believe the Anglo-Saxon is where he is today because he's been breeding truer to sex than other strains. So did the early Greek. So did the Roman. Crossbreeding is apt to produce lack of complete definement of sex. It's responsible for the decline of most once-powerful races. It was responsible for Emmet Junior. I knew it when I saw his face and heard his voice at the post-office window and watched his gestures as he took his mail.

"I didn't come in close contact with him for some time. I'd get a glimpse of him driving through town or meet him on the road somewhere in his car. I don't think I ever saw that car again without a girl in it. I'd heard that he was going to be a poet—or rather was a poet; he'd proved it by having some of his things published. Now we're about as much interested in poetry in Emmetville as in Sanskrit or the Einstein Theory; but some reviewer on a Philadelphia paper had spoken of Emmet Junior as the poet of the Poconos, and that got a purr out of us. Nobody had ever read any of Emmet Junior's poetry and nobody expected to, but anyone who could get us mentioned in a city paper wasn't altogether doless.

"I read some of Emmet Junior's verse by accident, in this way: August Firth had died two years before I got here. Mrs. Firth had turned Gaylord's into a boardinghouse after her father died, three years before that. She'd had tough going for six years and that summer she broke down—jaundice, neuritis, and general exhaustion. Her daughter Lucille— "

"You're speaking of my Mrs. Firth?" I broke in.

"Is she yours?" asked the doctor, twinkling. "Yes, that's who I mean."

"But you said her daughter. She's never mentioned a daughter to me."

Said the doctor, without any particular cheerfulness, "You've dragged me out of a stream with a big trout rising to tell you about certain events. If you'll just—"

I hastened to apologize. The doctor proceeded:

"Her daughter Lucille got an extra woman in to help and carried on after a fashion. Lucille was a pretty girl and a well-meaning one, I think; but selfish, with the natural selfishness of youth and her mother's encouragement. She was, for example, about the best-dressed girl in Emmetville. All her mother's doing; but then she accepted it. She also let her mother persuade her to keep ber hands out of dishwater and away from any dirty or tiring work about the house, and that her schooling was too important to be interrupted by the fact that her mother was slaving day in and day out. So she went through the local school and then through the high school at Stroudsburg, which is supposed to be better than ours, taking the morning train down and returning on the 5:10 each evening.

"Gaylord's is so close to my place that I'd generally drop in to see Mrs. Firth after my day's work. I'd got her liver to working and the neuritis had yielded nicely to treatment; but her strength didn't seem to come back as it should, and I was calling every few days. I stopped there about nine o'clock one night. Lucille let me in. Two or three boarders were sitting in the parlor to the right of the hall in front of a wood fire as I went up the stairs.

"Mrs. Firth was in that room you're in now. It was one of those chilly nights that we have up here every now and then in the middle of the summer. I'd just driven four miles without gloves and I walked over to the stovepipe to warm my hands before touching Mrs. Firth. Perhaps you know that if you stand close to that stovepipe you can hear everything that goes on in the kitchen—every sound, every syllable that's spoken."

"Yes," I said, "I've discovered it."

"Well, I heard a man's voice as I approached the pipe. I listened idly for a minute, and then he got my attention. He was speaking intently, in an overcultivated, affected manner that I'd heard every day at one time, but not since I'd hit the Poconos. His subject, I gathered, was free love—and he was for it. He was explaining that mating should be as untrammeled by convention as drawing the breath. 'We should mate impulsively,' he said. 'Like the birds or the shy deer or flaming tigers.' He went on to say that man, in his coarseness and stupidity, had hedged himself and woman—particulary woman—with a lot of vulgar, prudish, and unimaginative restrictions, and so stolen from the world the most beautiful thing that human life contained. 'But the new generation just becoming articulate,' he said, 'is cutting those restrictions away. You can see by the books we have been reading,' he said; 'you can see by this tremendous new novel we have been discussing tonight, that no one of any importance who is writing today will tolerate for a moment those stultifying bonds placed about us by the unthinking generations of an earlier, cruder civilization.'

"I stopped listening and went over and asked Mrs. Firth who was the man down in the kitchen. She told me weakly that it was Emmet Junior.

"'And Lucille?' I said.

"She said, 'Lucille and other girls. He's been very kind. He's organized a reading circle to help them understand the best writers.''

"I asked her who the girls were and she named them. I'll say this for Emmet Junior—he was some picker. This mountain air is good for anybody. Youngsters bloom in it. He'd culled the blossoms for his circle, make no mistake about that.

"When I left Mrs. Firth I took a chair at the head of the stairs and waited. What I'd heard via the stovepipe had interested me a lot. I wanted to hear from a member of the circle.

"They all came out of the kitchen at last—that is, the girls did—and giggled and chattered for a minute in the hall before they said good night. Lucille went back to the kitchen and I had a fairly long wait before she and Emmet Junior appeared in the hall together and she let him out the front door. I got up and walked downstairs.

Lucille was startled.

"'Is mother worse?' she asked quickly.

"I told her I thought her mother was a little better.

"'But you've been here all this time, she said.

"I told her I'd stayed to chat with her mother while she entertained her company.

"'Yes,' she said, curling her lip, 'in the kitchen. It's the only warm place in the house that isn't— ' She broke off and looked in at the parlor fire and the people sitting there.

"I said, 'I'm glad you were in the kitchen tonight,' and explained, when she looked at me puzzled, that a lot of Emmet Junior's lecture had come up the stovepipe.

"She blushed, but threw back her head in a challenging sort of way and said, 'Well, what did you think of it?'

"'What did you think?' I said. 'That's the important thing.'

"She said, 'I think it was wonderful. I think he's wonderful. He's so far above any of us here—so far above me that it makes me sick. I keep telling myself that it's only the advantages he's had—college and New York and everything—but it's more than that. Look at this.'

"She pulled a magazine from under her arm, opened it, found a certain page, and handed the magazine to me. On the page she'd found was a poem—I suppose you'd call it that—of Emmet Junior's. It didn't rhyme and the lines began with small letters. Some of the lines were long and some had only one or two words for no apparent reason. You know the sort of thing I mean."

"Oh, quite," I said.

"It was called "Throbbing Beads." I turned the pages of the magazine, after I'd read the poem, and found it full of drawings of deformed people afflicted with dropsy. They took me straight back to Greenwich Village, and drawings and paintings just like them tacked up on dirty walls in dirty rooms by the thousands.

"I found Emmet Junior's poem again and said, 'Well, what does it mean?'

"Lucille said, 'I don't know, but I'm going to study it until I get an impression. Then he'll tell me whether the impression is the one I should get.'

"I said, 'You think he knows what it means, himself?'

"'Of course; she said; 'every word in it is absolutely necessary in conveying the exact shade of color he wants.'

"'Color?' I said. 'I thought this was a poem.'

"'It is,' she said; 'but all the arts are alike now. They don't use form any more. That's all in the past—with advanced minds, that is.'

"'He has an advanced mind, has he?' I said.

"Lucille told me Emmet Junior was in the front rank of the new movement.

"'Well,' I said, 'he wants to be careful or he'll advance himself into a building at Scranton, with keepers and padded cells and things like that.'

"She took the magazine from me and folded her arms across it in a sort of protective gesture.

"'Of course you'd take it like that,' she said quietly, but her cheeks were flushed and her eyes fairly blazed. 'You just don't know. You just don't realize what's happening in the world.' Then she said good night and went back into the kitchen with the magazine. Stalked back, I should have said.

"On my way home I made up my mind that Emmet Junior's reading circle didn't belong in Emmetville any more than his car or himself. I was led to it by the impression he'd made on Lucille. In all probability the rest of the girls felt as she did. Emmet Junior, as I have said, was a pretty poor specimen; a sallow, thin-necked fellow with his eyes set close together. The girls he'd chosen for his circle wouldn't have given him a second look ordinarily; but he had the glamour of the city—of the great world—in the eyes of those country-raised maidens, and he'd topped this off with as exciting a line of propaganda as any healthy young female ever listened to.

"I drove up to the Mulhauser place next day and found Emmet reading in a hammock on the front porch. I sat in the car and he came out to the gate when I called. I told him who I was and that I'd been hearing something of his reading circle. 'I don't think you're doing those girls any good,' I said, 'and I've driven up here to ask you to stop it.'

"He'd been looking down at the wheel of the car, not meeting my eyes, but his head came up with a jerk.

"'Stop what?' he said. 'What do you mean?'

"I told him I wanted the reading circle called off.

"'Oh,' he said, and passing his fingers over his narrow forehead and through his long hair, with just the sort of gesture you'd expect.

'The Emmetville point of view,' he said. 'Amusing!' He put on a pair of nose glasses attached to a broad black ribbon and gave me a languid stare. 'The mothers of the girls' he said, in a tired voice, 'are, if I may say so, grateful that I'm giving their daughters a faint conception of modern literature.' He called it 'litrawchaw' and passed his hand through his hair again; then he said, 'You're getting out of your depths, if I may say so, doctor. Suppose you stick to pills.'

"One of the girls in the circle was Ruth Bascom, the daughter of Ed Bascom, sheriff of the county. Ed had been a Rough Rider under Roosevelt and a state trooper after that. He's covered with oak leather and filled with steel springs and dynamite.

"'You're not talking to anybody's mother now,' I said; 'you're talking to me. Unless you agree to cut out your literary activities with those girls, you and Ruth Bascom can explain all about it to her father, and we'll see what he thinks."

"Now birds of Emmet's feather sicken at the thought of standing up to anyone who might resort to physical violence. That's why I selected Bascom's daughter and mentioned Ed; but I wasn't prepared for what it did to Emmet Junior. He didn't turn white—he turned green. His glasses fell off and he had to take hold of the fence. His mouth opened and closed like the gills of a fish. I was startled. I didn't know any man—I don't mean man; I mean any human being—could be as yellow as that.

"When he could talk at all Emmet Junior promised to do anything I wanted if I'd say nothing to Bascom. 'Whatever he's done has been done,' I thought, 'and just an interview with Ed would kill this worm'; so I told him to call off the reading circle and I'd not go into it any further. I drove away and left him still hanging onto the fence.

"So I broke up the only reading circle Emmetville ever had." The doctor paused. A kingbird darted down from somewhere and zigzagged through a hatch of flies just coming off the stream. "I was too late," said he, his eyes on the bird; "too late!"

He picked up a stone and tossed it into the water. The head of Pocono Shot came up at the splash. He got to his feet, shook himself, and poked at the doctor with his nose.

"Not yet," said the doctor.

The dog turned to the stream, lapped a few swallows of water, then came and lay down again.

"Does he understand everything?" I asked.

"Pretty nearly, I guess. He'll bring me anything I mention that he can get hold of. Once I saw a stray kitten in the yard. I told him to bring it to me and he went out and brought it in—hardly ruffled its fur. He'll go uptown and bring me back the newspaper from the news-stand or the mail from the post office. All I have to say is, 'Mail,' or 'Paper.' He barks at the right place and they give it to him. He'll shut any door in the house or ring a doorbell for me if it's the pull kind. All that's just monkey business. When he has to use his nose is where he shines.... Lord, look at that sun! The best of the fishing is from now on, you know."

The sun was sliding stealthily down upon the crest of the ridge at our backs, but that meant little. We had a good hour of daylight left.

"In order to do any fishing right now," I said, "you'll have to lick me first."

The doctor sighed and went on:

"About two weeks after my talk with Emmet Junior, we got quite a shock in Emmetville. One morning about ten o'clock Ed Bascom and his daughter Ruth and Emmet Junior drove up to the courthouse and got a marriage license and walked down the street to old man Farrell's office, who was a justice of the peace. Ten minutes later Ruth Bascom was Mrs. Emmet Mulhauser, Jr. Ed drove the newly married pair up to the Mulhauser place and left them there, and that was that.

"Well, of course the town buzzed. The couple would have all of Emmet Senior's pile someday; but somehow nobody felt like discussing the marriage with Ed. Mrs. Bascom went everywhere explaining that Emmet Junior had persuaded Mr. Bascom into this sudden marriage because he wanted to take Ruth back to New York with him.

"But Emmet Junior didn't seem in such a hurry to get to New York. He didn't even take his wife on a wedding trip. They just stayed on at his father's, although he'd expected to leave Emmetville about that time. Mrs. Bascom began to explain that Ruth wasn't very well and that Emmet Junior was waiting until she was better before they left. Ruth wasn't ill enough to have a doctor, apparently. I knew that because Kittridge—he's the other M.D. here—asked if I'd been up to the Mulhausers' and when I said no, he said, 'Neither have I. What are you doing for your scarlet-fever cases?' An epidemic of scarlet fever had developed among the school kids and we both of us were on the jump just then. In the rush I'd let some other things go and I hadn't seen Mrs. Firth for some time.

"I was passing there one evening, dog-tired, but I thought I'd better go in and have a look at her. The front door was open, so I walked in and up to her room. She was sitting by the window, so much improved that I advised her to begin taking short walks in the fresh air and lengthen them a little each day. She said she didn't know about the walks in the fresh air, but that she'd been going downstairs for three days and that she thought she'd start doing a little something about the house next day.

"I said, 'You'll do no such thing. You'll let Lucille manage for at least another week.'

"She gave me a troubled look and said, 'Doctor, I believe Lucille is sicker than I am, this minute. She won't admit it; she wouldn't let me send for you; but something is wrong with her. She looks terribly. She doesn't eat and I heard her crying late last night. I went in to her and asked her what was the matter and she said 'Nothing,' and then clung to me as she did when she was frightened as a little girl. After a while she said she'd got nervous for no reason at all, and she came and helped me back to bed. I think I know what's wrong. I'm telling you as a doctor. I wouldn't have it known for anything on earth, and Lucille would sooner die. I think she thought a lot of that young Mulhauser. She's been like this ever since his marriage. I think it's affected her health. I'd like to have you see her. She's downstairs. Don't say I asked you to see her. Just find her and act as though you wanted to tell her that I'm so much better. Then say you don't think she looks well herself, and that will lead up to your finding out just what's wrong with her. Do you understand?'

"I said yes and went downstairs. I found Lucille sitting by a kitchen table. She was sound asleep, with her arms on the table. Her cheek was resting on the magazine she'd showed me. The pages were wet and tears were drying on her face. I put my hand on her shoulder and she moaned and sat up. When she recognized me she jumped to her feet and picked up the magazine.

"'Mother sent for you,' she said, backing away from me. 'There's nothing wrong with me and I won't have mother pretending there is. We've had enough doctor's bills in this house. Thank you for coming, but you needn't bother with me at all.' She'd been backing toward the door. Now she turned and darted through it and I heard her running up the stairs.

"She hadn't looked ill, especially—pale and tear-stained was about all—and she'd gone up the stairs a lot faster than I could have that night. After what she'd said about Emmet Junior and what her mother had just told me, to find her crying over the magazine seemed to indicate what a correct diagnosis would have been. There's nothing in the pharmacopœia for lovesickness that I know of, so I went up and told her mother not to worry and dragged myself home.

"The scarlet-fever epidemic hung on until partridge season opened. I was wild. Bill Trimble had asked me to come out as often as I could make it and—well, I guess you know how I felt."

"I can imagine," I admitted.

"I couldn't fix it to get away until Monday of the second week. I telephoned Earl Geiger Saturday evening—the Geiger farm isn't far from Bill's shack—to let Bill know I'd come out and spend Sunday night with him if nothing happened.

"Well, nothing happened. No new cases of the epidemic and nobody came down suddenly with anything. I got to Bill's shack about ten o'clock Sunday night. Bill was glad to see me, in his undemonstrative way, and we drank hot applejack toddies and talked for a couple of hours before we turned in.

"Monday turned out to be a soggy, cloudy day, almost warm, with no wind stirring. Hard shooting, with no sunlight to break the cover and a dark sky for a background, but just right for a dog's nose. There was no use to think about that, though, with this fellow—he nails 'em, wet or dry. We walked over from Bill's place to the nearest cover and Shot went straight down to the foot of the ridge and pointed in a patch of rhododendron. Two birds jumped. Bill got his. I missed mine in the poor light. We followed the line and Shot found in a swamp, but drew out carefully and started to go round, clear down on his belly. We knew what that meant—the bird was deep in the swamp and restless. Shot was going to try to come in from the other side and send it out our way. The bird flushed wild, for no reason, before he could get around. I took a crack at it to make it lie and was watching it rocket off over the trees, when somebody hollered from the top of the ridge, 'Is that you, Bill?'

"Bill yelled back that it was, and whoever it was asked him to come up there.

"Bill yelled, 'Have you got a gun?' He'd have called in Shot and headed in the opposite direction if he thought it was another hunter.

"Then the voice said, 'This is the sheriff. I want to see you right away.'

"I said, 'What have you been doing, Bill?' And he grinned and told Shot to heel and we worked up and found Ed Bascom on top of the ridge.

"'They tell me that dog will take a human trail and follow it if you tell him to,' Ed said. 'Is that right?'

"'That's correct,' said Bill.

"'I now swear you and this dog in as deputy sheriffs in this county,' said Ed. 'Come and get in my car. Sorry to spoil your hunt—and yours, too, doctor.'

"I said, 'What's happened, sheriff?' Bascom started toward Bill's shack.

"'Lucille Firth was murdered last night," he said."

The doctor turned and met my appalled eyes.

"I don't think anything I saw in France," he admitted, "gave me the jolt that those words did, and I saw some fearful things over there." He lapsed into silence.

As for me, I felt a curious tightening of the muscles of my throat, an unusual dryness of the mouth and lips. The doctor was such a wholesome, jolly-looking person. I had not expected him to shock me as he had. I thought of the silent woman at Gaylord's. I thought of Gaylord's itself. The staring, blindless house. The stare was one of horror! That was apparent now. And the grounds—bare maples ringed by wet sapsucker drillings above winter-killed, matted grass. Over that grass, beneath those maples, a child had toddled. Later, the surer tread of a schoolgirl had pressed down the grass; and later still the ardent feet of a glowing maiden. Those feet had borne her lightly through every part of the worn interior of the house. The chairs I'd sat in had held her slim young body; perhaps the very bed in which at night I lay—in that room with the stovepipe. Despite its grateful warmth, the smooth black cylinder grew sinister in my mind's eye.... The doctor's voice broke in upon my thoughts:

"The sheriff gave us the details as we crossed the clearing to Bill's shack. The girl had been killed close to the stream, just below the town, about ten o'clock the night before. Joe, the man at Gaylord's—you've seen him around there, of course—had come rushing into town, wet to the waist, with his hands and shirt covered with blood. He could speak just a word or two of English at that time and he was all but out of his head. None of the crowd that surrounded him could make out anything he said, but they gathered that something was wrong and somebody went for the sheriff.

"The Italian had managed to lead the sheriff and the crowd down to the bridge at the foot of the main rift and then down the edge of the stream to Lucille Firth's body, lying among some boulders. Her head had been beaten in with a stone that was lying beside her. The Italian wouldn't go near the body, Bascom told us. He fell on his knees when they approached the spot and began to cross himself and jabber what must have been a prayer.

"The sheriff had told the crowd to keep back as soon as he saw what had happened. 'I've got a guard there now,' he told us; 'but most of the town's been as close to it as they could get, and the coroner had to walk around some, and his men, too, when they carried her to his office. I don't expect it's any use, but I'd like to give the dog a chance, Bill. I'd have been here sooner, only there was some moves made to take the Eyetalian out of jail and lynch him, so I had to wait for some state troopers I telephoned for to get in.'

"'You've got the Eyetalian locked up?' asked Bill.

"Ed said, 'Yes, he's locked up all right.'

"'Well, what do you want the dog for then?' asked Bill.

"We'd got to the shack by this time and were standing by the door. The sheriff didn't answer—he just looked at Shot. The dog was watching the sheriff's face intently, with that wise look he has.

"'He's sure giving me the once-over, ain't he?' said Ed.

"'He's thinking over your talk.' said Bill.

"The sheriff stared at Shot for a minute, with Shot staring back, at him.

"'I'm darned if I don't believe it,' he said; 'and I'll tell vou something. If he's got the nose they claim and is half as smart as he lets on to be, I won't have that Dago in jail this time tomorrow.'"

· V ·

At that moment the doctor was violently, overwhelmingly interrupted. The sun was well behind the hill by now. The stream had become a painted mystery in the dimness that followed. Flies were appearing by thousands to drift before a faint breeze above chuckling rapids or solemn pool. Trout were breaking close to a ribbon of froth just above us, and a mirror of water below was scarred again and again by magic, ephemeral rings.

I had sat there absorbed by the doctor's story. At one point I had been absolutely stricken by his words. And yet from time to time I had found my glance resting on the spot in the stream made noteworthy by the trout whose rise had necessitated the removal of the rod. Such is the way—and such, thank God, it will remain—of the simple fly fisherman.

And now within a few feet of the fascinating spot came a cataclysmic upheaval. The previous trout had been large. This undoubtedly was his great-grandfather. The doctor gasped and was lifted to his feet by a power greater than mere muscular action. Pocono Shot stood tremblingly by his side.

Said the doctor, blending good sportsmanship with an unmistakable firmness, "Are you going after him?"

"I'll watch you," I said, and handed him his rod.

The doctor's third cast was rewarded. He struck; the rod bent and the shine of his spectacles grew dim in the greater light of his countenance.

"Got him," said he in a half whisper, as he fed out line.

I was prepared to witness a battle of the giants, and so, I think, was Pocono Shot, crouching tensely on the bank; but nothing, epoch-making followed. The spectacles reestablished their supremacy as the doctor mastered a ten-inch fish and the dog, obviously dejected, brought it to bank.

Once more the doctor waded into the stream. Again and again came the swish of the rod, the faint hiss of the curving line, and the all but imperceptible flicker of the flies taking water. So twenty barren minutes passed.

"You're fishing dry, aren't you?" said the doctor at last. "Go below and take a crack at it. I'll get out of here."

"I'd rather you went on with what you were telling me," I said.

"That'll keep till tonight. Why, God A'Mighty, man, he was two feet long!"

So for another twenty minutes I sent Cahills, Whirling Duns, Woodruffs, Fan Wings of various sorts, and many another deft arrangement of feathers to the foot of the miniature waterfall and watched them come bobbing down the riffle into the quietness of the pool. Whether the taking of the doctor's minnow had disturbed the leviathan, or whether the wisdom of age was too much for my most cunning cast, I do not know. At any rate, nothing happened; and the doctor and I and the sedate Pocono Shot wended our way toward Emmetville, silent, a little awed, by the unearthly beauty of the stream and the hills beneath a glory of rose and flame that was the sky.

"Glad to give you a bite at my place," said the doctor as we came, in the last of the twilight, to the street corner where we must separate.

"Thanks," said I; "but I want to get out of these waders and clean up a bit."

"Well, come over later then."

"You may depend on that," I assured him.

It was too dark to observe whether my new impression of Gaylord's held in the face of reality. The limbs of the maples were spidery tracings against a green sky in which a crescent moon and the evening star swam in pale serenity. The front of the house was only a ghostly shimmer, and the mellow light, streaming, from several windows, softened their stare.

"Bigga feesh?" asked Joe as he took my creel from me on the side porch.

"Not very," said I.

The light from a dining-room window streamed upon him to reveal the simplicity of his humble smile. It gleamed in his big, brown, faithful eyes.

So there had been some moves made to lynch this friendly, doglike soul. What an utterly monstrous thing a mob could be!

I found it hard to inspect, with a new though pitying curiosity, the silent woman of Gaylord's. I tried it as she served the table. My thoughts being what they were, my eyes insisted on dropping to my plate when she was present.

What a nightmare of horror the memory behind her astonishingly placid brow must hold! I could not account for that placidity. I could not account for her contented singing.... Suddenly the explanation came. Hymns! Always hymns! Of course! The thing she saw with her farseeing gaze was, as I had suspected, not of this earth. But I had been wide of the mark. I had fancied a dead husband, or even lover. Now I knew that no such recollection sustained her. She, who had found life so appalling, was thoroughly convinced of a better life to come. The ecstatic contemplation of its possibilities was what absorbed her. Looking after the comfort of anglers and drummers was purely automatic.

A phrase came to me out of the past—out of that past from which had come the memory of the hymns she sang: "The peace ... which passeth all understanding." I had never comprehended the meaning of those words. I would never fully comprehend it. But the silent woman of Gaylord's comprehended it; a blessing surely—an all but miraculous blessing—that for her the thing was possible.

· VI ·

"It's only lime juice, sugar, water, and Bacardi," the doctor was explaining an hour or so later.

We were safe in the consulting room attached to the wing of his house. I had been assigned a comfortably tipping desk chair. He had dragged in a chintz-and-wicker affair from the outer waiting room in which to dispose of himself. He settled into it, glass in hand, with a contented sigh.

"Only Bacardi,"

I exclaimed. "Only diamonds and pearls! Where do you get it?"

"Pal of mine is ship's doctor on a fruit steamer."

I missed the gorgeous presence of Pocono Shot and asked if he were in the house.

"No," said the doctor, "he's out in his kennel. He's restless in the house except in winter. Likes fresh air, I suppose. Glad of it. It's better for his nose."

"I should think he'd want to be near you," I suggested.

"He doesn't care anything about me."

I looked my surprise.

"Fact. He stays with me because he knows he's supposed to. He's friendly with me just as he'd be friendly with you; but care for me? Not for a minute! There's just one person in the world he cares about. If you were around him a little while you'd find it out."

We sipped in silence for a moment. "Well?" said I at last.

"Where was I when the whale came up?" asked the doctor.

"You were at the shack with the sheriff who'd come for the dog."

"Oh, yes. Did I tell you how Shot looked at Ed?"

"Yes, and what the sheriff said."

"Well, after that we drove to town. I followed the other car in the flivver. When we got to the bridge below the rift we left the machines and crossed the bridge on foot. About three hundred yards down the stream I saw two state troopers, each sitting on a rock fifty feet or so apart. There were people standing on the bridge watching the troopers, and an even bigger crowd along the railroad track farther down; men and boys mostly, with a few women. The sheriff led us down the stream to the nearest trooper. He said 'All right, Jake,' and we passed the trooper and came to a halt on a rock-strewn bar, with willows and laurel all along the land side except in one place. Here a narrow slide of shale flanked by willows and undergrowth pitched from the railroad right of way to the rocky bar below.

"'Now, Bill.' said Ed, 'right at the foot of that slide is an oblong stone about as big as your two fists. It has dried blood and a little hair on the side nearest the slide. There's a pool of dried blood on the other side of it toward the stream. The girl was killed with that stone. Take the dog over there and see what you can do. If you want to pick up the stone, lift it by the ends and keep your hands off the clean side. A pair of bloodhounds will get in from Wilkes-Barre on the 1:40. I hear they're not much good; but if your dog falls down we'll give 'em a chance. Don't move around over there any more than you have to.'

"Bill started for the slide with Shot at heel. Suddenly the dog stopped and stuck his head low and forward, sniffing. Then his hair went up on his back and he whined."

"'I know. Come on,' said Bill, and Shot followed him to the foot of the slide. Bill stood for a minute looking down, took a step or so forward, squatted, and lifted a stone to the level of Shot's nose.

"'Smell this!' he said.

"Shot whined, and backed away.

"'Come on, it's got to be done,' said Bill.

"Shot came to him and pushed him with his nose, whining.

"'Smell it!' said Bill.

"Shot smelled the side of the stone Bill held toward him and backed away.

"'Smell it good!' said Bill, and the dog came slinking and smelled the stone again.

"'Now, can you find him?' Bill asked.

"Shot gave a half bark, half growl.

"'All right,' said Bill. 'Let's go!' He waved his hand at Shot. The dog circled with his head in the air, stopped, and stuck his nose forward as he had when he came to the slide, lifted it high, his nostrils working, and bolted on a lope off through the scattered willows, downstream.

"'Slow!' yelled Bill. 'Slow!' And Shot came to a walk. 'He's got it, Ed,' said Bill, following the dog.

"The crowd up on the railroad had begun to move along in the direction Shot was taking. The sheriff yelled to the troopers to keep the crowd from following and started after Bill. I trailed the sheriff. I could hear the troopers yelling to the crowd to stand still, and one of them was threshing about in the thicket, swearing, as he tried to force his way through it up to the right of way. Shot led on down the stream for a quarter of a mile, swung left, and started diagonally through a lot of blackberry and wild rose vines. He crawled under a barbed wire fence along the right of way and climbed a steep slope of cinders up to the tracks.

"'Don't step in those,' I heard the sheriff say, and saw footprints in the soft cinders where someone had climbed the slope. Shot turned left again, up the eastbound track along the ties. He was heading straight for the crowd huddled in the right of way with a trooper acting shepherd over them.

"My heart was trying to jump out of my chest, with the climb and excitement, and my clothes were ripped and my hands bleeding from the briers we'd come through. I heard Ed begin to swear as he saw we were going, back to the crowd.

"'Every damned fool in the Poconos has rammed up and down that track in the last ten hours,' he said. As we got nearer, he yelled 'Get out of the way! Get off the track!' and the crowd scattered to each side. As we came nearer still, Shot stopped suddenly. He whined, turned, came back past us, and stopped again. He swung his head back and forth like a scythe, with his neck stretched out. You know how calm his expression is as a rule? Well, it wasn't like that then. It was tremendously intent and anxious, and you could hear his nostrils sucking at the air.

"'No hurry.' said Bill; 'take your time.'

"Shot went ten feet farther down the track, turned back, and then, for the first time in his life, I think, put his nose to the ground—or rather to the ties. He came up the track again, a step at a time, a tie at a time, with a deep sniff at every tie. He went that way clear to the station, right through a lane of people as though they hadn't been there.

"The trooper tried to hold the crowd where they were; but most of the boys and a lot of men broke away from him and trailed along after us, and the crowd on the bridge joined them as we passed. By the time we reached the station there must have been a mob of over a hundred following us. Shot's head came up at the station road. He broke into a lope as he started down it and Bill had to slow him again.

"The crowd started to yell. The sheriff stopped at the road and turned to them. 'I'll shoot the first son of a — that tries to follow past here,' he said. He spoke quietly. His voice wasn't any louder than the buzz of a rattlesnake — and not much more harmful sounding. We went on alone.

"Shot went down the station road, left it for the clearing at the end of the gorge, crossed the clearing, struck the west road through the gap, followed it to the Mulhauser place, turned in through the drive, went round the house to the side door, and stopped. He scratched at the door, looked up at Bill, and gave the same low half bark, half growl he had at the slide.

"'I'll make you a little bet the party you want is in here, sheriff,' said Bill.

"'I won't take it,' said Ed. His face was a frightening thing to see as he opened the door.

"Emmet Senior and Emmet Junior and Ed's daughter Ruth were in the room we came to at the end of a hall leading from the side door.

"'Why, father!' said Ruth; and then she saw his face, and her own face froze.

"Ed's eyes were on Emmet Junior, who came up out of his chair like a ghost. There was a brier scratch across his forehead and one on his chin. They looked redder than blood against the deadly white of his face.

"'I thought so,' said Ed, half to himself. Then he nodded to Emmet Junior and said, 'I want to talk to you. Come on outside.'

"Emmet brushed his hand through his hair exactly as he had with me. I remember being startled by the gesture. It didn't seem possible he could have an affectation left in him.

"Ruth rushed over to Emmet Junior. 'Emmie,' she said, 'what is it? Why does he act like this?'

"Her father said, 'You get on your hat and go to your mother! Wait there till I come!'

"'Why should I go home? What do you want with Emmet?' she said.

"Old man Mulhauser had been staring at the sheriff. Now he walked over to him.

"'What the hell do you think you're doing, Bascom?' he said.

"I remember seeing the sheriff's hand go out and sort of hover at his daughter's shoulder as he answered.

"'I'm sending my girl home,' he said. 'This dog took a trail from where Lucille Firth was killed last night, and came straight here. I want— ' He nodded at Emmet Junior.

"Ruth screamed and let go of Emmet Junior. Emmet Senior went brick red. He gave one look at Shot standing quietly beside Bill, watching Emmet Junior.

"'You crazy fool!' he yelled at Ed. 'You dumb idiot! Take that damn dog out of my house and don't you ever stick your nose in here again as long as you live!'

"The green look I'd seen once before had come into Emmet Junior's face. He began to sway. He muttered, 'She fell! She fell down the slide!' Suddenly he gasped out, 'I swear to God she fell!' and came smashing to the floor in a dead faint.... How about another drink?"

"No, thanks; not just now," I said; but my self-denial got me nothing.

"Well, I seem to be doing the heavy work—I think I've got one coming." The doctor rose from his chair. "Just as easy to mix two."

"Well—if you insist."

"There wasn't much to Emmet Junior's trial," said the doctor, his powers as a raconteur having been duly stimulated. "He'd scratched himself, charging wildly through the briers that night. The footprints in the cinders up to the tracks tallied with a pair of his shoes they found, with cinders in the eyelets and along the soles. Kittridge, who was coroner, testified about the autopsy, which made it clear why Emmet Junior was afraid to leave after his marriage, and why he had met Lucille down by the stream.

"It turned out that Lucille had really fallen down the slide, as Emmet Junior had declared before he fainted. He was waiting for her among the rocks below. She must have rushed down the slide in a sort of frenzy when she saw him. At any rate, she fell near the bottom and struck her head against a stone. As she lay at his feet, half stunned, or perhaps wholly so, Emmet picked up the stone and brained her. I'm certain he never intended to kill her. He hadn't the nerve for premeditated murder. Something she told her mother about wanting to go to New York to work leads me to think he intended sending her away when he was certain it was necessary. Then suddenly she lay helpless before him and a blind impulse to get rid of her did the rest.

"Joe, the Italian, had actually seen Lucille fall down the slide. He explained through an interpreter at the trial that he'd sneaked down to the stream to do a little night fishing out of season—fish laws meant nothing to him—and was sitting in the shadows on the bank below the bridge as Lucille passed over it. There was a three-quarter moon that night, but he didn't recognize her. He heard her start down the slide and saw her fall, and saw a man—he couldn't tell who—pick up something and pound her with it. He said he thought it was nothing but a man beating his wife, so he shrugged his shoulders, Italian fashion, and went on fishing. But the man went away, and the woman lay still so long that he walked down his side of the stream and looked at her. What he saw made him wade across, up to his middle, to the poor woman, who, he thought, must be unconscious. He tried to lift her up, saw that it was Lucille and that she was dead, and rushed, half crazy, into town.

"The most pitiful thing at the trial was the reading circle. Emmet Senior had employed a lawyer from Philadelphia and the best man in Stroudsburg. They decided to plead insanity. The prosecution set out to show that Emmet Junior was sane enough for planned and skillful seduction. Ruth, as his wife, escaped testifying; but the four other girls were put on the stand, one after the other, and those poor young things, stammering, weeping, with their cheeks like flame, were stripped, so to speak, in public.

"The defense claimed that the books that Emmet Junior had furnished the reading circle, as a basis for further developments, were the accepted novels of the day, and not regarded as harmful or obscene by authorities. They read reviews of the books to prove it. The prosecution came back by reading from the books themselves. You should have seen the faces of that Pocono jury at some of the passages.

"The defense pulled off a master stroke, however, along literary lines. They read some of Emmet Junior's poetry aloud. It saved him from the chair. Nothing could have persuaded the jury—or the judge, either, for that matter—that a sane man could have written it.

"When they gave Emmet Junior life imprisonment, Emmet Senior didn't take it to a higher court. I think his lawyers told him his son was a lucky boy.

"I've forgotten one thing. I've forgotten to tell you what happened at Lucille Firth's funeral. I don't know whether you know it or not; but anyone can come to a small-town funeral, and this one was crowded. It was at Gaylord's. In the midst of it old Jerry Gorsuch shambled into the parlor and up to the casket. The service was just beginning and everyone else was seated. Jerry is crazy and no mistake. Harmless, of course; but he goes around painting quotations from the Bible on fences and rocks. Suddenly he pointed into the casket and shrieked out, 'The wages of sin is death!' He kept on yelling it till they got him out. It was a tremendously shocking thing under the circumstances. You can imagine what it did to Mrs. Firth. But just the same, I'm inclined to think it was a good thing the old fool did what he did. She'd never been a religious woman, yet the day after the funeral she began her hymn singing and a few days later she was saved, as they say, publicly, at the Methodist church. She's kept up her singing and churchgoing ever since. I've a notion that when the Methodists saved her soul they saved her reason.

"About the only thing Emmet Senior did that was worthy of attention after the trial was to post his land against hunting, but that was surely enough. There isn't another foot of land posted anywhere around here. Public sentiment is against it in this section. Emmet had cut the heart out of the shooting within decent walking distance of town, and there was general cussing and protesting about it, especially when fall came around. Nothing was done about it because there was nothing to do. He had the legal right to post if he wanted to, and he never had cared a hoot what anybody thought of him. It was perfectly clear why he did it. He hated everyone who'd had anything to do with sending his boy away, and among them—the most prominent of the lot, when you stop to think of it—was Shot. You couldn't blame Emmet for not wanting to lay eyes on the dog again, and it's easy to imagine that any hunting dog, particularly a setter, would remind him of the whole terrible business. So he put up his signs to keep Shot, or anything that looked like him, off his land.

"I had counted on a lot of days with Bill and Shot that fall; but it did seem as if the cussed kids would never so much as sneeze till hunting season and then welcome the first germ that came along. This time it was measles. It didn't miss more than fifty children for five miles around; then to add to the general gayety, we got a touch of diphtheria, not especially virulent; but I hardly got my clothes off for two weeks. I came home to dinner one night and the girl told me that Earl Geiger had telephoned twice in the last half hour and that I was to call him the minute I got in. I said, 'I'll have some dinner before I call anybody'; but the phone rang while I was washing up and the girl said I was in, so I had to answer. It was Geiger. He told me to come to Bill Trimble's as fast as I could drive.

"I said all right, told the girl I couldn't wait for dinner, and went out to the car. Just as I was starting she came running out with three or four slices of hot roast beef. I ate 'em with one hand as I jounced and swayed up grade to Bobcat Mountain. Glad I did, too, although it was taking a chance on that road. I thought Bill must have hurt himself—broken a leg, maybe, hunting. I never thought of him being sick; not that tough old rooster.

"Geiger was standing in front of Bill's shack when I got there. I said, 'What's happened?" He said, 'You can see inside. I'm going home and get a bite.' I went to the shack and pushed open the door to the kitchen. There was a lighted lamp on the kitchen table. Bill was sitting in the middle of the floor, bathed in blood from his chin down, and the floor looked like a slaughterhouse. He was holding Shot's head in his lap. The dog seemed to be cut more than half in two, just ahead of the shoulder. The wound seemed to include the neck vertebra, but I put a hand on him and found he was still alive, so I knew the spinal cord hadn't been severed.

"I said, 'How did it happen?'

"'Emmet Mulhauser—with an ax,' said Bill.

"I asked him whereabouts and Bill told me up on the edge of Emmet's land, above the big swale.

"I stood looking down at the dog. I'm not given to emotion, and I was in France two years; but I found I couldn't see Shot or Bill. Queer, wasn't it? I stood there, with the tears rolling down my cheeks as though I'd gone back to boyhood. I suppose I was overtired.

"'Ain't you goin' to do nothin' except stand there?' said Bill.

"There's nothing I can do, Bill," I said.

"'No, I suppose not,' he said.

"He put his hand on Shot's head and began to stroke it gently, looking down at the dog. I was still standing there like a great soft lummox, when I heard the sound of a motor. It stopped in front of the shack and a minute later the sheriff walked in.

"'Hello, Ed,' said Bill.

"The sheriff said hello and stooped to the dog. 'Christ!' he said, then he looked up at me. 'He ain't alive, is he, doc?' And I said, 'Still alive.'

"Bill spoke up then. He said, 'I'd kind of like to stay for a while yet.'

"'Sure thing, Bill,' said Ed. 'Just as long as you're a mind to.'

"That brought me to myself with a jerk. 'What are you talking about? What's happened?' I asked.

"Before Bill could open his mouth the sheriff spoke up. 'Why, Emmet Mulhauser cut Bill's dog down and started after Bill,' he said. 'Bill had to shoot in self-defense. There was a Swede logger of Mulhauser's not far off that saw it. I've talked to him. He saw Emmet with his ax lifted. I've got to take Bill to town, but they'll turn him loose easy enough.'

'Mulhauser's dead?' I asked.

"'Never be anybody any deader!' said the sheriff. 'He stopped both barrels at five feet. Lucky you got him when you did, Bill. He'd have clove you down to the middle.'

"Bill stopped stroking Shot's head and looked up.

"'They ain't hardly any of that true, Ed,' he said. 'I'll tell you the facts.'

"'You ain't goin' to tell me nothin',' said Ed. 'Anything you say to me I've got to repeat under oath. You don't have to say nothin' to nobody. The Swede says he saw Emmet's ax raised. You've got a perfect case of self-defense. Now shut your fool mouth! Doc, you tell him!'

"The sheriff's right, Bill," I said.

"Bill went back to stroking Shot's head.

"'No, he ain't,' he said. 'He means well, but he ain't right. Facts is facts. If I've got to be tried, it's what I'll stand on. Here is the facts: I knowed I was close to Emmet's land, but a pa'tridge that flushed wild swung that way. I thought the bird would stop in the alders, thirty feet or so this side of the line, so I let Shot go after him. When we got to the alders the bird wasn't there, and Shot smelled him on the other side and went through and nailed him. I'd heard a ax as I come up and I hustled up the rise through the alders. I was goin' to pull Shot off his point if he was over the line. Well, he was over—barely. I seen him holdin' on the bird like iron as I got toward the edge of the alders. I didn't see Emmet till he showed up at Shot's side and brought the ax down on him, standin' there on point. When I got there Emmet stepped back from the dog. Shot was layin' like you see, with the blood pourin' out of him in a river. He—well, he wagged his tail at me. It rustled like, in the ferns, and his eyes said, 'Everything will be all right, now Bill's here.' So then I put both barrels into Emmet's belly and picked up Shot and come on home. That's the way it happened—just like I've said. You got me wrong, Ed, if you think I'd let a man cut old Shot down, him a-pointin', and then plead self-defense. If Emmet had of got away after he done it, I'd go after him tonight as soon as it was right for me to leave, and it would turn out just the same.'

"Bill hadn't more than finished telling us when the sheriff took out his watch, looked at it and said, 'Bill, we'll have to go right now. What you've just said makes things different.'

"Bill's hand stopped moving over Shot's head. He looked up at the sheriff—a long, slow look, he gave him.

"'I guess I've had you wrong, too, Ed,' he said. 'You swore old Shot in as a deputy and he tracked down our man for you through half the town. Ain't no livin' thing on this earth except him could have done it, and look where it's brought him. Now I'm askin' you to let him die with his head just where it is.'

"The sheriff never quivered. He just said, 'It can't be done, Bill. Come on—right now!'

"Bill laid Shot's head on the floor, knelt by him, whispered, 'Good-by, Bud,' and got to his feet. 'I'm expectin' you'll stay with him,' he said to me.

"My silly weakness had come back. I couldn't speak—I just nodded. Bill and the sheriff tramped out. I heard the car roar as it pulled out of the mud in front of the shack and grew fainter down the mountain. I sat there for an hour. Shot had stopped bleeding. There wasn't enough blood left in him to force the slight coagulation of the wound. Why he stayed alive was a mystery, but a stethoscope proved that his heart was still beating—just a pulse, but still beating. Earl Geiger came and stood looking down at Shot without speaking. I said, 'Bill's gone to town.' He said, 'Yes, doc, I know. I saw the sheriff's car go by. Can I do anything to help you?' I told him no, and to go home and get to bed, which he did a few minutes later.

"It was close to midnight when I heard a car again. It stopped in front of the shack and the sheriff walked in. He said, 'Still alive?'

"I said, 'Sheriff, I don't want to talk to you. I want you to remember that whenever I'm unlucky enough to meet you after this.'

"He pulled a chair out from under the kitchen table and sat down.

"'Now, doc,' he said, 'I'm going to kind of act a fool with you. You weren't raised around here; but I've seen something of you, and you've struck me as a pretty decent sort of a coot, with more than the ordinary amount of common sense. I'm going to tell you some things and let you draw whatever conclusions occur to you.'

"I didn't say anything. He looked down at Shot for a minute and then went on:

"'Bill Trimble hasn't ever been what you'd call a friend of mine,' he said. 'He's just a good, well-meaning wood rat that does the best he can. Now I'd go as far for a friend as the next man; but I wouldn't get on the stand and swear to a lie, not for my best friend—not for my brother. Well, that's what the situation seemed to call for, after Bill belched up to me like you heard. Even if he could of been persuaded to act sensible about pleadin' self-defense when he'd steadied down and got his judgment back, it wouldn't get him much after he'd told that story to me. I've been sheriff of this county for nine years, and the more I've seen of juries the more I've learned you never can tell what they'll do. They'll let a loose woman that's shot her husband in the back, and then come into court and sniveled about it, go scot-free. On the other hand, they'll give some poor devil who hasn't got money enough to hire a string of lawyers a hell of a dose, when the facts, outside the law, show in his favor.

"'Now look at the cold facts in this case. Mulhauser kills a dog on his own land, that's posted according to law, and gets shot down, on his own land, a minute later. It don't make any difference that every real man on the jury would have done the same as Bill under the circumstances. The average citizen seems to get all bogged down in the law when he sits on a jury. He can't seem to put himself in the other fellow's place. I don't say a jury wouldn't let Bill off—they might. But then again they mightn't. The prosecution would have to talk a lot about the sacredness of human life and Bill might end up with a long stretch.

"'Now I let Bill in for this, just like he said, and these hills won't look good to him for quite a while—he'll be seeing the dog everywhere he looks. This thing'll blow over some in a year or two, and I don't think the prosecutor, knowin' him as I do, will bust a lung tryin' to find Bill, and something tells me I won't. My term's up this year and I won't run again. If Bill ever wants to come back here I'll be a private citizen that'll take a sudden notion to visit Canada. I'll leave on the next train and they'll have to try Bill without my testimony.

"'Well, when I took Bill out of here in such a rush I knew there was a freight train headed east that stopped at the water tank about eight o'clock. Going down the mountain I explained all what I've said to you, to Bill, and told him I'd accidentally dropped a fifty-dollar bill down by the clutch somewhere that I'd pick up when we got down the grade. I clean forgot to pick it up before I had to get out of the car to fix my brake, about two hundred yards from the water tank. I had to get clear under the car to fix that brake, and when I crawled out Bill wasn't in the car. He wasn't anywhere to be seen. I looked in the brush on both sides of the road, the best I could, till that freight came in and pulled out; then I drove to town and told 'em Bill had jumped out of the car sudden and got away from me in the dark; which, as Bill says, is the facts.

"'I'm on the hunt for Bill right now. I've got a couple of deputies threshin' around, down the mountain; but I thought you might like to hear about Bill gettin' away from me so neat. Now, doc, if I've misjudged you, as Bill says, it'll be me and not him that a jury'll decide about—after our little talk. That's about all I've got to say, and now I'll be goin' along.'"

The doctor came to a full stop to twinkle at me.

"Splendid!" I exclaimed, for some reason. "Splendid! And Shot lived!"

"Yes," said the doctor, "though how I don't know. He lay, without so much as the twitch of a muscle for two days. I stayed right there. Mrs. Geiger cooked my meals and sent them over by Geiger or their boy. I had them telephone young Crosby, who was trying to get a foothold in Stroudsburg, to come up and handle things in town for me, which he was glad to do. I hadn't done a thing to keep Shot's heart going—afraid of hemorrhage. It just kept pulsing faintly away all those hours. On the morning of the third day the wound looked as though I might help the heart a little. I did it with a hypodermic of strychnine. Ten minutes later I saw Shot's eyeballs move slightly as I stooped over him. By the next day he could swallow a tablespoonful of brandy and milk, poured back of his tongue through a tube. After the first week he came along fast. No infection whatever. His neck was stiff for two or three months—scar tissue and severed leaders—but he worked out of it as you've seen."

"When was this—the shooting, I mean?" I asked.

"Last November."

"And when is Trimble coming back?"

The doctor's face clouded.

"I don't know," he said. "I don't know where he is. Of course, he thinks Shot is dead, and the sheriff was right in thinking Bill would want to stay away from these hills for a while if he believed that. I'm certain nothing would keep him away if he knew Shot had pulled through and was waiting here for him. The sheriff is out of office, and there's no reason why Bill shouldn't come back and stand trial right now. They'd never convict him. He'd keep still with Shot alive; I'll bet on that. The sentiment around here, as it turned out, is close to 100 per cent for him. People think he ran away through ignorance. You see, Shot is an institution in the Poconos. He's a matter of civic pride in Emmetville. He's like the courthouse or the new Presbyterian church. They think shooting was too good for the man who cut him down.

"Bill doesn't know all this. He's probably hiding somewhere, thinking they're after him, when there hasn't been a single move made to get him."

"Isn't there some way to let him know he should come back?" I asked.

The doctor was observing a felt slipper on the dangling foot of the leg that crossed his knee. Now he wiggled the foot and seemed lost in amazement at the articulation of his ankle joint.

"What do you do for a living?" he asked casually.

"Write—mostly," I said.

"You mean you're a writer?"

I admitted that I was. The doctor's face fell.

"Oh," he said, "then that's no good."

"What's no good?"

"Why, you wanted to buy the dog. The idea came to me that I might lease him to you for the season—it would have to be at a big price—and then I'd use the money to try to get word to Bill."

"How?" I asked.

"Run something in the Want Columns from New York to San Francisco about like this: 'Shot is alive. Doctor L.' I wouldn't say, 'Come home.' He might think that was a ruse. I'd just, say, 'Shot is alive.' I'd run it three or four days. It would bring him if he saw it."

"Yes," I thought, "it would." Aloud I said, "How much would it cost?"

"Enough," said the doctor gloomily. "I've thought of doing it myself, but I've still got one of the notes to pay that I gave for the practice, and the old flivver's about through. There's twice as much on my books as I've ever collected. That's the way it is with country doctoring."

I considered a moment. I thought of Pocono Shot; not long—just for the instant it took to recall his expression, his head, his carriage. Then I spoke.

"Doctor," I said, "I write, as I've told you. I try to write tales that a reasonably intelligent man or woman can read without knitted brows, or boredom or disgust. It's a quaint, old-fashioned custom; but some people still approve of it, and—I'd like to lease the dog. How much?"

The doctor sat up suddenly. His spectacles registered an emotion somewhere between doubt and hope.

"Why, man," he said, "it'll take five hundred dollars to run those ads!"

"Done!" said I, and held out my hand.

· VII ·

I had planned to spend the summer in Maine, on a little lake whose surface and hemlock-bordered coves ached with the loneliness of the north. That loneliness fills me with a peace that is like a pain. I fled from the Poconos toward it, just ahead of the summer season, which would tax the silent woman of Gaylord's to the utmost and fill the staring house and its porches with distressing chatter.

My five hundred had been hopefully expended by the doctor, but without avail. If the owner of the dog was still slinking about somewhere on the face of the globe, he failed to receive the electrifying message, conveyed through various leaded columns, that Shot was alive.

He was very much alive as he hauled me through the doorway of the club, with my full weight on the chain, as opposed to his straining shoulders and the click of his digging toenails on the marble floor of the hall; so gloriously alive that soon we were surrounded by a circle of members, with an outer fringe of bellboys, all paying homage to the dog's magnificence.

The adulation did not seem to meet with the approval of Pocono Shot, or perhaps, I thought, the smells and noise of the city, which he was encountering for the first time, had begun to disturb him. At any rate, his serenity, which had been perfect on the train, on the ferry, and in the taxicab, was gone at last. It had departed as we got out of the cab. Having literally hauled me through the door, he was now tremendously uneasy. He began to shake. He began to pant and to slaver. He tried to break through the inspecting circle about him with violent surges at his chain. I had difficulty in forcing him into the elevator. He gave a stricken moaning whine as it carried us up to my room.

"Quiet down," I told him. "We'll be out of this in a little while."

He refused to quiet down. I left him pacing the room like a wild thing when I went down to secure further impedimenta for the months in Maine.

I found the cellar empty. The furnace, no longer needed, was a black disk in the gloom. The draft arrangement on its door looked like the jetty teeth of a cold, fixed leer. Its lanky tender was gone.

I secured another duffel bag from the storeroom, pointed out a trunk I wanted to the porter, and returned to my room. I unpacked and repacked for two hours, while Shot paced back and forth, back and forth, before the closed door.

Having finished packing, and with an hour to kill before leaving for the station, I telephoned to the desk and asked for Gregory Trane. I was astonished to hear that he had sailed for Africa the week before.

"Are you sure?" I demanded, and was told by the clerk that there was no doubt of it whatever.

I hung up, wondering. Why had Trane gone back so suddenly to trekking and big game? Perhaps the batch of spring novels had done it! I smiled at the thought, but grew sober as my eyes fell on the pacing setter with the great scar showing at his glistening shoulder as he wheeled.

I telephoned to the kitchen for a plate of meat. Shot thanked me with a wave of his tail when the food was set before him, but refused to touch it. I offered him water. He turned away from it, then changed his mind and lapped greedily. When we departed at last, I had to haul him by main strength through the hall and out to the taxicab. He had come with me that morning in Emmetville readily enough. The doctor had simply handed me the chain and said, "Go along with him, Shot!" The dog had quietly obeyed. He had obeyed me perfectly on the way down, or rather he had done what was necessary in making the trip without being told. I had been enraptured. Now I was more doubtful.

I need not have been. He became a perfect companion in Maine from the moment we go there. He would lie at my feet if a mood for work struck me, handle himself in a canoe as circumspectly as I, and retrieve trout for me if I fished a stream. The most extraordinary thing about him was this:

The woods about were filled with partridges. The partridges, in turn, were filled with the tame stupidity that these birds show in the wilderness. On the first morning after our arrival a brood crossed a trail ahead of us and stood clucking not ten feet away as we passed. Shot gave them no attention whatever. He simply stalked by. I was dumbfounded. A wild suspicion of the doctor crossed my mind. Five hundred dollars for one season! Was it possible that spectacled, guileless-seeming M.D. was an easy fictionist who made my more labored efforts in that direction seem clumsy in comparison?

I hastened to try an experiment. I went back to the camp, unstrapped the first gun case that came to hand, and put the weapon it contained together, Pocono Shot gravely watching. I walked the length of the camp porch, gun in hand. As I stepped from the porch Shot was already swinging through the sunshine of the clearing on an easy lope. He swept toward the edge of a thicket of birch and melted into statuesque, high-headed immobility. As I persuaded a lazy cock partridge to blunder up reluctantly from his dust bath among the birch wands I blushed to recall my recent thoughts concerning the good doctor.

"So you don't waste your time without a gun," I said, as we watched the bird tilting with spread wings through the birch thicket and into the hemlocks beyond. "Come into heel—it's out of season. We'll go and put this up."

He obeyed, as always, instantly, with no effort to continue hunting. My will was his law in everything; and yet—well, I came to know what the doctor had meant when he had said Shot did not care for him. It showed in a certain wistfulness that would creep into his expression now and then. He would be sleeping in the sunshine on the porch. Suddenly his head would go up as he listened intently. In his dreams he had heard a longed-for footstep or perhaps a voice. He would turn and survey me wonderingly at last, a question in his look, and back of that a troubled yearning.

When fall came Shot and I journeyed to Vermont. I was to shoot over a vast preserve with a man who owned it and a great many other things. Among them—so he had informed me—were the two best partridge dogs that ever lived. This I doubted. Sometimes even multimillionaires fail to get the best of everything.

My host grunted when he observed that I was accompanied by a setter. A moment later, when the full symmetry of Pocono Shot dawned upon him, he whistled.

"Of course he isn't as good as he looks," he said.

"I've never shot over him," I explained deceptively, "but the man I got him from seemed to think a lot of his work."

My host brightened. He was the sort of man who would. He even grew hilarious.

"So the man who sold him to you liked his work, did he? Don't you know any better than to buy a shooting dog without seeing him in the field? Never mind. I have thirty in the kennels here—two of em, as I wrote you, world beaters."

I must confess it—I led him on. I encouraged him to expatiate on his two headliners. I heard of their noses and bird sense and staunchness and retrieving, all through an extremely elaborate dinner, and afterwards—until we retired, in fact.

Ultimately morning dawned. I insisted on taking Shot with us, although my host objected.

"You can find out about him tomorrow," he said. "Don't let's spoil the opening day. I've ordered out Craft and Bess."

Still I insisted. He could do no less than submit. He said that a gamekeeper—he had gamekeepers—would bring Shot in after I had tried him out.

It may have been an hour later—not much more than that—when their owner called the aforementioned gamekeeper and indicated Craft and Bess.

"Take those two back and shut them up," he said. "We don't want them messing about."

That was the last I either saw or heard of any of those thirty in the kennels.

Pocono Shot! Pocono Shot! The doctor had not told me half. I had given five hundred dollars for twenty days over him. A single day was worth it. A single, never-to-be-forgotten day, in which an awed plutocrat and I followed wherever a lonely, wise-eyed master of thickets led and did our anxious best.

I sat in the baggage car with him on the way to Boston, and again between Boston and New York. I could have done no less.

It was snowing in New York the afternoon we arrived; an early snow, which disappeared as it added to the level wetness of pavement and asphalt. The taxi could not draw up fairly before the club door, because of an ash wagon backing into the curb. Two iron doors sunk in the pavement close to the building rose and opened. As I got out of the taxi, I heard the rattle of an ash can somewhere below in the black square disclosed by the opening of the iron doors.

I was paying the taxi driver when Shot jerked his chain from my hand with an irresistible lunge. I turned in time to see him plunging down between the iron doors. I heard a crash, a rattle, and nothing more. Rushing to the opening, I saw an overturned ash can on the hoist ten feet below, and realized that the darkness beyond was an opening into the club cellar.

And then, at last, I knew. Oh, fool! Oh, idiot! Oh, groping human creature—at last I knew! I went into the club and descended the iron stairs.

The furnace man, as white as death, crouched on his wooden stool. His arms were wreathed, awkwardly, clutchingly about the head of Pocono Shot, which burrowed in his breast.

Trane has not returned from Afirca. This is disappointing. I want to tell him of my new knowledge of the effects he dwelt upon, one night. I also wish to admit that—to use his own expression—the modernists are not so damned forlorn. "Forlorn" does not describe the mongrel adventurers in neuroticism, whose mark may be found, so long as he lives, on the shoulder of Pocono Shot!